"In a manner both subtle and splendid, *A Fiction of the Past* detects the elusive shifts in culture and morality that underlie the sixties. Cavallo's book should be read by those looking for a comprehensive understanding of that era as well as for insights into what we have become since the sixties."

—David Burner, State University of New York at Stony Brook, author of *Making Peace with the Sixties*

"... fascinating ... his conclusions can startle ... Cavallo makes a convincing case for the American-ness of the '60s ..."

—*Kansas City Star*

"[A] superb synthesis ... [R]ich and stimulating ... [A] must-read for those interested in these years."

—*Choice*

"Well written and argued, this work presents a new view of the 1960s and will no doubt spark considerable discussion."

—*Library Journal*

"It is all too rare that *any* book on the 60s these days makes me really rethink the era, but Cavallo's succeeds brilliantly ... I am in complete agreement with the animating spirit of the book, which is that the 1960s have to be understood, for better or worse, as part of the grand sweep of American historical development—as culmination rather than aberration ..."

—Maurice Isserman, William R. Kenan, Jr., Professor of History at Hamilton College and author of *If I Had a Hammer ... The Death of the Old Left and the Birth of the New Left*

"Cavallo makes the 1960s into a real period in American history, not an exception, and that is an important accomplishment ... A persuasive interpretation of the period [and] a major contribution toward reestablishing that era as a period to study and not just denounce."

—James Gilbert, Professor of History, University of Maryland and author of *Another Chance: Postwar America, 1945–1968*

The end is in the beginning,
and lies far ahead.

Ralph Ellison, *Invisible Man*

A Fiction of the Past

THE SIXTIES IN AMERICAN HISTORY

Dominick Cavallo

palgrave

For JoAnn Drumheller Smith
and
Fred Weinstein

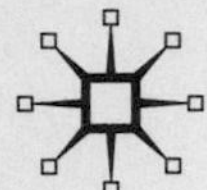

A FICTION OF THE PAST

First published 1999 by
PALGRAVE™
175 Fifth Avenue, New York, N.Y. 10010 and
Houndsmills, Basingstoke, Hampshire RG21 6XS.
Companies and representatives throughout the world.

PALGRAVE is the new global publishing imprint of St. Martin's Press LLC Scholarly and Reference Division and Palgrave Publishers Ltd (formerly Macmillan Press Ltd).

ISBN 0-312-21930-X hardback
ISBN 0-312-23501-1 paperback

Library of Congress Cataloging-in-Publication Data

Cavallo, Dominick, 1946-
A fiction of the past : the sixties in American history / Dominick Cavallo.
p. cm.
Includes bibliographical references and index.
ISBN 0-312-21930-X hardback—0-312-23501-1 paperback
1. United States—History—1961-1969. 2. United States—Social conditions—1960-1980. 3. Radicalism—United states—History—20th century. 4. Youth—United States—Political activity—History—20th century. 5. Subculture—United States—History—20th century. 5. Subculture—United States—History—20th century. 6. Youth—United States—Social Life and customs. I. Title.
E841.C33 1999
973.923—dc21 98-46179
CIP

Design by Acme Art, Inc.
First paperback edition: January 2001
10 9 8 7 6 5 4 3 2 1

Printed in the United States of America.

TABLE OF CONTENTS

ACKNOWLEDGEMENTS

I owe an enormous debt to those who helped me write this book. A number of colleagues at Adelphi University read and commented upon the work at various stages of its evolution. Fellow historians Lester Baltimore, Robert Devlin, Martin Haas and Carl Rheins were insightful and, thankfully, relentless in their criticisms. I owe them a great deal. I was fortunate as well to receive guidance from other members of the Adelphi community who read parts of the manuscript: Jeffrey Kane, Vincent Passaro, Nicholas Petron, Alan Sadovnik and George Stricker. The staff of the university's Swirbul Library were extraordinarily creative and resourceful in locating documents. I am especially grateful to Dean Eugene Neely, Gertrude Neubauer and Victor Oliva. And, as always, Carol Sabino was helpful in a variety of ways.

Other scholars and friends read the manuscript—I am especially indebted to Mel Albin, David Burner and Dennis Fagan; others engaged in ongoing discussions during which they helped me clarify my ideas about the sixties—thanks to Anita Cohen, Denise Schank, Cathy Tuohy and Martin Van Lith. Michael Flamini, Alan Bradshaw, and Jennifer Simington of Palgrave were extremely helpful, effective and understanding; and a special thanks to William Berry for his adroit, focused and tenacious copy-editing.

This book is dedicated to two people without whom it would not have been written. Fred Weinstein was there from the beginning. He spent countless hours patiently reading numerous drafts of each chapter. More than that, his incisive mind (and wit) kept me on my toes. But even more than that, his unique ability to juggle and blend the roles of teacher and friend, critic and advisor, sparring partner and trainer, enabled me to push on when I was tempted to drop the project (the burden for not dropping it rests, of course, solely on my shoulders). Everyone who has dealt with, been touched and taught by Fred during his distinguished scholarly career knows what I'm talking about.

JoAnn Smith was there from the beginning as well. For hours, which slipped into days, then months and finally years, JoAnn listened to my ideas about the sixties and plans for "the book." She owns the book as much or more than I. Though a baby boomer, she is not a child of the sixties; and perhaps that fact, along with her formidable intelligence, made me listen when she voiced skepticism about ideas which struck her as off the mark. We spent hours talking about the fifties and the Diggers, and hours more listening to the music. And dancing to it. The book is over, but we're still dancing.

ONE

Problems in Making Sense of the Sixties

[O]ur national life has been a running argument about, and with, the sixties.

George F. Will, Forward, *Reassessing the Sixties*

THE INCLINATION OF AMERICANS TO EXPECT AND ACCEPT CHANGE is perhaps their most commonly shared national trait. But no one old enough to vote or understand the issues debated by John F. Kennedy and Richard M. Nixon during the presidential campaign of 1960 could have dreamed how profoundly and unalterably their society would change over the next ten years. Or how deeply distressing those changes would be to so many of them. The assumptions that shaped some of their most valued, fragile or problematic relationships—those between women and men, children and parents, students and teachers, citizens and political leaders, black people and white—unraveled to one degree or another during the decade.

But few events during that whirlwind of movements, conflicts and upheavals known as "the sixties" took Americans more by surprise or enraged them as much as the insurrection of those who were young, white and college-educated. Perhaps no other movement was more maligned during the sixties. Certainly none has been more misunderstood since. In this book I explore various expressions of white radicalism during the decade with an eye toward answering two basic questions about them.

First, why did they happen? How was the initial stirring of discontent among a relatively small number of college students at the start of the decade related to their upbringing? Or, to ask the same question somewhat differently, how did the furiously chaotic sixties spring from the comparatively placid late forties and fifties? And why did millions of young people become alienated from mainstream American values by the end of the decade?

At the time, convincing answers to these questions eluded most Americans, including thoughtful radicals. In 1965 Paul Potter, the president of the radical campus group Students for a Democratic Society (SDS), gave a speech to an audience of college administrators at the University of California at Berkeley. One of the most intelligent and politically astute radicals of the decade, Potter told his audience that the young white students who organized the New Left in the early sixties were the "sons and daughters of the American dream." Most were raised in "comfortable" middle-class suburbs in the forties and fifties, within what he called a "permissive" family culture. Many enrolled in the country's elite colleges and universities. Hence the mystery. "Somehow," said Potter, "and for reasons that are not entirely clear to me, this group of young people, who had everything their society could give them, found that gift hollow and rejected it."[1]

More than three decades after Potter's speech, the reasons for their discontent remain "not entirely clear." This is so despite the estimable attempts to account for it by those who have studied those volatile years.

The second question concerns the historical significance of the radical youth culture. What can it tell us about the American experience, before and since the sixties? What were the historical precedents of the political ideas advanced by SDS, the largest radical student group in American history? Where does the hippie counterculture—that strange, paradoxical melange of communal bonding and "do your own thing" individualism—fit into the broad sweep of American culture and history? These historical questions and issues have not been systematically pursued by scholars. And to do so is to embark on a very different enterprise from simply describing the rebellions, or searching for their immediate origins in the post World War II years leading up to 1960.

For instance, both the Civil Rights revolution of the early sixties and the women's movement that gathered momentum toward the end of the decade had deep historical roots as well as tangible immediate causes. They were not only responses to blatant contemporary injustices, but had precedents in earlier reform and liberation movements. At least on the surface, that cannot be said of the cultural and political radicalism that took shape in the first half of the sixties. These movements were created by groups of relatively privileged white college students whose leaders—though by no means, of course, all their adherents—were almost invariably men. And their substantive criticisms of American society, which garnered little serious attention in the sixties (beyond their opposition to the Vietnam War) and are all but forgotten today, exist in historical limbo. Rather than being an integral part of the American saga, they remain the stuff of myth, warm nostalgia or cold disdain, depending on one's point of view. I will suggest that the most important ideas and values of the radical youth culture were firmly grounded in specific American historical traditions. Most of them originated long before the forties, fifties and sixties. Indeed, before the twentieth century.

In answering the two questions, especially the second, the book often moves back and forth in American time. And my approach is thematic rather than chronological. This is an unusual way of exploring the decade's history. It requires, therefore, an introductory chapter that describes both the problems of accounting for the rise of the radical youth culture and how I propose to connect it to the American past.

THE ORIGINS OF DISCONTENT

During and since the sixties, historians and social critics have tried to account for the origins of the radical youth culture. Much of their work is astute and insightful, and can be divided into three major themes (they are not mutually exclusive). One of them interprets the disaffection and domestic violence generated by the war in Vietnam as the major force behind the decade's radical movements. In his perceptive history of the era's numerous movements, Terry Anderson called the Vietnam War "the engine of the sixties." Without the war, "the decade would have remained a liberal reform era, not a radical decade, not 'the sixties.'"[2]

There is, of course, a good deal of truth to this. The war in Vietnam inspired hundreds of thousands of perhaps otherwise apolitical young people to join antiwar organizations or to sporadically participate in increasingly bold and violent protests against the war. As the war dragged on in stalemate year after year, despite the optimistic predictions of military and civilian officials, it caused many Americans of all ages to question the wisdom, even the integrity, of their leaders. And it prompted a legion of young people either to "drop out" of society altogether and join the counterculture or display their alienation from mainstream America by selectively adopting elements of the hippie lifestyle. Perhaps as many as 3 million of the 45 million young people who turned 18 between 1960 and 1972 became involved with the counterculture to one degree or another, at one point or another. Tens of thousands of others joined, or identified with, radical political organizations like SDS.[3]

But the American combat presence in Vietnam, greatly expanded by President Lyndon Johnson in the spring of 1965, did not inspire young people to create early New Left groups like Students for a Democratic Society or the Student Peace Union. SDS was organized in 1960, the SPU in 1959. Of course, the obsessive anti-communism that defined the country's Cold War foreign policy and made the Vietnam tragedy possible, if not inevitable, contributed mightily to the development of the New Left to begin with. Nevertheless, the New Left was there before the war. And though it attracted only a few thousand adherents in the early sixties, it became a conduit for political opposition once the war erupted.

The hippie counterculture was already stirring in the San Francisco Bay Area when Johnson raised the stakes in Vietnam. For the rest of the decade the counterculture, with its rock music, long hair, hallucinogenic drugs, experiments in communal living and colorful costumes, served as the main vehicle of protest for young people who sought refuge from a society they saw as equal parts violent and boring. The foundations of the New Left and counterculture were laid in the first half of the decade. The young people who created these movements were poised to rebel from the beginning, before the war made protests against the "establishment" popular. They have to be accounted for.

But so do the hundreds of thousands who joined them after 1965. The war may have been the crucial factor in their decision, but that doesn't account for their disposition to oppose it. There was nothing inevitable about the antiwar movement. Just 15 years before Vietnam, the United States became involved in another stalemated and futile Asian land war, in Korea. The two conflicts erupted under different domestic circumstances, including rules governing the draft, but similarities between the two are significant. The Korean war was just as undeclared by Congress as Vietnam. And it was just as driven by American fears (and fantasies) of a monolithic international communist conspiracy directed by the Russians and Chinese and bent upon world conquest. Korea claimed over 36,000 American lives, about 20,000 fewer than were lost in Vietnam. But it did so much more quickly, in about one-third the time. Yet Korea did not generate significant domestic opposition, from young or old. By contrast, during the sixties hundreds of thousands of all ages, especially the young, were willing to protest a war and challenge the authorities who made it. The war in Vietnam did not create either the alienation felt by many young people or their penchant to question authority, although it greatly increased both.

A second way of accounting for the rebellion of the young in the sixties focuses on how they were raised in the forties and fifties. While the emphasis differs from one historian to another, all of them agree that most alienated young people came from middle-class families, especially before the late sixties. Their parents usually had at least some college education and were professionals or business executives. Or if not themselves middle-class, they wanted their children to become college-educated professionals and raised them accordingly. Either way, the overwhelming majority of the disaffected young were middle-class by birth or aspiration. Historians target various aspects of middle-class family life as holding the key to explaining the discontent of its children.

Some trace the rebelliousness of young people in the sixties to the affluence and consumerism of the fifties. According to this theory, the quest for self-fulfillment and the outright hedonism of the sixties youth culture were legacies of the affluent forties and fifties. During those years middle-class families indulged their children by catering to their whims. Some believe affluent parents raised children permissively. They socialized them in the ways and means of a post World War II orgy of promiscuous consumption. For the children of affluence, things came too early and too easily in that time of plenty.

During the fifties, corporations saw a potential windfall in the huge new market created by the baby boom. Department store shelves brimmed with everything from toys based on Walt Disney film and television characters to 45 rpm records whose vinyl grooves spun out a new music called rock-and-roll. Parents who remembered their own deprivations during the Great Depression of the 1930s eagerly showered their children with a cascade of consumer goods. As a result, according to Stanley Rothman and S. Robert Lichter, the "requirements of work and self-discipline" were gradually undermined. By the time the children of middle-class prosperity came of college age in the sixties, they lacked the capacity for delayed gratification that characterized previous generations. What they wanted, in a word, was "fun."[4]

A variation of this theme holds that affluent parents encouraged their children to believe that a good education inevitably led to prosperous careers, and both would make their future reasonably stable and secure. The affluence of their parents allowed children to feel secure enough about the future to indulge themselves in the present. Historian Godfrey Hodgson said the problem with hippies was that they were raised in a "no problem society—not of the United States but of the relatively privileged part of American society from which they came. They were bored because there was no problem about money, no problem about sex, no problem about college, and no great problem if you dropped out."[5]

A final spinoff on the theme of the middle-class family seizes on its democratic, child-centered qualities. Professional middle-class parents earnestly cultivated their children's moral and intellectual faculties. They encouraged them to think for themselves. The sociologist Richard Flacks, a leading member of SDS, went so far as to suggest that the child-centered ways of the middle-class family unwittingly subverted the "bourgeois" values of the wider society. These families encouraged children to express themselves and embrace "humanism."

Consequently, they became "hostile to the self-denying, status-oriented individualism of bourgeois culture."[6]

There is at least an element of truth in all of these views. The problem is that none of them can explain why "the sixties" happened only in the sixties. The egalitarian, child-centered, status-obsessed, consumer-oriented and frequently liberal-minded professional middle class family has existed since at least the late nineteenth century, though there were then fewer such families than in the years following World War II. This version of the middle-class family continues to thrive in the 1990s, in even greater numbers than in the forties, fifties and sixties. Yet neither before nor since the sixties have significant numbers, or comparable percentages, of its children dropped out of society or become its critics. Much less have they challenged the hegemony of "bourgeois culture." More important, other than in the sixties American college students have never *created* major cultural and political movements to protest the status quo. Quite the contrary. And if there was a link between an American cult of consumption and the sixties counterculture, it is not as obvious as some might think. "It wasn't hard to drop out," said one hippie. "I had a lot of things to get rid of—a car, a hi-fi, a million useless things." These sentiments were common among serious members of the counterculture.[7]

A third view about the origins of the radical youth culture is especially important. The psychologist Kenneth Keniston was probably the first to advance it, in the late sixties.[8] Keniston said the young activists he interviewed usually fulfilled rather than rebelled against the political and moral values of their middle-class parents. According to Keniston, most of the white students who joined New Left groups, civil-rights organizations like the Student Nonviolent Coordinating Committee, or participated in antiwar protests were acting on values they had learned at home. They had been instilled with empathy for the oppressed and the poor by liberal or, more rarely, radical parents. Also, the democratic, relatively egalitarian atmosphere in professional middle-class households encouraged children to think critically and question figures of authority. Young people raised to think for themselves became disillusioned and alienated when they discovered the chasm between the America depicted by politicians, clergy or teachers in the forties and fifties and the one they encountered around 1960. The United States was not the paladin of democracy, equality, freedom and universal affluence they had learned about in their textbooks.

Without question, the young people who joined civil-rights and peace organizations in the early years of the sixties were motivated by moral outrage over the gulf that separated American ideals from American realities. Their activism was ignited when they discovered that the United States was riddled with racism and poverty. They were disturbed as well by the pervasive, irrational anti-communism that dominated American politics, stifled dissent at home and inspired a nuclear arms race that threatened human survival. I want to make it clear that I believe these issues played a major role in fostering their initial rumblings of alienation from American society.

Yet by themselves they cannot account for the origins of the New Left or the counterculture. Racism neither suddenly burst onto the American scene in 1960 nor disappeared after 1970. Why didn't comparable percentages of morally concerned, middle-class white college students join African American organizations in their struggle against institutionalized racism in the prosperous 1950s? Or during the boom times of the 1920s? For that matter, why are they holding back in the affluent 1990s? Issues dividing the races are different today than they were in 1960 but nonetheless remain explosive. The same is true of poverty and the inequitable distribution of income. Even during its most spectacular boom periods in this century, the United States economy has been marked by gross disparities in wealth and large numbers of poor people.[9] And as for the existence of government officials who ignore the country's democratic traditions and procedures in designing their foreign and domestic policies, what made the America of 1960 particularly unique in this regard?

The willingness of significant numbers of college-educated young whites to rebel in the sixties requires an explanation that includes but goes beyond the existence of these issues and inequities as they existed in 1960. And as we shall see in chapter 4, some of the white college students involved in the Civil Rights movement in the early sixties were quite conscious at the time of being motivated by urges that went beyond (but certainly didn't detract from) their sincere moral outrage over racial injustice.

In the three chapters that make up part I, "Sources of Ferment in the Forties and Fifties," I describe how the culture, economy and boundless expectations of the affluent, comparatively placid postwar years fed into the upheavals led by the young in the sixties. Like others who have tackled this issue, my focus is on how radicals were raised. But my interpretation of this process is very different.

A good deal of chapter 3 describes the child-rearing patterns in middle-class families of the forties and fifties. These children were obsessively doted upon by their parents, but they were also taught self-discipline. Their intellectual and moral faculties were energetically cultivated, though seldom with the goal of making them rebels. They were led to believe their lives would be self-fulfilling, adventurous and challenging, but only if they were competitive, hard working, self-reliant and willing to take risks.

These attributes were not nurtured in a vacuum. Middle-class parents encouraged their children to be intensely competitive and individualistic so they might take advantage of the extraordinary economic and personal opportunities created by the postwar economic boom. The unprecedented prosperity of those years was unexpected, coming as it did on the heels of the Great Depression and the dislocations of the war years. Its magnitude and longevity created the most widespread boom mentality in the country's history, a modern reprise of pre-twentieth-century American dreams of limitless frontiers of possibility. By contrast with most previous and subsequent eras of prosperity, the cornucopia of the postwar boom was relatively egalitarian; it swelled the incomes of millions of working class families and led them to believe that they or their children would attain middle class status (despite the fact that twenty percent of the population stagnated in poverty). It was as though the New World of incalculable economic frontiers and boundless personal horizons had been discovered all over again. Major technological innovations, expanded educational opportunities and developments in popular culture reinforced these sensibilities. They suffused the world of the young, at home, in school and through the media. In other words, various social and cultural trends reinforced the traditional American values of individualism, self-reliance and autonomy imbibed within the family. Along with their parents, the children came to believe anything was possible in America.

In 1960 President John F. Kennedy used the term "New Frontier" to describe the youthful daring of his administration. This historically evocative phrase is appropriate as well for defining the culture of limitless expectations that reigned within the postwar middle-class family and the wider society.

Many sixties radicals sprang from that culture, though most of their parents did not raise them to become disillusioned with their country, much less grow into radicals. But the traits instilled at home did arouse expectations about leading autonomous, adventurous lives in an egalitarian society. These sensibilities were out of step with the social and political conformity of the fifties. More important, they were sanctioned by powerful myths and values woven into American culture from the beginning. The mixture of the two proved combustible in the sixties.

I will argue that the New Left and counterculture were more than rebellions against a repressive, boring Cold War culture. In addition they revived older, mostly pre-industrial visions of work, individualism, self-reliance, community and democracy. In effect, they pitted a somewhat mythic (though real enough) America of open spaces, adventure and unpredictability against the modern managerial, bureaucratic and (from their point of view) staid society that they inherited as they reached college age in the middle of the twentieth century. The fear and furor created by the emergence of the sixties youth culture reflected an underlying struggle between two powerful, historically grounded yet contradictory versions of American life.

Part I links the child-rearing practices of the middle class in the forties and fifties to the values and behavior of young radicals in the sixties. A good deal of evidence is mobilized to support this view. But short of the impossible task of compiling biographies of every political and cultural radical mentioned in the book, the evidence is inferential, as it must be when drawing connections between childhood experiences and adult behavior. Not every sixties radical was raised by college-educated or affluent middle-class parents (or by working-class parents intent upon achieving professional status for their children). And by no means did everyone raised in such families become alienated from mainstream American values. The story told here is necessarily incomplete and inevitably immune to "scientific" validation. Hopefully it provides a reasonably convincing narrative of how and why this unprecedented insurrection among young Americans occurred.

THE SIXTIES IN AMERICAN HISTORY

The remainder of the book is an attempt to connect three important and very different expressions of the radical youth culture to the American past. The hippie movement, which started in San Francisco, is discussed in chapter 5, and the attitudes toward work of those who created the music of rebellion, sixties rock-and-roll, is the subject of chapter 6. Chapters 7 and 8 describe Students for a Democratic Society and the ambiguities and ideals of the American political tradition it reasserted.

The goal of these chapters is to weave the radical youth culture into the American experience. Unlike other major instances of turbulent internal conflict, such as the American Revolution and the Civil War, the sixties of youthful rebellion has not been sutured to the country's past. Rather than being explained by and made an integral part of that history, this crucial aspect of the decade dangles in time. It is generally unhinged from what went before, and painfully alien to what followed. It remains, therefore, inevitably misunderstood and misinterpreted.

This is evident in contemporary views of the radical youth culture. In the mass media the revolt of young people in the sixties is often portrayed as a bad memory happily fading as the decade recedes in time. For instance, some blame the tumult and violence of the decade on the "spoiled" children of middle-class affluence. In the words of a *Time* magazine columnist writing in 1996, they were "overprivileged, pretentious, self-righteous, self-important."[10] And although the only apparent links between the heinous acts of a serial bomber (known as the Unabomber) apprehended in the nineties and sixties radicalism are the facts that the Unabomber taught at Berkeley in 1967 and composed a "manifesto" studded with caricatures of sixties radicalism, a recent headline in the *New York Times* nonetheless reads, "Campus Turmoil of 60's Reveals Themes Echoed in Unabom Manifesto." And one in *Newsday* proclaims, "The Unabomber Is a Typical '60s Lout."[11]

Still others see the legacies of the youth culture as a host of social "pathologies": an ongoing drug problem, moral relativism, political correctness, multiculturalism, sexual promiscuity, high divorce rates, identity politics, mistrust of authority figures and disengagement from the electoral process. Allan Bloom's 1987 book, *The Closing of the American Mind,* placed a good deal of the blame for these conditions on the counterculture and New Left.[12] More directly, and minus Bloom's erudition, Republican congressman and majority leader of the House of Representatives Dick Armey asserted in 1995 that "all the [contemporary] problems began in the Sixties." Indeed, the upheavals of the sixties continue to inform the political animosities of the 1990s. During the 1992 presidential campaign Bill Clinton's patriotism was questioned because of his antiwar stance during the sixties, and in 1994 House Speaker Newt Gingrich referred to him as a "counterculture McGovernik."[13] Of course, running against "the sixties" in political campaigns is as old as the decade itself. Ronald Reagan's successful campaign for governor of California in 1966 was enhanced by his incessant warnings to voters that the Free Speech Movement at Berkeley in 1964 and the hippies of San Francisco were harbingers of anarchy and moral degeneration.

Focusing on the bizarre and irrational nature of the sixties youth culture (it possessed both qualities) allows critics (and most other Americans) to ignore its legitimate and still-relevant criticisms of American society. Some who were young, radical or otherwise "hip" during the sixties may recall it fondly. But they tend to engage in wistful nostalgia about lost opportunities to change the direction of the country. Or they invoke the decade as if it was a dream.[14]

Young people enrolled in the proliferating college courses on the sixties, like the one I teach, often seem envious of that generation's lust for freedom, commitment to causes and casual willingness to challenge authority. But contemporary students have difficulty fathoming the depth of that "older" generation's alienation from American institutions. Most do not entertain the possibility that the rebellions of the sixties may have been mobilized by issues that were inextricably tied to but went beyond the antiwar, Civil Rights or women's movements. Nor can they imagine how deeply etched in the American grain were even the most radical visions of the New Left and counterculture.

Drawing connections between events in the sixties and those of the distant past is a hazardous enterprise fraught with snares, both obvious and subtle. Some caveats are in order. I am not suggesting that ideas and circumstances that existed before the twentieth century were directly tied, in some causal continuum, to the movements discussed in this book. Or that terms like democracy, autonomy and individualism necessarily mean the same things in different historical periods. Nor do I argue that hippies, New Leftists and rock musicians looked to earlier movements in American history for inspiration. On the contrary, like most of their fellow citizens they viewed the past as an obstacle to transcend rather than as integral part of the present. They were typically American in believing a new and perfect world could be created from scratch and that they were the ones to do it.

At the same time, however, I would suggest that a people's myths of origination—its stories about where they came from, what they became and how both frame a projected future—are passed from one generation to another. As are ambiguities and conflicts about the meaning of the values and ideals contained in those narratives. They are adapted to the unique circumstances confronted by each generation and transmitted in various formats through an assortment of media.

For instance, when the sixties generation was growing up, the media were saturated with stories about the American Old West. Young people were inundated with novels, comic books, movies and especially television programs about the Wild West. They were surrounded by powerful, often historically inaccurate tales of the adventure, danger and individualism associated with the "conquest" of the West, and of its centrality to their country's identity. Young people diligently raised by parents to be individualistic in the extreme and trained to be poised for adventure and risk taking might well identify with these images. Or they might intuit how sharply these values contrasted with the emphasis on personal security and conformity during the fifties. Or both. Put another way, there was nothing inevitable about the prevalence within the counterculture of cowboy garb, unruly long hair on males, Indian lore and other images linked to the frontier and Old West. But it was far too pervasive to have been mere coincidence either. The question is, what did it mean?

The same is true of the democratic values espoused by SDS. It was not so much that they were socialized as children to value democracy and equality. So is every generation of young Americans, although those growing up during the most heated years of the Cold War might have heard more about their country's democratic heritage and why it was worth defending. What distinguished the experiences of young people in the forties and fifties were the implacable intensity and limitless optimism with which their parents and others urged them to become autonomous, take command of their lives and exploit new frontiers of post-war economic and personal opportunity. Because of this, they may have viewed the American idealization of democracy as the political coin that legitimated their need for autonomy and independence. They valued democracy not only as an end in itself, but also as a means of achieving control over their lives. Under certain circumstances, such as the apathy or violence with which most white adults responded to the early Civil Rights movement, they might also come to see that what passed for democracy and equality in their country were mere shadows of the real things.

Finally, the reasons for building the book around SDS, the counterculture and rock music should be explained. Especially since I largely ignore other movements that arguably were far more significant and undeniably had a greater impact on the country in the long run. For instance, the Civil Rights and women's movements are the decade's primary legacies. Unlike the counterculture and New Left, they still exert a powerful influence on society. They continue to challenge attitudes and institutional arrangements that historically consigned African Americans and women to second-class citizenship. Or worse. Also, involvement in the Civil Rights and women's movements was deeply entwined with the disaffection of young, middle-class whites, especially those in New Left organizations like SDS.[15] And isolating as I do the history of political and cultural radicals from the Civil Rights and women's movements, as well as from the anti-Vietnam War crusade, incurs the risk of artificially extracting them from the wider context of the decade's liberation and protest movements.

Despite this, I have decided to take the risk. A major goal of this book is to link the youth culture to the American past. Unlike the counterculture and New Left, the historical roots of the Civil Rights and women's movements have been thoroughly excavated by scholars. The sources of their discontent and their relation to previous reform movements now form an integral part of the American story. The history of both groups has been incorporated into high school and college textbook accounts of the American experience.

Also, in contrast to student radicals and hippies, an aura of political and cultural legitimacy surrounds the Civil Rights and women's movements. There were radical feminists and black activists who challenged the economic and social premises of American society. But the primary goal of most of their advocates was to achieve American equality: before the law and of educational and economic opportunity. Neither group has achieved full equality of opportunity, but the phrase "equality of opportunity" invests both movements with a legitimacy never enjoyed by the New Left or counterculture. The term embodies an ideal that goes to the heart of what the country means to most of its citizens. Equality of opportunity, along with more or less unfettered competition between individuals for wealth and status, defines what freedom means to most Americans. The vast majority of civil-rights and women's advocates reasserted ideals upon which the country was supposedly founded, and to which most of its people generally adhere. At least in theory.

This was not the case with the young men and women who were hippies, New Leftists or rock musicians in the sixties. They may have reprised myths and ideas that are touchstones of the nation's identity. And their dedication to liberty and democracy is shared by most of their fellow citizens, at least in the abstract. Indeed, Americans tend to think they invented them.

Yet for reasons touched upon throughout the book, most Americans recoil from the radical implications of the freedom, autonomy and democracy enshrined in their myths of national origins. In the sixties the youth culture revived and acted upon those myths. And for a fleeting, brutally contentious moment in American time, it made them all too real.

PART I

Sources of Ferment in the Forties and Fifties

What is happening in Eastern Europe and Spain, in Brazil and Argentina, is easier to understand: it is the fight for freedom. But what then do the student uprisings of the affluent world represent? The answer is not easy or clear.

Nathan Glazer, *Remembering the Answers,* 1970

[T]he civil rights and student movements had taken all political intellectuals by surprise. We were making a chapter of history no one had anticipated.

Tom Hayden, *Reunion: A Memoir,* 1988

TWO

The Cult of Security

Domesticity, religiosity, security through compliance with the system, that was the essence of the fifties.

Douglas Miller and Marion Nowak, *The Fifties,* 1977

A stench of fear has come out of American life, and we suffer from a collective failure of nerve.

Norman Mailer, *The White Negro,* 1957

CONTRADICTORY IMAGES OF YOUTH IN THE FORTIES AND FIFTIES

THE FOLLOWING VIGNETTES portray two views of young people during the 1940s and 1950s. They existed simultaneously and projected contradictory visions of American society and where it was headed.

Youth and Conformity

A cover story in the November 5, 1951 issue of *Time* was titled "The Younger Generation." Sounding alarms about contemporary youth that journalists and intellectuals would repeat throughout the fifties, the magazine proclaimed young people of the fifties a generation of conformists. *Time* had commissioned an extensive survey of Americans between 18 and 28. The results suggested that American traditions of "rugged individualism" and entrepreneurial drive were virtually extinct, especially among those born between the mid 1920s and mid 1930s.

According to the magazine, young people lacked the hunger for adventure and the burning desire for personal achievement that had animated previous generations. The amenities of life in an affluent society made them soft and satisfied. Contemporary young people wanted safe jobs and secure private lives; they not only distanced themselves from the daring individualism of their forebears, but acted as if "the frontiers of the U. S. economy have been reached." Even in the Far West, "only yesterday removed from the frontier," the pioneer spirit of independence was replaced by a "curious dependence on the biggest new employer—Government." Rather than creating new frontiers of opportunity, the young wanted to husband and enjoy the unprecedented prosperity created by a booming postwar economy. Mired in conformity, few of them were able to stand apart from the crowd by taking unpopular stands on political or social issues.

There were scattered exceptions to this trend. A young woman from Minneapolis expressed dismay over her generation's slide toward conformity in behavior and uniformity in outlook. "The individual is dead today," she said.

> But the young people are unaware of it. They think of themselves as individuals, but really they are not. They are parts of groups. They are unhappy outside of a group. When they are alone, they are bored with themselves. There is a tendency now to date in foursomes, or sixsomes. Very few dates are just a boy and a girl together. They have to be with a crowd. These kids in my group think of themselves as individuals, but actually it is as if you took a tube of toothpaste and squeezed out a number of distinct blobs on a piece of paper. Each blob would be distinctive—separated in space—but each blob would be the same.

Many students of American society during the fifties agreed with this view. The most pervasive (and perhaps overwrought) portrait of middle-class life in the fifties drawn by contemporary critics was that of the youthful "organization man" who was too "other-directed" to have a mind of his own and was easily recognized by his white collar uniform: the gray flannel suit.[1]

Youth and Non-Conformity

But something else was happening to children of the middle class who were born just prior to, during or immediately following World War II. Janis Joplin, one of the premier rock-and-roll performers of the sixties, was eight years old when the *Time* article appeared. She lived in Port Arthur, Texas, where her father was an executive with the Texaco company. Joplin's parents were among the relatively small number of Americans at the time who had attended college, though neither graduated. They were determined to raise children who were self-reliant and autonomous. For example, the toys they purchased had to do more than divert or entertain; they had to enhance the children's initiative and intellectual development. "We never got toys that did something on their own," said Laura Joplin in her biography of her famous sister. Their toys "were always raw materials that stimulated the imagination of the user. We had to provide the spark that made the experience fun."

Their mother stressed the importance of excelling in school and competing for superior grades. She told her children that inspired hard work was the only way to succeed. She would quote Abraham Lincoln on the importance of self-reliance: "'You cannot help men permanently by doing for them what they could and should do for themselves.'" Usually it was their mother who "cajoled, negotiated, stimulated, and oftentimes laid down the law about homework." But both parents encouraged the children to think about social and moral issues, and come to independent judgments about them.

> Reading and ideas defined our family life. No one hesitated to broach any topic during the dinner-table conversation, and our parents expected each child to contribute to discussions. Personal thought on a subject was paramount for Mom and Pop. They asked, "What do you think, Janis?" Then they listened seriously to our replies. In this way they taught us about personal integrity. If you could state your opinion and back it up, then you should stick to it.

Even when they disagreed with their children, Mr. and Mrs. Joplin encouraged their independence. In the mid sixties Janis Joplin left Port Arthur for San Francisco, where in a few years she would become the country's most celebrated female rock star. When her father visited Joplin, who at the time lived in San Francisco's bohemian North Beach neighborhood, he was taken aback by his daughter's determined immersion in the emerging hippie lifestyle. Rather than expressing his disappointment, however, he "affirmed that she was a beautiful person." "You will achieve," he told her.

Despite her chronic insecurity, Joplin more than fulfilled her father's prophecy. To a considerable degree, her success was founded on the self-reliance and on the lessons about hard work and the importance of striving for excellence she had learned while growing up. In a letter written to her mother in 1968 she said her rock group, Big Brother and the Holding Company, was "working, working, working, all spare time devoted to sleeping and eating. Mother, even w[ith] your incredible pace [you] would be amazed at all we've been doing." In another letter, composed a few months before her death from a heroin overdose in 1970, Joplin told her family that being "numero uno" in the music business means you "gotta break ass so nobody catches you! Catches you? Two years ago I didn't even want to be it! No, that's not true. I've been looking around and I've noticed something. After you reach a certain level of talent (and quite a few have that talent) the deciding factor [in attaining success] is ambition."[2]

In this and the following chapter these contradictory images of youth are described. The social conformity portrayed by *Time* and the competitive individualism encouraged in the Joplin household were responses to the extraordinary economic prosperity, technological innovation, corporate consolidation, enhanced educational opportunity and dedicated consumerism of the post–World War II years. But each reaction projected a different vision of American life. The cult of security, well documented in surveys of young people made during these years, imagined an America that was settled and stable. It conjured a country whose people held secure jobs and had stable, loving families that lived in safe suburban enclaves. They were united by their abhorrence of communist subversion at home and abroad, and they believed the post-war economic boom would continue as long as extreme expressions of competitive individualism were contained.

But the less well documented child-rearing strategies of families like the Joplins, garnered mostly from inferential but intriguing evidence supplied by parents during the fifties, implied a very different America. Far from being settled, the country was brimming with challenges, opportunities and unpredictability. It was, therefore, a theater of boundless possibility for those, like Janis Joplin, who were equipped to walk onto its stage, risk failure and aggressively seize the day. If, in fact, the fifties was an age of conformity, of a play-it-safe obsession with security, it contained its own negation in the way these children were raised. In other words, it harbored the seeds of rebellion that sprouted in the early to middle years of the sixties.[3]

THE CULT OF SECURITY

Political discourse in the late forties and fifties revolved around a coercive disdain for dissent fed by fears of international and domestic communism. An obsession with containing communist expansion abroad was complemented by fears of being overwhelmed by a subversive "red menace" at home. The diplomat George Kennan, an architect of the American containment policy toward the spread of international communism, made it clear that political conflict over basic issues at home would embolden communists abroad. Any "exhibitions" of domestic "disunity," he wrote in 1947, would have "an exhilarating effect on the whole Communist movement."[4]

Such thinking helped feed a terrifying hunt within the United States for alleged communist subversives. The search was spearheaded by government officials, congressional committees and influential journalists. Their assumption—that a Soviet-controlled and *widespread* domestic communist conspiracy existed—was ludicrous. A small number of American communists were, in fact, spies acting on orders from the Soviet Union. Some, like Julius and Ethel Rosenberg, who were accused of passing secrets about the atomic bomb to the Soviets, were exposed and prosecuted (the Rosenbergs were executed in 1953). But in the process of ferreting out a small number of actual American communists who spied for the Russians, the reputations and livelihoods of thousands of innocent people were destroyed. They were persecuted and at times prosecuted because of their past or present beliefs, not their behavior. Dissent from the political and social status quo was nearly eliminated; even opposition to laws sanctioning racial segregation was viewed as subversive. College officials hired so-called security officers, some of them former FBI agents, to attend classes and listen for hints of communist sympathies in professors' lectures. The House Un-American Activities Committee conducted hearings in a manner reminiscent of the Inquisition. Acting on hearsay or on evidence about an individual's past or present sympathies with leftist causes, committee members hounded citizens from a wide spectrum of backgrounds. The scope of their targets ranged from Hollywood screenwriters, directors and actors to teachers, professors and union officials.

Thousands of individuals were fired from their jobs or blacklisted. Over 6 million Americans were subjected to loyalty checks, usually without their knowledge. The domestic terror would subsequently be associated with the bizarre behavior and unsupported accusations of Republican senator Joseph McCarthy. But many other officials, Democrats and liberals as well as Republicans and conservatives, also exaggerated the threat posed by domestic communists. J. Howard McGrath, President Truman's last attorney general, said communists "are everywhere." They lurked stealthily "in factories, offices, butcher shops, on street corners, in private businesses—and each carries in himself the germs of death for society."[5]

Historian Godfrey Hodgson aptly called the forties and fifties an "age of liberal consensus."[6] (Of course, African Americans were excluded from the consensus, as were those who veered from the political and social mainstream.) A good deal of the consensus rested on this collective obsession with communism, but factors other than anticommunism helped forge the surface unity.

During this period of unprecedented economic prosperity and low unemployment, most Americans apparently shared a belief in the infinite productivity and beneficence of the free-enterprise system. They generally supported the relatively meager economic safety nets created by the New Deal, such as Social Security. And they were certain they were hitched to history's most powerful economic engine: all Americans were inevitably bound for universal affluence, or at least comfortable middle-class status. As Hodgson said, they seemed convinced that "a natural harmony of interests" united the country. They felt that "American society was getting more equal. It is in the process of abolishing, may even have abolished, social class. Capitalists are being superseded by managers. The workers are becoming members of the middle class."[7]

To some degree, social conformity and an obsession with security were handmaidens of this prosperity and confidence. Historian R. W. B. Lewis, writing in the fifties, said American society had become a "curiously frozen" place in which a chilling conformity had all but eliminated "opposite possibilities" of any sort.[8] High schools preached "life adjustment." Students who were different in appearance or behavior from their peers were often deemed uncooperative, even neurotic, by school officials. A frenzy of consumption—of new homes, new automobiles, and new toys for the children of the newly affluent—was complemented by an atmosphere in which students "didn't challenge any authority" or ask any questions.[9] And Marty Jezer pointedly titled his history of the period *The Dark Ages.*[10] As Benita Eisler remarked in her study of the fifties, those who came of age in that decade quickly learned that they had to curb "spontaneity, irrationality, individualism of any kind" to be accepted.[11] Many contemporary commentators were equally struck by the conformity of Americans, both at work and in their private lives. As much as any development of the time, the scores of more or less identical homes that dotted recently constructed suburban communities symbolized the drift away from the individualism and independence of spirit that had supposedly characterized earlier generations.

There was a good deal of justification for these views. In 1949 William H. Whyte, an editor of *Fortune,* analyzed the results of a survey of that year's graduating college class that had been commissioned by the magazine. In Whyte's opinion, this elite group wanted no part of the adventure and daring that inspired old-style entrepreneurs. "What they don't want" said Whyte of recent graduates, "is risk" of any sort. Contemporary young people sought the sure bet and the safe job. "Above everything else security has become the great goal." And they were convinced that security on the job, as well as stability in their family lives, was to be won by working for large corporations rather than striking out on their own. As one graduate said with absolute assurance, "I know that A. T. and T. might not be very exciting, but there will always be an A. T. and T." Whyte believed these young people were as dedicated to capitalism as previous generations, but they lacked the drive and ambition of traditional entrepreneurs. They were, declared Whyte, "interested in the system rather than the individual enterprise. They will be technicians" or managers in large companies rather than "owners" of their own enterprises. The class of '49, the "leaders of tomorrow," were described by Whyte as a security-obsessed, "settling-down generation."[12]

Similar views of the young and their lack of ambition were common in the fifties. In June 1957 *Life* magazine published excerpts of speeches made at college commencement ceremonies around the country. Some speakers echoed the sentiments expressed by Whyte in 1949 and *Time* in 1951, but their tone was harsher and more shrill. At DePauw University Thomas Watson, Jr., president of IBM, criticized the graduates and their generation for being more "concerned with security than integrity," and with "imitating" others rather than "creating" their own values. He scorned those who shunned a life of "free and fearless inquiry," or whose horizons were limited to becoming voiceless, faceless members of an "organization." Such individuals, said Watson, were like "jellyfish wrapped in Cellophane." Abram Sachar, president of Brandeis University, was more concise in summarizing the attitudes of the young. Alluding perhaps to the generation's political quiescence as well as its limited personal aspirations, he called their desire for "security" a "craven disguise for servility." And the president of Yale used the occasion of commencement to criticize both the graduates and their society. The United States was becoming "a whole nation of yesmen." Because they "spend so much of their time listening to somebody else," Americans were in danger of losing the capacity to behave autonomously.[13]

A year later, the distinguished sociologist David Riesman echoed these sentiments. Riesman, who popularized the term "other-directed" to describe the prevailing postwar American "character" in his 1950 book, *The Lonely Crowd,* mourned the loss of enterprise and innovation in the country. Riesman's tone was reminiscent of historian Frederick Jackson Turner's late-nineteenth-century pessimism about the country's future in the absence of a physical frontier. Riesman said the United States had become "a conservative country," whose people retreated from rather than eagerly explored new frontiers of opportunity and experience. Despite "our world-wide reputation for seeking novelty," Americans in the fifties were "unable . . . to envisage alternative futures" to the present.[14]

As late as December 1961, perceptions of the young as bland, stolid and beset by limited aspirations were reinforced by a Gallup Poll commissioned by the *Saturday Evening Post.* George Gallup and Evan Hill interviewed a diverse group of young people between 14 and 22. They ranged from high school and college students to blue collar workers. Gallup and Hill concluded that young Americans of the sixties would be as conformist and as immune to risk-taking as those of the previous decade. Those coming of age in the sixties were "most unlikely to rebel" or become involved in "crusades." According to Gallup and Hill, "our typical youth will settle for low success rather than risk high failure. He has little spirit of adventure. He wants to marry early. He wants very little because he has so much and is unwilling to risk what he has. Essentially he is quite conservative and cautious. He is old before his time."[15]

Surveys of college student attitudes were especially common during the fifties. Perhaps they were targeted because the opinions of working-class youth were considered unimportant by middle-class analysts. Or because fears about waning individualism among the nation's educated elite were particularly alarming. In any event, college students and graduates were usually described as insulated from the heat generated by burning ambition.

The March 9, 1957 cover story in the *Nation* was titled "The Careful Young Men." The *Nation*'s editors asked professors from 16 colleges and universities to describe their students' political ideals, intellectual role models and personal aspirations. Stanley Kunitz of Queens College said the "mass" of his students embraced lives of "quiet enervation." They "articulate caution" and strive "above all . . . to buy security for themselves in the full knowledge that the price is conformity." One of his students expressed gratitude to Senator Joseph McCarthy (presumably with irony) for "having taught his generation a valuable lesson: to keep its mouth shut." Stanford's Wallace Stegner said his students lived the "other-directed" conformity to peer group values described by Riesman in *The Lonely Crowd.* Professor Charles Fenton of Yale criticized his students, most of whom he derided as prospective "company men," for their uncritical dedication to the status quo. The University of Minnesota's Leo Marx expressed dismay that students lacked passionate commitment to anything, "perhaps even to passion itself." So it went, from one faculty member to another. Most admitted it was dangerous to generalize about an entire generation, and a few noted the presence of a small number of nonconformists on campus. But as the *Nation*'s editors remarked, the picture of American youth drawn by faculty portrayed a generation that was "prematurely aged." They were young people "old beyond their years" and bereft of "gaiety and a sense of life."[16]

In 1956 Riesman published the results of still another survey of college students in an article titled "The Found Generation."[17] Riesman said the survey was neither comprehensive nor "scientific." Nevertheless, "there is very little evidence in the interviews that the respondents have had to struggle for anything they want—or have wanted anything that would cost them a struggle." An affluent, secure, efficient and organized society had built a "floor under these men" and a "low ceiling over them."

Those interviewed for this survey, representatives of the class of 1955, projected futures for themselves that corroborated Riesman's caustic judgment. One of them justified his goal of working for a large corporation by saying he did not expect to be "making capital gains, even by 35," so "why struggle on my own [as an entrepreneur] when I can enjoy the big psychological income of being a member of a big outfit?" Another was convinced that large corporations were inherently "benevolent." They do "what's best for you and best for them," he said.

These young men were remarkably certain about what the future held in store for them. One predicted his future wife (he had yet to meet a suitable candidate for the position) would be "vivacious." While he would not "marry her until I'm twenty-eight," by the time he turned 36 they would have "two of the four children I hope for eventually. We'll be living in an upper-middle-class home costing about $20,000 by then, in a suburban fringe." Traditional gender roles were the ballast of these visions of future bliss and security. Another member of the class of 1955, also neither married nor acquainted with his future wife, predicted that by the time he was 35 his life would "not be a burden for me." He looked forward to being

> securely anchored in my family. My main emotional ties will center on my wife and family. I hope for five children. Yes, I can describe my wife. She will be the Grace Kelly, camel's-hair-coat type. Feet on the ground, and not an empty shell or a flake. Although an Ivy League type, she will also be centered in the home, a housewife. Perhaps at forty-five, with the children grown up, she will go in for hospital work and so on.

Their implacable determination to lead secure, settled, orderly, predictable lives was concisely summarized in the words of a Harvard graduate. "I think," he said, "contentment is the main thing."[18]

In 1958 psychologists Daniel Miller and Guy Swanson linked the apparent erosion of individualism in the young to two related factors: the increasing emergence of a corporation-dominated economy since the turn of the century, and a consequent shift in child-rearing practices that took hold toward the end of the 1930s. Miller and Swanson argued that working for large corporations or massive government bureaucracies led to a decrease in competitive individualism. Parents who wanted their children to succeed in a salaried, white collar, corporate and less entrepreneurial economy discouraged them from being overly "aggressive or too ambitious." These "qualities disturbed the corporation's course." Instead of creating "inner-directed," morally autonomous, competitive children, they geared their offspring to be cooperative and sensitive to the needs of others. They had to be attuned to subtle shades of intent transmitted by those above and below them in a complex chain of command. They needed to be sensitive to potential shifts of power and influence within the organization. Middle-class children were being raised to become "members of great organizations" rather than pioneers of enterprise. Since "their behavior will be guided and supervised through daily contact with others, there is less need for fathers and mothers to provide the child" with the "stern, self-propelling conscience" displayed by the rugged individualist of American lore.[19]

Stability at Home

Family stability and cohesion symbolized the cult of security as much as any other facet of social life in the fifties. As Riesman's survey of the class of 1955 suggested, family "togetherness" was universally idealized by college students. Their certainty about what the future held in store for them was inseparable from participation in an idyllic family life. They envisioned a life that was family centered and, therefore, secure, insular and private. And, of course, these projections in turn were based on the assumption that their wives would happily embrace traditional gender roles.

Their focus on family was not isolated. By the early fifties the idealization of family stability—a staple of American culture in any period—reached epic proportions. Every influential means of communication, including popular magazines, television, film, the pulpit, academic journals and government publications, praised the family as the linchpin of personal and social stability. And they railed against the forces capable of undermining family cohesion. Especially worrisome in this regard were divorce and infidelity. Women who harbored ambitions beyond marriage and motherhood were agents of family dissolution as well. The family was portrayed as a fortress of security and nurture in a world sizzling with conflict, anxiety and the prospect of nuclear war.

The post-1945 obsession with family reflected a widespread need for the stability and tranquility denied Americans during 15 years of economic depression and world war. In a remarkable reversal of demographic trends, Americans married at earlier ages and had children in quicker succession. The migration from city to suburb (by the mid fifties, 4,000 families made the move each day), the baby boom and the proliferation of home ownership reinforced ideals of domesticity and privacy. The suburban family ensconced in a newly purchased home was more than a symbol of stability and postwar affluence. As the editors of *McCall's* magazine said in 1954, the fifties family was a harbinger of a "new and warmer way of life." It created a "common experience" among its members and decreased the individual's sense of isolation in a complex, increasingly impersonal society. What *McCall's* glorified as family "togetherness" complemented the quest for a secure job in a large corporation. Both pointed to a life of serenity and "contentment."[20]

The idealization of family life helped solidify the image of the fifties as an age of conformity, especially when it was tied to the suburban lifestyle. Historian Loren Baritz claimed the lifestyle of the suburban family increased the susceptibility of Americans "to public opinion." The demographic, racial and social class uniformity of the suburbs, as well as similarities in patterns of consumption and architecture, elevated conformity in these middle-class enclaves to a "level approaching tyranny."[21]

Baritz's point may be valid, but idyllic images of home, family and suburb served other purposes as well. In her history of family life in the fifties, Elaine Tyler May suggested that a connection existed between the cult of female domesticity, the apparent decline of male individualism, and the country's obsession with communist expansion. May argued that the policy of "containment" toward the spread of international communism was mirrored on the home front in the desires of men to have secure jobs and stable families. The repression of aggressive masculine competitiveness on the job and the attempt to curb women's ambitions by limiting it to their maternal roles were means of "containing" domestic disorder and dislocation. A powerful longing for security and order dominated their lives—whether on the job or in the home, through clearly defined gender roles or from the threat posed by international communism.[22]

To some intellectuals at the time, the idea of domesticity symbolized not only orderly personal lives, but their accommodation to American society as well. For some, particularly former radicals, home and family served as metaphors for coming to terms with an American culture from which they had previously been alienated. In an essay written in the late fifties, the sociologist Daniel Bell traced the ideological trajectory of a number of intellectuals who, like himself, had been communists or socialists during the thirties.[23] As they came of college age during the thirties, economic depression in the United States and the rise of Nazism in Germany led Bell's generation of radicals to entertain visions of a transforming moment of revolution and redemption. They were committed to an ideological faith in the possibility of fashioning a utopia in which economic exploitation, ignorance and totalitarianism might be vanquished once and for all.

But lessons they learned in the late thirties and forties convinced them that "such chiliastic moments are illusions." Bell and other intellectuals—he named Reinhold Niebuhr, John Dos Passos, Sidney Hook, Alfred Kazin and Lionel

Trilling, among others—developed a more realistic, "ironic" and paradoxical view of human nature and its prospects. The depredations of Stalinism and the inexpressible horror of Hitler's gas chambers convinced them that human beings were "children of darkness" as well as "children of light," in the biblical phrase Niebuhr chose for the title of one of his books.

Accordingly, Bell and his cohort of radical intellectuals became a "twice-born generation." As young men they deplored the crude materialism of America's financial elite, the mediocrity of its popular culture and the anti-intellectualism of its democratic "masses." These traits still existed in the fifties. But "intellectuals found new virtues in the United States because of its pluralism, the acceptance of the Welfare State, the spread of education, and the expanding opportunities for intellectual employment." Bell and his colleagues enthusiastically sided with America in the Cold War, and were convinced that "Soviet Russia was the principal threat to freedom in the world."

What is interesting about Bell's tale of the "twice-born" intellectuals' journey toward accommodation to American culture was his use of domestic routine and imagery as metaphors for describing it. They exchanged their faith in the possibilities of living "at some extreme" of "genuine passion" for the "unheroic, day-to-day routine of living." They were, in Bell's words, the "prodigal sons" who "in terms of American culture had returned home." Bell employed the primary symbol of fifties domesticity to define the intellectuals' retreat from "passion" and their embrace of an American status quo premised upon moderation, incremental social reform, compromise, order and stability. Or "reality," as he called it. Whatever its imperfections or injustices, America was their "home." And "a generation that knows it has to be 'moral' and 'responsible,'" wrote Bell, "is a generation that is destined to stay at home."[24]

Norman Podhoretz, who became editor of *Commentary* in 1960, glorified home and family as ideals representing stability and social order, rather than as metaphors for coming "home" to American culture. Like Bell, Podhoretz saw domesticity as a symbolic haven from unrestrained passion and unrestricted personal freedom. In his 1979 memoir, Podhoretz recalled that as a young man in the fifties he longed for the stability of family life. "There was nothing," he remembered, "that appealed to me less than the idea of refusing to grow up and settle down." Like the college students described by the *Nation* as old "beyond their years," Podhoretz "couldn't wait to grow up," even when he was in his teens. There was "nothing that I wanted more than to take my rightful place as an adult among other adults." By the late fifties, he was married "and I believed in marriage; I had children and I believed in having them; I had a steady job and I believed in hard work."[25]

These paeans to domesticity and "hard work" were significant because Podhoretz made them while recalling his intense hostility toward one of the few public episodes of nonconformity during the fifties, the Beat movement. In 1958 he wrote an article, "The Know-Nothing Bohemians," in which he excoriated the Beat writers, especially Jack Kerouac. What he most disliked about Kerouac and the Beats was their "emotional intensity," their "primitive" hostility to "civilization," their "spontaneity"—"saying whatever comes into your head, in any order you happen to feel like saying it." The Beats' way of life made him "nervous" because it glorified improvisation. They had a "resentment against normal feelings." In other words, they were irresponsible. They didn't have regular jobs. They didn't marry. They refused "to grow up." Podhoretz implicitly created a polarization between adulthood, "normal feelings," domesticity, organized work and stability on the one side, and primitivism, "emotional intensity," spontaneity and freedom from responsibility on the other.[26]

Teamwork On The Job

"Togetherness" at home, whether as a haven of personal security or metaphor for the grand American consensus, was paralleled at work by an emphasis on being a member of a team. As we have seen, few of the young people interviewed in the various surveys wanted to start up or own a business. The dream of working for oneself, which had been in steady decline since the end of the nineteenth century, faded perceptively during the forties and fifties. It was replaced by the goal of working for a large firm and becoming part of a team that functioned within a complex organization and defined chain of command. William Whyte believed the self-propelled, competitive individualist was disappearing from the work place. "The future," he noted with dismay in 1953, "will be determined by Organization Man."[27]

The notion of work as a team effort was particularly prevalent in the white collar world inhabited by middle managers. In his 1959 book, *The Status Seekers,* Vance Packard said that those who wished to rise through the ranks of management had to "shed their rough edges of individualism" and become team players. Few chief executive officers went as far as the president of an aircraft manufacturing company, who referred to his managers as "teammates" over the intercom, but it was generally understood that the appearance of unshackled personal ambition was bad form. More than anything else, young middle managers had to project loyalty and be sensitive toward the needs of those above and below them in the company hierarchy. Especially those above them. The enterprising young manager needed to show that loyalty to the firm and the boss exceeded his desire for personal advancement. Since "team players were valued more highly than mavericks," the individual had to "take all signals" and "share all attitudes and prejudices of the men above him, as his wife tended to play the sports and card games favored by the boss's wife."[28]

If the zest for enterprise declined in the fifties it was not because the frontiers of economic opportunity were entirely closed. Ambitious, old-style entrepreneurs could still build economic empires. William Levitt did it in suburban construction, Eugene Ferkauf in bargain retailing (E. J. Korvettes), Kemmons Wilson with the Holiday Inn chain, and Ray Kroc through the McDonald's fast-food franchises. But the giant shadows cast by mammoth corporations increasingly eclipsed new economic frontiers of opportunity.[29]

In 1949 the historian Arthur Schlesinger, Jr., said that relatively few opportunities were available for ambitious young entrepreneurs. American traditions of innovation and individual enterprise required capacious fields of opportunity upon which to roam. He conceded, however, that "big" government and corporate consolidation were both inevitable and integral to the nation's economic well-being.[30] In 1953 the radical sociologist C. Wright Mills observed that the daring and independence of nineteenth-century pioneers, farmers and entrepreneurs had not "carried over in the contemporary population." The white collar salaried employee, the fastest growing segment of the work force in the fifties, was "always somebody else's man," never his own.[31]

In addition to fears of communist subversion, the cult of security rested on two major factors: the legacies of the Great Depression of the thirties, and the extraordinary and unanticipated performance of the economy after 1945. It is impossible to measure the psychological impact of the Depression years on those who were in their teens and twenties in the late forties and fifties. But it is reasonable to assume that memories linked to the anxieties and dislocations of those years lingered into the postwar era and to some extent shaped the attitudes of college-aged individuals in the fifties. Whyte was convinced the specter of the Depression haunted the graduates he studied in 1949. In his 1956 book, *The Organization Man,* he said that contemporary college students were "almost psychotic on the subject of a depression." It conditioned their fear of risk taking and accounted for their desire to have secure jobs in large corporations. These young people, said Whyte, longed for "a depression-proof sanctuary."[32]

This was not the only legacy of the thirties. Some economists during the Depression decade believed that the future growth of the economy would be relatively limited. It might rebound from the collapse of the early thirties and recapture some of its former vibrancy, but they viewed the industrial base of the economy as "mature." In other words, its capacity for expansion was limited by comparison with the extraordinary growth of the industrial base during the nineteenth and early twentieth centuries.

To some degree, this perception of the economy's limitations informed the New Deal's response to the Depression. The New Deal cast a limited but unprecedented array of economic safety nets over American society, such as Social Security and various social welfare programs. These programs were designed not only to deal with the immediate crisis, but also to provide a small margin of security against the prospects of relatively limited growth in productivity in the future. They implied restricted economic horizons for some, perhaps many, Americans. Franklin Roosevelt said as much when he suggested that the New Deal had amended the traditional American "definition of liberty." Historically, liberty meant the individual's right to act with minimal interference from government, and within an economic field perceived as limitless in terms of potential growth. But the Depression altered these assumptions, and Roosevelt said the New Deal broadened the concept of individual liberty by guaranteeing "greater [economic] security" for those whom he called "average" citizens. One of the implications of the welfare state was that neither economic growth, nor dreams of universal affluence garnered through a competitive free-enterprise system, were boundless. As one New Deal supporter said in 1939, personal freedom was fine, but people need to "eat regular." You "cannot fill the baby's bottle with liberty."[33]

It is possible that this perception of the economy's vulnerability and limitations survived the war years, despite the fact that between 1945 and 1960 more Americans enjoyed more affluence than any previous generation in the country's history. During those 15 years, over 19 million families bought new homes in the suburbs. By the end of the fifties, and for the first time in modern American history, the majority of families lived in dwellings they owned. That broad, amorphous economic group called the middle-class, whose annual family income in 1960 ranged from $5,000 to $10,000 or so, had doubled since 1939. The devastation wrought by war in Europe and Asia removed much of the competition for American-produced goods. By the late forties, American companies produced over 50 percent of the world's manufactured products, nearly 60 percent of its steel, over 60 percent of its oil and 80 percent of its automobiles.[34] Only 8.5 percent of blue collar workers and 17.5 percent of white collar employees received paid vacations in 1946; this increased to over 40 percent for each group by 1951.[35] In 1953 *Business Week* noted the dramatic improvements in working conditions, salaries, medical and pension benefits, and paid vacations in a naively titled article, "The Leisured Masses."[36] By the late fifties, most Americans earned enough money to allow their children to complete high school. Over 85 percent of the baby boomers completed high school, compared with slightly more than 40 percent of the preceding generation. College enrollments increased as well, from about 12 to 15 percent of high school graduates in 1940 to approximately 40 percent in 1960.[37]

Despite these figures, 20 percent of the population lived in poverty during the fifties. Even so, economists, most of whom were pessimistic about the country's prospects at the end of the war, fell over themselves to praise the magnitude of the boom. One of them noted that the level of prosperity was unprecedented in American history. He called it the "crossing of a great divide in the history of humanity." The United States "truly became an affluent society" during the fifties, said another economist. Given the disaster of the thirties, the recovery was one of the "swiftest and most thoroughgoing changes in economic history."[38] In 1949 *Fortune*'s editors, who described the American boom as capitalism's version of a "permanent revolution," endorsed a Brookings Institution forecast of an 800 percent increase in American living standards over the next one hundred years.[39] To many it seemed evident that poverty was on the brink of extinction, and the "trend toward a universal middle class" irreversible. As Loren Baritz said in retrospect, the centuries-old American Dream of affluence was "coming true," at least for the burgeoning ranks of the middle class. "America was delivering, at last."[40]

Thus the cult of security: why disturb the course of an expanding, consolidated, comparatively regulated (perhaps even depression-proof) economy by espousing the aggressive, competitive individualism of the early industrial era? Why not settle down and enjoy the postwar cornucopia within a society marked by stability, prosperity and general accord on major political issues and anti-communism? Why not embrace the minimal but unprecedented security net provided by the welfare state, as well as the steady jobs and generous benefits garnered through negotiations between labor unions and large corporations?

Even behavior that on the surface seemed expansive and adventurous reflected the quest for stability. This was true of the tidal waves of early marriages and births that flooded the country in the two decades following World War II. Over 76 million children were born between 1946 and 1964.[41] Americans also unburdened themselves of long-standing fears of personal indebtedness. In addition to incurring long-term debts for purchasing homes, they applied for the new credit cards aimed at middle-class consumers issued by Diner's Club, BankAmericard, American Express and Carte Blanche.[42] But daring though the early marriages, high birth rates and indebtedness might seem, they in fact represented a commitment to domesticity that complemented the cult of security.

Obviously, these trends were not universal. John Diggins, William O'Neill, Scott Donaldson and other scholars have argued persuasively that conformity was not as widespread in the fifties as many assumed.[43] Neither the suburban lifestyle, despite its surface uniformity, nor the repressive political atmosphere told the whole story. And as Daniel Bell said in 1955, while many social critics insisted that a democratic "mass" society fostered "excessive conformity" and mediocrity, it was "hard to discern who is conforming to what." Who, after all, defended conformity in America? "[E]veryone," said Bell, "is against it."[44]

Bell was exaggerating, but he had a point. Even in the corporate world, where conformity and the cult of security seemed most pronounced, there were contrary tendencies. This was especially true of ambitious, hard-driving individuals intent upon reaching "the top." William Whyte, that relentless critic of the organization man, admitted that raw, competitive individualism was alive and well in the executive suites of corporate America. In a 1954 article describing his interviews with executives, Whyte said presidents and vice-presidents of corporations projected a "keen sense of self." They were intense, driven, competitive individuals who approached work as a means of "self-expressive" achievement. Though executives viewed crude expressions of aggressive individualism as unseemly, "beneath" the "modulated exterior of today's executive" loomed an "ego as powerful as drove any nineteenth-century [business] buccaneer."[45] In her 1986 book on the fifties, Benita Eisler also took note of this ambivalent attitude toward individualism. Behavior that was overtly competitive or egotistical was seen as bad form. Many associated it with the greed and ruthlessness of 1920s businessmen, whose rapacious economic behavior supposedly brought on the Great Depression. But aspiring, college-aged young people in the fifties received other messages as well. Beneath the surface suggestion to rein in overt expression of personal ambition, resided a more subtle message: "you had better be a success."[46]

Nor was the goal of working indefinitely for the same company shared by everyone. Graduates of elite institutions like the Harvard Business School expected to move from one company to another as their prospects and ambitions warranted. By the mid fifties there was more movement of high-level executives between major corporations than there had been during the prosperous 1920s.[47] The movement of managers and executives from companies in one state to those in another transformed ostensibly stable suburban communities into what Whyte called a "series of way stations."[48]

The flux created by families moving in and out of suburban communities was complemented by incessant jostling within them. In 1959 David Riesman noticed that beneath the apparent uniformity, order and "tidiness" of the suburbs, a subtle but characteristically American penchant for disorder survived. The uniformity and convenience of suburban shopping centers gave the impression that Americans had created an orderly suburban idyll. But the anarchic shuffling of cars, and the constant blaring of horns borne of impatience and stress as shoppers pushed their way in and out of parking lots, told a different story. It "almost looks," he said, "as if every victory of efficiency and planning in America was won at the expense of an underside of disarray."[49]

As powerful as the urges for order, certainty and stability may have been, they did not monopolize life in the fifties. Nevertheless, the cult of security was pervasive enough to inspire alarm among some Americans. Among other things, they believed it undermined the masculine aggressiveness they associated with the country's traditions of individualism, technological innovation and spirit of enterprise.

THE ORGANIZATION MAN, AMERICAN MASCULINITY AND THE WILD WEST

The "organization man" did not exist. He was a sociological abstraction, a myth constructed from the reification of a host of discreet sensibilities. He craved economic security, easily assumed the slavish mien of the conformist and readily cooperated with fellow workers. He set the fire of personal ambition on a low flame, tuned into the nuances of a supervisor's tone of voice or body language and longed for a personal life centered on family cohesion and suburban tranquility. Whether someone harboring all of these attributes actually roamed the corridors of corporations or the neatly carved tracts of suburbia is beside the point. He had to be invented because the organization man was the antithesis of traditional, equally mythic images of American masculinity. And enough men robed themselves in one or another of the traits associated with the cult of security to threaten not only the ideal of competitive individualism, but also the stereotypes of masculinity that fueled it.

The myth of the organization man was the polar opposite of the myth of American manhood as incarnated in historical images of the independent, morally autonomous, risk-taking, individualistic explorer-pioneer-hunter-farmer-entrepreneur. Worse still, the cult of security, and the organization man's aptitudes for sensitivity, empathy and cooperation, reproduced historical stereotypes associated with femininity. Insofar as the male of the forties and fifties was perceived as less than aggressively poised for daring, ambition, competition and achievement at work, he was by definition less than definably "male." The two were historically linked.[50]

His role within the family was also problematic. If his wife did not work outside the home, she raised the children, negotiated their moral dilemmas and generally managed the household. Traditional patriarchal roles within the middle class had been altered by companionate marriages and "democratic" family relationships since the nineteenth century. But the pressures of working as a salaried employee in complex, hierarchical organizations, along with the strains of commuting to and from work for those who lived in suburbs, raised fundamental questions about the role of the husband and father within the modern family.[51]

In the fifties, intellectuals made the connection between waning individualism and truncated masculinity. In a 1958 article, "The Crisis of American Masculinity," Arthur Schlesinger, Jr., suggested that American men had become "unmanned" during the fifties. They seemed devoid of "spontaneity" and self-confidence. Unlike the supposedly inner-directed, individualistic men of the eighteenth and nineteenth centuries, their modern counterparts lacked self-assurance when "apart from the group." At work and at home they were less manly than the men of the past:

> The organization man [works] by day in immense business concerns, sleeping by night in immense suburban developments, deriving his fantasy life from mass-produced entertainments, spending his existence not as an individual but as a member of a group and coming in the end to feel guilty and lost when he deviates from his fellows. Adjustment rather than achievement becomes his social ideal.[52]

This had political as well as social and economic implications. Two years later, in "The New Mood in Politics," Schlesinger linked the organization man's torpor and "passivity" to the country's inability to "beat" the Soviet Union in the space race. The Russians were out-manning existentially flaccid Americans through the powerful "thrust of their missiles" and their "penetration of outer space."[53]

Paul Goodman also saw a relationship between waning individualism and the erosion of traditional images of manhood. In his acclaimed 1956 book, *Growing Up Absurd,* Goodman argued that the urgency, opportunity and uncertainty that inspired old-style entrepreneurs was declining in contemporary society. Ideals of teamwork and efficiency on the job were destroying what Goodman called the "open space" of contingency within which the creative or ambitious individual might freely roam. American males were constricted psychologically and emotionally by a daily regimen of managed time, managed lives and managed imaginations. Devoid of an "open economy, some open mores, some activity free from regulation," men pulled back from the precipice of "risk" that sparked "the heroic age of capitalist enterprise" in the previous century. America in the fifties, concluded Goodman, was "lacking in enough man's work." It was "not easy to conceive of a strong husband and father who does not feel justified in his work" or is not an "independent," autonomous individual.[54]

The experiences of men in the corporate world frequently justified Goodman's concerns. Some executives believed it was as important to control a male employee at home as on the job. As one corporate executive lamented, the company "controls a man's environment in business" but loses it "entirely when he crosses the threshold of the home." Supervisors developed strategies designed to "liberate," as he put it, the husband's "total energies for the job." They were unlikely to enhance the employee's self-esteem or sense of "manhood."[55]

For instance, some executives sent letters to wives of employees, informing them of the valuable "prizes" and hefty "bonuses" their husbands could win. Of course, in order to get them the employees had to work diligently and effectively. The letters might include information about how they were doing "at the moment." The usual evaluation (and, of course, the reason for sending the letters to begin with) was "not as well as he should be." Other executives were candid about their uneasiness with the ideal of family "togetherness." A man's primary focus should be his job, not his family. "Successes here," said an executive in 1951, "are guys who eat and sleep the company. If a man's first interest is his wife and family, more power to him, but we don't want him."[56]

The perception that American manhood in the fifties was being lost somewhere in the middle-class commute between a job that was less than "manly" and a family that needed his salary but might get along nicely without his presence was expressed in popular culture as well as by intellectuals. Especially intriguing was the emergence and enormous popularity of "adult" television westerns in the mid fifties. Of course, there were popular television series which portrayed an idealized middle class suburban family, such as *The Adventures of Ozzie and Harriet, Father Knows Best* and *Leave It To Beaver.* These series captured the postwar dedication to the cult of security and family "togetherness," and are the television programs most frequently discussed by those who study the fifties.

But what can be made of the even greater popularity of television westerns? These programs generally portrayed circumstances and behavior incompatible with the cult of security, family togetherness or the mentality of the "organization man." While westerns might portray an idealized version of cohesive family life, they often did so in the absence of wives and mothers (*Bonanza* and *The Rifleman* are prime examples). Television westerns celebrated male camaraderie, and often pitted rugged, individualistic men against a lawless, insecure, spacious and adventurous physical environment.

Between 1955 and the mid sixties, network television westerns annually generated a 33 percent to 40 percent share of the weekly prime-time audience. Approximately 60 million viewers said they watched them.[57] In 1958 five of the ten highest-rated weekly series were westerns. In the next year they accounted for seven of the top ten shows.[58] The titles of the programs conjured visions of a preindustrial, unregulated, mythological America. They portrayed a West dominated by violence and personal freedom, male aggressiveness and daring, geographical mobility and restlessness, and winning big one day and losing it all the next. Among them were *Gunsmoke, Wyatt Earp, Bonanza, The Texan, Wagon Train, The Rebel, Frontier, Cheyenne, The Californians, The Rifleman, Maverick, Tales of Wells Fargo, The Virginian, The Outcasts, Wanted: Dead or Alive* and *Have Gun, Will Travel.*[59]

At a time when books by C. Wright Mills, Paul Goodman, William Whyte and others portrayed fifties America as staid, boring and lacking "enough man's work," millions of people gorged themselves on programs that recalled a very different American experience. Every evening of television viewing presented one or another version—fanciful and ahistorical though they usually were—of the American conquest of a continent. They told tales of uprooted, courageous pioneers who settled the frontier, and of brave lawmen who tamed it. They depicted ruthless bounty hunters, gamblers, and a rogues gallery of rootless, marginal characters who roamed a capacious landscape. And they portrayed the scouts and trappers who explored and exploited it for material gain. Nor were television characters associated with the winning of the West limited to programming. What may have been the most famous television advertisement of the fifties also featured a cowboy. The "Marlboro Man" of cigarette-commercial fame became a cowboy in 1954. Previously he had been portrayed as a sea captain.[60]

The western saga did not suddenly become popular in the fifties. Since the official demise of the western frontier at the turn of the century, literary and film portrayals of the western migration recreated for the imagination what the actual winning of the West destroyed: the prospect of escaping from the economic and social constraints of the "civilized" East and "starting over" in the untamed West.

That most easterners did not move west, either prior to or during the twentieth century, was irrelevant. Westerns were popular because they preserved the idea of an open space in which escape, endless movement and adventure were possible. Western expansion was entwined with some of the most important myths about the origins of American culture and the qualities of American manhood.

Historian Robert Athearn pointed out that the significance of a mythological West to urban, sedentary twentieth-century Americans had little to do with the region's actual history. The West treasured by modern Americans was what Athearn called a "West of the spirit." It was a space occupied by the imagination that harbored valued traits of "national character," nearly all of which were irrelevant to the daily routines of urban-industrial society.[61] The West portrayed in most twentieth-century novels and films played, in Jane Tompkins's apt phrase, to a "Wild West of the psyche." Westerns reminded the civilized, urbanized, urbane denizens of a bureaucratic, corporate culture of the primitive sources of their country's identity. The West represented not only adventure, but the "desire to test one's nerve, physically, as a means of self-fulfillment" and masculine self-definition.[62]

The popularity of westerns ebbed and flowed during the twentieth century. A staple of the Hollywood picture mill during the silent film era, westerns received stiff competition during the thirties from romantic comedies and detective and gangster melodramas. But western novels and films made a comeback after World War II. In 1950, 25 percent of the movies produced in Hollywood were westerns. During the fifties, western novels sold at an annual rate of 35 million copies.[63] Television westerns competed with prime-time programs that glorified the arch symbol of stability and security, the middle-class suburban family. *The Donna Reed Show, Father Knows Best* and similar programs reinforced the ideal of family "togetherness," of the household as a private kingdom of nurture and tranquility. The middle-class family was presented as a conflict-free haven of mutuality, tolerance and ethnic anonymity. It portrayed the middle-class life toward which all Americans were supposedly headed. It was a world in which parents did not divorce or raise their voices. Children were never abused and fathers never experienced stress at work or were fired from their jobs. Mothers were always understanding and comforting. No one had sex. And everyone was white.[64]

If these programs projected the need to celebrate and settle down within a society defined by prosperity and consensus, the westerns presented viewers with an alternative America. It was not an alternative that portrayed the West realistically. And the programs' plots and characters neither questioned nor challenged the political or social status quo of the fifties. But television westerns recreated a pre-corporate world of rugged individualism, violent masculinity and male bonding. It was fathers and sons against the untamed West, male camaraderie within a setting of adventure, danger and opportunity.

In westerns, "manhood" was often defined as the willingness to take a stand, to be one's "own man," sometimes in opposition to the "crowd" and usually outside of marriage and the family. In a 1955 interview, Clint Walker, the star of *Cheyenne,* reflected on the relationship between the western character he portrayed and American manhood. "A hundred years ago," he said, "every citizen had to have some of the good stuff cowboys are made of—if he wanted to survive. It's the kind of heroism that makes it possible for a man to live alone and at peace with himself, or to do what seems right whether it comes easy or hard, to stand up for what he believes in, even if it's going to be the last time he stands up."[65]

James Arness, who played Marshal Dillon in the enormously popular series *Gunsmoke,* told *TV Guide* in 1958 that his program was successful because his character did not "come home and help his wife with the dishes." He had a job that routinely exposed him to danger and unpredictable situations, but he lived without the stability offered by a wife and family. A westerner, said Arness, "wasn't tied down to one place or one woman." Nor was he hampered by the constraints of modern civility. "[W]hen he got mad he hauled off and slugged someone."[66]

Men of the West were neither subservient to women nor obsessed with job security. "[W]ork is all right for killin' time," observed one of the gambling, roving, unmarried Maverick brothers on *Maverick*. "But it's a shaky way to make a livin'."[67] In other words, "real" men were risk takers. They were willing to live (or die) by their own devices. They didn't depend on employers or worry about the ups and downs of the economy. Most of all, they scorned the job routine that was the handmaiden of personal security. They stood apart from powerful institutions and public opinion. When the star of *Lawman* was asked by an interviewer to define the character he portrayed, he described traits opposed to that of the white collared organization man. A westerner was not supposed to be "winning or witty, or do anything else to make people like him."[68]

Fears that affluence, the cult of security, "organization man" conformity and settling down to family life were undermining masculinity surfaced in some Hollywood films as well, both westerns and nonwesterns. In *Rebel Without a Cause* (1955), the adolescent angst and confusion suffered by the James Dean character was caused to some degree by the absence of a strong male role model in his family. Dean's mother dominated her upper-middle-class household. His father was an affluent professional portrayed as timid, indecisive, overly concerned about "what the neighbors will think" and resolutely subservient to his wife's opinions. "She eats him alive," said Dean's character about his mother's domination over his father, "and he takes it."[69]

Other films reasserted traditional male prerogatives by having their characters "stand up" to their wives. In the western *High Noon* (1952), Gary Cooper played a small-town sheriff. Although a westerner without much formal education, he marries a Quaker schoolteacher from the East. The film opens with scenes of their marriage and imminent departure from town. The sheriff has resigned from his dangerous job and is ready to settle down by opening a store. But as they are leaving town, Cooper is told that members of a vicious gang whom he sent to prison years earlier are headed for town seeking vengeance.

His new wife, played by Grace Kelly, urges Cooper to leave. As a practicing Quaker and a civilized easterner, she abhors violence. But Cooper tells her he has to do what "is right." "I've never run from anybody before." He stays, she leaves. Abandoned by the townspeople he protected for years—they are portrayed as a conformist, meek and exceedingly "lonely crowd"—Cooper fights alone. He is the solitary male individualist who doesn't need his wife or anyone else to tell him right from wrong. In the denouement his wife returns to his side and implicitly renounces both her religious imperative against violence and her eastern civility. She not only supports her husband's determination to do the right thing, but becomes a true westerner in the process: she shoots one of the outlaws in the back.[70]

The same theme of a dominating wife put back in her proper place by the reasserted manhood of her husband was portrayed in the film version of Sloane Wilson's novel *The Man in the Gray Flannel Suit* (1956). The main character, played by Gregory Peck, is a talented, self-possessed individual who has the ability to succeed in the upper reaches of the corporate world. Perhaps lacking the drive or the instinct for power needed to make it as an executive, he prefers working for a nonprofit foundation. His wife incessantly reminds him his choice is unmanly, that his unwillingness to reach for the money and power offered by the private sector proved, as she put it, that he had "lost his guts." She claims to be "ashamed" of him because he settled for a safe job. Their comfortable but modest suburban home symbolizes "ugliness," "depression" and "most of all . . . defeat."

Inspired by these pep talks, Peck quits his safe job and goes to work for a major broadcasting company, an apt symbol of American technological prowess in the postwar era. The head of the company is a dynamic, old-style captain of industry. "Big, successful companies are built by men like me," he says. They are men who take risks, do things their own way and give "body and soul" in the quest for success. He contrasts himself to the "nine-to-five" white collar men who play it safe by living off the enterprise of the creative entrepreneur. Peck's character is successful in his new job but appalled by the immorality of executives at the top and by the obsequiousness of the organization men in the middle. In the end he quits and returns to the nonprofit foundation, where he can achieve the balance he seeks between spending time with his family and doing useful work. And like the Grace Kelly character in *High Noon,* in the end Peck's wife supports his courageous decision to be his own man.[71]

Postwar threats to traditional male prerogatives were sometimes raised even in films in which they were not central to the plot. In the courtroom drama *Twelve Angry Men* (1957), a "liberal" jury member played by Henry Fonda argues with a "conservative" one portrayed by Lee J. Cobb. They disagree about the motives and ultimate causes of a young defendant's criminal behavior. Fonda seeks the roots of the defendant's antisocial behavior in an abused childhood: "Ever since he was five years old, his father beat him regularly." But Cobb views the alleged crime as symptomatic of a generalized assault upon authority, beginning with the lack of respect given by young people to men and fathers. "It's the kids, the way they are nowadays. Listen, when I was his age, I used to call my father 'sir.' You ever hear a boy call his father that anymore?" Somewhat taken aback, Fonda weakly replies, "Fathers don't seem to think it's important anymore."[72]

Finally, in the western *Shane* (1953), the central character, played by Alan Ladd, symbolized how the link between individualism and manhood was severed by the settlement of the West and the course of national progress. Shane is a professional gunfighter. In his younger days he roamed a sparsely settled West, plying a trade dependent upon the anomie of the landscape. But his time is running out. The Wild West of his youth, like the entire country since the middle of the nineteenth century, was being tamed by economic progress, civility and law and order.

Shane becomes involved in a conflict between recent settlers who farm small plots of land and a large landowner who wants their property for raising livestock and is willing to use violence to get it. Shane allies himself with the small farmers. One family in particular attracts him. He is attracted to its stability, loving domesticity and "togetherness." At the same time, as an individual whose identity was inseparable from the violent, untamed western landscape, it is too late for him to become a family man. Nor is his gunslinging future very bright. In the film's final scene, Shane tells the family's young son that he has to move on, even though the family wants him to settle down with them. "I gotta be going on," he tells the boy. "Man has got to be what he is. Can't break the mold. There's no going back."[73]

At that moment Shane embodies the cul-de-sac of American masculinity in the 1950s as well as in the Old West. His life of rootless solitude, adventure and criminal violence, all vital sources of his rugged male individualism, were incompatible with the routines of work and orderly family life that ultimately tamed the West of his youth. He could neither settle down nor live "like a man" in the new West. So he rides off alone, toward the proverbial western sunset, an American individualist without a country.

In their own way, television and film westerns of the fifties sounded the same alarm as intellectuals like Mills, Goodman, Schlesinger, Whyte and Riesman. The historical sources of American masculinity and individualism—the country's physical and psychological open spaces, its frontiers of unexplored opportunity—were evaporating. In their place was a congested landscape inhabited by civil, cooperative, regulated, affluent and security-bound family men.

In *Gunfighter Nation,* historian Richard Slotkin wrote that the popularity of westerns in the fifties was tied to the confrontation with the Soviet Union. Bloodshed and militaristic themes in westerns reminded both Americans and their communist foes abroad of the redoubtable determination and extravagant violence that "won" the West in the nineteenth century. The same attributes might contribute to winning the Cold War in the twentieth.[74] But fifties westerns served purposes closer to home as well. They were powerful remembrances of American things lost during the course of American progress.

The most significant challenge to the cult of security didn't come from intellectuals. Or from television and film westerns—though as we shall see, myths associated with the west had a profound impact on the sixties youth culture. The most powerful negation of the tepid, conformist fifties was brewing in an unlikely place: the affluent, status-obsessed households of the professional middle class.

THREE

Middle-Class Child Rearing and the Renaissance of American Individualism

So his speech to the Yippies and children assembled was of value, since he learned for the record of his report that they were a generation with an appetite for the heroic, and an air not without beauty had arisen from their presence; they had been better than he thought, young, devoted, and actually ready to die—they were not like their counterparts ten years ago. Something had happened in America, some forging of the steel.

Norman Mailer, *Miami and the Siege of Chicago,* 1968

A CHILD OF THE PROFESSIONAL MIDDLE CLASS

IN THE LATE FORTIES, the psychologist Else Frenkel-Brunswick interviewed scores of American families from a variety of social-class and regional backgrounds. The interviews were part of a project to study relationships between family variables, such as social class, and the development of racial and ethnic intolerance in children. One of Frenkel-Brunswick's interviews was with a middle-class family consisting of two professional parents and their 12-year-old daughter, excerpts of which were published in 1955.[1] They shed considerable light on the child-rearing practices of the postwar professional middle class.

Both parents were college graduates with "liberal" views about politics and race. They frowned upon what the father called "any radical movement," but they supported legal political dissent, especially efforts to combat racism and racial segregation. During their discussions with Frenkel-Brunswick, they spoke at length about how they were raising their daughter, whom the psychologist called "Peggy."

The parents worked energetically to instill self-confidence and autonomy in their child. "I feel," said the mother, "that I can help [Peggy] by giving a lot of trust and confidence in the girl." But Peggy had to earn her mother's "trust and confidence." She had to work hard and successfully in school and act responsibly at home. The mother admitted that "at times in the past" she probably demanded "too high a performance" of her daughter. Perhaps she pushed Peggy too hard, and "for the sake of my own gratification." Nonetheless, the mother believed prodding was essential for nurturing her daughter's independence. Peggy had "always been given more responsibility than the average [child]." Nor in her opinion had her constant exhortations to earn superior grades in school "seem[ed] to be a strain" on Peggy. Asked by Frenkel-Brunswick what her daughter should avoid as an adult, the mother said she would "hate" to see Peggy take "a job she didn't like for the sake of money or caring too much for the acquisition of material things." Fulfilling work was more important than making money.

Peggy's father agreed, adding that parents should not impose specific career goals on their children. "Whatever she wants to choose—that's her business," although he took for granted her choice would be a profession. According to the father, the most important contribution parents could make to a child's future was to cultivate her self-confidence and self-reliance. "If we can bring her up with self-assurance," he told Frenkel-Brunswick, "and [teach her] not to give up at the first obstacles, we will be doing something." The "something" he referred to was "to get the best out of herself" and to "be happy with herself and with other people."

The parents believed physical punishment of children was cruel and counterproductive. The rationales for their household rules were patiently explained to Peggy, and her transgressions calmly discussed by the three of them. Peggy's parents did not agree about everything—they had recently divorced. The father said his former wife may have begun Peggy's toilet training too early. Like other middle-class parents at the time, the mother began rudimentary toilet training for Peggy about six months after birth, and completed it around the eighteenth month. In the end, however, the father admitted the training had been successful because their daughter was encouraged to believe she had "regulate[d] her own training." Both parents had wanted Peggy to feel that in this, as in other areas of her life, discipline and self-control came from within herself rather than being imposed from without. As a result, the father believed her independence and self-reliance had been enhanced.

Both parents were pleased with what they had wrought. Their daughter was intelligent, self-disciplined and autonomous. The mother was delighted that Peggy had a "philosophical interest" in people and public issues, was forthright in advancing her opinions and confident in expressing them. The father liked Peggy's "strength of character," along with the fact that she was "intelligent and liberal." Like his former wife, he was impressed with Peggy's willingness to express her likes and dislikes "emphatically" and with self-assurance.

After interviewing Peggy, Frenkel-Brunswick was similarly impressed. The 12-year-old was a self-confident, independent youngster. She was not prone, as Frenkel-Brunswick put it, to uncritical "submission to authority." Peggy was not intimidated by the authority of parents, teachers or peers. When asked to describe the "ideal" teacher, she said it was someone who can "understand you, be a friend to you, someone you can confide in, someone you like." She did not like teachers whom she described as "dumb," like those who yelled at their students or told them to "shut up." Nor was she seduced by peer pressure. Peggy expressed disdain for female classmates who were "silly, stupid, giggle all the time and never get their work done but say they do." What made her angry? "When people pick on someone else, even dogs or animals, or when they tease Negroes and call them dirty names."

Arbitrary authority, racial prejudice and injustice were as anathema to this young girl as they were to her parents. Her notion of a good father was someone who was "a good friend to you, understanding and nice. Just a person." She saw her father in this light. Her perception of her mother was equally nonauthoritarian. "My mother just talks to me. Children should never really be punished, but have things explained to them." Peggy was asked to describe the "worst" thing that could happen to a boy. "To have his life planned," she responded, "to be what he doesn't want." And for a girl? "Same as for a man." As for her own goals, she wanted to become "an artist, a poet, a writer, and a dancer."[2]

"Peggy's" parents raised their daughter in a way that was common for professional middle-class families of the forties and fifties. Their child-rearing experiences are described in the following section. Before discussing this issue, three questions related to Peggy's upbringing should be addressed. How did the traits and sensibilities cultivated in Peggy differ from those associated with the cult of security? What was the relationship between her parents' attitudes and anxieties regarding child rearing and their status as middle-class professionals? And how did their approach to raising children differ from that of blue collar families?

The cult of security rested on the assumption that it was possible to reduce, though not totally eliminate, the contingencies and uncertainties inherent in a dynamic, democratic, capitalist society. Job security could be achieved by working for large companies. Rational control over a sprawling, free-enterprise economy could be attained through bureaucratic planning implemented by cooperative administrative hierarchies in the private and public sectors. And personal stability could be won by immersion in a family life securely rooted in socially homogeneous suburbs. A paradox haunted this vision of life in the United States. Virtually all Americans maintained their allegiance to a free enterprise economy, however modulated by the welfare state. At the same time the cult of security was ultimately an attempt to drastically limit the perpetual insecurities associated with living in a free-wheeling, market-driven economy and society.

Peggy's upbringing implicitly challenged these assumptions. With a good deal of determination and anxiety, her parents were intent upon making their daughter versatile, confident, competitive, self-reliant and open to new, unanticipated challenges. They assumed, even welcomed, the prospect of uncertainty and wanted Peggy to confront it with assertive self-assurance. This was evident in her father's reluctance to push Peggy toward a specific career, as well as in her mother's hope that she would not settle for a job simply because it paid well. Peggy herself saw a "planned" life as among the "worst" things that could be inflicted upon a child. The three of them seemed to feel it was wrong to cultivate specific skills geared toward securing a safe niche in life or a job. The parents believed that self-confidence nurtured by strenuous self-cultivation (they marvelled at Peggy's precocious intellectual development), determined self-reliance (they made it sound as if she had toilet trained herself) and competitive achievement in school (she frowned upon students who didn't do the work) would prepare their daughter for whatever life might bring her way.

While the parents did not directly address the state of the postwar economy, it is possible that their qualms about placing Peggy on a specific career path were related to new career opportunities percolating throughout the economy. But it was impossible to anticipate what these opportunities might be. What seemed relatively certain was that postwar innovations in electronic media, computers, space exploration, chemical engineering and numerous other fields were going to alter the scope of some professions and create new ones. Just as Peggy's parents groomed her to be tolerant of the "unknown" in terms of racial and ethnic differences, it is possible they wanted her to be receptive to unanticipated change and the challenges presented by an unpredictable, innovative economy.

Nor, finally, was Peggy prone toward the social conformity that seemed so prevalent in the fifties. She disdained classmates who were frivolous. She looked askance at peers who didn't do their school work. And she was encouraged by her parents to question received opinions and rules.

The second question is, why were professional middle-class parents like Peggy's intent upon raising their child in this fashion? A clue resides in the peculiar cluster of aspirations and anxieties that sociologist Barbara Ehrenreich said are part of the "inner life" of the professional middle class. In her 1989 book, *Fear of Falling: The Inner Life of the Middle Class,* Ehrenreich described how the social status enjoyed by professionals rested on their achieved educational credentials rather than on "ownership of capital or property."[3] While significant disparities in prestige and income prevail among professional groups—engineers, physicians, professors, lawyers, corporate executives, scientists, therapists, architects, schoolteachers and so forth—all share a common trait. The doors of professional status opened for them once they successfully navigated years of strenuous competition in school.

Obviously, professional status cannot be inherited. It has to be earned. In order for children to follow the professional path of their parents, they need to reproduce the intellectual, psychological and emotional qualities that made their parents successful. Professionals are relatively autonomous on the job—they require the confidence to make independent judgments and on-the-spot decisions. They must possess the self-assurance necessary to supervise others. They also need the self-discipline and competitive edge required for success at all levels of schooling. Entrance into the professions presumes possession of undergraduate and graduate degrees. And entry into the most prestigious, influential and highest-paying spheres of a profession usually means attending colleges and universities of the first rank. Acceptance to these colleges requires the ability to compete with the best and brightest of one's generation. In other words, from the opening bell of childhood, parents of would-be professionals need to promote self-reliance, a bent for competition and self-confidence in their children.

In any decade these pressures would make middle-class child rearing singularly anxiety provoking. But they may have been especially acute in the late forties and fifties. New economic and professional opportunities were spawned by a supercharged economy, which, in turn, was driven by extraordinary technological innovations. The stakes and rewards were greater than they had ever been. And expanded educational opportunities for Americans since the end of World War II made competition for admission to the best schools more intense than ever. It is not surprising, then, that a study made in the fifties found that parents who had graduated from college read more child-rearing literature than any other group. It also revealed that professional middle-class couples experienced more anxiety and a greater sense of inadequacy in raising children than the rest of the population. They understood that there were no guarantees their children would succeed in reproducing their status.

A final problem confronted by status-conscious middle-class parents should be mentioned. Preparing children to internalize the attributes of prospective professionals requires that parents delicately juggle a series of emotional balancing acts. Self-confidence and self-esteem are vital for creating the feeling that one is entitled to compete and worthy of the success it brings. Parents, then, need to be intensely child-centered in order to nurture these sensibilities. At the same time, however, they cannot be solicitous to the point of making children "soft" and dependent, else they may fail to develop the self-discipline and competitive edge needed for success, especially in school. Instilling discipline and control is essential. But so are "democratic" relations between parent and child. In order for children to develop autonomy and critical awareness, as well as the capacity to adapt to change and progress, they should be encouraged to question the rationales of the rules and restrictions imposed on them.[4]

These quandaries and tensions were evident in Peggy's parents. They were willing to allow their daughter to question the conventional ways and means of her world, including their household rules and regulations. In effect, they asked Peggy to compel them to justify their authority over her. Simultaneously, and with considerable anxiety about pushing Peggy too hard, too soon or not hard enough, they wanted her to become autonomous by imposing self-control upon herself. This was most obvious in the early age at which the parents commenced toilet training, as well as in their desire to make Peggy as "responsible" as possible as soon as feasible. Unable to transmit their status to their daughter, they instilled in Peggy aptitudes and attitudes that a young achiever needed in order to earn it.

Finally, in evaluating the consequences of middle-class child rearing it is worth noting the differences between an upbringing like Peggy's and that of blue collar children. During the forties and fifties, social scientists who studied child-rearing practices found significant differences between the two groups. It is important to bear in mind that these middle-class students of working-class behavior were often condescending toward blue collar families. At times they referred to working people as "lower-class." More important, they often viewed the values and aspirations of middle-class professionals as normative for all Americans.[5]

Studies of child-rearing practices in working- and middle-class households from the early forties to the late fifties usually drew sharp contrasts between the two. Middle-class mothers commenced toilet training earlier, placed greater emphasis on "individual achievement," and encouraged their children to become as independent as possible as quickly as possible.[6] "If we call [the children] when they are doing something," said one middle-class parent, "we don't expect them to drop what they are doing right that minute and come. Their activities are important, too, and they should be able to finish what they are doing."[7] Another said his child should feel "directly" responsible for his behavior and "come to his own understanding" of right and wrong.[8] Still another middle-class parent claimed obedience was important but should not be won at the expense of stifling the child's sense of freedom and independence. "You have to let them know that if they do something wrong, it's all right and not too important."[9]

By contrast, blue collar families usually waited well past six months to start toilet training.[10] Their children were not taught household responsibilities "until an age at which [the tasks] become relatively easy."[11] Working-class parents demanded obedience, promptness and neatness from their children. Most of all, they expected young people to automatically defer to adult authority. Where middle-class parents promoted "internal standards for governing one's relationship with other people," working-class parents usually relied on compliance with external authority and popularity with the peer group.[12]

MIDDLE-CLASS CHILD REARING

Descriptions of child-rearing practices within middle-class professional families, which comprised about 10 percent of the working population in the fifties, were seldom as revealing as those of Peggy's parents. One that came close was compiled by psychologist Bruno Bettelheim of the University of Chicago.[13] Between 1948 and 1952, Bettelheim supervised biweekly discussion groups with young mothers. Over that time, scores of young women attended the sessions. They were middle-class women, many of whom were married to graduate students or junior faculty at the university. Most were students or college graduates. These were not therapy sessions. Rather, Bettelheim, one of the country's most distinguished child psychologists, wanted young mothers to discuss with one another the problems they faced in raising children in postwar America.

One mother asked the group for advice about how she should respond to a problem her four-year-old son brought home from nursery school. A "bully" had gratuitously punched him. Her son wanted to retaliate, and she did not know what to tell him. She didn't want to encourage violence. "I don't want him to hit," she told the group. She was deeply disturbed by the animosities, wars and bloodshed that gripped the twentieth century. At the same time she worried about the consequences of imposing her own views on her child. In addition, she was afraid he might become passive toward unprovoked aggression if she compelled him to turn the other cheek. "What to do about it?" she asked the group.

"The first thing," said Bettelheim, was to convince her son that "you respect his opinion and are interested in it." It was wrong to impose her values on him. The mother agreed. She said it was important to treat her four year old as "a human being and not a baby." "That's right," Bettelheim responded, "and he wants to hear from his mother that his own feelings count more with his mother than what civilization says" about retaliation, aggression or pacifism. He also pointed out how "hard [it is] to instill our own values in a child when they contradict the values of the community." In the end, the participants agreed that the best approach was for the mother to discuss the matter openly with her son and allow him to decide on his own course of action. As the mother said, her son should "take some of the responsibility" for making this decision. "That's most important," said Bettelheim. "And after you've made sure that he understands that, then he can take care of the situation on his own, as he thinks best."[14]

The belief that children should learn as soon as possible to think and act on their own was a prominent feature of stories and advertisements in magazines targeted toward middle-class women, such as *Ladies' Home Journal* and *McCall's.* The mother of a family described in *Ladies' Home Journal* in 1950 said she routinely discussed important social issues, such as race relations, with her children. She wanted them to believe in the ideals of toleration and the "equality of all souls." But like the mother in Bettelheim's session, she stopped short of imposing her values. She told her children they would have to "think it out for yourselves. Any fool can follow a crowd. It takes a real man to stand up for what's right."[15]

Some advertisers in these magazines claimed that their products enhanced the independence of children. A 1955 ad in *McCall's* touted the home "playground of tomorrow." It said toys should not be diversions for children. A good toy must "challenge" children's "creative powers" so that they might "learn how to cope with the unexpected."[16] The following year the same magazine featured an article that informed parents how they could measure the emerging intelligence and independence of young children. By the end of the child's first year, "clues" about his future character and level of "smartness" could be seen in the way he played. Parents should not merely encourage their children to play, but purchase toys that enhanced "mental alertness" and independence.[17] Nor should they worry if their children were untidy during play. Scolding a child about "messing up" the house sent a message that being "neat and clean" was more important than being creative and autonomous. It might even make the child "unnaturally" dependent upon his parents. The creation of "self-sufficient boys" should be the goal of serious play and committed parenting.[18]

Encouraging autonomy in their children was supplemented by laying the intellectual and emotional foundations for success in school. Long before their children were old enough to attend school, middle-class parents cultivated their offspring's intellectual skills and zest for competition. One of Bettelheim's mothers kept "count" of her 18-month-old son's progress in learning vocabulary. "[H]e learns every day," she told the group of mothers, "at least two [words] a day. I've got a whole list of them. . . . it's a matter of pride." Bettelheim warned her that it was dangerous to pressure the child to perform beyond his years. She disagreed. "I've just accepted the fact that my kid's a genius! I don't even think about it anymore."[19]

Neither her ardor in cultivating her son's verbal skills nor her joy in his success were unusual. Middle-class parents who were anxious to find out how "bright" and "quick to learn" their infants might become could test them. A *McCall's* article, "I. Q. Tests for Babies," told parents about new techniques for measuring the intelligence of infants developed by Ivy League social scientists.[20]

An affluent couple from a Connecticut suburb did not need this test. They toiled diligently to create a home environment that stimulated their son's mental and emotional development. They "never stop marvelling" at the speed with which he developed. According to his parents, the child was "inquisitive to a point that sometimes frightens his mother." They were impressed as well by his "ingenious" ability to get his hands and mouth on what he wanted. To balance his already acute mental faculties, their son possessed "a sense of humor that is a constant delight to his parents." The child was one year old.[21]

By contrast, the fear that the one's child was less than a "genius" compromised the expectation, as one mother put it, that her children were supposed to be "clever and verbal and fun and perfect." "I had this horror," she said, "of having a stupid child. It seemed almost morally bad, reprehensible to me."[22]

Parents continued to hone their children's intellectual skills after they started school. Some believed the extra work gave their children an edge in the competition for good grades. Others, fearful that most schools fell short of providing a first-rate education, supplemented school lessons at home. Still others were convinced that it was necessary to "work" the young mind, day and evening. Sometimes these attitudes caused friction between parents or their children on one side, and teachers and school officials on the other. One sixties radical recalled a conflict with his second-grade teacher. His father, a graduate student at the time, often supplemented his son's school lessons. Lessons learned at home could conflict with those imbibed at school.

> I remember when I was in the second grade, the second grade teacher said, "The sun is ninety-three million light years from the earth." I raised my little paw and

> said, "No it isn't, it's ninety-three million miles." You know, she sent me to the principle for insubordination. You know, kids are perceptive, so it wasn't too hard to figure out that it was the educational system that was fucked up.[23]

A 1950s study of the attitudes of public school teachers toward classroom organization found that many of them encouraged peer conformity in their students. "Teamwork," obedience to authority and "life adjustment" were more likely to be stressed by teachers than autonomy or nonconformity.[24] This caused problems for young people whose parents urged them to think and behave independently. Janis Joplin was criticized by teachers because she frequently asked them to justify their assertions in class (just as she and her siblings were required to do at the dinner table). She was torn between her parents' admonitions to be her own person, to think for herself and always "try for excellence," and the desire of teachers to foster compliance in students.[25]

Sometimes confrontations occurred when the desire of parents to stimulate their children's autonomy and independence clashed with the requirements of order in the classroom. In the mid fifties a mother who wanted her children to "be themselves" and "know their own minds" had a dispute with a teacher about the behavior of her 11-year-old daughter. The teacher claimed the child was "maladjusted" and, therefore, a disruptive influence in class. She sent a note to the parents urging them to do "something" about their daughter's "personality." The student came from a lower-middle-class family, but the mother was determined that her children would become professionals. In a heated confrontation, she told the teacher to change *her* personality rather than force students to blindly conform to a single standard of behavior. "Try to get along with your students instead of asking me to turn my daughter into something else like she's a robot. What's the difference between being maladjusted and having a strong personality?"[26]

Parents who wanted their children to become professionals saw schools as arenas of competitive individualism. They were quick to voice displeasure when their children failed to achieve superior grades. One mother from a "highly upwardly mobile family" was disappointed when her daughter did not receive "all A's" in her courses. "I'm afraid I'm not very satisfied. She doesn't get all A's in school. She doesn't perform her tasks to perfection."[27]

Competition for superior grades could occur between families as well as students. Jerry Rubin, one of the most famous radicals of the sixties, was born in Cincinnati in 1938. His mother came from a prominent local family and was a college graduate. Her family felt she married "beneath" herself when she wed Rubin's father, a truck driver who eventually became a white collar official with the Teamsters union. When Jerry Rubin completed primary school, his grades fell short of admission requirements to the city's elite high school, Walnut Hills. His cousins on his mother's side were admitted to that school. According to Rubin, "nobody" in his mother's family let him "forget that." They encouraged "competition among the cousins." Angered by the comparisons with his cousins and shamed over his failure, Rubin worked furiously during the next two years and was eventually admitted to Walnut Hills as a junior. He was successful, but paid a price. He developed an "achievement drive" that, he said in the sixties, "is too damn high for my own sense of balance."[28]

The writer Midge Decter captured the spirit of these colossal expectations and pressures in a book published shortly after the sixties. Decter's book, addressed to the young radicals, was a strident attack on the values of the youth culture. But she understood the child-rearing goals of their parents, whom she called "enlightened" professionals.

> As children of this . . . enlightened class, you were expected one day to be manning a more than proportional share of the positions of power and prestige in this society. . . . It was at least partly to this end that we brought you up, that we attended so assiduously to your education, that we saw to the cultivation of every last drop of your talents, that we gave you to believe there would be no let or hindrance to the forward, upward motion into which we had set you from the day of your birth.[29]

By the mid fifties some child-care experts were warning parents about the dangers of pressuring young children to achieve exceptional grades. A 1955 article in *McCall's* claimed this was a pervasive problem in middle-class families. The author gave an example of a "highly successful" professional couple who were infuriated by their child's less-than-stellar performance in school. The mother was "worried, disappointed, angry" that her child was not doing better. The author said that too many parents were forcing children to put their self-esteem on the line at too early an age. As a middle-class professional herself, the author understood the importance of instilling a bent for competition in school-aged children. She was concerned, however, about doing so before a child was mature enough to handle the pressure. She even cautioned parents to wait until their children entered the fourth grade![30]

A year later the same author wrote an article about cheating among pupils at all levels of education. She said it was a pervasive national problem, caused to some extent by parents who placed too much pressure on children to bring home "better and better report cards." Many parents were "short on patience" with their children's performance in school "but long on ambition" in terms of their future prospects.[31]

Parents largely ignored these warnings. They tended to view schools as crucibles of competitive individualism. In 1954 *Ladies' Home Journal* surveyed parents on their views of schools and student performance. Those surveyed overwhelmingly supported the idea that schools should be arenas of achieved status through competition. Nearly 80 percent thought it wrong to automatically promote everyone from grade to grade. Those who failed should be left back. Approximately the same percentage were against "watering down" curricula and grading standards. A large majority favored a tracking system that separated "above average" students from those "below average." And 72 percent believed those who "aren't getting anything" from liberal arts studies should be compelled to take vocational course work.[32]

During the sixties, some young radicals recalled the intensity with which their parents stressed competition and achievement in school. One antiwar activist remembered his parents inundating him with extra reading when he received grades they deemed "too low." "We had subscriptions to twenty-five different magazines at one time at home, and I used to read them all."[33] Another antiwar organizer said his parents put "a lot of pressure on me" to earn superior grades. They would not settle for less than "perfect" report cards: "You have all A's but one B. What about that B."[34] Still another recalled his parents "would constantly feed you ideas, ways of expressing yourself. . . . They put that together with a very demanding sense of achievement, and for utilization of your talent."[35] A woman activist said her mother "demanded" too much of her when she was in school. At the time she resented it. But once in college "I felt much more mature. Because I had much more demanded of me."[36] Still another recalled parents who drummed into him the notion that achievement in school went hand in hand with becoming an autonomous individual.

> You can do it the best [they told him] therefore you should do it yourself. . . . My parents were just always pushing us, academically and in other ways—specifically academically—to do better, to do better, better. So there was a great deal of self-confidence in terms of your now being able to go out and do the thing, whatever it was.[37]

It was one thing for middle-class parents to imbue children with the drive and independence needed for success in a meritocratic society. It was quite another to instill them with the confidence and self-assurance to explore the outer boundaries of their ability. As Peggy's father told Frenkel-Brunswick, "self-assurance" was perhaps the most valuable asset he and his wife bequeathed to their daughter. Convincing children that they should expect success if they worked for it was crucial to middle-class child-rearing strategies.

This was reflected in the relative equality between parents and children that permeated middle-class households. In the mid fifties, years before he achieved notoriety as the high priest of LSD, Timothy Leary taught psychology at Berkeley, and was the father of two young children. He and his wife were intent on becoming what he called "a new breed of parents." The couple treated "our kids as equal, independent, privileged human beings." They "would not stunt their [children's] growth with restrictions." Rather, "[w]e would deliberately indulge them, make them the center of the universe."[38] The young Dr. Leary and his wife were typical of professional middle-class parents of the time.

This indulgent attitude toward children is responsible for the perception that "permissiveness" was the rule in middle-class families during the forties and fifties—especially those containing a copy of Dr. Benjamin Spock's book on child care. In his history of the American middle-class, Loren Baritz criticized parents in the fifties for replacing "old fashioned parental authority" with a "democratic," egalitarian approach to raising children. Those who catered to their children's whims by submitting themselves to the "subtlest vibration from the newly imperial infant" courted the prospect of creating self-centered children.[39]

In the late sixties, the psychologist Kenneth Keniston suggested that the young radicals he studied possessed a "sense of specialness," cultivated during their childhoods, that made them different from their nonradical contemporaries.[40] And in 1970, amidst the chaos and factiousness generated by the upheavals of the late sixties, Philip Slater blamed the willingness of young protestors to "make a scene" in public on the "permissiveness" practiced by their "Spock-taught parents." When they were children their parents frequently indulged displays of bad manners. "As a result," wrote Slater, "their children have grown up feeling that human needs have a validity of their own."[41] This view was corroborated in the late sixties by Jerry Rubin. Rubin claimed he relied on the same tactics as a radical confronting the American "establishment" that he used as a child in making demands on his parents. "If I cried I'd get my way, if I screamed I'd get my way."[42]

Despite these views, permissiveness, however defined, was not the goal of middle-class child-rearing. As we have seen, parents were concerned about discipline. They did indulge their children, treated them more or less as equals and gave them significant leeway regarding obedience to household rules and other aspects of behavior. But the purpose of these strategies was to gird the confidence and self-esteem of the young, to make them believe an innate legitimacy clung to them and their aspirations. Put another way, the goal was to invest children with a level of confidence equal to the discipline and competitive drive and autonomy needed by prospective professionals.

Imparting these sensibilities was an arduous and anxious experience for parents. In 1953 a child-care expert told the story of a mother who refused to use negatives with her infant son. She believed expressions of negativity—especially verbal or emotional cues which signalled disapproval of the child—would make him feel "insecure and rejected." Yet, she wanted him to be well behaved and to obey her rules. She was especially concerned about his tendency to pick up and play with dangerous household objects, which he liked to do. She devised a strategy to restrain him from such mischief, yet make it appear as though he was the source rather than the object of the restraint. The mother created a "no-song." Instead of reminding him to stay away from pointed objects, she taught him to sing "no, no, no" when tempted to play with them. Because he said "no" to himself, she hoped her son would feel self-empowered rather than a victim of external restraint. This lesson in autonomy, concluded the child-care expert, would fortify his self-confidence in the future, and enable him to "try new adventures, to make friends, or to stand up for his own rights."[43]

The young mothers who attended Bettelheim's sessions in Chicago constantly raised issues about discipline. How could parents discipline children without compromising their self-esteem or inhibiting their freedom to explore their environments? One mother asked the group to assess "the full cost" to discipline if a parent tried to "reason" with a recalcitrant child rather than simply "slap him." Bettelheim, who did most of the talking at these sessions, told her she would be "creating a fool's paradise if you never said 'no' or 'don't' to a child." But an enlightened parent should never resort to physical punishment.[44]

At a subsequent meeting the issue was raised again. One mother asked how she could discipline her four-year-old daughter without making the child feel rejected or insecure. She described her efforts to convince the child that some behavior was "naughty" and if she persisted in acting that way she would be punished. At the same time, this mother struggled with deciding what "naughty" meant. "I'm having a hard time defining it." She told the group of mothers that "there are some things I disapprove of, and I tell her that, but I don't consider it naughty if she does them against my wishes."

She was caught in a classic middle-class bind. She might disapprove of her child's behavior, but found it difficult to impose her own views on the child. In other words, the mother implicitly assumed she and her child were equals. She possessed the power, authority and sufficient reason to punish her daughter when she misbehaved, but found it distasteful and possibly harmful to do so. Bettelheim told her to give the child "specific reasons" why certain behavior was deemed "naughty." He also defined the crux of her dilemma. "I don't think you have to approve of everything a child does, but you have to approve of the child."[45]

Bettelheim's mothers were particularly concerned about how their children would manage to retain the confidence borne of the love, approval and encouragement they received at home, given the slings, arrows and restraints the world beyond the home inevitably held in store. They were afraid that the self-assurance and autonomy they instilled in their children might be compromised in school and afterwards.

During one session a mother went to the heart of the issue. "Where should a person draw the line on the amount of love a child gets at home, as opposed . . . to the affection he's not going to get when he's not at home any more?" She found it "very easy to give a great deal of approval [to her child] and I'm wondering it that's not too much," in light of the slights and rejections that accompanied adulthood. A second mother responded to this by saying a person fortified with self-esteem from infancy and who knew he was a valued individual was unlikely to experience a "jolt" in the "real" world that would undo what his parents had wrought. "I think," she said, "it's very much easier to take this [cruelty and contingency] from the outside world if you know that at least somebody you like is approving of you." At this point Bettelheim intervened. "Finally, I start to harvest results from my labors."

During this session he told the group it was important to avoid conveying a "defeatist" attitude in their children. If a child was convinced he and his surroundings were "good," he would have "more courage . . . to face the world." During this exchange a third mother said she thought it might help the mother who initially expressed concern about making her child "too happy" if she could "think of the child in terms of say, a young sapling. I always feel that the more sun and the more light and rain a young sapling gets, the better it can withstand the battering of the storm it will get later on. And I think that this thinking can be applied to the child."[46]

At times, the efforts of Bettelheim's mothers to buttress the self-esteem of their children was surpassed only by the anxiety they felt during the process. Nearly all of those who attended Bettelheim's sessions agreed with his idea that a parent "shouldn't suppress your child if you can help it." They constantly spoke of the tightrope they walked and the Herculean efforts they made to ensure their offspring would feel loved, focused upon, autonomous—and well behaved.

At one meeting a mother told the group about a problem she was having with her little son. He constantly reached for the kitchen stove when it was hot. She and her husband were concerned that he might hurt himself. But they were reluctant to declare the stove off-limits to the boy because it might stifle his curiosity and freedom of movement. They wanted him to roam freely in his environment, to feel he could go where his interests and curiosity might lead him. Their solution to the problem was to avoid using the stove when the child was awake. "[I]t works," she told the group. "And now if the baby's awake, we eat sandwiches. . . . That's all you can do."[47]

Awareness that their children's egos were fragile and easily damaged could inspire unusual behavior in some mothers. "I had the idea," one mother of the fifties recalled years later, "that every little thing I did could have this terrific impact on this tender little psyche." Her anxiety was so great that she was afraid to show affection toward her youngest child while the older one was present, even though the older child had never shown a trace of jealously toward her younger sibling. "The worst was when Nick, my second child, was born. I was so concerned that my two-year old, Lisa, not be jealous, that if she came into the room and found me hugging or caressing the baby, I'd literally jump guiltily, and have an impulse to put the baby down and act as if I didn't care about him."[48]

Middle-class couples knew that their brand of child-rearing was a delicate process haunted by uncertain outcomes. Accordingly, some mothers felt that they alone should oversee the development of their young children. Even when they needed and could afford household help, these mothers were loath to surrender exclusive control of their children. One mother agonized for weeks about hiring a nurse to take care of her baby during the daytime. She finally did so, but could not find one who pleased her. "I wanted the nurse to conform to my liberal ideas about [child] training." The first nurse she hired was let go because "she did not pick up the baby often enough." What the mother meant by "often enough" was "every time she cried" or otherwise sought attention. A second nurse was fired because she fed the baby food the child "did not like."[49]

The reluctance to use intermediaries between mother and child went beyond domestic help. Another mother, hounded by endless household tasks and harried by a peripatetic baby, thought about buying a "playpen" for her son. It would keep him out of harm's way while she worked around the house. In the end, however, she decided against it. A playpen would limit her son's ability to "explore" his surroundings at will. Also, it might give him the impression that he had done something wrong and had to be placed in what the mother called a "prison."[50] Parents went to great lengths to stimulate their children's curiosity by allowing them to roam about the house without undue restrictions. It was as though their homes harbored an imaginary, expansive American space within which their children might explore new frontiers of experience.

The lengths to which they went to cultivate autonomy, self-esteem and competitiveness in their children aroused fear in some parents that discipline might fall between the cracks. Typical of such parents was a 28-year-old Manhattan mother. She was alarmed by her 5-year-old son's chronic misbehavior, but would ask "the children's own advice" about appropriate punishment for their misdeeds.[51] She wanted her children to be both autonomous and well disciplined.

CONCLUSION: MIDDLE-CLASS CHILD REARING AND SIXTIES RADICALISM

It is hard to measure with anything approaching precision the extent to which the child-centeredness described in this chapter was a radical departure from previous middle-class practices. In every historical period, widely divergent approaches to raising children have existed in the United States, even within a given social class. Religious values, ethnicity, the region of the country in which families live—as well as social class—foster diverse child-rearing practices throughout the country. As do unanticipated shifts in the economy, technological developments, political events and other factors.

The child-centered middle-class ideal of the forties and fifties was a sharp departure from the austere, authority-centered, behavioral approach to child rearing advocated by the psychologist John Watson in the first third of the century. Yet it was a logical extension of the late-nineteenth-century middle-class ideals of companionate marriage and relatively democratic household relationships. It is possible that the exorbitant child-centeredness and overwrought anxiety exhibited by parents in the forties and fifties became widespread within the middle class sometime between the late 1930s and the end of World War II.[52]

Whatever its lineage, the middle-class family of the forties and fifties was a cradle of self-reliant, competitive individualism (as the next chapter describes in its discussion of young radicals). But self-reliance and individualism are politically neutral traits. They include demands for privacy, autonomy and freedom, but in and of themselves these traits do not imply anything about an individual's political values. What, then, is the relationship between middle-class child rearing and sixties radicalism?

It is important to remember that the leftist youth culture was not the only brand of radicalism that attracted college students in the sixties. In 1960, the same year that Students for a Democratic Society and the Student Nonviolent Coordinating Committee (SNCC) were established, the right-wing Young Americans for Freedom (YAF) was founded. Created with the help of older conservatives like William F. Buckley, Jr., YAF was a college-student organization passionately opposed to communism and liberalism, with almost equal degrees of zeal. While YAF played a minor role in galvanizing support for the candidacy of conservative Republican Senator Barry Goldwater in the 1964 presidential election, it attracted only a small fraction of the attention garnered by SNCC or SDS in the sixties.

But as John Andrew III pointed out in his important book on YAF, the young conservatives believed that the New Deal welfare state and the liberalism of Lyndon Johnson's Great Society undermined the individual's self-reliance, self-respect and independence (many New Leftists agreed). And YAF members were as critical of liberal elites and as committed to grass-roots organizing as those in SNCC, SDS and the counterculture. Unlike the New Left, however, YAF was adept at political organization. Its ideas continued to play important roles in the conservative wing of the Republican Party long after the sixties, and some of its members served in the administrations of Richard Nixon and Ronald Reagan.[53]

It seems, then, that young Americans destined for college in the sixties were well trained in the ways of competitive individualism, regardless of their political orientations. At least with regard to being autonomous, self-reliant and competitive, it is difficult to tell the difference between baby boomers who turned leftward in the sixties and their age peers in Congress who helped lead the "Republican Revolution" in the eighties and nineties.

How, then, can we distinguish between those who created the cultural and political left and those committed to YAF in the sixties? As pointed out earlier, the evidence suggests that most young whites who organized the New Left and counterculture in the first half of the sixties were raised in middle-class households by professional, relatively liberal parents.[54] Peggy's parents and the mothers who participated in Bettelheim's "dialogues" reinforce this view. How Peggy herself and the actual offspring of the Chicago mothers turned out in the sixties is, of course, impossible to know.

Nor with the exception of notable radicals, is it possible to trace the social class backgrounds and family environments of the tens of thousands of individuals who became cultural or political radicals. Was their faith in American democracy buffeted when they were in high school in 1957, as they witnessed the televised spectacle of white adults screaming "Go back to the jungle" at the black children who integrated Little Rock's Central High School? Did doubts about the veracity of American Cold War rhetoric surface during their college years, when they learned their country supported regimes every bit as oppressive as the Soviet Union—as long as they were anticommunist? One can speculate endlessly. There may have been almost as many reasons, both personal and political, for becoming radical in the sixties as there were radicals.

At the same time, there are some documented and intriguing differences between the liberal-to-left Berkeley students who joined the Free Speech Movement (FSM) in 1964 and those who organized YAF. For example, the 773 Berkeley students arrested in the largest FSM protest, the sit-in at the university's administration building in December of 1964, were more Jewish and less Catholic than the student body as a whole. In the general student population at Berkeley 20 percent identified themselves as Jewish, 44 percent as Protestant and 15 percent as Catholic. Those arrested in the FSM protest were 32 percent Jewish, 36 percent Protestant and only 6 percent Catholic. The protesters claimed they were less religious, or at least less likely to attend religious services, than the rest of the student body. They had higher average grades, were more likely to major in the humanities (none majored in business) and were characterized as unusually "independent" in their attitudes toward authority.[55]

The profile of students who joined Young Americans for Freedom was quite different. There were YAFers who came from upper-middle-class backgrounds, but the majority hailed from lower-middle- and working-class families. Their parents worked hard to send their children to college and prepare them for professional careers. Many YAF members were religious and the organization was particularly popular at Catholic colleges. Somewhere between 26 percent and 33 percent of its membership was Catholic (by one estimate members of that faith accounted for about 50 percent of those who joined the ultra-right-wing John Birch Society in the sixties). YAF's Jewish membership, if it had any, was negligible. Less than 10 percent of SDSers were Catholics. While most early New Leftists majored in the humanities, YAFers were more career oriented and leaned toward professional majors. They were particularly attracted to business, law, pre-med and the physical sciences. And they were less likely to be enrolled in elite colleges and universities than those in the New Left.[56]

Ultimately, the differences between the individualism of the radical youth culture and right-wing organizations like YAF rested on the former's open-ended approach to experience and genuine commitment to egalitarianism. Political and cultural radicals embodied traits instilled in their middle-class families and described in this chapter (beyond that of individualism). They were spontaneous, open to new experiences and willing to endure unpredictability. Their family experiences implicitly exposed them to the ideals of fair play and equality: every person should be autonomous and have the opportunity to become a fully developed human being. Their parents thought it important to encourage them to be wary of arbitrary authority and received wisdom. And they allowed children to roam unrestrained in their homes as a means of nurturing their curiosity and freedom to explore their world. Young radicals felt free to exercise those freedoms in the real world beyond the family, come what may.

By contrast, members of YAF knew the "truth" from the beginning and were obsessed with social order and personal stability. They rejected the authority of liberal government in the name of self-reliance and individualism. But they relied without undue qualification on other forms of authority. This was especially true of religious dogma, the dictates of the free market, the patriarchal family and the values of (nonliberal) elites such as William F. Buckley and Barry Goldwater.[57]

The cult of security and the resurgent individualism nourished by middle-class child rearing were extreme reactions to the remarkable prosperity of the late forties and fifties. But they were more than vastly different responses to the bounty of the postwar economic boom. They were opposite ways of imagining life in the United States, mid-twentieth-century expressions of contrary strains of belief and behavior deeply rooted in the country's history and culture. The historical sources of these American polarities, and how tensions between them helped shape a rebellious generation in the sixties, are the subjects of the next chapter.

FOUR

New Bottles, Old Wine: An Archeology of Rebellion

[American society] is deeply imbued with the sentiment of order. It has been nurtured in the hatred of the old political divisions of Europe, but a feeling of the need for self-restraint runs through its veins.

Michael Chevalier, 1836

And he hunched over the wheel and gunned her; he was back in his element, everybody could see that. We were all delighted, we all realized we were leaving confusion and nonsense behind and performing our one and noble function of the time, move. And we moved!

Jack Kerouac, *On the Road*

One is Hip or one is Square. One is a rebel or one conforms, one is a frontiersman in the Wild West or American night life, or else a Square cell trapped in the totalitarian tissue of American society, doomed willy-nilly to conform if one is to succeed.

Norman Mailer, *The White Negro*, 1957

THE AMBIGUOUS LEGACY OF MIDDLE-CLASS CHILD REARING

In 1972 Paul Potter published a political memoir of the rise and fall of the New Left. Potter played a major role in the creation of the New Left a decade earlier, and served a term as president of Students for a Democratic Society. A recurring theme in his book was the intense animosity of early SDSers toward middle-class values. Even though most young activists came from middle-class backgrounds, Potter said they rejected its economic individualism and materialism. And they refused to participate in its relentless hunt for influence, power and professional status. Potter nevertheless argued that members of SDS were inspired, as well as put off, by their middle-class heritage. Their radicalism both affirmed and negated the middle class worldview. They were products of an ambiguous legacy.

> Most of our parents were at least a little embarrassed by the vacuous materialism they raised us in. If they fed on and helped to create the cult of the expert and personal possession, it was still within a framework of consciously wanting something more for us, even as they became resigned to the notion that whatever it was, it was not for them. Stated most positively, the social and political aspirations of the American middle class are for the completion of the American revolution—the creation of a society of equality, liberty, and the inviolable integrity of the individual—and from that social vision, which was projected so strongly onto us, came our first sense of hypocrisy and injustice, our first commitment to set things right.[1]

Potter's words captured a glaring irony of sixties radicalism. To a considerable degree, the alienation of white youth during the first half of the decade was produced by contradictions in the vision of American life held by the modern middle class. On one side was the non-economic "expressive" individualism that middle-class parents persistently encouraged in their offspring. As we saw in the previous chapter, parents taught their children to see the future as an adventure in self-development. Their lives would be experientially rich as well as professionally and economically rewarding. Life should be an endless stream of personal challenges and opportunities that, if properly handled, would lead to personal fulfillment. Toward this end they nourished their children's independence, self-esteem and assertiveness.

On the other side of the modern middle-class value system were commitments to economic mobility, social progress and order. Since the last third of the nineteenth century, middle-class intellectuals, experts and policymakers have engaged in what historian Robert Wiebe called a "search for order."[2] They promoted economic individualism because it fueled the country's dynamic, opportunity-laden, free-wheeling economy. But they tried to limit its potentially destructive impact through "rational" social planning, scientific management and other strategies. The professional middle class played a central role in the development of bureaucratic processes and planning throughout American society. And it helped spread the agenda of liberal reform in the twentieth century by creating the managerial values and techniques of large-scale planning embraced by activist state and federal governments.[3]

For the past century the middle class has been the primary advocate of what Potter disparagingly called the "cult of the expert." It organized the various professions into discreet vessels of expertise. Middle-class intellectuals helped legitimate the roles of unelected experts—economists, physicians, psychologists, social workers, lawyers and academicians—in the formulation and execution of public policies. They designed educational standards for entry into the professions and fashioned codes of conduct for practitioners. Its engineers initiated the movement for industrial efficiency. Its psychologists and sociologists devised strategies for measuring the intelligence of individuals and for evaluating and controlling their behavior.[4]

Thus the middle class is the carrier of a series of behavioral, emotional and intellectual polarities. It promotes personal freedom and hierarchical chains of command; autonomy and submission to external standards of behavior and knowledge; the ideal of equality and the prerogatives of achieved status; individualism and conformity; competition and cooperation.

During the forties and fifties, the parents discussed in chapter 2 cultivated competitive individualism in their children. But they also conveyed to them, explicitly and forcefully, the ideas that self-development and personal freedom were ends in themselves. They were concerned about discipline, but the expressive, developmental side of the middle-class ethos was promoted in tandem with its orderly, "rational" side. "Mother laid out possibilities like a three-course meal," recalled the sister of Janis Joplin. But she "never talked about limits."[5] Competitive individualism was the means of pushing back the boundaries of possibility, whether personal or social. In his autobiography Jerry Rubin said that after "the sixties ended . . . I discovered that though I rebelled against my parents, I had in fact reproduced their psychic structures inside me." These "psychic structures" involved a hunger for self-fulfillment and the competitive individualism necessary to achieve it. "You taught me," Rubin told his parents, "to compete and compare, to fear and outdo. I became a ferocious achievement-oriented, compulsive, obsessive, live-in-my-head asshole."[6]

The message sent to their children was that they were independent. Control of their lives and destinies should be in their hands, and theirs alone. One of the young women who participated in Bruno Bettelheim's "dialogues with mothers" expressed this attitude and the contradictions it harbored. This middle-class woman rejected the notion that her three-year-old daughter should be controlled by what she called "middle-class" conformity. She told Bettelheim's group that pressures to conform to accepted standards of femininity were already being aimed at her daughter by peers and family members. At the tender age of three her child was told she should look "pretty." A proper young lady should wear dresses instead of the more comfortable "overalls" that enhanced her freedom of movement and were preferred by her mother. "I'm afraid," said the young mother, "she'll turn into what I've seen her cousins turning into. They're all, I hate to use the word 'middle class,' but that's what it is." Bettelheim asked her what was wrong with being middle class: "What do you want her to be, a proletarian?" "I want her to be a rebel," countered the mother.[7]

The life of the middle class was riven with such ambivalence. The attitudes of its children toward competition is an important case in point. For example, as Potter pointed out, the early members of SDS constantly expressed contempt for the competitive ethic of the middle class. They believed ruthless competition was the ballast of an amoral free-enterprise economy. It justified destructive egoism and turned human beings into economic predators instead of mutually supportive members of a cooperative, humane society. Unregulated economic competition transformed potentially gratifying work into mere "careers." Worse still, the social Darwinism that fueled the middle-class "rat race" fostered gross disparities of wealth and power. It made poverty and frustration inevitable for millions of people. Tom Hayden, a major leader of SDS in the early sixties, said it was hard to exaggerate the extent to which "this movement was a rebellion against middle-class careerism." It was the "perfect organizational formula for the suppression of middle-class ambition" and competitiveness. He claimed that SDS was an antidote to these values. The organization served as a model for a cooperative, egalitarian social order. Important decisions were arrived at through open discussion among equals. Rather than mere majority rule, SDSers tried to achieve a "consensus" on matters great and small as a way of solidifying cohesion within the group. In SDS, said Hayden, "the ego of the individual" was "submerged in the group as just one ego among many."[8]

In fact, however, powerful, often destructive urges to compete pervaded SDS. Charismatic, articulate and invariably male "movement heavies" like Hayden usually dominated meetings. Decisions about the organization's positions on major issues and strategy often evolved more from a battle of clashing male egos than from a democratic consensus.

Todd Gitlin was another key player in early SDS; since the sixties he has been a distinguished sociologist, historian and social critic. In 1970 he observed that middle-class radicals harbored "internal deformations and diseases" rooted in the egoism they had been "taught" since "the cradle." Their resulting "arrogance, elitism, competitiveness, machismo, ruthlessness, [and] guilt" prepared them "to devour each other."[9] These traits fed the factionalism that riddled the organization in the late sixties and contributed to its demise in 1969.

Hayden himself, for all his talk about "submerged" egos, said, "I have always been more of an independent catalyst than equal member of any collective or group."[10] Indeed, decision making through consensus reflected this reflexive individualism. An individual's wishes or ideas could not be contravened by mere majority rule. And Paul Potter said that radicals imbibed the "middle-class image of the good society," which for their parents meant a society "at its most competitive." To prepare them for future struggles for power, wealth and status, middle-class children were exposed to "constant grading and evaluation" by teachers and parents. It was a destructive experience. Middle-class competitiveness, according to Potter, might help create economic "progress," but it did so in a moral vacuum.[11]

Yet as we have seen, Potter understood that the middle-class version of competition empowered as well as deformed young radicals. It had another dimension. The autonomy encouraged by their parents made them feel "reasonably potent in influencing our personal milieu." While in high school and college, future radicals were usually able to withstand peer pressures to conform and were immunized against blind submission to their teachers' arbitrary exercise of power. A "careful socialization to upper-middle-class values has ill-prepared [them] to accept" such pressures. Because of their upbringing, "we are in a much better position to challenge a society that promises to make us impotent." In other words, a society that threatened their autonomy. "As a group," wrote Potter,

> the men who were attracted to SDS, particularly early SDS, were highly motivated, success oriented, competitive men. Perhaps one of the reasons some of us got into SDS was because we didn't like the modes of competition that had been set up, thought that they were too destructive, in fact wanted some more fraternal set-up for that to take place in, and also wanted more control than you have if you go to work working your way up somebody else's hierarchy. . . . So it [SDS] was both fraternal and competitive, but everybody talked about fraternalness, nobody talked about competition.[12]

Young radicals rejected the careerism, expertise and achieved status offered by the middle class. They did not turn away from its summons to strive and compete, to take risks and welcome challenges.

To some degree the non-economic, expressive side of the middle-class value system was detached from its status-seeking, hierarchical side in young radicals. Whatever the immediate causes of the rupture—the hypocrisies built into American race relations, the transparencies of Cold War rhetoric, the incongruities between the cult of security and their upbringing—expressive individualism gave shape and definition to their alienation from American society.

The autonomy and intellectual independence they were taught as children enabled them to question, even disobey, the authority of parents or public officials. A young man who violated the draft law in 1968 to avoid service in Vietnam said his parents had encouraged him from childhood to be self-reliant. "I was fortunate to have been raised by strong parents, who gave me a clear sense of goodness and self-worth, and an ability to get things done." Yet, when his parents (who were against the war) accused him of acting "impetuously" in avoiding the draft, of committing a "crime" and getting himself "in deep trouble with the government," his response was telling. He didn't need their permission to violate the draft laws. "I didn't need their approval. I had to do what I thought was right for me."[13] After all, that was how he was raised. The parents of a young woman encouraged her to question authority when she was growing up. They told her it was wrong to be a "good German" by obeying authorities who issued immoral commands. Nevertheless, they were upset when she became an antiwar activist. She might be arrested. Her career might be jeopardized. She went her own way. "There's always a double-edged sword," she said, "when you bring people up with the notion that you should take positions on things. You never know where they'll come out."[14]

Bruno Bettelheim saw this coming long before it happened. The mothers he worked with in the late forties were perhaps too intent upon encouraging autonomy in their offspring. "[T]hey have invested their small children with this power to judge them."[15]

Judge them they did. From the early sixties, young radicals mocked the staid, privileged lifestyle of their middle-class parents. And, not surprisingly, they felt guilty about their own privileged status. Seeking expiation for the entitlements of their middle-class backgrounds was a mainstay of sixties radical chic. It could be expressed humorously. Richard Flacks described an SDS "fund-raising orgy" that occurred on the final day of the group's national convention in 1963:

> The scene might have been written by Genet; it was worthy of filming by Fellini. A young man, well clothed and well groomed but with his shirt collar open now, and his tie pulled down, shouted to the audience like an old-fashioned revivalist: "Come up," he cried, "come up and confess. Put some money in the net and be saved!" And they came. The first youth, clutching the

> green pieces of paper in his hand, recited for all to hear: "My father is a newspaper editor. I give twenty-five dollars." His penitence brought cheers from the assembly. The sin of the next young man was a father who was assistant director of a government bureau. He gave forty dollars. "My dad is Dean of a law school," confessed another, as he proffered fifty dollars for indulgence.[16]

Rituals like these may have served to distance them from their backgrounds. But they could not eradicate other legacies of their childhood, of which most seemed blithely unaware (Potter and Gitlin were exceptions). They were driven by the individualism and competitiveness that marked their early years. They needed to be self-reliant, autonomous and paid attention to. The problem—and the irony—of their condition was that the magnitude of these middle-class expectations could not be redeemed in an impersonal, bureaucratic, hierarchical, managerial (that is to say, middle-class dominated) society.

By the early sixties, this contradiction bubbled to the surface and helped spawn the first signs of disillusionment in the young.

EXPECTATIONS UNBOUND

Their alienation surfaced by the late fifties and early sixties, as children born between the late thirties and the war years came of college age. In his autobiography Tom Hayden recalled the amorphous, gnawing uneasiness he felt toward the end of his undergraduate years at the University of Michigan in 1961.[17] As a child his parents encouraged him to value education and strive for success in school. He was taught "enterprise" and tolerance toward others. Hayden graduated from high school with "heady expectations" of the intellectual excitement college held in store. He looked forward to experiencing a life of "enrichment and adventure" beyond his time at the university.

As a senior in high school he read Jack Kerouac's new novel, *On the Road.* Kerouac's book affirmed Hayden's "heady expectations" about his future. He understood Kerouac's main point: American freedom was the odyssey of taking to the road and opening himself to the unexpected experiences, tales and people he would find there. These thoughts fortified Hayden's "deep desire" to "take risks and journey into an emotional and intellectual wilderness." He identified with the novel's peripatetic Dean Moriarty and described him like a hero of a 1950s television western. Moriarty was "a powerful rebel, a combined image of the cowboy/explorer" trying to bust out of the "new suburbia that now occupied the once-vast American frontier."

These expectations were dashed by the time Hayden was a senior in college. Instead of being challenging and stimulating, American society was passionless and stolid. In a word, fifties America was "boring." Everything about it, including the prospective futures of its most privileged and educated children, seemed "prearranged," controlled and inevitable. Success in college was a prelude to a life of meaningless work. The future stared back at him in his college courses and textbooks, most of which were bereft of intellectual excitement and challenge. Beyond the campus, the country was devoid of an experiential "wilderness," some open road to freedom that might be explored by a curious, conscientious individual. "A fine, normal upbringing in America," Hayden said, "had left me anticipating a lifetime of unfulfilled expectations."[18]

Jerry Rubin experienced a similar disillusionment. As a child his parents "instilled in me a deep expectation of living for the future," along with powerful "expectations" of what it held in store for him. Rubin's assumption that excitement and adventure lay ahead was supplemented at home and in school by stories that depicted "America's promise" through tales of daring, individualistic heroes. Rubin learned about and admired "Columbus, George Washington, Paul Revere, the pioneers, the cowboys." They took chances, lived in exciting times and welcomed adventure and the uncertainty it entailed. By the early sixties, however, it was clear to Rubin there was no place for daring heroes in an affluent, settled, bureaucratic society. In place of adventure, modern America offered the best and brightest of its youth a track to predictability and ennui: "get good grades . . . get a degree, then get a job. . . . But kids aren't satisfied with that." They wanted excitement, challenge, and the prospect of earning a place in a world of their own making. "They want to be heroes," Rubin declared.[19]

When they were children, influences beyond family and school fed their impression that America was a field of exciting possibilities for the daring individual. Among them were science-fiction comic books, the federal government's space program, and television and film westerns. By the fifties, the prospect of travel in "outer space" was more than the product of the science-fiction writer's imagination. As Geoffrey O'Brien recalled in his evocative memoir of growing up in the fifties and coming of age in the sixties, imaginative children in those years could envision the day they might "walk on Mars" or swim "through the air."[20] Another child of the forties and fifties dreamed of growing up and participating in "space operas."[21] And a young writer for the underground press in the sixties remembered his fascination with westerns and cowboy shows in the fifties. They sparked in him the vision of the American as a passionate "adventure-crazed pioneer in fringed leather and long blond hair charging across the western plains." Fearless cowboys and risk-taking pioneers embodied his idea of "the American values of individualism."[22] Rubin was also fascinated by the image of the loner cowboy dispensing justice in an anarchic West. He once remarked (tongue only slightly in cheek) that his radical ideas were "more influenced" by "the Lone Ranger [television series] than by Mao or Che or Lenin."[23]

As they approached college age, however, the "new frontier" explored by the space program seemed less than exciting. A young man observed in 1961 that the government's space program feigned adventure and mocked genuine individuality. It didn't conjure the daring exploits of new "Lindberghs flying the ocean alone." It was just an efficient bureaucratic effort that had nothing to do with real individualism. The "astronauts are not people," he said with despair, "they are a team."[24] And, of course, in the security-obsessed fifties the Old West was not only a memory but so were the daring individualists who supposedly tamed it. In the late sixties, Yippie leader Abbie Hoffman suggested that American manhood played itself out in the West of the nineteenth century, and was submerged in the twentieth by the organized boredom and routine of "plastic-coated America." "America lost its balls on the frontier," said Hoffman, "and since then there have been no mighty myths" to inspire or challenge the imagination.[25]

Time and again they voiced their disappointment over the gap that separated their childhood expectations from their young-adult realities. Peter Coyote was a member of the Diggers, the theatrical group that helped make the Haight-Ashbury the mecca of the counterculture during the mid sixties. Coyote said that by the early sixties it was clear that "kids" raised by Depression-era parents, in what he called the affluent, "permissive loony bin" of the forties and fifties, were "being shortchanged." Instead of the "vital stuff" they had been promised by society, they were getting sterile substitutes.[26] Grace Slick of the Jefferson Airplane rock group, the daughter of a wealthy investment banker, said parents in the fifties told their children their lives would be "wonderful." But American society was not "awfully exciting." The security offered the children of the affluent classes was "boring," and the response of its best and brightest to the kinds of status offered "well-educated kids" was simply, "'I don't think so.'"[27]

They expected to fly, to be challenged, noticed—as they had been as children. Instead, by the time they were ready for college, they encountered a society committed to eradicating the unexpected. Mario Savio, one of the leaders of Berkeley's Free Speech Movement in 1964, said American society was run by bureaucrats who believed "nothing new happens." Students in the early sixties were not only alienated from society, but were "strangers in their own lives." College students had expected "to learn, to question, to grow." But "American society in the standard conception it has of itself is simply no longer exciting. . . . America is becoming ever more the utopia of sterilized, automated discontent. The 'futures' and 'careers' for which American students now prepare are for the most part intellectual and moral wastelands."[28]

In the early sixties, the burgeoning Civil Rights movement provided Savio and hundreds of other white college students with an outlet for their trammelled energies and hunger for adventure. They were already alienated. This does not mean their involvement with the African American struggle for equality was motivated only by their need to be challenged or to escape from boredom. The Civil Rights movement was not only a watershed in the history of African Americans, but ignited in thousands of young whites what Paul Potter called their "first sense of hypocrisy and injustice" in American life.[29] Their decision to join the African American cause was fueled by moral outrage over racism and by the desire to create a just society. The distress they experienced over the prospect of leading less-than-fulfilling lives dovetailed with a commitment to racial equality. Both played a role in their decisions to join the movement.

In February of 1960, African American college students launched the first sit-ins against segregated lunch counters in Greensboro, North Carolina. Television, newspaper and word-of-mouth accounts of young African American women and men being harassed and beaten for trying to purchase a cup of coffee energized the Civil Rights movement. Young blacks from the South and the North joined the nonviolent struggle against segregation. Within months sit-ins spread throughout the south and thousands were arrested. In April of 1960 young African Americans organized the Student Nonviolent Coordinating Committee (SNCC). The stage was set for a full-scale assault on institutionalized racism in the South.

Hundreds of young whites joined the movement as well. Some of them were southerners, more came from the North. Many were like "Peggy," the twelve year old we encountered in the preceding chapter, whose parents openly decried racism. Most whites who joined SNCC or participated in the sit-ins, boycotts, freedom rides and voter-registration drives of the early sixties, were children of liberal, middle-class parents. Whatever their family backgrounds (not all of them were offspring of middle-class or liberal parents), these young people were inspired by moral outrage. The injustice and inhumanity of racism moved them to go to the South and "put their bodies on the line."[30] Once there, they faced incessant threats, frequent beatings and even death in virulently segregationist states like Alabama and Mississippi.

They were deeply disillusioned by the discrepancy between the American ideal of equality before the law and the American reality of discrimination sanctioned by the law. For young people like Paul Potter (who went south in 1961 and was beaten by racists in Mississippi), the idea of equality transcended its political, economic or even racial connotations. Equality was the linchpin of their upbringing. It legitimated middle-class child rearing and was woven into the fabric of their worldview. The "middle class projects equality so vividly into the future and onto its children," observed Potter, because it is the ideological fuel that drives individualism, competition and achievement. For the middle class, equality of opportunity was "supposed to make it all make sense."[31]

Most of all, perhaps, many of them were inspired to work in the movement because they hoped its call for integration, love and nonviolence would become the model for a redeemed, more communitarian society. They wanted to live in a society in which cooperation and intimacy were valued. This was the counterpoint to their determined individualism. They had, after all, spent their formative years as members of apparently tightknit, bonded families. The America they entered around 1960 was as bereft of intimacy and community as it was of passion and adventure. People like Potter wanted to experience both genuine individualism and life in a close-knit community. "We do not want to be complete, autonomous men—not quite," observed Potter. "Part of us wants to need, and openly acknowledge the depth of need, for other people."[32] As Todd Gitlin said of his first encounters with early SDS, he was attracted to it because it was a "fused group" bonded by intimacy and friendship. SDS, he said, was more like an "extended family" than a political organization.[33]

The need for community and intimacy that bonded those who worked in the southern Civil Rights movement, along with its compelling call to moral witness, attracted people like Potter and Gitlin. Young whites in the movement were struck by the dignity of the "ordinary" African Americans they encountered in the deep, rural South. Usually poor, often unlettered, these courageous people risked their lives and livelihoods in opening their homes and churches to civil-rights insurgents, who were viewed by segregationists as "outside agitators." Sandra "Casey" Hayden, a white southerner and SNCC organizer, was deeply moved by the dignity and humanity of rural African Americans. Neither the savagery of racism nor the scourges of poverty had broken the spirits nor undermined the dignity of rural blacks. The dignified carriage of these people, along with the sight of young blacks and whites working together to fight racism, suggested to Hayden that the Civil Rights movement was more than a struggle against institutionalized racism. It portended the creation of what SNCC activists called "the beloved community," a haven of colorblind sisterhood and brotherhood beyond the movement, the struggle and the south.

> We were the beloved community, harassed and happy, and poor. And in those little, hot black rural churches, we went into the music, into the sound, and everyone was welcome inside this perfect place. We simply dropped race. . . . And we did love each other so much. We were living in a community so true

> to itself that all we wanted was to organize everyone into it, make the whole world beloved with us, make the whole world our beloved.[34]

More than anything else, this vision of an America at once egalitarian, morally redeemed and communitarian inspired young whites to enlist in the Civil Rights movement. But the desire for lives marked by intensity, danger and daring moved them as well. The perils of going south offered a way out of the boredom and security that imprisoned them. Sandra Hayden recalled how "exciting, liberating, [and] spicy" it was for activists to work in a hazardous, hostile environment. It "was all underground, illegal, dangerous." And in a telling echo of Kerouac's celebration of the American highway to freedom, she noted the movement was "on the road," far from home, where they were on their own.[35]

A sense of exuberance in being challenged, experiencing danger and diving into life on one's own terms pervaded accounts of going south in the early sixties. A young white man from the North participated in the most dangerous civil-rights activity of the time, the 1964 "Freedom Summer" effort to register African American voters in Mississippi. He wondered if the goal of racial equality was his only motivation. He wanted to be assigned to the most isolated rural areas of the state, where violence against civil-rights advocates was not only condoned by law-enforcement officials but frequently committed by them. "But this naturally suggests to me," he wrote in his journal, "some unpleasant and unresolvable questions about my own motivations for being down here." Searching for "adventure isn't exactly the highest idealism."[36]

Others who went to Mississippi in the summer of 1964 were similarly introspective and ambiguous about their motives. In a letter to his parents, who feared for his safety, an activist said, "I feel the urgent need, somehow, to enter life, to be born into it." The movement offered him the opportunity to do so, and he refused to return "home where everything is secure and made for me." It would be like choosing "a kind of death."[37] Another college student who participated in "Freedom Summer" wrote to her parents, who were fearful she might be killed. She rejected their demand that she leave the South. The letter is a testament to the sensibilities instilled in middle-class children during the forties and fifties. She was their equal. "I hope you will accept my decision even if you do not agree with me." She was autonomous. "There comes a time when you have to do things which your parents do not agree with." She was self-confident, assuming her values should be acted upon. "Convictions are worthless in themselves. In fact, if they don't become actions, they are worse than worthless." And she was intent upon immersing herself in life, taking chances, letting the chips fall where they may. "I think you have to live to the fullest extent to which you have gained an awareness or you are less than the human being you are capable of being. This doesn't apply just to civil-rights or social consciousness but to all the experiences of life."[38]

David Harris, the future anti–Vietnam War activist, left Stanford University as a sophomore in the fall of 1964 to work for racial equality in Mississippi. In his 1982 autobiography he confessed he "still didn't altogether understand why, out of nowhere, I jumped at that opportunity." More than anything else, he wanted to be part of the struggle for the creation of a colorblind society. But something else gnawed at him as well. He needed to escape the boredom of routine and the irrelevance of much of his college studies. Harris also needed to quench his thirst for "adventure," to put himself on the line and be "tested." He longed for a "hell-bent, wild-west" sort of "manhood."[39] Mario Savio put it more starkly. Going to Mississippi had as much to do with what he called "middle class" expectations about living intensely and being challenged as it did with the moral imperatives of the Civil Rights movement. Perhaps more.

> I thought about it and my own involvement when I went to Mississippi where I could be killed. My reasons were selfish. I wasn't really alive. My life, my middle class life, had no place in society, nor it in me. It was not really a matter of fighting for constitutional rights. I needed some way to pinch myself, to assure myself that I was alive.[40]

Savio's feelings captured the irony faced by alienated youth in the early sixties. Their capacity to tolerate an uncertain future and welcome unanticipated experiences clashed head-on with their society's attempts to narrow the range of uncertainty. This tension assumed a variety of forms. For one, it fed their negative responses to their college experience. A well-documented problem existed at large public universities. Children of the middle class, used to being "the center of the universe" at home, felt lost and ignored in a morass of mega-university impersonality and red tape. They complained about being processed in massive "knowledge factories" like Berkeley. As one Berkeley student said in 1964, he was "just a number," unknown to his professors, lodged in immense classes. He was an anonymous face "in the sea of a thousand faces."[41]

But even some students at small, liberal arts colleges like Smith and Mount Holyoke felt alienated and "lost." Their classes were much smaller and they knew their professors. Nevertheless, some felt "reduced to less than human beings" because their studies were "lifeless," as one student put it.[42] The curriculum was less a challenge to learn, question and grow than a bureaucratic piling on of course credits. And it was suffused by what one of them called "desiccated irrelevance."[43] The curriculum spoke to neither their expectations nor their aspirations. It was almost as easy to feel lost or irrelevant in small colleges as in "multiversities" like

Berkeley or University of Michigan. One student at a small liberal arts college said that if she suddenly disappeared from school, "no one would really miss her."[44]

The alienation of students had a number of causes. One was the difficult transition in moving from child-centered families to an impersonal, meritocratic society. Also, students who came from families in which parents were politically liberal or radical found little correspondence between their studies and important issues like civil rights, poverty, the Cold War and nuclear disarmament. Most of all, perhaps, college didn't challenge them beyond competition for grades, a skill already finely honed from their earlier educational experiences. Like the society and careers that beckoned after graduation, college was too safe and secure, its promises of status and material gain too predictable and unchallenging.

During his term as president of SDS, Tom Hayden addressed these issues in a speech to students at Ann Arbor in March 1962. He chided them for their hesitation to "take risks." Most students, he said, were afraid to set "dangerous goals" for themselves. But the structure and purpose of the university were also at fault. It was as oppressive and impersonal as other institutions. Both the assembly-line quality of the curriculum and the arbitrary rules imposed upon students by administrators and professors were preludes to what life after college held in store. College prepared young people for lives of conformity and prepackaged career options. Hayden told the students that "man is meant to live, not to prepare for life," much less be processed through it. The primary goal of the university was identical to that of other major institutions: it forced individuals to assume identities "made in the image of others." Its impermeable bureaucracies augured a lifetime of work within equally impersonal "mass organizations." And its fragmented curriculum paralleled the narrow, leaden "specialization" required by most jobs, which had little to offer the independent, self-reliant or creative individual. Hayden's remedy for this malaise was telling. "The time has come," he told his audience, "for a re-assertion of the personal."[45]

Hayden did not explain what he meant by a "re-assertion of the personal," but the phrase was significant. For one, it linked a burgeoning introspection and interest in personality among the young to the individualism nurtured during their upbringings. And it was prophetic, since projecting "the personal" onto everyday social interactions and political issues was a touchstone of cultural and political radicalism. It assumed numerous forms, all directly or indirectly linked to their expectations of being autonomous and of cutting their own path through life. More than anything else, it fueled the belief that the way they lived and the values they espoused should be products of their own experiences. The past, if not altogether irrelevant, was something to transcend. After all, they had learned during childhood that the world was undergoing rapid, unpredictable change. Old ideas might prove less than useful. They might even be harmful to individuals trained to transform the unpredictable events life threw their way into opportunities for self-development and achievement.

The belief that people should respond to an event or issue on its own terms and view it through the prism of their own experiences played a major role within the New Left of the early sixties. In his autobiography, Hayden said the one assumption shared by all members of early SDS was that "politics should flow from experience, not from preconceived dogmas or ideologies." One of the unique features of SDS before 1965 was its refusal to be categorized through the established frameworks of the Marxist Old Left, contemporary liberalism, or postwar democratic socialism. The activists in SDS "were determined to study all the [political] philosophies through the lens of our own experience, . . . searching for a language of our own." This reflected the feeling of young radicals "that the individual mattered in history, that nothing was entirely determined, that action created an evidence of its own."[46] Of course, he meant their "action."

The assumption that "nothing was entirely determined" was central for cultural radicals as well. The Grateful Dead's lead guitarist, Jerry Garcia, felt comfortable with the idea of the future as "less predictable" than "straight" people hoped it might be. "The trick," he said, "is to be as adaptable and changeable as possible."[47] This sensibility informed the counterculture idea that the individual could define and incessantly redefine her identity. There was no more powerful instance of a "re-assertion of the personal" during the sixties than the hippie attitude that through thoughtful deliberation or sheer whim the individual could alter her received identity and reinvent a new one. An inherited identity, like the past in general, meant little. The individual could become whatever she wished, and assume new identities with the frequency that hippies tried new drugs or new color schemes for their clothing. She could become "self-made," in the words of the traditional and quintessential American success story.

One of the hippies interviewed by sociologist Lewis Yablonsky in the sixties—most of whom, he discovered, were the children of "lawyers, doctors, businessmen, professors"—said "life is so groovy" because "there's so many ways to go through it." It was "really neat," he declared, "to try them all."[48] One of the shortcomings of American society, according to Jerry Rubin, was its failure to give everyone the opportunity to "change our personalities." Life would be far more interesting if it included the prospect of "abrupt new beginnings." Individuals should have the right to "start our lives all over again" as new needs or circumstances warranted.[49]

Thus the society they inherited around 1960 was triply disappointing. It was hypocritical, especially regarding race. It was too organized, secure and predictable to satisfy their cravings for adventure and autonomy. And it was too impersonal and corrosively competitive to gratify their needs for mutuality and cohesion. Disaffected young people frequently articulated their alienation through words and ideas that conjured an individualism and sense of adventure associated with the cowboys and Native Americans of the Old West. They spoke of open spaces and open roads in ways that recalled an older, less settled, more challenging and, most of all, more mobile America. (Of course, imagery tied to the Old West was neutral politically. It was used by the right and center as well as the left. Note how John F. Kennedy wrapped his Cold War rhetoric around the idea of a new frontier, or how Lyndon Johnson compared the American stake in winning the war in Vietnam to the struggle at the Alamo.)

The language used by those in the New Left and the counterculture often contained images and metaphors associated with movement, especially the idea of moving through a physically and psychologically spacious landscape. And it harbored a world of experience that at once was definably American, yet out of place and time with the country they inhabited.

METAPHORS OF "MOVEMENT" AND "SETTLEMENT"

The America imagined by the alienated young, in contrast with the one that existed in 1960, contained plenty of room to roam, literally and figuratively. It was more than coincidence that political radicals called their collective challenge to the status quo "the movement," or that they tried to change society through "direct action" protest. Or that those enamored of psychedelic drugs referred to their internal journey toward freedom and self-discovery as "trips."

The United States they conjured was defined by freedom of movement, psychological boundlessness and immersion in a seemingly endless succession of unexplored frontiers of new spaces and new experiences. "Our message," said Abbie Hoffman, "is always: Do what you want. Take chances. Extend your boundaries."[50] The ability to push beyond known or acceptable "boundaries" assumed the initiative to move, act directly and travel beyond the familiar, the routine, the expectable. "Action," declared Rubin, was an end in itself. "I support everything which puts people into *motion,* . . . which creates chaos and rebirth." For Jerry Garcia, musical improvisation was a way of discovering an "infinite cylinder" of new "open-ended . . . space."[51]

As we have seen, the activists in early SDS held that dogmatic, ideological descriptions of the world could never capture the complexity and shifting nature of "reality." What was original about their New Left was its fluid, nonideological posture toward a world whose possibilities they saw as open-ended and plural. Even their notion of participatory democracy was not a political doctrine but, according to Al Haber, the first president of SDS, "a charge to action. It was how to be. To be out there doing."[52]

Tom Hayden claimed the doctrinal assumptions of the Old Left were deterministic. SDS shunned the traditional Marxist left because its dogma placed absurdly precise limits on how the future might unfold. They shied away from contemporary liberalism because its shibboleths failed to account adequately for the moral and political possibilities of the present. Nothing was determined, said Hayden. Only the role of "becoming an actor in history instead of just a passive object" provided definitive "evidence" about what was possible and how to respond to it.[53] The activists in early SDS felt comfortable with the idea that life was full of surprises. Its possibilities would be revealed through direct action upon it, and the consequences of their actions could neither be predicted nor assumed. They sought to usher in a "new sense of mobility" in American society, wrote Potter in 1963, "a self-conscious sense of the ability of the people to move in society, up and down on the social structure, in and out of roles, in and out of class conditions."[54]

Thinking of freedom as exploration and movement was particularly pronounced within the psychedelic drug culture. Those who took "trips" on LSD, peyote or "magic" mushrooms incarnated the idea of "movement." Consciousness-expanding drugs enhanced the capacity of trippers to explore and map their interior spaces, much like the scouts, frontiersmen and trappers of an earlier era helped open the American West to exploration and eventual settlement.

The analogy is appropriate. Advocates of psychedelic drugs frequently employed metaphors and imagery related to movement through space, especially the country's westward expansion, to describe the significance of the trip. The novelist Ken Kesey orchestrated the improvisational "acid tests" that popularized the use of LSD in 1965. Kesey used a mathematical term that measures spatial relationships to describe the way hallucinogenic drugs reveal "internal" and "external" experiences otherwise unavailable to consciousness. The "geometrics of humanity," observed Kesey, were hidden within "worlds that have always existed" but whose frontiers could not be breached without the aid of psychedelics.[55] Jerry Garcia, whose band in its pre-Grateful Dead incarnation performed at Kesey's acid tests, called them "our first exposure to formlessness." The improvisational psychedelic experience was an act of breaking "down the old order and old forms," where "you suddenly find yourself in a new space with new form and new order."[56]

Timothy Leary was the most famous advocate of LSD in the late sixties. Though much older than other cultural radicals, he was the product of a professional middle-class family from whose values he had rebelled in the forties. Leary consistently described the effects of LSD in ways that evoked the epochal western trek of American pioneers. Sounding like a modern version of Horace Greeley, who urged the young to "go west" in the nineteenth century, Leary exhorted them to seek their destiny by leaving the confining, settled, dreary spaces of middle-class America. LSD would enable them to get closer "to reality, to direct experience. Go out where things are really happening. Go out to the frontier."[57]

According to Leary, LSD opened up a "limitless" internal world of "space-time dimensions." The drug was a "road map" that detailed "interior territories." But the trip within had social consequences. Psychedelic drugs revealed a hidden America, a free space shrouded from those who were obsessed with finding security, who needed to "march in step . . . to go to offices . . . to sign up on the installment plan . . . to climb aboard the treadmill." The other America, the one explored during the trip, was an endlessly shifting, kinetic theater of "Movement. Change. Flashing Images. Simultaneity. Multiple Choice." In effect, the drug recreated the hoary American quest to discover what lay beyond the next range of mountains, forests or plains. Leary asked those whom he referred to as "LSD frontiersmen" to pioneer a "new page in the story" of human freedom and evolution. It would be, he said, a "highly American" thing to do. "The expansion process in human affairs is defined in terms of the word 'freedom'. . . . Freedom to move in space. Freedom to explore. Freedom to get high. Freedom to let go. . . . The uncharted realm lies behind your own forehead. Internal geography."[58]

Obviously, experimentation with psychedelics during the sixties had other, less benign consequences. Many used them recklessly. Some used drugs as a means of exploiting the naive. Still others sold them for profit. But the idea of the hallucinogenic trip, as it was used by Kesey, Leary, the philosopher Alan Watts and thousands of their younger acolytes, was another matter. It connected the expressive, individualistic side of middle-class values to important, formative orientations in American culture. The solipsistic illusions that often occurred while under the influence—"I am the nuclear image of eternity," "my body is the universe," "with a flick of my wrist a new cosmos begins," said various young trippers—were extreme incarnations of American individualism.[59] The interior trip could be a voyage toward self-sufficiency, the psychedelic equivalent of self-reliance.

Leary made this clear (more or less) in one version of his famous slogan, "Turn On, Tune In, and Drop Out." To drop out, he observed, meant choosing "movement" and "self-reliance" over the stagnation and security offered by American affluence. The internal explorations ignited by LSD helped individuals to choose "expansion" over "stability." The aware tripper was bent on achieving "self-reliance, a discovery of one's singularity, a commitment to mobility, choice, and change" over the dominant inclination of most Americans, which, Leary said, was to "settle for less." In other words, the thoughtful tripper could pull himself up by his own bootstraps, become self-made, be born again. "I was taking acid and I began to recognize a new self," said a hippie who lived in a rural commune:

> I recognized that if I centered myself into being, I could be Einstein or anything I wanted. . . . I broke myself down to one light—to my soul. And it was from that point I chose to put myself back together again piece by piece. And each piece that I put back together would be a piece that I liked and wanted. . . . LSD just made it happen that much quicker. I was pushing for a breakdown because I was looking for a whole new identity.[60]

The aspirations of cultural and political radicals, then, were frequently framed by images related to movement through open spaces, whether external or internal. They reflected desires to achieve autonomy, moral rectitude or self-reliance through self-exploration and direct action. And if metaphors or images related to movement spoke to some of the aspirations of young radicals, the opposite tendency, a disposition toward "settlement," embodied much of what disturbed them about their society. Settlement conjured the attitudes and lifestyle that middle-class child rearing did not prepare them for: stability, predictability and the uncritical acceptance of things as they were. In other words, for the cult of security. As Leary said, the choice was between a "commitment to mobility" and Wild West adventure, or a life of stability and "settling for less."[61]

"Movement" and "settlement" as metaphors for experiencing America can help to place the sensibilities of youthful discontent in the sixties—*in their broadest expressions*—into the *general sweep* of American history. These figurative terms do not contradict the fact that real social, political and moral issues inspired rebellion in the sixties. They can, however, shed light on how predispositions toward rebellion, abetted by contradictions in their middle-class upbringing, were linked to underlying tensions and ambiguities in American history and culture.

Movement and settlement, whether conceived as modes of behavior or metaphors for elemental tensions within American culture, are among the most basic points and counterpoints of American history. By themselves, they do not, of course, define the culture. Nor do they encompass all of the swirling ambiguities or twisted ironies of the American experience. But they come as close to doing so as any other set of opposing tendencies.[62]

Immigration and the endless migrations of people back and forth across the continent—movement toward and through America—are perhaps the most elemental forces of the country's history. On the plane of physical reality, the prospect of roaming over and settling upon the continent's open spaces of pristine and relatively inexpensive land drew millions to these shores prior to the twentieth century. But in addition to such concrete expressions of movement, the entrepreneurial drive of Americans has been imagined in phrases and images associated with mobility. Americans go up or down the social ladder; they move beyond their inherited social status or sink beneath it. Beyond economic issues, movement is associated with daring explorers who penetrated the "uncivilized" interior spaces of the country, who took to the road in search of adventure or a new start in life. Finally, movement conjures the sheer size of the country. It symbolizes its capacity to absorb those who for whatever reasons needed to move beyond their current conditions in life. Or their pasts.

By contrast, settlement symbolizes more than the physical process of rooting oneself in an American destination. It represents the needs for community and intimacy in a nation whose ethnic, regional and religious diversity can make strangers of fellow citizens. Or it can symbolize social stability in a country seething with economic uncertainty. As a metaphor, settlement might be associated with continuity and tradition, family and community cohesion, moderation and order. Or even of relatively limited economic ambition, of settling for just enough to get by.

"Movement" in American History

In *Democracy in America,* the book about the country he visited for nine months between 1831 and 1832, Alexis de Tocqueville called attention to a "double movement" of people that "never halts" as a defining factor in the evolution of American "character." First, Europeans arrived on the eastern seaboard of the continent. Then some of them, along with thousands of the native born, moved westward through the continent's succession of frontiers.

> [I]t starts from the depths of Europe, continues across the great ocean, and then goes on through the solitudes of the New World. Millions of men and women are all marching together toward the same point on the horizon; their languages, religions, and mores are different, but they have one common aim. They have been told that fortune is to be found somewhere toward the west, and they hasten to seek it.[63]

Toward the end of the nineteenth century, the historian Frederick Jackson Turner suggested that the country's economic and political development, along with the "character" of its people, were products of its incessant western migrations.[64] Turner's thesis was and remains controversial. There is no doubt, however, that from the beginning the idea of movement across the American landscape captured the flux and dynamism of the country's democratic ferment. It defined as well the bustling ambitions of its enterprising people. A spacious landscape and social progress were intertwined. "My hope" for the country's economic prospects, wrote Thomas Jefferson in 1817, "is built much on the enlargement of the resources of life going hand in hand with the enlargement of territory."[65]

Also from the beginning, however, it was difficult to separate movement inspired by economic gain, by far the most important motivation, from movement as a search for adventure, new experiences or escape from confining circumstances. It was difficult to separate the economic from the experiential. Movement meant a new start in life, which usually but not inevitably involved economic opportunity.

Jefferson's agrarianism is a case in point. His most well known vision of the new nation's future revolved around the creation of a relatively static American landscape. Self-sufficient, frugal, independent farmers who settled permanently on land they owned would be the backbone of a stable democratic commonwealth. Yet many pioneers in the eighteenth and early nineteenth centuries settled farmsteads only to move again and again. They did so even when they had prospered in their original communities.[66] Some of them had an implacable urge to move. In 1772 a British official reflected on this restlessness. In an observation echoed by others before and since, he said Americans possessed an incorrigible "avidity and restlessness. . . . They acquire no attachment to Place; but wandering about seems engrafted in their Nature; and it is weakness incident to it that they should forever imagine the Lands further off, are still better than those upon which they are already settled."[67]

Their tendency to move may have been caused by what Tocqueville called a passion for risk. Americans were attracted, he said, to "all undertakings in which chance plays a part."[68] They moved time and again, usually seeking a bigger economic payoff, but also because of what historian Marvin Meyers called their desire for adventure "steered only by a bold imagination."[69] And, as the writer Timothy Flint observed in the 1820s, the constant shifting of populations in and out of midwestern communities made it difficult to achieve social cohesion. "Everything shifts under your eyes," he declared. "The present occupants sell, pack, depart. Strangers replace them. Before they have gained the confidence of their neighbors, they hear of a better place, pack up, and follow their precursors." This behavior, he concluded, "adds to the instability of connexions."[70]

Although movement was normally focused on a quest for material gain, it also reflected the desire of individuals to engage chance and experience change beyond the realm of economics. One might even become independent of "connexions," as Flint put it. Eighteenth- and nineteenth-century narratives of the exploits of pioneers and explorers like Daniel Boone emphasized their roles in helping make an untamed West a place of civility and permanent settlement. But some narratives also celebrated Boone's plunge into the western wilderness as sagas of untrammelled personal freedom.[71] Movement by solitary explorers into the country's sparsely settled interior spaces symbolized freedom, however temporary, from the constraints and obligations of family and society. Movement was freedom. Why, asked Henry David Thoreau, in his aptly titled essay "Walking," should a man be bound to a law, or any other obligation for that matter. He could simply "walk" away from it. Why not "live free" like "a child of the mist?"[72]

In other words, freedom of movement suggested independence from organized society. It implied escaping what George Gatlin, the nineteenth-century Philadelphia artist famous for his portraits of Plains Indians, called "the killing restraints of society."[73] Movement could symbolize the quest for personal independence, the desire (whether acted upon or merely imagined) to carve zones of separation from others. Gordon S. Wood, the distinguished historian of the American Revolution, summarized the feelings of a New Yorker in 1800 who was disturbed by the seemingly endless flux created by his countrymen. He called it "the problem" of Americans. Everybody in the country wanted independence: "first independence from Great Britain, then independence of the states from each other, then independence of the people from government, and 'lastly, [that] the members of society be equally independent of each other.'"[74]

Movement could signify still another type of independence: from the limitations of time and history. The move to the New World and incessant migrations across the continent allowed Americans (more than just symbolically) to imagine that in some ways they had severed their ties to the past. Theirs was a "new" world of possibility and experience. By the mid eighteenth century, if not before, traditional monarchical relations slackened, as did the feudal ideals of mutual dependency and obligation they entailed, as people dispersed through American space. "[E]verywhere in the colonies," according to Wood

> the sudden increase and movement of people in the middle decades of the eighteenth century shattered traditional monarchical relationships that were often not very strong to begin with [in the colonies]. People were freed from customary connections and made independent in new, unexpected ways. This demographic explosion, this gigantic movement of people, was the most basic and most liberating force working on American society.[75]

Movement through the continent created emancipation not just from European notions of social cohesion, but potentially from tradition and history as well.

"We have outgrown tradition," Orestes Brownson said in 1836 about his peripatetic, enterprising, dynamic fellow countrymen.[76] The freedom to move might sever ties between children and parents. Equally important, it could shatter the symbolic connection between the idea of family and its relationship to tradition and personal continuity. In either case, movement emphasized the present rather than the past. "Is the parent better than the child into whom he has cast his ripened being?" asked Ralph Waldo Emerson. "Whence then this worship of the past?"[77] Movement meant perpetual youth, a new start for every generation. As Thoreau wrote in *Walden,* "Old deeds for old people, and new deeds for new."[78]

In innumerable ways movement, as an idea, fantasy or literal fact, created a wall of space between individuals and their pasts. In 1847 Francis Parkman published his famous history of the westward migration, *The Oregon Trail.* Confronted by the unanticipated perils of the journey, Parkman's pioneers were sometimes forced to discard furniture and other belongings representing links to their pasts. In a poignant passage, Parkman described how relics symbolizing family history were discarded along an endless succession of American roads, destinations, and dreams. He found

> shattered wrecks of ancient claw-footed tables, well waxed and rubbed, or massive bureaus of carved oak. These, some of them no doubt the relics of ancestral property in the colonial time, must have encountered strange vicissitudes. Brought, perhaps, originally from England, then, with the declining fortunes of their owners, borne across the Alleghenies to the wilderness of Ohio or Kentucky; then to Illinois or Missouri; and now at last fondly stowed away in the family wagon for the interminable journey to Oregon. But the stern privations of the way are little anticipated. The cherished relic is soon flung out to scorch and crack upon the hot prairie.[79]

It was ironic that Thomas Jefferson also pursued the idea of movement to an extreme. His vision of a more or less static, agrarian society idealized "settlement" and social stability more powerfully than did perhaps anyone else's in the eighteenth century. Yet in a 1789 letter to James Madison, Jefferson argued that it was a violation of "natural rights" for one generation to bequeath a legacy of public debt to the next one. "I set out on this ground which I suppose to be self-evident," he declared, "'That the earth belongs in usufruct to the living,' that the Dead have neither powers nor rights over it." But his aversion to one generation binding the next went beyond accruing public debt. Neither the laws, customs nor governing constitutions composed by one generation were binding upon subsequent ones. "[B]y the law of nature, one generation is to another as one independent nation to another."[80]

Thirty-five years later, Jefferson reiterated his belief that the earth belonged to the living. One generation should not be bound by the decisions or the values of preceding ones. But this time he added a phrase that suggested contempt for the past and disdain for tradition, rather than simply the right to be free of them. The "dead," he said, "are not even things."[81]

Movement meant freedom from the dead hand of the past, for the individual and society. Like Thoreau's sojourn at Walden Pond or Mark Twain's description of Huck Finn's and Jim's adventures on the raft, the nonconformist or the oppressed could flee into American space. The country was brimming with Waldens and rivers of escape, in its myths as well as in the actual West. There were plenty of places where a free spirit could escape from organized society, which Thoreau dismissed as a league "for mutual defense." It was the "prudent" and the "timid of whatever age or sex" who craved security and were incessantly pursued by nightmares of disorder.[82] They spent most of their waking hours dreading life's uncertainties and possibilities. Or, at the other extreme, the enterprising American might move up the economic ladder and transcend the economic status into which he was born. Either way movement meant self-invention, the democratic prospect of starting from scratch and creating a new self.

"Settlement" in American History

By the early nineteenth century Americans enjoyed a freedom from government restraint, and to a less extent from intrusions by fellow citizens into their private lives, that was unique among Western nations. Unbridled self-interest in economic matters was gradually evolving into a hallmark of daily life. And though few were inclined to join Thoreau and Emerson in celebrating expressive, non-economic forms of individualism, they were nonetheless free to do so. But this version of individualism, divorced from economic enterprise and glorifying footloose personal freedom, repelled far more Americans than it enticed. Freedom to move through the open spaces of the continent and in and out of community bonds threatened social cohesion and personal stability. Pushed to its logical extreme, the urge to move and the radical individualism associated with it might compromise personal stability and social order.

If, as Jefferson said, the dead (and by implication the past, tradition and continuity) were "not even things," where could the country's principles of cohesion be located? What unified the sprawling, dynamic, ethnically diverse nation? Where were the common threads, the shared values? The extraordinary democratic flux and uncertainty of American life promised unlimited opportunity. But it also harbored the potential, perhaps unprecedented in the history of civilized societies, of making daily life routinely unstable and chaotic. According to historian William R. Taylor, Americans in the first half of the nineteenth century were brimming with optimism about the spread of democracy and economic progress. The New World worked. But they were equally anxious about the threat to order and cohesion posed by their commitment to individual freedom.

> If men were naturally self-centered and rapacious, bent on pursuing their own private ends . . . then what was there in the classless and open society of America to prevent its becoming a social jungle the equal of which the civilized world had never seen? What was to preserve the sanctity of home and family, upon which it was felt depended the stability of society, from the forces which were daily tearing it apart? What, finally, was to provide the nation at large with a coherent set of common aims which could prevent its breaking up into a number of armed bands and hostile factions each bent upon satisfying its wants at the expense of society as a whole?[83]

These anxieties persisted, even though the actual process of mobility was far less chaotic than it appeared. For the most part, groups, not "rugged individualists," led the way west during the eighteenth and nineteenth centuries. "Movement," for the vast majority of pioneers, did not represent a rejection of community, family or social order. Often it was a way of preserving them in the face of economic instability in their original settlements.

In addition, as early as the eighteenth century Americans rationalized their thrusts into the continent's primitive interior as a temporary but necessary step in the process of bringing civilization and Christianity to the wilderness and its "savage" inhabitants, whether white or red. In his *Letters from an American Farmer,* the French immigrant Hector St. John de Crevecoeur observed that the people who pioneered movement along "our extended line of frontiers" in the eighteenth century were usually the dregs of the settled communities from which they originated. Failures to begin with, they wandered into unsettled territories and lived like "carnivorous animals of a superior rank." They were primitives in a pristine American wilderness. But they served the purpose of opening up unsettled areas, and within a decade or so were followed by more "respectable" people, mostly farmers. They brought law, order and civility to the "barbarous rudiments" of the wilderness.[84] In other words, movement led to settlement. Movement was a brief, chaotic, but essential moment in the inevitable process of civilizing a "barbarous" continent.

Nevertheless, the specters of chaos, disorder and anarchy that movement symbolized were not easily exorcised. Although movement was the essential ingredient in the very freedom Americans celebrated as their unique heritage, most of them nevertheless recoiled from it. The freedom to move away from settled, orderly communities was part of what Howard Mumford Jones called the "anti-image" of the new world held by some Europeans in the sixteenth and seventeenth centuries. It provoked fears that Euro-Americans would shed their patina of civility by emulating the supposedly savage and rootless Indians. Stripped of their sense of order, decency and Christian rectitude, they might be enveloped in the moral vacuum of American space. They could be devoured, like Jonah in the whale, within the "incredible, the immeasurable, the unpredictable, and the horrifying" vastness of an amoral wilderness.[85]

Consequently, in addition to their dedication to what they call "law *and* order," Americans created idealized images of certain institutions and social relationships to counteract the fragmentation associated with freedom of movement. They developed ideals of continuity and stability—of settlement—to restrain non-economic expressions of individualism and movement. Most Americans never seriously questioned the moral or social legitimacy of a free enterprise economy, though at times they were alarmed by its excesses. But in order to live with the anxieties provoked by a ruthlessly competitive, largely unregulated and brutally unforgiving free-market economy, they needed to limit the threats to stability posed by expressive, or "cultural," forms of individualism. They did so by glorifying ideals to which most people would readily adhere, regardless of their ethnic or religious heritage.[86]

Thus family life was idealized. From the early nineteenth century family life was anchored by the ideal of feminine domesticity, and the nurture, cohesion, continuity and emotional bonding it symbolized. The idealization of maternal love and family "togetherness" helped compensate for the paucity of shared values among Americans of different social classes, religions, regions and ethnic groups. The romanticized version of the family, along with the "cult of true womanhood" it rested upon, created a mythological reservoir of tradition and continuity, of roots and stability, in a mobile, dispersed society.[87]

Life in the small town was also mythologized. Often this was because of, rather than despite, the social conformity associated with it. Since a knowing whisper could destroy an individual's reputation, idiosyncratic behavior might be restrained, though not entirely eliminated. Small-town life could be inhibiting and intrusive. But it also offered a sense of place, mutuality and community within a dynamic, often anonymous wider society.[88] A related ideal was that of the "simple life." This assumed various forms. It was reflected in the numerous utopian movements that have marked American history, from the eighteenth-century Shakers to twentieth-century hippie communes. Or the simple life might take the form of "settling" for a modest but sufficient slice of the economic pie, like Jefferson's yeoman farmer. Seeking security through a modest lifestyle was an antidote to the anxiety-provoking and potentially unsuccessful ambitions to endlessly earn, ceaselessly achieve or boundlessly experience more and more.[89]

"MOVEMENT" AND "SETTLEMENT" IN THE SIXTIES

"Movement" and "settlement" represent certain tensions and conflicts in American history. They are metaphors, not "causes." As such, they neither account for nor explain that history. Nor, of course, did they cause the rebellions and upheavals that rocked the sixties. The idea of settlement can, however, be used as a figurative and broadly historical representation of the cult of security that developed in the aftermath of World War II. And the notion of movement distills the varieties of personal freedom available in American culture. It ties the expressive individualism nurtured by middle-class child rearing in the forties and fifties, and its flowering in the early sixties as alienation and rebellion, to wider issues in American history.

For instance, underlying themes of movement and settlement were evident in external symbols of rebellion during the sixties, and in the negative responses they inspired in most Americans. Since radicals spiced their language with references reminiscent of the wilderness, the frontier and the West, it is not surprising that many of them adopted fashions and hairstyles that recalled that far away time, along with the individual freedom associated with it. Both the styles and the freedom were frequently modelled on stereotyped, ahistorical images of the Old West portrayed in television and film sagas about Indians and cowboys.

Mythical or otherwise, there was a primitive quality to the long, often slovenly hair, beards and mustaches worn by men in the counterculture (and adopted by millions of young men who were not hippies as the sixties progressed). Some of the clothes worn by hippies and weekend hippies also had a western or wilderness flavor about them. Not all of the clothing worn by the hip and the young of the sixties fit this description. They might don long Victorian-era dresses or microminiskirts; purple bell-bottoms with flowing hems or embroidered, multicolored robes; and military jackets emblazoned with peace symbols or tie-dyed shirts. Hip garb was a bizarrely eclectic enterprise.

But in the fashions and hairstyles adopted by many hip young men and women there was more than a hint of the Old West or of the unexplored wilderness inhabited by Indians and trappers. The young wore buckskin shirts and jeans; boots and beads; cowboy hats planted with feathers, and headbands. And there were shaggy beards and drooping mustaches. Most of all, perhaps, there was long, often ungovernable hair, flowing south toward the hips or twisted skyward in piles of natural curls.

The reaction to long hair on males is especially intriguing. In the seventeenth and eighteenth centuries the sight of long hair on Native American males instilled discomfort and loathing in Euro-Americans. English colonists in particular associated long, disheveled hair on Indian males with overweening pride and intractable individualism. The English saw long, unruly tresses on Indians as signs of their stubborn independence and sexual promiscuity. They linked it to the free and supposedly rootless movement of Native Americans through the forests of the Northeast. The English were equally outraged by white trappers and frontiersmen who adopted the long hair, buckskin clothing and other elements of Native American culture. More than any other artifact of Indian culture, however, long hair on males symbolized primitive, unrestrained individualism. Fear of long hair was likely a projection of English fears that the plunge into the amoral American wilderness might strip the "civilized" European of self-control.[90]

There was a logical historical connection between the fashions and hairstyles that recalled a less settled and more spacious society—psychologically and physically—and the determined individualism of the young in the sixties. By adopting these external signs of disaffection, the young unwittingly embraced historical artifacts associated with autonomy, adventure and independence. Jerry Rubin observed that "our long hair hurts/offends them more than anything else we can say or do." As usual Rubin overstated the case, but he had a point. Long hair, he noted, symbolized the young's rejection of a "White Bread" America and "Cleanliness-as-Godliness."[91] In other words, it substituted the archaic styles of long hair, scraggly beards and buckskin shirts for the protocols of personal neatness associated with contemporary middle-class sobriety and professional status. Long hair suggested primitivism and ungovernability. It symbolized their refusal to embrace the rationality, moderation, security and orderliness that modern society expected from the best and the brightest of its young. The message of the "cultural revolution," said Abbie Hoffman, is "fantasy is freedom. Anybody can do anything." Genuine freedom and personal autonomy implied the right to "let go," "lose control," and do "what pops into my mind."[92]

Hoffman connected these attitudes with wearing long hair. In 1969 the federal government indicted Hoffman, Rubin, Tom Hayden and five others on trumped-up charges of "conspiracy to riot" in Chicago during the 1968 Democratic National Convention. When he heard of the indictment, Hoffman said he wanted to be tried not just for his radical beliefs but, among other reasons, "because I have long hair."[93] To some degree he was. After the conspiracy trial, in which they were found guilty, one juror remarked that the verdict was justified because of the defendants' "appearance, their language and their life style." Another juror said the verdict was sound because they needed "their hair cut."[94]

He got his wish. After their sentencing, Hoffman, Rubin and Hayden were sent to the Cook County jail, where their long tresses were immediately cut. The county sheriff, the brother of President Richard Nixon's personal secretary, Rosemary Woods, held a press conference at which he "triumphantly displayed" the radicals' shorn locks.[95]

Reactions to the way hippies looked were often emotional, sometimes violent and often tied to the cult of security and "settlement." This was evident in the attitudes of working people toward hippies and the rebellious young. In a distant echo of Jefferson's self-sufficient yeoman farmer, working-class Americans in the sixties frequently referred to themselves as "plain," "average," "ordinary" people who simply wished to "get by" economically.[96] Rather than trying to set the world on fire, their ambitions were usually limited to securing a safe, settled niche in the economy. They valued America because it provided people like themselves—factory and construction workers, firemen and policemen—with a comfortable if modest living. At least since the end of the World War II.

"I'm happy," said the wife of a welder, "I don't want a lot." Her husband agreed. "It's a rat race, it is." And the "more you make, the more you spend, the more you have to make."[97] They were willing to settle for a modest lifestyle rather than risk failure or experience emotional stress by entering the "rat race." In a remark that was as characteristic of "middle-American" attitudes as those of this couple, the owner of a marginally profitable gas station said he hoped his children would obtain "a good, safe job—so long as no one's on their backs all day long."[98]

The attitudes of the working class toward hippies and anti–Vietnam War protesters were grounded in this view of themselves and their lot in life. Most were morally offended by the brazen hedonism of the counterculture. And they viewed antiwar activists as unpatriotic. A good deal of their anger was rooted in social class antagonisms. Middle Americans routinely used words like "rich" or "spoiled" to describe college radicals. They assumed all activists were the children of "influential" and "liberal" parents.[99] The parents of protesters, according to a policeman, passed to their children a legacy of grasping, aggressive, ill-mannered egoism. While policemen came from "plain, ordinary families," hippies and protesters had parents who "make all kinds of money by climbing over other people until they get to the top."[100] In other words, people who moved up the social ladder by any means necessary, no matter the cost to those less powerful or influential than themselves.

Accordingly, middle Americans focused on long hair and hippie garb as symbols of moral breakdown and potential social disorder, of "movement" unbound. Social class resentments merged with disgust for youth culture fashions. "Maybe you envy these kids because they are smarter than you were, or because they have more opportunities," declared a clerk. "But what nauseates the average guy is the long hair and those goofy costumes."[101] The sight of hippie outfits and long hair induced images of moral disarray. A working-class resident of Kent, Ohio, said the "thing I can't stand [about protesters] is the way they dress." He immediately followed this observation by noting his "disgust" at the "way the [college] girls sleep around."[102] Primitive costumes and sexual promiscuity flowed from the same stream of licentiousness. Long, unruly hair generated much the same reaction in the sixties as it did in English colonists in the seventeenth century. Neatness, morality, sobriety, hard work, order, routine, predictability—all were threatened by the specter of long hair. "We have got to clean up this nation," said an irate woman in 1970. "And we'll start with the long hairs," whom she described as "lazy," undisciplined, "dirty," unwilling to work and always "doing nothing."[103]

Some liberal intellectuals were equally appalled by the appearance and behavior of young people. The intellectuals were as middle class as most hippies and New Left activists. For the most part, their ire was focused on the expressive individualism of the youth culture. The liberal intellectuals were committed to what they called "moderation" and "reason" in their pursuit of social reform. Change was fine, as long as it was "planned" and "orderly." In other words, they championed the ideas of rationality and expertise as advanced by the professional middle class.

A good deal of their criticisms of young radicals were couched in the metaphor of movement. Thus the writer Diana Trilling said New Leftists were wrong to "move" toward "direct action." They willfully ignored the "limitations imposed upon the individual by emotional and social reality."[104] The diplomat George F. Kennan decried the "primitive chaos" created by the counterculture's refusals to accept "an obligation to cultivate order, not chaos; cleanliness, not filth, self-abnegation, not self-indulgence, health, not demoralization."[105] And Norman Podhoretz used the term "expansionism" to describe the tendency of young rebels to push beyond "moderate" means for achieving orderly change.[106]

The sociologist Daniel Bell got even closer to the real issue, though not exactly the truth. He defined sixties radicalism as a "post-modern" expression of "modernist" impulses. Those impulses were directly related to what he termed "movement." In Bell's view, "modern man" was buffeted by the experience of "temporal-spatial dislocation." Advanced technology and modern means of transportation shattered traditional notions of "continuity" and community. They created a sense of ceaseless movement upon an incessantly "changing landscape." In short, modern life was "a blur of motion." The capacity to move rapidly through space and change "scenes" with ease fed the "modernist" need for self-realization and for "exploring" the new, in art and personal experience. For Bell, hippies and New Left activists, with their raucous music, plunge into sexual "perversity" and utopian political ideals, embodied this quest for "self-infinitization." Young radicals reflected "the modern hubris," which Bell defined as "the refusal to accept limits, the insistence on continually reaching out."[107]

Sixties radicalism was not a "post-modern" expression (whatever that means) of "reaching out," although, as Bell and other intellectuals suggested, it did refuse "to accept limits." Cultural and political radicals transcended the limitations of their society by "reaching" backward toward a less confining past. It was not premeditated. It was all inadvertent. And it happened within a technological, social and political world markedly different from that of the past. Yet their language, appearance, behavior and values frequently reprised pre-twentieth-century images of American democracy, individualism, freedom and even entrepreneurial aggressiveness. It was old wine poured into new bottles.

But it wasn't the same wine in every bottle. The major expressions of rebellion among the young in the sixties revolved around their desires to be autonomous and to experience lives of challenge, risk and adventure. That is, of movement. But these aspirations were poured into distinct forms of rebellion, which, in turn, flowed from different historical sources.

PART II

The Sixties in American History I: The Counterculture and Rock-and-Roll

The young man, on entering life, finds the way to lucrative employments blocked with abuses. The ways of trade are grown selfish to the borders of theft. . . . Has he genius and virtue? [T]he less does he find them fit for him to grow in, and if he would thrive in them, he must sacrifice all the brilliant dreams of boyhood and youth as dreams; he must forget the prayers of his childhood and must take on the harness of routine and obsequiousness. If not so minded, nothing is left him but to begin the world anew.

Ralph Waldo Emerson, "Man the Reformer," 1841

FIVE

"It's Free because It's Yours": The Diggers and the San Francisco Scene, 1964–1968

Our first act of freedom, if we are free, ought in all inward propriety, to be to affirm that we are free.

William James, *Essays In Pragmatism,* 1907

Do your own thing. Be what you are. If you don't know what you are, find out. Fuck leaders.

The Diggers, 1966

The individual in America has usually taken his start outside society.

R. W. B. Lewis, *The American Adam,* 1955

The key to the puzzle [of changing America] lies in theater.

Abbie Hoffman, 1968

THE DIGGERS TAKE THE STAGE

It started in the waning days of October 1966. Leaflets containing provocative, often bizarre messages were placed on building walls and storefronts in San Francisco's Haight-Ashbury neighborhood. They were posted by a group calling themselves "The Diggers." No one in the city had heard of them. Most of the broadsides were distributed in Haight-Ashbury, the birthplace of the hippie counterculture. But hundreds of the mimeographed postings were handed to pedestrians throughout the city, including the downtown financial district. Some leaflets announced events, like one that offered free food to all comers every afternoon at Golden Gate Park's Panhandle, an elegant strip of lawn and trees on Ashbury Street. (See Leaflet at right.)

Digger broadsides targeted the mind as well as the stomach. Most of them had an anarchistic edge. "There must not be a Plan. We have always been defeated by our Plan," said one. Another message warned: "Watch out for cats who want to play The System's games, 'cause you can't beat The System at its own games." Still another proclaimed: "Autonomy is Power! I mean you've got to make up your own mind." One leaflet, a distant echo of Thomas Jefferson's observation that the dead were "not even things," exhorted the young to "wipe out the old—simply wipe it out." A message with the title "Money Is An Unnecessary Evil" offered amnesty to those who had it. "As part of the city's campaign to stem the causes of violence the San Francisco Diggers announce a 30 day period beginning now during which all responsible citizens are asked to turn in their money. No questions will be asked."[1]

Some Digger bulletins were subtle and insightful, others crude and scatological. They blended the machismo that pervaded the counterculture with the intelligence, street savvy and wicked humor of their authors. Hundreds of pedestrians throughout the city were handed this epistle about the threat long hair on young males posed to "straight" Americans:

> Are the mothers of America avatars of Delilah? Those preferring clippers to tresses have reacted with the sort of righteous indignation one could expect if their own balls had been threatened. The shorn men are jealous because they think you're getting laid more. They're right, but they must also realize it's your whole way of being and not just the hair or else they'd be home nights pulling at their hair instead of their dicks. Yeah, it's jealousy baby. Don't get bugged—just be beautiful and long may it wave![2]

In response to a suggestion by Haight-Ashbury merchants that neighborhood residents invite policemen to dinner as a way of easing tensions

Free Food Good Hot Stew
Ripe Tomatoes Fresh Fruit

Bring A Bowl and Spoon to
The Panhandle at Ashbury Street

4 pm 4 pm 4 pm 4 pm

Free Food EVERYDAY Free Food
It's Free Because It's Yours!

the diggers.[3]

between hippies and city authorities, the Diggers peppered the district with this poem:

Take a cop to dinner.
Racketeers take cops to dinner with payoffs.
Pimps take cops to dinner with free tricks.
Dealers take cops to dinner with free highs.
Unions and Corporations take cops to dinner with post-retirement jobs.
Schools and Professional Clubs take cops to dinner with free tickets to athletic events and social affairs.
The Catholic Church takes cops to dinner by exempting them from religious duties.
The Justice Department takes cops to dinner with laws giving them the right to do almost anything.
The Defense Department takes cops to dinner by releasing them from military obligation.
Establishment newspapers take cops to dinner by propagating the image of the friendly, uncorrupt, neighborhood policeman.
Places of entertainment take cops to dinner with free booze and admission to shows.

Merchants take cops to dinner with discounts and gifts.
Neighborhood Committees and Social Organizations take cops to dinner with free discussions offering discriminating insights into hipsterism, black militancy and the drug culture.
Cops take cops to dinner by granting each other immunity to prosecution for misdemeanors and anything else they can get away with.
Cops take themselves to dinner by inciting riots.

And so, if you own anything or you don't, take a cop to dinner this week and feed his power to judge, persecute and brutalize the streets of your city.[4]

Throughout the fall of 1966 the Diggers engineered street "happenings" in Haight-Ashbury. Many were bizarre, even by the standards of that hippie haven. One of them led to the arrest of five Diggers, and the incident made the front page of the *San Francisco Chronicle.* Two Diggers brought a huge wooden frame, twelve feet square and painted in bright yellow, to the intersection of Haight and Ashbury Streets. They called it a "Frame of Reference." Dozens of yellow three-inch replicas of the "Frame" were handed to passersby; the small frames were hung on straps so they could be worn around the neck. People were urged by the Diggers to look through the small squares so they could experience the event through their own "frames of reference." Two giant puppets appeared. Each was about eight feet high and manipulated by two men. The puppets, along with the rest of the Diggers, invited scores of pedestrians to participate in a "play" called "Fool on the Street." The Diggers organized people in polygons and had them crisscross the streets in opposite directions. The purpose of the play was to block automobile traffic as a protest against the pollution created by American technology.

It worked. When the police arrived to untangle the knot of pedestrians and stalled cars, a cop inadvertently created a memorable moment in the history of the Haight-Ashbury. "We warn you," he addressed one of the puppets, "that if you don't remove yourselves from the area you'll be arrested for blocking a public thoroughfare." The puppet responded with a question: "Who is the public?" "I couldn't care less; I'll take you in," shot back the officer. "I declare myself public," said a Digger's voice from behind the puppet. "The streets are public—the streets are free."[5]

In addition to their street happenings, the Diggers opened a "free" store on Page Street called the Free Frame Of Reference. The store stocked clothing, furniture and other goods. All of the items were free. "Customers" could take whatever they wished, in any quantity they desired. Indeed, if a customer wished, he could empty the entire store. The only rule in the store was etched on a sign not far from a box containing cash and labeled "Free Money." It read, "No Stealing."[6]

Within weeks of their first mimeographed broadsides and street "plays," the Diggers became the most celebrated and influential voice within San Francisco's hip community, although few in the city knew their identities. Anonymity was the group's first principal. "Free means not copping credit," read one of their leaflets.[7] The Diggers believed love and commitment should be given without strings attached, including the hope for fame or fortune. Nor did they wish to become media celebrities, thereby risking what they called "co-optation" by the "establishment."[8] Their instant notoriety within San Francisco, which quickly spread to "hip" communities in the rest of the country, made people curious about who the Diggers were. In response to queries about their identities a Digger sent a letter to a local underground newspaper. "Regarding inquiries concerned with the identity and whereabouts of the Diggers, we are happy to report that the Diggers are not that." The letter was signed "George Metevsky."[9] (It was the misspelled name of George Metesky, the so-called Mad Bomber who terrorized New York City in the fifties, and was a sort of folk hero to those Diggers who came from the New York area.)

Most of the Diggers, in fact, were actors who worked for the San Francisco Mime Troupe. The Mime Troupe was an alternative theater company that presented plays for free in an abandoned church in the Mission District and in the city's parks (a hat was passed through the audience at the end of a show). The Mime Troupe had a varied repertoire, ranging from Shakespeare to Beckett, but specialized in the ribald, class-conscious medium of sixteenth-century commedia dell'arte. Perhaps those members of the Mime Troupe who at one point or another called themselves "Diggers" stumbled upon the name when performing in a play from the seventeenth or eighteenth centuries—the original Diggers were mid-seventeenth-century English agrarian radicals.[10]

Although the Diggers of San Francisco were short lived, lasting barely two years, their impact upon the style and substance of counterculture protest during the second half of the decade was significant. As a historian recently noted, the Diggers were the "high priests of the counterculture."[11] Their iconoclastic broadsides, free services, community events and guerrilla theater street happenings were emulated by cultural radicals later in the decade. As their caper of the Fool on the Street demonstrates, the Diggers believed that consciousness could be jarred and moral "frames of reference" altered by staging theatrical confrontations between symbols of freedom and authority. This had a seminal influence on the media-oriented style of protest created in the late sixties by Jerry Rubin and Abbie Hoffman. When Hoffman began his career of protest in New York City's East Village in the mid sixties he called himself a Digger. This chagrined the original Diggers, who saw Hoffman as little more than a media-obsessed publicity hound. And when Hoffman, Rubin and the satirist Paul Krassner created the far more famous Yippies in 1968 they used the Diggers as their model. More important, the Diggers distilled the chaotic urges of the counterculture during its early days in San Francisco. They brought a sort of intellectual cohesion to the embryonic hippie impulses to seek new identities, new experiences and new lives.[12]

But the significance of the Diggers goes beyond their impact on the counterculture, within or beyond the Haight-Ashbury. Nor does it rest on their criticisms of American society. Their views more or less mirrored those of other sixties rebels, even though the Diggers disparaged most forms of political and cultural radicalism. They called the New Left self-righteous and "puritanical," and dismissed Timothy Leary's psychedelic drug culture as naive and devoid of moral direction.[13]

The Diggers are important for understanding the counterculture because of the method they used to protest American limitations on American freedom: theater and acting. The Diggers used theatrical formats, especially the self-conscious acts of performance and improvisation, as metaphors for personal freedom and as practical means of enacting that freedom.

Diggers referred to their street plays as "life-acts." These included the free stores, the daily free food service (where the "customers" had to pass through the large "frame of reference" to get the food), and the various street happenings they organized. Digger life-acts were plays in which the most radical implications of American liberty were "performed."[14]

Digger radicalism was based on an intuition. They never made it explicit, but it pervaded their ideas and behavior. American freedom, particularly the right of the individual to alter and refashion his identity, was an improvisation, like the Digger style of theater. The self-reliant individualism at the heart of the American version of personal freedom was based on the unspoken assumption that the individual's identity was malleable. It could be improvised, altered at will. In theatrical terms, it was an "act." American individualism, indeed the very idea of being American, was an improvised act of self-creation. "Acting" American and making yourself up as you went along were essentially the same things. History and scripts were irrelevant to both. Creating an identity in America was a process through which the individual presented (that is, staged) an invented self (or role) to his public (the audience). And the play could be endlessly restaged.

From the Diggers point of view, the idea that the individual could be self-made, become the product-in-process of his autonomous right to be what he wished, implied a performance. And if he was a conscious life-actor, he became the independent director of his own play. He could change scripts, roles and identities as he saw fit.

This had radical implications. Whether expressed in secular or religious terms, the American idea that one could be "born again" or become self-made presumed the malleability and mutability of individual identity. This was implicit in one of the grand American myths: personal identity was a willed invention rather than a fixed condition determined by an individual's family or personal history. Indeed, the Diggers viewed American culture as a stage upon which neither the "props" nor the scripts were permanent. An American life could be a consciously performed series of improvised roles. The only permanent lines in the script of American culture were the rights of individuals to create themselves and the continent's expansive stage upon which that freedom was enacted. For the Diggers, history, whether personal or collective, implied old roles for old plays. If an American wished to be free of the past, he simply needed to "act" that way.

The Diggers represented the values and dynamics of cultural radicalism in their purest, most articulate and explicit forms. They provided a (more or less) coherent rationale for the tendencies of counterculture youth to explore unchartered regions of the mind and to experiment with new forms of social relationships. Along with the use of hallucinogenic drugs, this included the hippie traits of trying on new costumes or adopting new names as ways of experimenting with novel identities. It meant "acting out" in front of others—"doing your own thing," as they said in the sixties—through self-revealing, public displays of normally private desires and fantasies. The star of Digger theater was the individual's pristine freedom and autonomy, unleashed from social controls. The antagonist of their life-acts, frequently portrayed with brutally stark condescension, was the cult of security, and the staid, settled personal life it incarnated.

This chapter describes the Diggers' performance of American freedom and their role in defining the cultural radicalism that was forged in San Francisco during the mid sixties, before it spread to the rest of the country. It also shows how their performance was linked to, and in one dramatic instance inadvertently reenacted, pre-twentieth-century literary myths about the wilderness origins of American identity, freedom and "manhood."

The Diggers were an act that combined the antics of Marx Brothers and Dead End Kids films of the thirties and forties with the tactics of shock and surprise employed by New York's "Mad Bomber" in the fifties. Theirs was a performance by determined, articulate, radical actors whose purpose was to kick away the modern props of an undemocratic, bureaucratic, materialistic culture. They offered a primitive alternative, informed by mythic visions of pristine American freedom, to the sterile roles and the repetitive, uninspiring scripts of a settled, hierarchical twentieth-century society.

The Diggers designed many of the counterculture's props. But they did not build the stage. The hunger for enhanced personal freedom was percolating among young people in the San Francisco Bay Area before the Diggers took the stage in the fall of 1966. It began in the early sixties, with student political activism at Berkeley and experiments with hallucinogenic drugs by the novelist Ken Kesey and his band of proto-hippies called the Merry Pranksters. An outline of these events, and why San Francisco provided a congenial environment for their development, is the necessary setting for describing the history of the Diggers.

THE SETTING

The San Francisco Bay Area was not the only geographic setting in the United States where the counterculture could have originated. But from a historical perspective it was the most fitting. From its frenzied, chaotic and violent inception during the Gold Rush of the late 1840s, San Francisco (and the area surrounding its capacious bay) was a place where, as one historian put it, "the bottom fell out" of nineteenth-century assumptions about moral order and progress.[15]

In some ways, the history of San Francisco undermined an important assumption about the American advance to the West: that it fostered moral elevation as well as national greatness, economic opportunity and social progress. "Manifest Destiny," the idea that a transcontinental America was tantamount to a divine charter for the creation of a new empire, implicitly linked moral and economic progress. The transformation of untamed wilderness and uninhabitable desert into cultivated farms and vibrant, commercial cities represented not only the triumph of progress and order over an anarchic wilderness. It promised as well, in the words of Walt Whitman, "immense spiritual results."[16]

On the moral plane, this marriage between commerce, nationalism and Christian rectitude was compromised somewhat by the daring and determined sensuality exhibited by San Franciscans throughout the nineteenth century. From the beginning it was an open city, where behavior deemed deviant or scandalous by nineteenth-century standards was not only tolerated, but at times even admired. This was not unusual for frontier boom towns. But well past the city's frontier stage, San Franciscans openly professed their relish for the pleasures of the flesh. A number of its streets were named for notable madams who ran the city's numerous houses of prostitution. The city also possessed a determined predilection for feeding the senses. Its citizens were as famous for their insatiable desires for good restaurants and fine wines as they were for openly negotiating sexual companionship in saloons. San Franciscans boasted of their city's luxurious hotels and its ornately appointed theaters and opera houses.

Toleration toward others, and inclinations toward a life both sybaritic and sophisticated, characterized the city from the start.[17]

To some degree, these conditions were a legacy of San Francisco's almost overnight transformation from a sparsely inhabited town to a major city. Its population soared from 1,000 in 1848 to nearly 30,000 five years later.[18] And the city's ethnic diversity made sharp contrasts in behavior inevitable, and toleration of different cultures (with the notable exceptions of Asian immigrants and African Americans) an imperative of survival. Gold, adventure and the willingness to start life anew made San Francisco a magnet for immigrants from Chile, China, Italy, Ireland, Scotland, Spain, England, Australia, France, Canada and Russia. The city's architecture, a mosaic of cultural styles drawn from scores of cities around the globe, reflected the diverse national origins of its inhabitants.[19]

The thousands of native-born Americans thrown into this mix were as alien to the area as the numerous non-Americans. American nationals were in no position, therefore, to impose their values upon white ethnic groups from other countries or to overtly discriminate against them. For example, San Francisco did not replicate the discrimination aimed at Irish Catholics during the middle of the nineteenth-century in New York, Boston and Philadelphia. The simultaneous settlement of the Bay Area by native-born Americans and white foreign nationals compelled the former to be more tolerant than they otherwise might have been.[20]

Because San Francisco rested on the western edge of the continent, its isolation from the populous cities of the East and the farming communities of the Great Plains provided its inhabitants with the freedom to create their own version of America. In some ways, the early denizens of San Francisco turned American assumptions about propriety and decorum on their heads—almost as gleefully, publicly and scandalously as would their colorful heirs in the Haight-Ashbury one hundred years later.

> At the Parker House or the El Dorado women dealt the cards, a brass band or banjo music played, and gold nuggets were piled high on the tables. One could take a brandy-smash at the bar, then stroll the crowded streets rakish in hussar boots, corduroy pants, red flannel shirt, and sombrero. Costume was posturing and romantic.[21]

As the nineteenth century progressed, the city's combination of refined hedonism and toleration toward white newcomers and the morally deviant was institutionalized rather than eliminated. Its inhabitants managed to balance acceptance of the ongoing rowdiness, robust sensuality and raw individualism characteristic of San Francisco since its Gold Rush days with a sense of civic pride for the city's sophistication and the refined tastes and civility of its citizens.[22] To be sure, the majority of its citizens were temperate, church-going folk. They complained about the sensuous ways of a city that by the 1890s had justly earned its title as the Paris of North America. There was much to complain about. San Francisco possessed a saloon for every 96 inhabitants, along with an untold number of brothels and opium dens.[23] But challenges to these and other infractions of Victorian-era morality, a staple of moral reform movements in New York, Chicago and other cities at the time, were tempered in San Francisco. Its citizens were inclined to define themselves as a people liberated from the country's Puritan heritage.[24]

By the late nineteenth century this comparative tolerance, along with a heritage of living on the continent's western and, perhaps, moral edge, made San Francisco the country's first enclave of bohemia. Avant-garde painters, novelists, dancers, actors, sculptors and photographers from around the nation and the globe gravitated there. After the earthquake of 1906 many of them, including Isadora Duncan, Gertrude Stein, Jack London and Frank Norris, moved to Carmel, a hundred miles south of San Francisco, and commuted between the two sites.[25] As Richard Miller pointed out, San Francisco's unique heritage of toleration, "Wild West traditions" and European sophistication made it a port of entry into the United States for European bohemianism. San Francisco

> was the epitome of the Wild West refined by Paris. In San Francisco the American frontier tradition of the self-reliant free spirit combined with Europeans and college-bred Argonauts, with seamen and French sporting girls, with savage criminals from the slums of Sydney and New York, and learned how to read and write and build a city.[26]

San Francisco's bohemian ways continued into the twentieth century. In the thirties the city's North Beach section became its bohemian quarter. In 1955 Allen Ginsberg gave the first reading of his epic poem *Howl* at the Six Gallery in North Beach (his friend Jack Kerouac supplied the wine).[27] In the twentieth-century, as in the nineteenth, San Francisco possessed "a culture of civility" that, according to sociologists Howard Becker and Irving Louis Horowitz, was unique among large American cities. More than any other American city San Francisco was a "natural experiment in the consequences of tolerating deviance." Its inhabitants "know that they are supposed to be sophisticated and let that knowledge guide their public actions, whatever their private feelings."[28]

San Francisco's traditions of civility and tolerance would experience their most challenging tests in the 1960s—and came close to cracking under the stress.

In the early years of the decade a surge of political activism among students at the nearby campus of the University of California at Berkeley challenged the political repression of the fifties. And from 1965 on, the center of the city's cultural radicalism shifted from North Beach, with its enclave of Beat writers and bohemians, to the Haight-Ashbury district. The fixtures of the small Beat movement—poetry, jazz, alcohol and discreet use of marijuana and amphetamines—were replaced by tens of thousands of hippies who lived in communes, listened to and created new forms of rock music, openly displayed their sexuality and boldly experimented with hallucinogenic drugs.[29]

The Free Speech Movement

In the early sixties, two unanticipated and very different forms of rebellion erupted among young people in the Bay Area. Their impact would ripple through the rest of the country during the remainder of the decade and to a great extent define for many Americans what the sixties youth culture represented: incessant political unrest among college students and a Dionysian hippie dance of abandon choreographed by hallucinogenic drugs and rock music.

Prior to 1964, most Americans viewed college students as a privileged class poised for a future of security, affluence and influence. One of the first public signs that some students viewed themselves in a different light—in fact thought of themselves as oppressed victims of an impersonal, repressive, boring society—appeared across the bay from San Francisco. In the fall of 1964 the Free Speech Movement (FSM) erupted on the campus of the University of California at Berkeley.

The FSM was a response by Berkeley students to new restrictions on student political activity imposed that fall by the university's administration. The restrictions were pushed by conservative members of the university's Regents. As early as 1960 conservative Regents were upset by the involvement of Berkeley students in left-wing causes. Students from Berkeley had played a prominent role in the massive demonstrations against the House Un-American Activities Committee that occurred in San Francisco in May 1960. In the early sixties, they were active as well in efforts to end both capital punishment in California and *de facto* racial segregation in the Bay Area.[30]

Since the beginning of the Cold War, political activity on campus had been generally prohibited. This was especially true of activism perceived by the university administration as "left wing," which in the repressive climate of the fifties meant almost any form of protest against the status quo. By the early sixties this included civil-rights activism. For instance, the new regulations prohibited students from engaging in off-campus acts of civil disobedience, a tactic regularly used in civil-rights protests. Also, students were prohibited from proselytizing or passing out political literature on city-owned sidewalks at the main pedestrian entrance to the campus, the intersection of Telegraph Avenue and Bancroft Way, where student political activity had traditionally been tolerated by the university.[31]

On October 1 the civil-rights activist Jack Weinberg and others defied the ban. Weinberg was arrested for distributing literature for the Congress of Racial Equality. When police placed him in the back seat of a squad car, hundreds of students surrounded it. In the first, and perhaps most memorable, act of massive student defiance toward campus authorities in the sixties, the squad car was prevented from moving for 32 hours. While Weinberg remained in the car, and the crowd surrounding it grew to a few thousand, dozens of students took turns standing on its roof, making speeches about the pros and cons of the ban on political activity. Most of the speakers removed their shoes to avoid damaging the squad car. And a few weeks later, FSM leaders voluntarily collected over $400 from students to pay for repairs to the vehicle.[32]

The outrage created by the university's prohibition on student political activity, along with the arrests of Weinberg and others, created a semester-long uproar on the campus. The lies and duplicity of a feckless university administration, which portrayed the dissidents as little more than puerile adolescents engaged in a fraternity-style lark, made matters worse. From the students point of view, they were fighting to secure their First Amendment rights to freedom of speech and assembly. Acrimony and frustration mounted on both sides, and on December 2 Sproul Hall, the university's administration building, was occupied by nearly 1,000 student protesters who staged a sit-in.[33]

Edward Meese, Berkeley's assistant county prosecutor (and later attorney general in President Ronald Reagan's administration) told Governor Pat Brown that the students were "busting up" Sproul Hall. Meese was being less than truthful. The occupation of the administration building obviously disrupted the campus. But the demonstrators, unlike many campus protesters later in the decade, carefully avoided abusing university officials or damaging property. They spent the day singing FSM-inspired folk songs ("Don't know if I'm subversive," went one, "just want to say what I please.") Some studied for final examinations, while others watched Charlie Chaplin movies. Jewish students organized a Chanukah service. The governor ordered the police to remove the students, which they did at 3 A.M. on December 3. Nearly 800 students were taken into custody in the largest mass arrest in California history. A campus-wide student strike ensued. Finally, on December 8 an overwhelming majority of the faculty voted to support the FSM's claim that the First Amendment guaranteed students' rights to freedom of speech and assembly on the campus. The administration caved in, lifting the prohibition on student political activity. The students had won a stunning, nationally publicized victory.[34]

On the surface, the Free Speech Movement was an ardent defense by students of their right to enjoy fundamental freedoms guaranteed by the Constitution. For this reason, even politically conservative student groups, such as the Young Republicans, supported the FSM (most of whose spokespersons were liberal to left) and participated in its rallies. But as the crisis deepened during the fall, issues unrelated to free speech unexpectedly surfaced among some of the leftists involved in the movement. These students began to question the right of the university to restrict their behavior in any fashion, except when the well-being of others was clearly imperiled. In their view, the university's traditional power to act in *loco parentis* was illegitimate.

More significantly, these students started to see themselves as fodder for an educational system—and a society—determined to mold them into efficient and compliant components of what FSM leader Mario Savio amorphously but ominously referred to as "the machine" of American society.[35] White middle-class college students saw a contradiction between their expectations of becoming autonomous, independent adults and the ultimate purposes of their education as it was defined by the society. In a famous metaphor, the president of the University of California, the liberal Democrat Clark Kerr, called Berkeley a "knowledge factory." Berkeley and the country's other major research institutions were what he called "multiversities." They promoted diverse forms of knowledge that not only reflected "middle-class pluralism," but were also, according to Kerr, "instrument[s] of national purpose" as well.[36]

Some students took a dim view of Kerr's vision, and of the impersonal nature of the university's academic and administrative environments it tacitly sanctioned. They saw it as proof that they were perceived by society as "products" and "resources" whose destiny was to serve the needs of an undefined "national purpose" not of their choosing. Particularly those students involved in or sympathetic to causes for social justice saw a parallel, however inexact, between themselves and victims of racial discrimination and economic inequity. Their sense of being "oppressed" was rather vague and undefined, but it brought to the surface powerful undercurrents of resentment. "For the first time," FSM leader Michael Rossman said years later, "the question becomes, What about us? For the first time we took the conditions of our lives, the institutionally determined conditions of our own lives, not as a base from which to address others' problems but as the ground of our own oppression. When people began to make this sort of connection, the floodgates opened."[37]

Ken Kesey and the Merry Pranksters

On June 14, 1964, while some of the Berkeley students who would lead the FSM in the fall were being trained to participate in the Mississippi Freedom Summer project, Ken Kesey and thirteen companions, who called themselves the Merry Pranksters, boarded a colorfully painted bus at his ranch in La Honda, California. La Honda was a small town located on the southern part of the San Francisco peninsula. Ostensibly, they were headed east, for New York City. Their actual destination was wherever the drug LSD might take them.

Kesey had purchased and refurbished the bus with money from the sales of his 1962 best-selling novel, *One Flew over the Cuckoo's Nest.* The exterior of the bus was painted in swirls of bright primary colors. The destination sign in the front was deliberately spelled "Furthur." The warning on the bus's rear door read, "Caution: Weird Load." The interior contained bunk beds, benches, a sink and a refrigerator. A sophisticated wiring system linked record players and microphones to exterior speakers, allowing those inside the bus to broadcast their music and conversations to the outside world. Exterior microphones captured the sounds of America, transmitting them to those inside the bus. The Merry Pranksters had sobriquets (a common practice in the counterculture they helped create) that captured new dimensions of their identities revealed by LSD. Among them were: "Intrepid Traveller," "Hardly Visible," "Stark Naked," "Mal Function," "Zonker" and "Highly Charged."[38]

The principal driver of the bus was the legendary Neal Cassady, called "Sir Speed Limit." In the fifties version of the "trip" across America, captured in his friend Jack Kerouac's novel *On the Road,* Cassady was the model for Dean Moriarty, who drove the car at furious speeds back and forth across the country. Kesey, called "The Chief" or "The Navigator," purchased expensive camera equipment to make a movie of the voyage. He called the 45-hour filmed chronicle of the trip "The Merry Pranksters Search For The Cool Place."[39]

The "trip." It was a powerful metaphor linking an LSD-inspired interior journey to the historic American inclination to take to the road in search of another place, "cool" or otherwise. But Kesey's bus trip reversed the historic direction of American movement. He and the Pranksters went from west to east. They wanted to discover what might happen to themselves and the country when the East experienced what had been uncovered in the West a hundred years after the Gold Rush: the liberating qualities of LSD.

Kesey was an accomplished novelist and a charismatic, rambunctious westerner—equal parts intellectual and cowboy. A native of Eugene, Oregon, Kesey was a drama major and on the wrestling team during his undergraduate years at the University of Oregon in the late fifties. He was exposed to LSD in 1959, while working as a psychiatric aide in a veteran's hospital in Stanford. The experiments there were part of a secret operation funded by the Central Intelligence Agency to determine the potential utility of hallucinogens as weapons in the Cold War. Hospitals and psychiatrists across the country, carefully selected by the CIA, conducted these government–sanctioned and financed experiments on patients. Many individuals were unaware they were being given the drugs. Others, like Kesey, were volunteers.[40]

LSD, peyote and other hallucinogens were revelations to Kesey. Unlike other enthusiasts of LSD, such as Timothy Leary, Alan Watts and Richard Alpert, Kesey was not interested in studying the drug's biological, neurological or psychological effects. Nor did he care about its potential for enhancing spiritual insight.

Kesey used LSD as a catalyst of personal liberation and social interaction. Drawing on both his wrestling experience and his college major, he had an action-oriented, theatrical, muscular approach to the drug. The individual should "act" in public while under its influence. Spontaneous public performances while under the spell of LSD was a way of uncovering, exposing and enacting elements of personality normally hidden from consciousness. Equally important, it was a means of tapping into interior spaces of personality that might be immune to social control. The drug might liberate the individual from both the limitations of normal consciousness and the constraints of social conventions and conformity. In effect, Kesey viewed LSD as a chemical bridge that connected hitherto unchartered realms of the mind with unexplored spaces of social territory.

The purpose of the bus trip was to see what might happen when spontaneous behavior inspired by hallucinogenic drugs confronted what Kesey saw as the dreary conformity and dismal rationality of American society. The Pranksters were like the Indian Chief in *One Flew over the Cuckoo's Nest,* who escaped from the superficially benevolent but manipulative and ultimately brutal state-run insane asylum. The asylum reflected what Kesey saw as the banality, conformity and violence at the core of American culture. The bus trip was a way of telling the country that the strange-looking, drugged young "inmates" on the brightly painted bus were "breaking out" of their American confinement. To where, or toward what end, was unclear. They assumed, as had so many peripatetic Americans before them, that the road would reveal everything they needed to know.

As the bus made its way through Arizona, Texas, Louisiana, New York and other states during the two-month trip, it is doubtful that people who encountered the Merry Pranksters understood what was happening. Few

Americans in 1964 had heard of LSD, despite the Central Intelligence Agency's extensive testing of the drug on thousands of people in the fifties and early sixties. This changed after the bus trip, when Kesey and the Pranksters returned to California and initiated the "acid tests"—Kesey used the word "acid" as a shorthand for LSD. Initially held at homes of friends, then in large halls rented by Kesey, the acid tests brought together hundreds of people and ample supplies of LSD-spiked punch. The acid tests also included two phenomena that seemed natural complements to the hallucinogenic state: light shows created by overhead projectors and strobes and rock music (embryonic "acid rock"). The music at the acid tests was usually performed by Jerry Garcia, an early Kesey acolyte, and his band the Warlocks. The band would shortly change its name to the Grateful Dead.

The acid tests were soirees of spontaneity. People confronted each other, displaying normally inhibited qualities of their personalities liberated by the drug. The point was to summon the courage to expose in public the "natural" self unlocked by LSD. As Kesey put it, unless "you get very near that precipice where you're likely to make a fool of yourself, you're not showing very much of how you feel. You're playing it safe."[41]

The Pranksters' "trip" and the acid tests were the genesis of the counterculture. Both were designed to reveal the "authentic" self that lay beyond the claims of convention, conformity and personality. The right to exhibit this natural self took precedence over socially acceptable behavior. As Kesey told the Pranksters at the start of the bus trip:

> Here's what I hope will happen on this trip. . . . All of us beginning to do our own thing, and we're going to keep doing it, right out front, and none of us are going to deny what other people are doing. If saying bullshit is somebody's thing, then he says bullshit. If somebody is an ass-kicker, then that's what he's going to do on this trip, kick asses. He's going to do it right out front and nobody is going to have anything to get pissed off about. He can just say, "I'm sorry I kicked you in the ass, but I'm not sorry I'm an ass-kicker. That's what I do, I kick people in the ass." Everybody is going to be what they are, and whatever they are, there's not going to be anything to apologize about. What we are we're going to wail with on this whole trip.[42]

Bill Graham and the Fillmore

More than anyone else in San Francisco, Bill Graham grasped the potential for transforming the various media used in the acid tests for the purposes of mass entertainment. Graham took the disparate features of the acid tests—electronic music, strobe lights, film, slide projectors and, by implication, hallucinogenic drugs—and transformed them into a new form of entertainment: the psychedelic dance-hall experience.

Graham was an unlikely candidate for this enterprise. He was New York tough and brash, rather than San Francisco civil and tolerant. Graham was also "straight." He avoided drugs in those years and had a temper that was as volatile as its threshold was low. If these traits were not sufficient by themselves to distance Graham from San Francisco's emerging hippie "love scene," they were supplemented by an obsession with the economic bottom line and a genius for money making that frequently inspired the wrath of the city's radicals, especially the Diggers.[43]

Graham was indeed different from San Francisco's cultural avant-garde, and not solely because he came from the New York area (so did the most notable Diggers). His toughness was hewed from personal travail and tragedy. He was born Wolfgang Grajonca in 1931 to a Jewish family in Berlin. He escaped the Nazi fury in 1939, fleeing first to France, then to Spain, on a long march with 63 other Jewish children, including his sister. Living mostly on oranges and relentlessly pursued by the Germans, only 11 of the children survived the journey (Graham's mother was murdered by the Germans; his sister survived Auschwitz). The ten-year-old Graham made it to the United States in 1941, where he experienced a painfully long stay in an orphanage before being adopted by a Jewish family from the Bronx. He changed his name to Graham as a teenager by searching the telephone book for an Americanized approximation to Grajonca.

Hoping to become an actor, Graham moved to southern California in the late fifties. He didn't make it in Hollywood, and eventually headed north to San Francisco. R. G. Davis, the director of the San Francisco Mime Troupe, hired Graham as the theater company's business manager. Davis's theater company, which performed for free, was perennially impoverished, and Graham quickly gained a reputation within the city's music and artistic communities as a creative, driven and successful organizer of benefit shows produced to raise money for the Mime Troupe. But the experimental theater group also needed money to pay the hefty legal fees incurred from ongoing battles with the city's Parks Commission. Notwithstanding San Francisco's hoary reputation as an urbane citadel of tolerance, Davis and his actors were hounded by censorious city officials. Mime Troupe performers were repeatedly arrested on charges of nudity and obscenity during their performances.[44]

Toward the end of 1965, Graham convinced some of the city's artists, poets and musicians to perform in benefit shows to raise money to defray the Mime Troupe's legal expenses. The Mime Troupe benefits were so successful that

Graham was asked to organize the legendary three-day "Trips Festival" at the Longshoremen's Hall on the weekend of January 21, 1966.

The Trips Festival was the supreme acid test. It was the formal "coming-out" party for the LSD experience, the event that helped launch LSD and San Francisco's hippie scene into the national spotlight. It included Kesey and the Pranksters. The music was provided by the best of the emerging San Francisco rock bands, including the Grateful Dead and Jefferson Airplane. Another new band, Big Brother and the Holding Company, which would shortly hire Janis Joplin as their lead singer, also performed at the festival. The music was deafening, as bands played simultaneously at both ends of the hall. There were vats of acid-laced Kool-Aid and light shows. Films were projected on ceilings and walls. And a play produced by a group called America Needs Indians was performed. All of this was going on at the same time. A poster advertising the event said the Trips Festival would include "Revelations—nude projections, the God Box. The endless explosion. The Congress of Wonders, the Jazz Mice, liquid projections, etc., and the unexpectable."[45] Perhaps as many as 6,000 young San Franciscans, most of them "stoned," passed through the doors of the cavernous hall that weekend. They were dressed, as a journalist who covered the festival for the *San Francisco Chronicle* noted, in styles reminiscent of old San Francisco:

> Long-haired girls in trailing dresses skipped along the street. Tall men with mustaches, long hair a' la Bonnie Prince Charles or, sometimes, Buffalo Bill Cody, wearing high boots and Stetson hats. They all seemed to be cued into [San Francisco's] Frontier Days and [their dress] ranged from Velvet Lotta Crabtree to Mining Camp Desperado.[46]

Graham had no interest in hallucinogenic drugs and, at this time, precious little in the visceral, improvisational music blasting from the Grateful Dead's amplifiers. But he understood that something new was happening among the young of San Francisco, and that there was money to be made from it. Lots of money. This was not simply "fun" or drug-inspired hedonism, though both were central features of the experience. It was also what Graham called "living theater," a free-form exhibition of the spontaneous self.[47] It was self-exploration unself-consciously carried on in public. No one seemed "uptight" or repressed, much less constrained by social convention. And, he was convinced, people would pay to be part of it.

Within a week of the Trips Festival, Graham leased an old beige brick building on 1806 Geary Street in the Fillmore district, a predominately African American neighborhood. The building housed storefronts on the street level and a spacious ballroom above them. It had a stage, a balcony in the rear, a large dance floor and a huge turn-of-the-century bar. Graham staged his first show, modeled on the Trips Festival, at the Fillmore Auditorium in February 1966.

> From the Mime Troupe to the Trips Festival to my first show in February [in the Fillmore] I realized what I wanted to do. Living theater. Taking music and the newborn visual arts and making all of that available in a comfortable surrounding, so it would be conducive to open expression. What I saw was that when all this truly worked, that space was magic.[48]

By the end of 1966 Graham's Fillmore, along with his rival Chet Helms's Avalon Ballroom on Sutter Street, had created the sixties dance-hall experience. At the center of the light shows and the drugs was the live music performed by scores of San Francisco rock and acid-rock bands that developed from 1965 on. The music they composed and played, the "San Francisco Sound" as it was called, was an indigenous American music combining blues and hard rock with electronic guitar feedback. The feedback often created a distortion evocative of the hallucinogenic state. The bands that emerged in San Francisco during this period had a seminal impact, along with Bob Dylan and the groups of the "British Invasion" like the Beatles and Rolling Stones, on the development of rock music for the rest of the decade. From 1965 on they included the Charlatans, the Grateful Dead, Jefferson Airplane, Big Brother and the Holding Company (with Janis Joplin), Hot Tuna, Moby Grape, Quicksilver Messenger Service, Sly and the Family Stone, Country Joe McDonald and the Fish, Santana, the Steve Miller Band, Creedence Clearwater Revival and many other groups.[49]

Beginning in 1966, the San Francisco Sound was a powerful medium for disseminating to the rest of the country what had been going on among the Bay Area's young people since 1964. Bill Thompson, the road manager for Jefferson Airplane, described the impact of the group when it played in Iowa during its first national tour in 1966:

> You should have seen it when we came out to play. We had a light show. But all the girls were in ruffled dresses all the way down to their ankles with corsages, and their families were there. We started the light show and we had three sets to do that night. The first set, it was like we were from Mars. Guys with their hair cut like Dobie Gillis were standing there and staring at us. The parents were all farmers. They were looking at one another and saying, "What the hell is this stuff? Too loud for me, Maude. Time to go home and milk the goat." So they all left. The second set, people started dancing a little bit. They started getting into it. The third set, people went nuts. Off came the corsages. Shoes

were coming off. Guys were ripping off their ties. They went nuts. It was like the turning of America in a way.[50]

The Scene Is Noticed

By 1966 the expressions of unrest percolating within young people in San Francisco were ready to move east. The rest of the country would be infiltrated by the sense of oppression and alienation among college students that had exploded during the Free Speech Movement; by the extreme "do your own thing" individualism exhibited by Kesey and the Pranksters during the bus trip, the acid tests and Trips Festival; and by the experiences of personal and collective ecstasy produced by the music and light shows of San Francisco's Fillmore and Avalon dance halls. The San Francisco scene, with its odd combination of seething rage, quests for personal liberation and the hippie spirit of "free love" and community, worked its way through America in the second half of the decade.

In a way, San Francisco's relationship to the rest of the country had come full circle since the middle of the nineteenth century. Restlessness, nationalism, a hunger for wealth and adventure and the search for a new life precipitated the country's "Manifest Destiny" to the Pacific Ocean in the previous century. "We go eastward to realize history and study the works of art and literature, retracing the steps of the race," wrote Henry David Thoreau in 1862. But "we go westward," he continued, "as into the future, with a spirit of enterprise and adventure."[51] That adventurous western spirit was about to head east in 1966.

In the early months of 1966, the national news media descended on San Francisco. Reporters from *Time* and *Newsweek,* as well as correspondents from network television news programs, did stories on the Trips Festival, the acid tests, the San Francisco Sound, the dance halls and the first Human Be-In, held in Golden Gate Park in January 1967.[52] Most of all they focused on the Haight-Ashbury and its hundreds of young, long-haired, bizarrely dressed denizens. A San Francisco columnist had recently christened them "hippies."[53]

The hippies looked as though they came from another time, or another country. This inspired a bus company to launch a tour of the Haight-Ashbury. It was immensely popular with tourists. Each week hundreds of visitors from around the country were driven through the strange scene that was Haight-Ashbury. The bus company advertised the excursion as "the only foreign tour within the continental limits of the United States."[54]

What the tourists saw must surely have struck them as "foreign." Many of the huge, run-down but still stately Victorian homes of the neighborhood had been transformed into hippie communes. They contained hippie "crash pads" and rehearsal halls for bands who lived in the district, like the Grateful Dead and Big Brother. The tourists were driven past the many recently opened shops that catered to the counterculture. There were the I-Thou Coffee Shop and Love Burgers, where hippies and other young people purchased or panhandled meals. And the Wild Colors Boutique, where they bought Victorian-era clothes, cowboy hats and the new "mod" bell-bottomed pants that hung low on the hips. Observant tourists on the bus who looked into the boutique's large display window might see an employee sitting on a mock throne and dressed as the pope. Her job was to sell penny "indulgences" on a piece of paper to shoplifters as they left the store. The indulgence read "You Are Forgiven."[55]

As the bus drove past 1535 Haight Street the tour guide pointed out the most famous "head shop" of the sixties, the Psychedelic Shop. The Psychedelic Shop was the creation of Ron Thelin, a "hip" Haight merchant who made it the general store of San Francisco's counterculture. It sold drug paraphernalia and tickets to Graham's Fillmore dances, books on transcendental meditation and the Kama Sutra. The Psychedelic Shop featured a bulletin board where hundreds of young runaways from around the country could get messages from their parents. And Thelin set aside a "meditation" room, where one could search for inner tranquility or experience more sensual delights.[56]

The tourists might also see the recently organized Diggers, who created a mime play in which Haight-Ashbury hippies surrounded the tour bus. The hippies aimed mirrors at the people on the bus. The mirrors reflected back upon the tourists the wonder, shock or fear they experienced when they saw the unbridled freedom enjoyed by hippies of the Haight. In effect, the Diggers were asking a silent question of the American tourists who had stumbled on what must have struck them as so un-American a place: who, indeed, were the real "foreigners?"

THE DIGGER PLAY

Most of the notable Diggers were members of the San Francisco Mime Troupe. The Mime Troupe was founded in 1959 by R. G. Davis, a native of Brooklyn, New York, who had moved to San Francisco earlier in the decade. Davis believed the experience of radical theater could move an audience to question its assumptions about politics, society and their lives. His goal was to push American society beyond what he called the "stagnation of the fifties." Davis wanted to create a relationship between performers and audience that transcended the escapism of "bourgeois" theater and the pedantic pseudo-realism of the theater of the Old Left. "My own theatrical premise," wrote Davis, was that "Western

Society Is Rotten in General, Capitalist Society In the Main, and U.S. Society In the Particular."[57]

By the mid sixties, when many of those who would become Diggers had joined Davis's company, the Mime Troupe emphasized what Davis called a "Guerrilla Theatre" approach to its productions. In part this was inspired by the idea of the "theatre of cruelty" developed by the French playwright and director Antonin Artaud in the twenties and thirties. Toward this end, the Mime Troupe specialized in theatrical formats that satirized the status quo, particularly mime and commedia dell'arte, which originated in the sixteenth century. In Davis's view, commedia dell'arte was theater from the "working-class viewpoint."[58] It was an inherently risqué and antiestablishment form of theater in which the anonymity of the masked characters (all commedia players wore masks except the hero and heroine) permitted them to mock social norms and economic elites with impunity.

Like commedia dell'arte, mime was historically associated with attacks upon the status quo. In addition, mime fulfilled one of the goals of the "theatre of cruelty" by emphasizing physical movement and improvisation over adherence to the play's text. In mime the play's message was signalled to the audience by physical movements and facial expressions that drew upon the actors' visceral, raw emotions rather than scripted dialogue. The physical gestures of the actors, performed within what Davis called "a motivated frame of reference," were supposed to change the audience, not inspire them to think. As Davis put it, words might "sharpen and define" issues but the "substance" of a play's "meaning is in action." "There is no such thing as acting," said Davis. "One does and one is."[59]

The idea behind both mime and commedia, said Davis, was "that all action on the platform was fake, masked, indicated, enlarged show biz, while everything off stage was real."[60] Theater, in short, should move rather than entertain the audience. It took a certain kind of actor to perform Davis's version of guerrilla theater. He had some types in mind. "I personally like to work with the kooks, the emotionally disturbed, the violent ones, the fallen away Catholics, non-Jewish Jews, the deviates. . . . They do what the well-trained actor can never do—they create."[61]

Many of those who called themselves Diggers in 1966 and 1967 worked at one time or another for the Mime Troupe. During the Diggers' brief history perhaps 20 to 25 men and women belonged to the group. Three individuals who met in 1965 while working for Davis were most responsible for developing the Digger's ideas and staging the group's "life-acts." All were born in the New York area.

The most famous, flamboyant, mercurial and mysterious was Emmett Grogan. Grogan was born Eugene Grogan in Brooklyn in 1944. His father apparently held a midlevel white collar position with a Wall Street brokerage company—Grogan's talent for inventing his history makes it difficult to be precise, or to separate fact from fiction when discussing his life. Especially when he was the source of the "facts." By the time he was 16, according to his autobiography, Grogan was an accomplished and cunning street fighter, loner, thief and heroin addict. After a brief stint in prison for stealing jewelry, an extended sojourn in Europe, and a short time in the army (he said he was discharged after feigning mental instability), Grogan went to San Francisco, where he acted in a few Mime Troupe plays. Peter Cohon, who was known as "Coyote" in the Diggers (and since the sixties as the successful film actor Peter Coyote), was born to an upper-middle-class family in New Jersey and graduated from Grinnell College. Peter Berg, called "the Hun" by Grogan, was born in 1937 and raised in a politically radical family in New York. Berg was a writer and director with the Mime Troupe.[62]

When Berg, Coyote, Grogan and others decided to leave what Coyote called the "safety-net" of the Mime Troupe's stage and bring improvisational theater to the streets of San Francisco, the influence of Davis upon the group was evident. It is possible that the Diggers' tactic of anonymity was to some degree inspired by the masks worn by commedia actors. Their notions that the "play" should be "free," that the gestures made by actors should jog the audiences' "frames of reference" and that the purpose of acting was to inspire the audience to "act," were all Mime Troupe perspectives.

The Diggers brought their own unique slant to these ideas, especially to Artaud's notion of the "theatre of cruelty." Artaud's purpose in developing this approach to theater was to invest the European stage with unmediated physicality, the "inescapably necessary pain without which life could not continue," as he put it. Artaud believed that twentieth-century Western society was soft and overly rational. Affluence, the scientific and industrial revolutions, and the rationalism spawned by the Enlightenment had created an emotionally sterile culture. Western society was dominated by a desiccated intellectualism and a narrowly framed rationality. Artaud wanted to create a theatrical experience that portrayed "life lived with authenticity. Life without lies, life without pretense, life without hypocrisy. Life which is the opposite of role-playing." A life, in short, in which intellect was informed by "action instead of making actions coincide with thoughts."[63]

The Diggers may have revered Artaud's basic propositions but they reversed his direction. Rather than create the experience of a "real," emotionally charged life in the theater, they brought these elements of the stage into the streets. Their implicit—and very American—assumption contrasted sharply with that of the European Artaud. Personal freedom was legitimated by American culture; it didn't have to be staged in a theater. In theory at least, the individual in America already possessed almost complete freedom of expression, and was invested with nearly total responsibility for the moral and economic decisions she made. If an American wished to make absolute autonomy the premise of her behavior, and to break free from the social and moral "roles" into which she had been "cast" by fate or by others, all she needed to do was "act" that way in "real" life. In other words, the Diggers' goal was to stage the improvisational elements of American culture. If the individual wished to act as though she were free from the constraints, traditions and limitations imposed by history, ethnicity, family and social class, who or what could stop her? What prevented her from directing and staging her own play of self-creation. Or from filling in the blank spaces of personal freedom, the tabula rasa that is American democratic culture, with her own "frames of reference"?

The Diggers were convinced the surge of rebellion and self-expression among young people in the Bay Area since 1964 provided the raw material—the "scripts" and "props"—for staging a real-life drama whose main character was unfettered American freedom. They believed that the New Left and the hippie music and drug culture missed the point. According to Grogan, the New Left was "as full of puritanical shit as the country's right wing was cowardly absurd."[64] New Leftists were not only self-righteous, but needed to dress themselves in the ideological armor provided by Marx, Lenin, Che or Mao. Instead of simply assuming and enacting their own freedom, they talked endlessly about power. They were more interested in robing themselves in a prefabricated, ideological version of the truth than in acting to liberate themselves. (There is a story about a Digger who attended a New Left conference in 1967. During one meeting he suddenly removed all of his clothes. When asked why he had stripped he replied, "Somebody has to be naked around here.")[65] As Coyote wrote years later:

> From our perspective, ideological analysis was often one more means to forestall the time and courage necessary to actually manifest an alternative. Furthermore, all ideological solutions, left and right, all undervalued the individual, and were quick to sacrifice them to the expediencies of their particular mental empires. We used to joke amongst ourselves that the Diggers would be "put up against the wall" not by the CIA or FBI, but by peers on the Left who would sacrifice anyone that created an impediment to their being in charge.[66]

The Diggers were equally disdainful of what Grogan called "the absolute bullshit implicit in the psychedelic transcendentalism" promoted by the "tune-in, turn-on, drop-out jerk-off ideology" of Timothy Leary.[67] The "salaried hipness" of the psychedelic self-awareness movement, and the media celebrity enjoyed by Leary and millionaire rock stars, made a mockery of their criticisms of American life. While supposedly critical of the blandness of "the middle-class man," they covered their audiences "in the warmth of [false] security until we masturbate ourselves into an erection of astral rapaciousness and grab whatever pleasures we might in the name of Love."[68]

The Diggers did not believe capitalism, or any other institution, was the real problem. The problem and the solution resided within American culture itself. The problem was the inability or fear of Americans to act upon the freedom their culture claimed to endorse and, in any case, legitimated. The solution was to simply improvise one's freedom, to act viscerally and theatrically. As Coyote said, "the Diggers knew what was wrong with the culture and believed that if we created enough examples of 'free-life' by actually acting them out on the streets, without the safety-net of the stage, then people would have alternatives to society's skimpy menu of life choices."[69]

Among the "alternatives" offered by the Diggers were free stores and free food. The Diggers also provided free legal and medical services, donated by lawyers and physicians who worked with them. The services were given to poor people and hippies who were harassed by police or haunted by the epidemic of sexually transmitted diseases in Haight-Ashbury. But the free goods, services and food were not acts of charity. The point was to create moments of theater in which people were compelled to put aside their "normal frames of reference" and cultural scripts concerning hierarchy, property and authority.

For example, at their free stores on Page, Frederick and Cole Streets (the last, called Trip Without A Ticket, was the most famous) a variety of goods were displayed. They included clothing, blankets, shoes and, at times, household appliances. Many of the goods were new and possibly stolen. "Customers," regardless of their appearance or incomes, could enter the stores and take whatever they wished, in whatever quantities they desired. There were no cash registers. If a customer asked to speak with someone in charge, he was told, "You're in charge."[70]

The Trip Without A Ticket free store was run by Peter Berg, who called it a "social art form" and "ticketless theater." According to Berg, the free store was an example of guerrilla theatre, the creation of a free space of theatrical "territory," designed to "liberate human nature."[71] It did this by forcing people to perceive the store and its goods as props and the positions of customers and consumers, clerks and owners as roles that they performed without thinking. Once they became conscious that their roles could be changed simply by altering the script, anything was possible.

Coyote, who took his turn as "manager" of the Trip Without a Ticket, said the point of the free store was to show the "customers" that one's "life was one's own, and if you could leap the hurdles of programmed expectations and self-imposed limits, the future promised boundless possibilities." "There was," he declared, "no one or system to blame" if you failed to assume your own freedom. "The condition of freedom," after all, "had been presented as an actual possibility" in the free store "play."[72] In Berg's view, the example of buying and selling involved moral and hierarchical (as well as economic) assumptions that "prop" up the social system. People and objects were categorized in a way that legitimated, consciously or otherwise, the status quo. The free-store experience was supposed to bring all this out into the open. "First free the space, goods and services," wrote Berg, then

> let theories of economics follow social facts. Once a free store is assumed, human wanting and giving, needing and taking, become wide open to improvisation. . . . No owner, no manager, no employees and no cash register. . . . When materials are free, imagination becomes currency for spirit. . . . The question of a free store is simple: What would you have?[73]

As it turned out, some "customers" answered Berg's question by emptying the free stores of all their goods.[74] Many free-store life-actors did not understand the Digger distinction between the goods as "props" and property. But there were moments, painfully rare ones to be sure, when the Digger version of freedom hit home. "One day, on my shift as 'manager,'" recalled Coyote,

> I noticed an obviously poor black woman, furtively stuffing clothing into a large paper bag. When I approached her she turned away from the bag coolly, pretending that it wasn't hers. In a conventional store, her ruse would have made sense because she knew she was stealing. Smiling pleasantly, I returned the bag to her. "You can't steal here" I said. She got indignant and said, "I wasn't stealing!" "I know" I said amiably "But you thought you were stealing. You can't steal here because it's a Free Store. Read the sign, everything is free! You can have the whole fucking store if you feel like it. You can take over and tell me to get lost."
>
> She looked at me long and hard, and I went back to the rack and fingered a thick, warm sweater. "This?" I queried. She looked at it critically then shook her head, "No, I don't like the color. What about that one?" We spent a good part of the morning "shopping" together. About a week later, she returned with a tray of donuts, "seconds" from a bakery somewhere. She strolled in casually, set them on the counter for others to share, and went to browse the racks.[75]

But for the most part, and despite their many admirers in the Bay Area, Digger exhortations to "act" free were met with hostility, bewilderment or indifference. Their free services were subject to constant police surveillance and harassment. The police periodically closed the free stores because they lacked a business permit (the stores would then resurface in another location). The police were also an intimidating presence at the daily free food distribution at the Panhandle. Nor did the Diggers succeed in convincing many people that the free food, free stores and free medical services could be the basis for "the people to set up an alternative power base." Despite these problems, the Diggers persisted in advancing the notion that "freedom means everything is free."[76]

Ironically, the Digger belief that everything should be free was inseparable from a naive and rather traditional faith in the power of American abundance and technological ingenuity to solve social problems. Like many cultural and political radicals of the sixties—and other thoughtful Americans since the mid nineteenth century—the Diggers assumed American enterprise and technology could create unlimited abundance and leisure for everyone. They inadvertently hitched their radical dreams to the wagon of American enterprise, affluence and innovation.[77]

They believed machines would liberate most blue and white collar workers from boring and routine labor. "Give up jobs so computers can do them," read a Digger leaflet. "Computers render the principles of wage-labor obsolete by incorporating them," went a more cryptic broadside.[78] One Digger said that within ten years "machines and computers will do most of the work," making people lords of their time.[79]

The Diggers' view of American technology as ultimately benign and liberating was cast in a classic pastoral motif by the poet (and Digger advocate) Richard Brautigan in the poem "All Watched over by Machines of Loving Grace." Brautigan, who admired the Diggers for their free services to the needy, "gave" them the poem, which they reproduced and distributed throughout the city. Unlike the Diggers, Brautigan was not naive about the implications of technology: he envisioned a future in which humanity was "watched over" by God-like machines of its own creation. But much like the Diggers, his poem spoke of a computer paradise where human beings were liberated from routine, boring labor. Brautigan's poem conjured up a futuristic "cybernetic forest," a plugged-in, harmonious ecological utopia in which people, animals and machines peacefully co-existed amid a pristine, naturalistic setting of "pines and electronics." Human beings were not only freed from labor but also reconnected to nature. This was a landscape of reconciliation, a middle ground between the mythic freedom associated with the primitive American forest and what the Diggers and others in the counterculture saw as the sterility of modern American life. In Brautigan's poem, nature, human beings and their machines existed in "mutually programming harmony." It was the quintessential American Eden: social concord achieved through technological progress, a Digger-world devoid of the rat race, careers and endless quests for status and power.[80]

To some extent, the Diggers' assumption that American technological innovation was boundless, and that the economic bounty it created was limitless, informed their hope that money was nearly antiquated. They organized a street pageant in Haight-Ashbury to celebrate the "death of money." Bills and coins were placed in a coffin. Hundreds of marchers and spectators were given penny whistles, flowers, incense, bags of (lawn) grass, and signs that read "Now!"

> Three hooded figures carried a silver dollar sign on a stick. A black-clad modern Diogenes carrying a kerosene lamp preceded a black-draped coffin borne by six Egyptianesque animal masks. Other Mime Troupers . . . all made up like cripples and dwarves from the Middle Ages—walked down the sidewalks in two groups on either side of the street.[81]

Within a few months of their debut the Diggers were well known in San Francisco and Berkeley. They were widely admired for their efforts to provide food, clothing and legal and medical services for those in need. Some people mistook the Diggers for a hip version of the Salvation Army. San Franciscans who witnessed the daily free food service at the Panhandle in Golden Gate Park would offer money to Grogan and the other Diggers. They said the money should be used to purchase food and continue their work (most of the food was stolen or donated). The Diggers thanked the donors, asked them to wait a moment, then produced a match and burned the money. Charity and philanthropy, they told the donors, were "indulgences" for the conscience, "cheap" ways of avoiding commitment.[82] When Allen Ginsberg, Gary Snyder and other writers organized a benefit for the group at a North Beach bar, the Diggers refused to accept the money. "The only type of benefit that could be thrown for the Diggers," Grogan told Ginsberg, "is one where everything is free."[83]

A group called the Love Conspiracy Commune held a dance at the Winterland Theater called the First Annual Love Circus, featuring the Grateful Dead. The Diggers picketed the show, as they often did Graham's Fillmore. They claimed that the word "love," along with the music and other features of a supposedly revolutionary youth culture, were being transformed into commodities. They carried signs that read "Suckers buy what lovers get for free" and "To Show Love Is To Fail." The Diggers told the "marketers of expanded consciousness" that "Love isn't a dance concert with a light show at $3 a head."[84] "Whose trip are you paying for?" inquired a Digger leaflet aimed at the young people who purchased tickets to listen to "their own" music at the Fillmore and the Avalon dance halls:

> How long will you tolerate people (straight or hip) transforming your trip into cash?
>
> Your style is being sold back to you. New style, same shuck, new style, same shuck, new style, same shuck.
>
> The Diggers will not pay for this trip. As you buy a ticket, you kill the Digger in yourself . . . yourself.[85]

By the middle of 1967 the Diggers' notoriety had spread to the East Coast. Their antics and free services were described in publications with national circulations. Groups calling themselves Diggers opened free stores in New York and other cities.[86]

Meanwhile the original Diggers explored new and more bizarre territory. In June 1967 they acted like thugs while disrupting a Students for a Democratic Society conference in Michigan.[87] A few weeks later a New York television talk show host named Alan Burke expressed interest in interviewing Emmett Grogan. Peter Berg went on the Burke show accompanied by a woman he introduced as "Emma Grogan." It seemed, Berg told the audience, that people had the wrong impression. The famous Digger named Grogan was a woman. As Burke spoke and the cameras rolled, Diggers in the studio audience ran onto the stage and hit Burke in the face with cream pies. Berg stood up and addressed the television audience as he moved toward the exit: "I am in a box looking at you through a box. And you are in a box, watching me through a box. I am leaving my box and the things which make up my box. I've made my decision. What are you going to do about the box you are in?"[88]

Despite their outrageous behavior, the Diggers were more than the sum of their frequently bizarre life-acts. And more than the decade's most adroit choreographers of the anarchistic deed. They connected their generation's amorphous, powerful urges for autonomy, self-invention and independence to a medium compatible with radical expressions of American freedom: theatrical improvisation. The Diggers said their goal was to "jog consciousness" by inspiring people to "break addiction to identity, to money, to job, to whatever." This meant that the individual in America who was willing, as Coyote said, to assume responsibility for his behavior could act as he pleased, and change roles as the spirit moved him. In the free stores "not only the goods were free but the roles as well." The individual could become his "own poem" if he approached his life as "a social art form."[89]

The Diggers understood the potential hidden within the ideal of individual liberty if pushed to its American democratic extreme. "There are no leaders," said the Diggers. "I'd like to have a life that is free," said Coyote, "so I begin living that life."[90] It *was* that simple. (The Diggers and some accomplices set up a table on the side of a freeway during rush hour. They arranged four places. Crystal glasses, linen and champagne graced the table. Two of them sat in chairs, reading a newspaper. Two chairs were empty. It was a silent invitation to drivers robotically crawling to or from laborious jobs and pointless or painful family lives. Anyone driving by who wished to leave his car, and his life, and join the Digger repast was "free" to do so.) "Motives don't matter," they said. "The act, not the reasons," was the thing. "Conditioning can be de-conditioned," went a Digger saying. "How, is a miracle."[91] Or, perhaps, simply an act.

The Diggers' notions about freedom would not entice most Americans (the two empty chairs on the side of the freeway remained empty). But the ways and means of Digger images of personal freedom, and their inclination to view it as an "act," did resonate with some pre-twentieth-century concepts of American liberty. The claims for individual liberty that animated the democratic impulses of the American Revolution were largely inspired by the ideology of English radical Whigs. As one of them said in a sentence that could have been composed by the Diggers two centuries later, freedom was the individual's right to "pursue the Dictates of his own Mind; to think what he will, and act as he thinks."[92] The idea of "acting" free, of approaching life as though it was a play, was among the motives that inspired Henry David Thoreau's move to Walden Pond. Thoreau retreated from the constraints and pretensions of "civilized" society into the solitude and "wildness" of Walden, where, he said, "I can have a better opportunity to play life," and not "when I came to die, discover that I had not lived."[93]

The Digger connection between life-acts, purposeful, morally informed action and American liberty was presaged in Ralph Waldo Emerson's 1837 essay "The American Scholar." In this essay Emerson staked a claim for the independence of the American intellectual from the "courtly muses of Europe." The American was distinguished by his inclination to "create through action." "Life"—that is, action—"is our dictionary," Emerson said. By contrast, abstract thought was relatively meaningless unless "catalyzed by action." It might be true, Emerson conceded, that in this new and raw country the American scholar lacked the traditional "organs or medium" possessed by Europeans. Nevertheless, "to imprint his truth" he could "fall back on this elemental force of living them. This is a total act. Thinking is a partial act."[94]

Although William James would have been scandalized by the anarchic behavior of the Diggers, the brand of pragmatism he articulated toward the end of the nineteenth century had something in common with the Diggers inclination to view freedom as an indeterminate, open-ended process. "Pragmatism," as James pointed out, was derived from the Greek word for "action." As a philosophy, pragmatism assumed that "our beliefs are really rules for action." By contrast with rationalist abstractions and "bad" a priori reasoning, pragmatism leaned toward "concreteness and adequacy, towards facts, towards action. . . . It means the open air and the possibilities of nature, as against dogma, artificiality, and the pretence of finality in truth." Among other things, James believed pragmatism lent support to the idea that "chance" and freedom were possible, in spite of the determinists, who questioned the existence of free will. "Chance," as James suggested in another sentence the Diggers might have composed, was a precious thing, for when chance appeared it came "as a free gift or not at all."[95]

Of course, the Diggers were not inspired by these thinkers, and they operated in very different social and economic universes. But, along with Thoreau and Emerson, the Diggers saw America as an endless empire of open spaces that the individual was free to fill according to his emotional needs, long-term aspirations or momentary whims. They believed that freedom was attained through action—by "doing it" as those in the counterculture put it—and in the process, by tolerating what James called the "open air" of uncertainty.

But unlike James, the Diggers and other cultural rebels of the sixties assumed individual freedom preceded the requirements and demands of social life. The moral claims of personal liberty were superior to those of the collective society. Digger acts, like their street happenings or the free stores, were meant to make explicit (and bring into the "open air") the tension between personal freedom and social conformity. Their antics were media for testing people, for compelling them to make the choice between assuming command of their lives or living the roles imposed upon them by others. "[O]ne wants to be real," said Peter Berg, "to feel that one's being is actually there."[96]

To some degree, this explains the crude behavior of the Diggers. The requirements of formal civility carried cultural cues about status, hierarchy and obedience to authority. According to Berg, the individual needed to push himself past "the crap of recognition. You know: 'Yes-sir-no-sir-thank-you.'"[97] Digger life-acts were deliberately crude and sometimes cruel devices for bringing to consciousness the idea that the individual need not submit to the pretense and domination implied by formal civility. The Diggers would have agreed with Emerson, who said that the "world is his who can see through its pretension. What deafness, what stone-bred custom, what overgrown error you behold is there only by sufferance—by your sufferance."[98]

Digger behavior was crude, implicitly violent and anarchic both because they acted that way and because they perceived the obstacles to freedom in modern America as nearly insurmountable. The children of the forties and fifties, Coyote pointed out, were raised in a "loony bin" that was at once "permissive" and stultifying. Postwar affluence, the cult of security, political oppression and sexual repression deprived them of "adequate tests of personal worth" and self-knowledge. The Diggers, he said, were members of a generation who needed their own "wild turf" as a way of "measur[ing] themselves." They needed to take a journey into an "emotional and intellectual wilderness" they could call their own.[99]

The most important and symbolically rich example of a Digger foray into the "emotional and intellectual wilderness" was described in a lengthy portion of Emmett Grogan's autobiography. Grogan claimed that in the spring of 1967 he met a Pueblo Indian named Larry Little Bird in the Haight-Ashbury apartment of a fellow Digger. Little Bird was described by Grogan as a "black-pearl-eyed" 25-year-old from the hill country of New Mexico. The Indian was "as graceful and strong as a birch tree dancing in the wind." According to Grogan, within 30 minutes of their introduction Little Bird invited the "white man" to return with him to New Mexico. Grogan struck Little Bird as "a man who could learn what every man needs to learn about himself and what every Indian like Little Bird [already] knows."[100]

Grogan accepted Little Bird's invitation. The two of them set out on what would become a month-long sojourn in the still-pristine hills bordering New Mexico and Colorado. The ostensible purpose of the trip was for Little Bird to teach Grogan how to hunt, kill and skin animals. In fact, however, Grogan's narrative of his hunt in the wilderness reenacted mythic stories of the historic encounters between the "civilized" white man, the "savage" (noble or otherwise) Indian and a primitive American environment. Grogan, the supreme life-actor, self-consciously improvised a "play" in which a white man alienated from organized society retreated into the open spaces of the wilderness in order to forge a new identity for himself. In the process he experienced a spiritual and intellectual rebirth. Like Thoreau at Walden over 100 years earlier, Grogan discovered a new way to "play" American life. He would confront the country's open spaces of freedom by undertaking an adventurous, and in this instance dangerous, foray into the American wilderness.

The story of Grogan's hunt with Little Bird is fascinating because it restaged American literary myths associated with a variety of relationships: between the wilderness and the sources of national "identity," between the hunt and the ideal of masculine individualism, and between Euro-American values and Native American culture. It both re-created and fulfilled what historian Richard Slotkin defined as one of the purposes of literary myths: to act as "narratives that dramatize the world vision and historical sense of a people or culture, reducing centuries of experience into a constellation of metaphors."[101]

Grogan's narrative described the New World as a space both vast and, in cultural terms, empty. Within that space a white man could fashion an endless series of new beginnings for himself. Ultimately, that is what the counterculture represented: the reconnection of individual autonomy with images and myths, however ahistorical and fanciful they might be, of pre-twentieth-century notions of American freedom.

THE LEATHERSTOCKING FROM BROOKLYN

Whether the hunting experiences recounted by Grogan actually happened is another matter. He was an inveterate liar. As Peter Coyote wrote in the introduction to a posthumous edition of Grogan's autobiography in 1989, "Don't believe everything you read." But, he immediately added, "don't be too quick to doubt either."[102] What matters about Grogan's odyssey into the wilderness is not its status as history but its role as mythology. Grogan retreated into the wilderness, and embraced the prospects for savagery, death, adventure and freedom it offered, as a means of transforming himself. And of distancing himself from the sterility of contemporary American society. In effect, Grogan inadvertently fashioned his own twentieth-century version of a James Fenimore Cooper "Leatherstocking" tale.

Before leaving San Francisco, Grogan (who referred to himself in the third person in the autobiography) and Little Bird purchased clothing. All "the clothing was bought with the silence of the hunt in mind, and Little Bird painted the sneakers green and brown and spotted the same colors in the pants and shirt to make them blend even more with the background of the Springtime forest, as their wool texture would soundlessly harmonize with the quiet of the forest."[103]

During their first days in New Mexico, the garrulous Grogan and the reticent Pueblo "seldom spoke." They spent most of the time wandering in the hills, with Grogan watching Little Bird's "every quick but careful movement, learning as much as his Indian brother wanted to teach him." In the evening, they returned to Little Bird's cabin, where their female companions (Little Bird's wife and Grogan's "Digger woman," known by her hippie name, Natural Suzanne) cooked for the men. After dinner, each couple shifted to their respective areas of the cabin where they made love "for an hour or so until it was beautiful to stop and fall asleep to dream about what the next day might bring."

> Emmett followed Little Bird's eyes during their first week . . . and saw the many different creatures who lived there, who sensed their presence but were not alarmed because of their quiet way and the scent Little Bird spread on their camouflaged clothing—a scent that came from tiny sacs of liquid above the hind hooves of deer. Little Bird had acquired and saved this liquid from the many deer he had slain over the years. It was Little Bird's knowledge of the ways of the wilderness and Emmett's careful attention to his teacher's planned style of movement that allowed them to approach and get within yards of the splendid animals of the land.

Grogan was especially attracted by the deer. "Each one of those magnificent stags was strikingly individual and solely responsible for his small herd—and the sight of them charged Emmett with a deep feeling that one of them was to be the answer to the question that brought him to New Mexico."

One deer in particular caught his eye. Almost every night after dinner Grogan thought about this "buck":

> He picked the buck from dozens he saw on his walks with Little Bird through the woods, because there was something about the stag that told Emmett it was him. Emmett would sometimes stand outside under the stars and listen to the howling of the coyotes and the whistling of the mating calls and understand that whatever it was he was about to discover, it would be soon. This made him feel warm and open to the smells carried by the brisk, dark air, but nervous, that there was so much to manhood and being a man.

Ten days after their arrival in the hills their food was nearly gone. It was time to hunt. They would hunt like Indians rather than white men, and observe Native American's traditional reverence for their prey.

> Of course, they had always carried their weapons with them on their walks, but even though they sometimes had been only a few feet away from an animal, Little Bird had never used his bow or Emmett his rifle, because no meat had been needed for the table. However, now there was a need, and the rabbits they had only been watching they now were hunting.

At first, Grogan and Little Bird hunted for snowshoe rabbits. They shot the rabbits, and Grogan noticed that his gun, with its terrifying thunder and the odor it emitted when fired, was unnatural in that place. It was very different from the "clean sound of the snapped string" of Little Bird's bow. After the kill, Little Bird cleaned their quarry.

> Emmett watched with a certain amount of amazement as Little Bird deftly moved his fingers around the insides of the rabbits, examining their innards and skillfully handling their entrails, searching for some trace of disorder. His amazement was caused by the obvious excitement that Little Bird was experiencing as he dealt with the warm bodies of the freshly killed animals. His eyes were wide and alive with a sort of spiritual enthusiasm, and in fact his whole body seemed involved in a climaxing orgasm that wasn't sexual, but rather religious. Sweat poured out of him and his muscles trembled and his mouth watered and his face jumped and twitched, while his whole body shook with the death experience.

They did not speak, but Little Bird's "reaction to the kill," his demeanor while cleaning the rabbits, spoke of its "enormity." Grogan began to understand something about the hunt. Its real object was the hunter, not the hunted.

> The words of an Indian song which Little Bird had translated to him one evening started to beat their message into his brain: "I aim my golden bow; I pull on my golden string; I let fly my golden arrow; and it strikes the heart of the target, and I fall dead. For I am the target. And the target is me."

"The target is me." Grogan felt himself becoming "more and more one with the creatures he hunted." He treated the animals with the "same respect" he would have for himself had he "been the target." Sensing this change in Grogan, Little Bird realized his "pupil" was ready "to learn what he brought him there to teach."

Finally, nearly a month after they left San Francisco, Grogan was ready to hunt in the hills. He hunted alone. He and Little Bird knew that was the only way. Walking for hours, wandering far from the cabin, Grogan did not rest until he reached a spot where he "sensed the presence of his buck." He stayed in the spot for some time, waiting.

> He would do absolutely nothing to startle the buck to his feet. . . . He didn't want it to be that way. He wanted to hit the animal as he calmly rose from his sleep, so that the kill would be the cleanest of kills, and the deer would not have to suffer a moment's shock of apprehension. Emmett loved this stag he had come to hunt. . . . Emmett wondered whether animals like his young buck felt loneliness in some way at all. He didn't feel silly in supposing that they did sense something similar to man in their instinct toward life, and he looked up at the clouds and watched them roll and lumber around the blue sky for what seemed like hours until a formation appeared in the mass of white billow and separated itself from the rest of the cumulus puffs to stand alone and apart—a cloud shaped like his antlered stag deer.

It was the buck. Grogan observed the "handsome face and taut-muscles beautifully framed in a hard body." As he prepared to "squeeze off the round," the Pueblo song resonated in his mind. "For I am the target. And the target is me." He fired and the explosion "momentarily blurred the vision of himself falling, gracefully, but hard, dead to the ground, the target of the bullet he had just fired." Grogan looked at the deer "and saw himself," how it would be "when the time came for him." He waited at a distance, respectfully, allowing the "splendid buck to die in peace and in private." Assured that "the magic of death had ended," Grogan knelt beside the fallen creature and felt "an overwhelming oneness with the deer."

Grogan, the good pupil, remembered how Little Bird taught him to clean his kill. He "slit the animal's belly neatly open and gutted him like a good surgeon." Then he tied the deer's legs and hoisted the two-hundred-pound animal onto his shoulders. Grogan was not a particularly big man, but the past month of "stalking in the woods" had "strengthened his body to a point where he could feel the difference in himself." So he lifted and carried the deer. He walked haltingly and painfully for three long hours back to the cabin. Like a modern Jesus he carried his cross of redemption, the instrument of his own death. Grogan pushed on, refusing to stop despite the agony that suffused his body. He was fortified by

> the enormous energy which Emmett Grogan has discovered within himself that seemingly timeless afternoon. A vital, spiritual energy which surged through his body, filling him with an invisible physical strength from the moment he aimed his rifle at the wilderness within himself and fired on the target of his own animality.

When he finally reached the cabin, Little Bird saw "the magnificence" of the buck and how effectively Grogan had eviscerated the animal. He was proud of his pupil. "'Good,' was all he said." The women also admired Grogan's prize and "were proud of Emmett for now he was a hunter—which was what his being there was all about."

After skinning the deer and treating it, the women cooked steaks and the four of them ate what Grogan believed was "the finest meat he had ever tasted." The taste lingered:

> Afterwards, each couple went to their section of the cabin's divided main room where they lay down together. Emmett was too completely exhausted to talk with his woman, but she understood and kissed him with her juice-filled mouth, softly raising his cock hard with her lips and tongue, easing forth an ejaculation that burst full-loaded wet against the inside of her cheeks, splashing like a hot wave down her slender throat and sedating Emmett into the slumber of a long, deep sleep.

The following morning Grogan knew it was time to leave. He had to return "to the valley where the earth is covered with cement and where the people lived their lives hoping for a moment's relief, and show his brothers and sisters what he saw." Grogan packed, but he left behind the gun used for hunting and killing his former self. Instead he took the bow and arrows Little Bird had given him. Grogan was now a native to America, and "satisfied that he had made no mistakes in picking and choosing what to leave behind and what to take with him." For all we know, he left Natural Suzanne behind as well. Nor did he say goodbye to Little Bird. "He didn't have to."

> It took him four days and all the eighty-five cents he had in his pocket to get back to Frisco with only the heavy deer scent on the Black-Bear, Rain-tite jacket Little Bird had given him to protect his senses from the immediate, hard, cold, unnatural assault of the city and its streets. Emmett kept one of the lapels tucked under his nose, using the perfume of the wilderness to defend himself against the industrial smell of progress and modern civilization. . . . Emmett walked because he wasn't tired and because he wanted to let the feel of the city work him over and massage him back into the shape he would need if he was going to pick up where he left off.[104]

Grogan's strange adventure distilled the ways in which the counterculture reprised an imagined preindustrial America. His odyssey was a symbolic union between the desire of cultural radicals for unfettered autonomy and the freedom of the solitary, "self-made" mythic American male. Grogan had to temporarily retreat from the constraints of organized society in order to taste the freedom offered by the savagery, adventure and struggle for survival in the ancient American wilderness.

Grogan told his story in the self-consciously dramatic fashion appropriate to the heroic process through which his identity and "manhood" were reinvented by means of the hunt. Whether Grogan was aware of the American literary traditions associated with these themes is an open question. There is no way of knowing whether he was familiar with nineteenth-century literary works, such as the Cooper tales, that portrayed a tension within American "character" between the settled, civilized ways of the East and the lures of freedom and primitivism represented by the forest or the West. Nor is there evidence that he knew about the history of the mountain men of the first half of the nineteenth century (except, perhaps, as portrayed in television westerns), whose actual wilderness experiences might not have differed significantly from the one he described.[105] And it is altogether unlikely that Grogan had knowledge of the historiography of the American frontier, even though he reenacted Frederick Jackson Turner's late-nineteenth-century belief that the European is transformed into an American when he "strips off the garments of civilization" and dons the "hunting shirt and the moccasin."[106] The idealization of Native American culture was, however, a primary feature of the counterculture and the Haight-Ashbury hippie community. Obviously, Grogan was keenly aware of this.

One thing is certain. Grogan was a thoroughly urbanized son of the city streets who consciously orchestrated his ascension to manhood by plunging into the wilderness. And when his travail was over, he saw himself as a sort of Moses of the counterculture. He returned to San Francisco with the "scent" of the hunt, the unmediated odor of pristine American freedom on his clothes, ready to be sniffed by his "people." The rebirth detailed in his story, then, is not only Grogan's. Symbolically it is that of a generation that needed to connect with primitive sources of individualism and freedom that were alien to contemporary American society.

The implications of Grogan's tale and its significance for understanding the counterculture are tied to issues that go beyond them. Grogan's self-invention through his "performance" as a symbolic American hunter in a pristine forest is linked to a number of historical issues. These include traditional American attitudes toward the wilderness, Native Americans and the significance of the hunt.

As we saw in chapter 4, from the beginning of European settlement, confrontations with the wilderness and frontier were invested with profound cultural significance and ambivalence. American attitudes toward the western migration, and the progressive recession of one frontier after another in the eighteenth and nineteenth centuries, were deeply ambivalent. On one hand, movement west suggested the inevitable march of progress. It symbolized the triumph of "settlement." American farmers and their plows replaced the Indians, hunters and trappers who wandered in the wilderness. Each town settled or farm staked negated the "savagery" and "anarchy" of the frontier and eradicated the moral dangers it represented. In the eighteenth century, Crevecoeur described hunters and frontiersmen as "unsocial" and "ferocious" individualists immersed in a "sort of lawless profligacy." He believed these Euro-Americans had sunk so low on the scale of civilization that they made the customs and manners of the Native Americans appear "respectable" by comparison.[107]

On the other hand, by the late nineteenth century the taming and settlement of the West inspired a feeling of loss in some Americans, especially easterners. The "conquest" of the West extracted from American life a symbolic arena of adventure and freedom. This sense of loss was intensified by the emergence of an urban, industrial, hierarchical and commercial civilization. The industrial city created the potential for widespread security and affluence. But its regulated, "settled," sedentary and congested way of life seemed to limit the horizons of American individualism and manhood. To some degree those qualities had been linked to the encounter with the wilderness and westward expansion. Masculinity and individualism had been cultivated by the struggles and dangers inherent in pitting oneself against the formidable dangers of frontier and forest.[108]

By the turn of the century some Americans tried to recapture this sense of danger by hunting and vacationing in wilderness settings "preserved" by acts of Congress. A congressman of the time said that after a "kill" the hunter felt like "a barbarian, and you're glad of it to. It's good to be a barbarian and you know that if you are a barbarian, . . . you are at any rate a man."[109]

As historian R. W. B. Lewis pointed out, perceptions of the West and the frontier as symbols of a descent into moral anarchy were challenged somewhat by writers in the nineteenth century who viewed the wilderness as a boundless and timeless "arena of total possibility."[110] The historian Francis Parkman, James Fenimore Cooper and Thoreau, among others, viewed the existence of an untamed, unsettled West as a necessary antidote to the intellectual, physical and moral limitations created by industrial progress and urban congestion.[111] One hundred years before Grogan proudly carried the scent of wild animals back to San Francisco, Thoreau said he "would have every man smell so much like a wild antelope, so much a part and parcel of nature, that his very person should thus sweetly advertise our senses of his presence. . . . I feel no disposition to be satirical when the trapper's coat emits the odor of musquash even; it is a sweeter scent to me than that which exhales from the merchant's or the scholar's garments."[112]

To a remarkable degree, Grogan's approach to his wilderness experience mirrored these perceptions of the West and the wilderness as an escape from the constraints of a settled, secure life. Grogan's adventure and his attitudes toward the wilderness recapitulated some of the sentiments of Cooper's Natty Bumppo in the five "Leatherstocking" tales, as well as the nineteenth-century narratives of Daniel Boone's career as a hunter and pioneer. Slotkin suggested that the mythological elements of the Bumppo and Boone tales revolved around the hero's ability to extract "moral value from the wilderness ordeal." But this would happen only if the individual possessed an innocent receptivity to the experience. He had to be willing to immerse himself in the wilderness environment and put aside, at least momentarily, his ties to the past.[113]

From the beginning of Grogan's narrative, he indicated the need for an experience modern society could not provide, something "every" Native American "already knows" but that eluded middle-class whites. Upon meeting Little Bird, Grogan put aside his past (and present) and rather innocently and naively placed himself in Little Bird's hands. The Native American taught Grogan how to become a "man." In effect, Little Bird was a cultural bridge between the settlement and security offered by contemporary society and the primitive, unfettered freedom supposedly harbored within the American wilderness. Natural Suzanne is Grogan's only tie to his urban world. But her dramatic function in Grogan's narrative is merely to give domestic feminine witness to his manhood, a characteristic attitude of radical males toward women in the sixties.[114]

The most important link between sixties radicalism and the mythic elements in Grogan's tale was Little Bird. There was a logic of sorts in the fact that Grogan and Little Bird met in the Haight-Ashbury neighborhood. The hippie-commune-drug culture lifestyle that took root there before penetrating the rest of the country was heavily influenced by white middle-class stereotypes of the American Indian.

Few symbols of unity between people, or between human beings and nature, captured the imaginations of cultural radicals as powerfully as that of Native American tribalism. A few months before Grogan and Little Bird met, the first "Human Be-In" of the sixties was held on the Polo Grounds of Golden Gate Park. The Be-In was sponsored by a coalition of Berkeley political radicals, such as Jerry Rubin, by counterculture figures associated with Haight-Ashbury and Beat writers, including Gary Snyder and Allen Ginsberg. The Diggers provided thousands of "free" sandwiches for the event. The Be-In's official poster called it "A Gathering of the Tribes." The center of the poster contained a drawing of an Indian on horseback. A press release on the Be-In called it a "pow-wow" convened by "every tribe of the young" who were dedicated to forming a "new" American nation.[115]

To a considerable degree, the ideals of this new nation were associated with Native American tribalism. Cultural radicals admired the communalism and communism of Native Americans, the supposed "simplicity" with which they lived and their respect for nature. Most of all, perhaps, they were intrigued by the noncoercive, apparently voluntary nature of Indian communalism.[116] Two centuries earlier, Thomas Jefferson noted much the same thing. Indian society was bereft, said Jefferson, of "any laws, any coercive power, any shadow of government. Their only controuls are their manners, and that moral sense of right and wrong."[117] For these reasons, many of those who lived in Haight-Ashbury saw themselves as "the reincarnation of the American Indian," in the words of the editor of the district's underground newspaper, *The San Francisco Oracle.*[118]

Grogan's perception of Little Bird reflected these views. But the real "role" played by Little Bird in Grogan's life-act was to be the instrument through which Grogan recreated himself. His identification and kinship with the Indian, whom he called "my brother," allowed Grogan to blend certain elements of American and Native American cultures into his new identity, while remaining independent of both.

In the end, Grogan is neither a Native American nor an American attuned to the values of contemporary society. His relationship with the Pueblo had an affinity with that of Hawkeye and Chingachgook in Cooper's *The Last of the Mohicans.* At the end of this tale Chingachgook, forlorn over the death of his son and the end of his tribal line, cried, "I am alone." Hawkeye, the white man who felt more at home in the forest and with the ways of the Indians than with his own people, replied, "No, no, not alone. The gifts of our colors may be different, but God has so placed us as to journey in the same path. I have no kin, and I may also say, like you, no people."[119]

Grogan had "no people" either. He and other cultural radicals embraced a version of American freedom that inevitably marginalized them in their own society. Little Bird, like Chingachgook, a symbol of pristine America, was the instrument through which Grogan articulated his rejection of modern American culture and reasserted the claims of a primitive American liberty. Grogan's new identity was concocted from selective elements of both cultures and suggested something entirely new. It can be said of the relationship between Grogan and Little Bird what D. H. Lawrence said of Hawkeye and Chingachgook: "This is the new great thing, the clue, the inception of a new humanity."[120] The American.

Grogan earned the right to claim his new identity by becoming a hunter. The actual target of the hunt, as he made clear, was his former self—the buck was Grogan. The danger inherent in the hunt was not just that the hunter could be injured or killed, but that he might fail to summon the courage necessary to prove his "manhood." In this context, the manhood to which Grogan referred symbolized the courage necessary to confront and destroy what he viewed as a morally decadent society. Put another way, the bravery necessary to combat and topple contemporary American society was forged through an adventure in the primitive American wilderness. The weapon used to destroy modern America was its own history.

The hunt was a parable in which an avatar of sixties radicalism ritualistically severed his ties to society by "performing" an act of mythic renewal and rebirth. It was an old American tale. As Slotkin pointed out in his extraordinary study of the mythology of the American frontier, *Regeneration through Violence,* the "myth of the hunter . . . is one of self-renewal or self-creation through acts of violence."[121]

Notwithstanding his admiration for both Little Bird's culture and its reverence for nature, Grogan's views of the wilderness and the hunt were typically American. They were instrumental and "white," not inclusive and "red." When ready to kill, he repeated the words of the song Little Bird taught him, "the target is me." But Grogan missed the point of the Indian song. For Native Americans, identification with the target reflected their belief that all creatures were spiritually related. The act of killing an animal, even for food, was symbolic suicide. But for Grogan, he, rather than the buck, was the issue. The deer was merely the means through which Grogan enacted his ritual of self-creation.

In the end, Grogan made it clear that his "weapons" of choice for combat with contemporary America were those of the primitive American forest. His rebirth as a hunter was a sign that, if necessary, he could shoot and kill as effectively in the city as in the hills. At the same time, however, Grogan left the gun behind. This symbol of the Euro-American conquest of the continent was replaced by the pre-Columbian bow and arrow given him by Little Bird. Leaving the gun behind expressed the counterculture's ideals of "peace" and "love." But keeping the bow and arrows, the killing of the buck and the savage relish with which Grogan dissected and devoured the venison spoke of something else. Thoreau captured this American ambivalence in a passage in *Walden*:

> Once or twice . . . while I lived at the pond, I found myself ranging the woods, like a half-starved hound, with a strange abandonment, seeking some kind of venison which I might devour, and no morsel could have been too savage for me. I found in myself . . . an instinct toward a higher or, as it is named, spiritual life . . . and another toward a primitive rank and savage one, and I reverenced them both. I love the wild not less than the good.[122]

Grogan's wilderness adventure enacted the repetitive process from civilization to frontier that occurred during the first three centuries of American history. "American development," suggested Frederick Jackson Turner in 1893,

> has exhibited not merely advance along a single line, but a return to primitive conditions on a continually advancing frontier line, and a new development for that area. American social development has been continually beginning over again on the frontier. This perennial rebirth, this fluidity of American life, this expansion westward with its new opportunities, its continuous touch with the simplicity of primitive society, furnish the forces dominating American character.[123]

One needn't agree with Turner about primitive forces "dominating" the character of Americans to perceive the San Francisco scene beginning in 1964 as an attempt on the part of young people to reinvent or rediscover an American frontier of their own. Thus the archaic qualities of Digger life-acts, the free-fall plunge into psychological and social frontiers by Kesey and the Pranksters, the centrality of Native American tribalism for cultural radicals and Grogan's odyssey into the wilderness. Radicals needed, as Coyote said, their own "wild turf."

Middle-class child rearing in the forties and fifties placed extraordinary emphasis upon autonomy, independence, exploration, risk taking and competitiveness—in other words, on "testing." In the sixties, millions of young people, with varying degrees of commitment to the hippie movement, took up this challenge. They attached themselves to culturally sanctioned myths or primitive experiences that tested their abilities to respond to challenges and to take the risks necessary to explore their world and themselves.

Digger "life-acts" and Grogan's wilderness experience were improvised performances suggesting that the sources and means of expressing these needs resided within the culture itself. American liberty could be rediscovered simply by heading "west," metaphorically or literally.

THE DIGGERS AND THE HAIGHT-ASHBURY EXIT THE STAGE

Grogan returned to Haight-Ashbury in time for the legendary "Summer of Love" in 1967. Tens of thousands of young people from across the country, many of them barely into their teens, headed for San Francisco that summer. They were lured there by two years of media hype about what they would find: radical politics at Berkeley, endless supplies of inexpensive hallucinogens, the stirring rhythms of the San Francisco Sound, the collective ecstasy produced in the dance halls and the open sexuality displayed by the hippies of Haight-Ashbury. These attractions, along with San Francisco's reputation for tolerating "deviant" lifestyles—though this tradition had withered considerably by 1967, as city officials and the police came down hard on the hippie hordes—made it the destination of those seeking new experiences, a new life or simply a new day. (A Digger leaflet proclaimed: "Today is the first day of the rest of your life".) Police estimated that a total of 75,000 young people squeezed into a densely packed Haight-Ashbury that summer. The Diggers and other neighborhood activists intensified their efforts to feed and house these American refugees.[124]

In July the Diggers changed their name to the Free City Collective. The new name was a reaction against the "expropriation" and exploitation of the word "Digger" by other radicals and the media. Even Hollywood had heard of the Diggers. Advertising copy for *The Love-Ins,* a 1967 film about the Haight-Ashbury, warned America that "the hippies and the diggers are here!" In the fall, the Diggers organized their last major parade. They called it "The Death of Hippie." Pallbearers carried a coffin filled with beads, hair, incense and flowers.[125]

It was not a premature farewell. The "Summer of Love" was the beginning of the end of the Haight-Ashbury, both as a bohemian neighborhood and a viable community. The influx of long-haired, runaway teens wasn't the only problem. Two years of Dionysian abandon had undermined, though not quite destroyed, hippie dreams of creating an empyrean urban haven where one might taste both personal freedom and shared ecstasy. As an army of young people and tourists invaded the district in 1967, many of the original Haight-Ashbury hippies fled. Like Grogan, they headed for rural areas, though not to hunt. Hundreds of Haight hippies founded new, mostly short-lived communes in the countryside.[126]

Many of Haight-Ashbury's new residents had neither the intellectual curiosity nor the spiritual ideals of the original hippies. A journalist who visited the neighborhood in 1967 reported that many of the young people who came there in 1965 and 1966 had gone to college and came from upper-middle-class backgrounds. They were the "children of chairman of the boards of the largest corporations, the most successful lawyers, the richest stockbrokers."[127]

Those who came in the spring and summer of 1967 hailed from more diverse backgrounds. They ranged from children of professionals to runaways from abusive or repressive families. The new Haight residents were a motley brew of high school dropouts, religious fanatics, naive "flower children," callous drug dealers, thugs and pimps. Rape and other forms of assault and exploitation greeted young women who ventured into the neighborhood. Some of them were as young as 14. "Rape is as common as bullshit on Haight Street," said the Diggers in 1967. They were accurate on both counts. Venereal disease and vaginitis were epidemic. The murder rate and incidents of physical assault soared. Robbery and burglaries became commonplace. In perhaps the most pointless robbery in the history of the United States, the Diggers' Trip Without a Ticket free store was burglarized![128]

By the end of the summer, heroin, barbiturates and other "body" drugs vied for popularity with consciousness-altering and less-expensive drugs like LSD and marijuana. The profitability of hard drugs led to an outbreak of violent crime. When police arrested a notorious heroin dealer, they found a suede bag in his car. The bag contained the severed arm of a drug dealer who had been murdered. When asked about the bag and its contents, the "stoned" drug dealer told police, "I'm very, very, hazy about that arm."[129]

In retrospect, perhaps the most telling sign of the decline of the Haight-Ashbury and the counterculture was the arrival late in 1967 of Charles Manson, recently paroled from prison. Two years later Manson embarked on the most infamous murder spree of the decade. The son of a Cincinnati prostitute, Manson met some of the young people who became his acolytes and accomplices in murder during his stay in Haight-Ashbury. He also experienced his first LSD trip there. The counterculture's "anything goes" toleration made it easy for anyone, including psychotics, to join up. His drug experiences fortified Manson's ambition to become a rock-and-roll singer-songwriter. One of his compositions was titled "The Ego Is a Too-Much Thing."[130]

The Diggers, or Free City Collective, continued to exist into 1968, although with far less fanfare and notoriety, and substantially diminished creativity. During their halcyon days in 1966 and 1967, Digger pageants, free food, free stores and free services invested the counterculture with moral concreteness. It provided moral substance to a hippie "love" ethic that often amounted to little more than self-absorption, hedonism and solipsistic trances masquerading as "self-exploration." Of course, the Diggers were radical individualists as well. Years later, Coyote called them "social safe-crackers, sand-papering our nervous systems and searching for the right combinations that would spring the doors and let everyone out of the box."[131] Yet they tried to integrate personal autonomy with a sense of civic responsibility. But the Diggers were no more successful than other radical groups of the sixties in harmonizing individual liberty and community.

Unlike most other sixties radicals, however, the Diggers, actors who had performed historical plays during their days with the Mime Troupe, possessed a sense of history as an unfolding drama. They knew that what had evolved in the San Francisco area since the early sixties was a celebration of American freedom deeply at odds with the way most Americans preferred to live their lives. The turmoil that ensued implied that the country might be at a crossroads. Down one road was the freedom associated with the West, down the other was the desire for security linked to the East: movement and adventure versus settlement and fear of the unpredictable. The Diggers sensed that with nowhere left to go, with no physical "West" of freedom remaining to explore, Americans might finally be compelled to confront what they had wrought. In 1967 they distributed a leaflet that had an apocalyptic edge. "Always before, there was somewhere to go. . . . Man has always moved westerly, now is piling up on the Pacific Cliffs, and Japan is flooding back on us. It is all One. At last."[132]

Ken Kesey, whose explorations of social frontiers anticipated the Diggers' life-acts, would have understood the historical significance of this broadside. In 1964, on the bus loaded with LSD headed east, he called the Merry Pranksters the "unsettlers of 1964, moving backwards across the Great Plains. . . . All of these things," said Kesey, "have a mythic story."[133]

Sometime early in 1970, when the hippie dream was all but over, the Brooklyn native Emmett Grogan gave up on the West. The most famous Digger decided to go back to the East. He had "done all he ever could in California with its people, at least for 'Free!' anyway."

> The west had become his home, and he pushed it as far as it could take him without dying. . . . He decided to head back to where it all began, when he was supposed to have been a boy. He decided to return to New York and Brooklyn, and he was going to walk all the way because he wanted to listen carefully to whatever sounds America was making. Everything he ever heard about America was true.[134]

He was going to walk to New York. As usual, Grogan opted for the grandeur and literary lilt of myth rather than the flatness and accuracy of fact. An avid reader of Beat literature, Grogan may have been familiar with a passage in Kerouac's *On the Road.* During a respite from their frenetic excursions back and forth across the country in a car, Dean Moriarty suggested to Sal Paradise that they walk to New York from San Francisco. "Let's walk to New York. . . . And as we do let's take stock of everything along the way."[135] Or as Grogan suggested, freedom was the experience of taking to the road and listening carefully to "whatever sounds America was making." For it was all "true." Whether on foot or behind the wheel, the road guaranteed there was always something new to discover or experience in America. Always some other place to go. And start over.

Whatever his means of transport, Grogan made it back to Brooklyn. In 1978 he died from an overdose of heroin. His body was found in a New York City subway car. On the Coney Island line.[136]

CONCLUSION: THE LEGACY OF THE DIGGERS AND COUNTERCULTURE

Measuring the long-term impact of the counterculture is not easy. Some historians and critics believe the hippie movement liberalized American culture (whether or not they view this as beneficial depends on their political and moral values). Counterculture attitudes toward sexuality, drugs and work challenged the supposedly work-obsessed, sexually repressed ways of mainstream America. Conservatives bemoan these changes, which they believe led to a crisis of values and the ensuing culture wars of the 1980s and 1990s. Others view the hip movement of the sixties as heralding a sea change in lifestyles. It shamelessly displayed and ultimately institutionalized the hedonism at the heart of twentieth-century consumer culture.[137]

The vast majority of Americans in the sixties rejected the counterculture as a way of life, but over time both they and the marketplace selectively absorbed some of its wares and values. In one form or another, rock-and-roll, new age therapies, sexual liberation and self-fulfillment as a way of life seeped from the counterculture into the mainstream. The suppliers and buyers of instant gratification transformed a leisurely stroll through a festive Haight Street in the sixties to an endless shamble though a bland shopping-mall culture in the nineties. And the hippies' attempt to explore their sexuality—however questionable their means—was transmuted over time into, among other things, a pseudoerotic obsession with sexuality.

All of these views have some validity because, during and since the sixties, there were so many motives for becoming hip and so many ways of expressing hipness. Many hippies seriously searched for secular enlightenment or spiritual salvation amid the fads, flowers, flashbacks and fleshpots of the counterculture. There were others who, so to speak, let their hair down only on weekends. It *was* fun. And there were still others, like those who joined Charles Manson's "family" of killers, the forlorn, hopelessly insecure souls desperately seeking meaning, any meaning, in their lives. Unable to devise one of their own, they looked to "gurus," benign or otherwise, to do it for them. Gurus were easy to find: the counterculture oozed exploitative, charismatic figures of one sort or another.

Easily lost sight of in this jumble of conflicting styles, motivations and interpretations was the concrete moral challenge to the established American order posed by the Diggers and others like them in the counterculture. The Diggers did more than champion anarchy, though they would have agreed with Emerson that a "man contains all that is needful to his government within himself."[138] And they were more than directors of some rousing plays in which primitive acts of American freedom were performed, though Grogan's hunt, like any serious play, was for real.

More than anything else, and more than most in the sixties, the Diggers intuitively grasped an abiding irony of the American experience: Americans either condone or acquiesce to near anarchy in their economic behavior but generally retreat from it in other areas of their lives. Or, for that matter, in other people's lives.

The most significant, culturally approved displays of improvised freedom in the United States occur within its largely unrestricted economic marketplace. The fruits of liberty aren't harvested in some wilderness of the free soul but on the Wall Street of bulging stock portfolios. "Free" enterprise—the "performance" of buying and selling—is the only "play" in which Americans can pretty much "act" as they please. Beyond the economic realm, there is a traditional and ongoing obsession with controlling spontaneous or idiosyncratic behavior, especially in matters of sex, drugs, dress, unpopular beliefs and general comportment. Thus an American can do as he pleases with his material possessions, but is not free to legally marry someone of the same sex. The accumulation and disposal of private property is one's own business; the enactment of one's private life may or may not be. After all, Americans implicitly ask themselves, how much anarchy can a society tolerate while still remaining viable?

Grogan, Coyote, Berg, other Diggers and serious hippies did more than challenge this equation. They reversed it. For a brief interlude they turned their little piece of America on its head. They substituted a free life for free enterprise. Their versions of self-reliance and of becoming self-made had nothing to do with work, careers, economic competition, possessions or status seeking.

At the same time, "It's free because it's yours" was not a call for socialism. Political ideologies and the hierarchies and organizational structures they require were anathema to the form of individualism advertised in the Diggers' most famous slogan. Rather, it was a call to explore an interior New World, a twentieth-century summons to stake a claim to a mythological American freedom lodged somewhere within the wilderness of the self. It was improvised, unalloyed "movement": away from modern economic striving, hierarchy and social control, and toward a lost, perhaps imaginary, unexplored frontier where one might create infinitely plural personal identities and social territories.

"It's free because it's yours." It was as un-American as any mythic American phrase could be.

SIX

Rock and Work: Another Side of Sixties Music

I am a writer and a singer of the words I write. I am no speaker or any politician and my songs speak for me because I write them in the confinement of my own mind and have to cope with no one except my own self.

Bob Dylan, 1965

[T]he deeper he dives into his privatist, secretist presentiment, to his wonder he finds this the most acceptable, most public, and universally true. The people delight in it; the better part of every man feels, This is my music, this is my self.

Ralph Waldo Emerson
"The American Scholar," 1837

ROCK AND WORK

"LIFE IS A STRUGGLE," Bob Dylan told the poet Allen Ginsberg during a conversation about Dylan's music and films. If "you want to do business and create work, then you struggle; if your struggle shows, then you make it," said the most influential rock musician of the sixties. "It's all about hard work."[1]

Dylan's words revealed an important and easily overlooked aspect of sixties rock-and-roll. Rock was work. Young performers of the time were far better known for their innovative music, wild antics on stage and prodigious sybaritic exploits than for their work ethic or entrepreneurial skills. With good reason. They exposed genitalia during performances (Jim Morrison of the Doors); asked an audience to volunteer who "has the biggest cock" (Grace Slick of Jefferson Airplane); dosed a horse with LSD before rides (Mickey Hart of the Grateful Dead); and appeared for a concert with a wad of cocaine dangling from a nostril (Neil Young).[2]

Less obvious and public was the relentless work ethic of these young musicians. Those who, in Dylan's words, wanted to "create work," "do business" and "make it" in a ruthlessly competitive industry worked obsessively at their craft. Their attitudes toward work and success, more than the political content of their songs or their libertinism, made late sixties rock-and-roll an expression of rebellion.

The North American musicians who composed and performed the most popular and enduring music of the second half of the sixties and early seventies—Dylan, Neil Young, Frank Zappa, Jimi Hendrix, the Band, the Doors, Jefferson Airplane, David Crosby, Steven Stills and the Grateful Dead, among others—approached their work both as artists and as determined, idiosyncratic entrepreneurs. Unlike previous popular entertainers, including earlier rock-and-roll performers, they demanded artistic control over every significant aspect of their labor from record companies. Minimally, this meant control over the music's composition, content, studio production and performance. It might include as well a role in the record's packaging and distribution.

Most of them wanted money and fame. But these artists were equally intent upon achieving personal autonomy through their labor. Sixties rock musicians rebelled against a long-standing division of labor within the popular music business, a fragmented work process typical as well of most blue and white collar work in the twentieth century. As a result, they changed profoundly the way popular music was conceived, produced and perceived. At the height of their creativity and the music's popularity, the most successful of them altered, for a brief time, the economic and power relationships between themselves and the corporations that owned record companies.

Their views about business matters and their audiences were equally unique. It seems odd to think of these counterculture figures and idols as entrepreneurs. But many of them had attitudes toward work and success that would have been more appropriate in a less corporate, pre-twentieth-century world, when many businesses were family owned or run by independent entrepreneurs. Or when artisans made the products they sold and to some degree controlled the pace of their labor. Many rock musicians disliked the rules, impersonality and hierarchy of the modern corporations that employed them. They acted like the independent, intensely competitive entrepreneur who started his own business and conducted it his own way (exactly the sort of young person thought to be extinct in the fifties).

In addition, there was an innovative, experimental quality to the work of rock artists. They experimented with new electronic technologies in the studio and on stage. Many of the most successful, especially those who composed and performed their own music, had little formal training. They were self-taught in their craft. There was a "pull yourself up by your own bootstraps" aura to the success and enormous wealth they achieved.

But their version of the old-style capitalist "ethic" was idiosyncratic, to say the least. In important ways it was out of touch with contemporary business practices. They scoffed at modern research-based marketing, which attempts to determine the preferences of consumers in order to give them want they want. Rock performers offered their wares to the public, and hoped it would buy and be moved by their "product." But they did it on their own terms. The decade's most successful rock musicians showed little concern for what the consumers of their products said they wanted. In effect, they told their audiences to "take it or leave it."

There was another key element in their approach to creating rock-and-roll music. Many of the most notable performers of the decade altered recorded versions of their songs, especially during live performances. At times, the changes were substantial. The reconfiguration of previously recorded material reflected two needs. One was to avoid the modern work-related problems of "burnout" and boredom. The second, shared with others of their generation, was a refusal to be defined or bound by the past, whether as artists or human beings.

Like the Diggers and Students for a Democratic Society, rock musicians rebelled against the dominant values of contemporary America. But they did so primarily through their attitudes toward work, rather than through theatrical explorations of personal freedom like the Diggers or radical politics like SDS. The musicians' demand for autonomy on the job implied more than a revolt against the managerial and hierarchical features of their society. It suggested as well a revulsion against the undemocratic nature of the American way of work. In gaining at least some control over their labor, rock artists compromised the power of the "boss" (derived from the Dutch word for master) to determine who will work for what wages at whose pace. In the process, they created an unprecedented form of white popular music.

This is not the way music critics and fans viewed the music during the sixties. They focused on its content, or the way it affected audiences. Seldom did they think about the music as a product of purposeful work, or as a revolt against alienated labor. Some were convinced the music itself was a form, or at least a fomenter, of rebellion and revolution. This was the view of San Francisco music critic Ralph Gleason, one of the founders of *Rolling Stone* magazine, which was launched in 1967. Gleason said rock music was "the single most potent social force for change" in the United States.[3] The fanatical, violent Weatherman faction of SDS took its name from a line in Bob Dylan's song "Subterranean Homesick Blues" ("You don't need a weatherman to know which way the wind blows").

John Sinclair, a poet, member of the White Panther Party (a white auxiliary of the Black Panthers) and manager of the Detroit rock group MC5, viewed rock-and-roll as a major weapon in the revolutionary struggle against American capitalism. Sinclair claimed the primitive, visceral qualities of the music, as played by "guerilla" bands like MC5, would encourage young people to "run out into the streets and tear everything down." The music was a "total assault upon the culture." It transformed young people into "free mother-country maniacs in charge of our own lives." (MC5 eventually replaced the political activist Sinclair with a manager who said "when you are making records you are making business").[4] The idea of rock-and-roll as a vehicle of political rebellion was captured in a message sent by a group of California radicals to the Rolling Stones during one of the band's West Coast tours:

> Greetings and welcome Rolling Stones, our comrades in the desperate battle against the maniacs who hold power. The revolutionary youth of the world hears your music and is inspired to even more deadly acts. . . . [T]hey try to make us war on our own comrades but the bastards hear us playing you on our little transistor radios and know that they will not escape the blood and fire of the anarchist revolution. We will play your music in rock 'n' roll marching bands as we tear down the jails and free the prisoners, as we tear down the state schools and free the students.[5]

Obviously rock-and-roll music was the backbeat for the youth culture's dances of alienation and ecstasy during the sixties. In the dance halls that sprouted around the country after 1965, young people used their bodies to decipher the Dionysian message implicit in the music. They moved as it moved them. In San Francisco's Fillmore and Avalon halls, Philadelphia's Electric Factory, the Tea Party in Boston, Chicago's Kinetic Playground and hundreds of less famous venues in scores of less populous cities, rock was a medium through which one could let go in public and, in the process, make a political statement of sorts.[6] The legendary Woodstock festival of 1969 remains a monument to that relationship.

It is something else, however, to claim that the music itself was a vehicle for social change. And even more difficult to define with precision what was "radical" about it (beyond the musical innovations of its creators). Rock was probably the most pervasive feature of the youth culture. It drew into its frenzied orbit millions of young people eager to liberate themselves from a society they viewed as repressive. But most fans of the music had little interest in fomenting revolution, at least the political variety. Janis Joplin was more on target about the social implications of rock-and-roll than those quoted earlier when she said, "[M]y music isn't supposed to make you riot. It's supposed to make you fuck." And it is impossible to know how millions of young people listening to compositions by Dylan or Grateful Dead lyricist Robert Hunter interpreted their words. Or whether most even bothered.[7]

If there was anything radical about rock-and-roll it was the attitudes of the musicians toward the production, performance and permanence of their work. In discussing these issues I focus exclusively on the attitudes of North American artists. A comprehensive history of sixties rock (which is not my purpose) cannot be written without describing the pivotal contributions made by British groups like the Beatles, the Rolling Stones, Cream, the Kinks, the Who and others. There were significant similarities between young British musicians and their American counterparts. In terms of the issues raised here, however, there were even more significant differences.[8]

CREATING AND PRODUCING THE MUSIC

The rock-and-roll associated with cultural and political rebellion was made between the mid sixties and the early seventies. The young musicians who created it made dramatic changes in the ways rock music had been produced and performed from its inception in the mid fifties. By contrast with most previous rock-and-roll performers, many musicians from 1965 on composed the music they sang. They might arrange and produce it, play the instruments that brought it to life and perform it "live" (rather than lip-sync songs) in front of audiences. Also unlike their rock-and-roll forebears, they sought control over, or the legal right to be consulted about, most aspects of the technical and business processes through which their music was produced and marketed. Many of them engaged in mammoth struggles with record companies to gain control of these functions, often successfully. Some founded their own record labels to ensure they would have the final word in these areas, as well as a larger share of the profits. To avoid a long-standing industry practice of cheating songwriters on royalties—a painfully common occurrence in the fifties and sixties—musician-owned song publishing companies were established as well.[9]

These performer-initiated changes in the ways and means of the music industry were inseparable from their approach to work. By contrast with rock pioneers like Elvis Presley, Little Richard and Jerry Lee Lewis, they did not think of themselves solely, or even mainly, as entertainers intent upon "making it" in show business. Late-sixties musicians hungered for success, but only if it came on their own terms. That included elevating their function as artists over their role as entertainers. Bob Weir, the rhythm guitarist for the Grateful Dead, said it would be "a stone gas" to make money from their music, but only if the band had the freedom to direct its own musical odyssey. If the "[music] industry wants us," Weir said, "they're gonna take us the way we are" or not at all. Robbie Robertson, the lead guitarist and principal composer for the Band, claimed the group's music was an "intense" and "serious" affair. It was designed "to come right inside your soul and your imagination." The presentation of the music wasn't the occasion for "a party," said Robertson. "It was a joyous experience but we were never going to be smiling at nothing. That was not allowed in this church." As Frank Zappa observed, rock musicians like himself wanted to be viewed first and foremost as artists because their music was "original, composed by the people who perform it, created by them—even if they have to fight the record companies to do it—so that [it] is really a creative action and not a commercial pile of shit thrown together by business people who think they know what John Doe and Mr. Jones really want."[10]

This was a major departure from the public attitudes of rock-and-roll performers of the fifties and early sixties. To be sure, early rock was potentially subversive music. It was a direct descendant of African American rural acoustic blues and urban rhythm and blues. ("The blues had a baby and they named it rock 'n' roll," said the great bluesman Muddy Waters.)[11] Fifties rock-and-roll, steeped in African American music (with elements of white hillbilly music thrown in as well), was marketed to white teenagers. The sexual innuendoes, the aura of defiance toward social norms and the raw emotional voltage of the music sent a very different message to fifties teens than did the standard popular music aimed at white audiences. Some feared its powerful vibrations might penetrate the great wall of prejudice, constructed by white America, that separated the races. It was not surprising, then, that adults in the fifties saw rock-and-roll as an invitation to juvenile delinquency or even a communist plot to subvert the morality of teens.

By the late fifties, however, the hard edge of early rock-and-roll was blunted. For one reason or another (and for varying periods of time), rock-and-roll pioneers such as Chuck Berry, Little Richard, Presley and Jerry Lee Lewis were exiled from the scene.[12] Their sexually provocative, defiant African American–inspired rhythm and blues music was replaced by a bland, white and tame pop rock performed by non-threatening whites such as Frankie Avalon, Fabian, Pat Boone and Lesley Gore. Bowdlerized versions of sexually charged lyrics—a common practice as early as the mid fifties—were the rule in covered versions of songs originally performed by African Americans but later targeted to the white teenage market. (In his effort to sanitize even the non-sexual elements of black music, Pat Boone tried to change the title of Fats Domino's "Ain't That A Shame" to "Isn't That A Shame" in his cover version of the song.) And the intensity that artists like Little Richard and Chuck Berry invested in their performances gave way to vapid presentations that eviscerated the music's passion (compare Little Richard's original version of "Tutti Fruitti" to the covered one by Boone). This pale, suburban, middle-class shadow of the powerful African American and hillbilly-inspired original rock-and-roll dominated the youth music market from about 1957 to the mid-sixties.[13]

But both in its original and tamed forms, the music was largely the product of a complex division of labor. Before 1965 or so, rock-and-roll songs were often composed by nonperformers and brought to the attention of record companies by music publishers. If a company was interested in producing a song, it was placed under the supervision of the company's "Artists and Repertoire" executive, who oversaw its creation. The "A & R man" (these executives were invariably male) selected the performer and the studio musicians, as well as the arranger, the recording engineers and the graphic artists who designed the record sleeve or album cover.[14]

By the late fifties, many rock-and-roll hit songs were formulaic creations of divided labor hatched in New York's Tin Pan Alley. Some Tin Pan Alley publishing companies were small operations run by one or two individuals. They scouted talent or hoped an unknown writer or singer might walk in off the street with a potential hit song. Other companies, like Aldon Music, started in 1958 by Don Kirshner and Al Nevins, employed 15 to 20 writers and created its own songs. Aldon Music was housed in a building across the street from 1619 Broadway, the address of the famous Brill Building, the spiritual heart of Tin Pan Alley. Kirshner said the idea behind Aldon was "to build new writers" whose job was to create songs aimed at the teenage market. His writers were between 19 and 26, young enough to be in touch with the tastes and values of teenagers. The most successful writers on Kirshner's staff earned $150 a week, a modest salary at the time.[15]

The Aldon staff included well-known hit makers like Gerry Goffin, Cynthia Weil, Ellie Greenwich, Barry Mann and Jeff Berry. It also employed Carole King (Goffin's wife) and Neil Sedaka, who subsequently made names for themselves as performers, a rare crossover in those years. Their job was to produce superficial lyrics hung on catchy tunes that captured the longings and angst of "teenagers in love." Gerry Goffin, Carole King and the other Aldon writers put out a string of immensely popular adolescent love songs, including "Will You Love Me Tomorrow," "Today I Met The Boy I'm Going to Marry," "Then He Kissed Me" and "He's Sure the Boy I Love." As Goffin said, the lyrics created by the Aldon group avoided topics that were too complex, "too adult" or "too artistic." Darlene Love, lead singer of the Crystals, for whom the Aldon group composed a string of hits, said the singers called these tunes "bubble gum" songs. The lyrics were "really not even teenage," according to Love, but more appropriate for "10 to 12" year olds.[16]

Many rock-and-roll hit songs from 1958 to 1964 were built on the teen-love themes adopted by Aldon and Tin Pan Alley in New York and Motown Records in Detroit. They were produced and/or distributed by the large record labels like RCA and Decca. The Tin Pan Alley songs in particular were prefabricated products created through a strict division of labor among writers, publishers, engineers, arrangers and performers, all overseen by A & R men. Irwin Pincus, a successful Tin Pan Alley publisher of rock-and-roll songs in the fifties and early sixties, described the process:

> The publisher was the link, the available ear, the conduit for the majors [large record companies] and the material, the one who would listen to anyone off the street and through whatever contacts he had, try to get a song made, without necessarily knowing who was going to be singing. The labels picked songs from demos, matched them with artists, decided who should arrange it, how it should be packaged, when it should be released. Artists weren't writing much in those days, and for the most part writers weren't performers.[17]

There were notable exceptions to the division of labor between composer and performer. Chuck Berry, Ben E. King of the Drifters and Motown's Stevie Wonder wrote and performed their music, though the bulk of the publishing royalties went to their managers and record companies. For the most part, however, the two functions were separated. "I quickly learned," said Aldon writer Jeff Berry, "that once you were a songwriter, it was almost impossible to jump out in front, on stage, and be a performer. There were performers who did that, only that, and it was your job as a writer to supply them [with material]."[18]

After 1965 the creation and production of rock music changed dramatically. To some extent this was a result of the different attitudes toward show business held by pre- and post-1965 rock performers. Those from the late fifties and early sixties were frequently products of what can be termed "managed" success. They were "discovered" by managers, A & R men, publishers or other denizens of the recording industry who were attracted by the performers' talent, mannerisms, stage presence or looks.

These performers were carefully groomed for success and usually did what they were told by managers, promoters, record companies and even disc jockeys. (Even the most independent of them fell in line. In order to get his first hit, "Maybelline," played on the radio, Chuck Berry had to share publishing credits and royalties with powerful disc jockey Alan Freed, whom he had never met.) Most early rockers wanted to "make it" in show business. For example, from the beginning of his career Elvis Presley said his goal was to be the next Dean Martin. In other words, and by contrast with his defiant, sexually volatile original stage persona, Presley's ultimate goal was to become a carefully packaged singer of pop tunes. Managers frequently made artistic as well as business decisions for performers, and record-company public relations departments created an appropriate "image" designed to market them to the widest possible audience.[19]

Most of the successful rock performers of the late sixties were not interested in making it in terms defined by the maxims of traditional show business. Nor had they cut their musical teeth as public performers on fifties and early sixties rock-and-roll. Many had been drawn to rock-and-roll as teenagers by the musical passion and the charisma of Buddy Holly, Little Richard, Jerry Lee Lewis, Chuck Berry and the early Presley. Those encounters were stored in their musical memory banks and would be drawn on after 1964. But some of the most famous performers of the second half of the decade played folk, blues, jazz or bluegrass music in the early sixties. Among others, these included Bob Dylan, David Crosby, Neil Young, Steven Stills, Marty Balin and Paul Kantner of Jefferson Airplane, Joe McDonald, Roger McGuinn of the Byrds, Jerry Garcia and Phil Lesh of the Grateful Dead and John Sebastian of Lovin' Spoonful. Although attracted to rock-and-roll as teenagers, they disdained the vacuous lyrics and teen-love themes of late fifties and early sixties pop rock.

Most of these young performers were drawn back to rock-and-roll by 1965 because of the Beatles' innovative electronic guitar work and immense popularity. But their approach to composing lyrics was influenced by Bob Dylan, who pursued themes in his writing that went beyond the teen-love tales composed by most rock acts at the time, including the Beatles. Given their different musical pedigrees, these budding rock stars retained their suspicious attitudes toward the shallowness of the popular music audience, the pieties of traditional show business and the bottom-line orientation of large record companies.[20]

Frank Zappa

An idiosyncratic individualism and insistence on artistic autonomy informed rock musicians' views of show business and record companies. After Frank Zappa signed with his first label, MGM, he constantly fought with executives over budgets for studio time, censorship, musical taste and artistic control. Zappa, whose father was a metallurgist and teacher, had eclectic musical tastes and roamed in a variety of genres. He first achieved fame by writing and performing commercially successful electric-guitar-driven music. His lyrics conveyed caustic, iconoclastic humor in songs like "Don't Eat the Yellow Snow," "My Guitar Wants to Kill Your Mama" and "Titties and Beer." Zappa also composed symphonic music performed by major European philharmonic companies, including the London Symphony Orchestra and the Residentie Orchestra of the Hague. He experimented with electronic technology in search of new sounds. In his 1969 album, *Trout Mask Replica,* Zappa tried to create a primitive, pristine sound, evocative of an "anthropological field recording." Instead of recording in the studio, he wired an eight-channel mixer in his house and placed instruments in different rooms. Drums were placed in the bedroom and a bass clarinet was played in the kitchen, while vocals were recorded in the bathroom.[21]

Whatever musical genre or technique he explored, MGM executives wanted Zappa to produce commercially viable albums as cheaply as possible. To hold down the cost of producing his records, they wanted Zappa in and out of the studio as quickly as feasible. "If the master doesn't sound right," he declared, "what the fuck do they care? It goes out anyway—it's only a 'product' to them."[22] With his characteristic sarcasm (and insight) Zappa summarized the tastes of most record company executives and fans:

> They say: "Gimme the tune. Do I like this tune? Does it sound like another tune that I like? The more familiar it is, the better I like it. Hear those three notes there? Those are the three notes I can sing along with. I like those notes very, very much. Give me a beat. Not a fancy one. Give me a Good Beat—something I can dance to. It has to go boom-rap, boom-boom-rap. If it doesn't, I will hate it very, very much. Also, I want it right away—and then, write me some songs like that—over and over again, because I'm really into music."[23]

Zappa's problems with MGM included censorship as well as disagreements over studio time and aesthetic issues. Prior to releasing Zappa's album *We're Only in it for the Money* in 1968, the company's executives excised some of his lyrics without informing him. For example, as Zappa noted in his autobiography, three lines were cut from the song "Let's Make the Water Turn Black":

And I still remember Mama,
With her apron and her pad.
Feeding all the boys at Ed's Cafe.

Zappa eventually discovered the reason MGM omitted these lines:

> I couldn't understand why anyone would chop that out. Years later I learned that an MGM executive was convinced that the word "pad" referred to a sanitary napkin. He became obsessed with the idea that a waitress somewhere was feeding sanitary napkins to people in a restaurant, and demanded (in violation of our contract) that it be removed.[24]

Such incidents happened routinely, and not only to Zappa. He eventually left MGM and founded his own record label, Bizarre, Inc., as a means of gaining complete artistic control over his music. A number of performers did the same, including Jefferson Airplane and the Grateful Dead.[25]

Neil Young

Rock artists saw their compositions and their lives as Whitmanesque songs of the self. They sculpted music according to their idiosyncratic visions. They did so even when it threatened the commercial prospects of their records. In describing his artistic muse, Dylan said, "I'm part of me, the me that's inside me, not part of society in any way." When Jimi Hendrix looked for artistic inspiration, he turned inward as well. "One of the worst statements people are making is 'no man is an island,'" he said. "Every man is an island."[26]

No musician was more intransigent in this regard than Neil Young. Young was born in Toronto, Canada, in 1945. His father was a writer. His mother was a television celebrity and the daughter of American-born parents. Young came to the United States in his late teens to pursue a career in rock-and-roll. He remained in America because it was where "I felt most at home."[27]

During an extraordinary career spanning parts of four decades and a series of musical incarnations, Young forged an idiosyncratic stardom and public persona. He drove to his early "gigs" in a 1948 Buick hearse. He "loved the hearse," he said, because his band "could be getting high in the front and back and nobody would be able to see in because of the curtains." And the coffin tray "was dynamite." He liked to draw startled looks from people as he drove the hearse to a concert and pulled out the coffin tray holding his guitars and other equipment.[28]

Young's sense of humor was more than matched by the extraordinary talent and unstinting passion he brought to his craft. During some concerts in the sixties, especially after performing his signature frenzied electric-guitar solos, Young would experience grand mal seizures. "Rock and roll," he observed, "is reckless abandon." To "really feel" the music "you have to burn as brightly as you can until you turn it off altogether." Before it "kill[s] me."[29]

In the sixties and early seventies, Young performed solo, as well as with Buffalo Springfield, Crosby, Stills and Nash, and his own band Crazy Horse. During those years he looked and behaved like the quintessential hippie. (Young still sported long hair and wore "grunge" clothing into the 1990s.) His 1970 song "Ohio" was a stirring rock-and-roll indictment of President Richard Nixon, whom Young held ultimately responsible for the killing of four students at Kent State University in May of that year. Yet, because he shared Ronald Reagan's commitments to "rugged individualism" and a strong national defense, Young endorsed him for president in 1980 and 1984. In 1988 he veered in the opposite direction by supporting the left-liberal presidential candidacy of Jesse Jackson. A determined follower of his own muse, Young saw no contradictions in these chaotic meanderings back and forth across the political spectrum.[30]

The same idiosyncratic individualism informed his musical career. From the beginning, Young wanted "lots of money and fame," and was intelligent and shrewd in business matters. Yet he never compromised himself as an artist. His records were, in fact, "records," vinyl documentaries which presented who he was and what he felt during a given moment of reflection and creativity. "Every one of my records to me is like an ongoing autobiography."[31] And if a life is lived reflectively and its course subject to changing interpretations, then the demands of record companies and audiences that the artist endlessly recreate successful musical formats, or that he play over and again the same hit song in the same way, were unpalatable. "There are artists," conceded Young, "who can. They put out three or four albums every year and everything fucking sounds the same. . . . That isn't my trip. My trip is to express what's on my mind." Young had the same attitude toward his musical collaborators. During his days with Buffalo Springfield and Crosby, Stills and Nash, Young engaged in epic ego battles over artistic issues, especially with Steven Stills. He always went his own way. His music, he said, "is my fucking trip and I don't have to listen to anybody else's."[32]

What was on Young's mind or where his "trip" might take his music at a given moment were not necessarily what record company executives wanted to market or audiences wished to purchase. Like most other rock musicians of the sixties, Young craved fame and wealth, yet was afraid commercial success would stifle his freedom to explore new, less commercially viable musical territory. Young dealt with this by following his commercially successful records with albums that took risks musically and topically. In the 1980s, billionaire record and movie mogul David Geffen sued Young, who was under contract to Geffen's eponymous label. Geffen claimed the singer deliberately made albums he knew lacked commercial appeal. The suit, according to Young, proved the company "saw me as a product. . . . They didn't see me as an artist." Young continued to play his own song. The "more they tried to stop me the more I did it. Just to let them know that no one's gonna tell me what to do."[33]

This implacable individualism and desire for artistic autonomy were common among rock musicians of the late sixties. Such traits fed into a reflexive egalitarianism that affected the dynamics and longevity of rock groups as well as their relationships with record companies. Most of the successful rock-and-roll acts of the sixties were groups. Fans, record companies and occasionally individual artists viewed the most popular performer as the group's "leader." But a persistent, disruptive egalitarianism set the tone for most successful groups. Each member of the Grateful Dead, Crosby, Stills, Nash and Young, Jefferson Airplane and Big Brother and the Holding Company had an equal voice in musical and business decision making. Charismatic, determined individuals in a band and alliances among key members of groups often compromised this ostensible equality. Heated disagreements over artistic and personal issues were common. But so was their instinctive egalitarianism. On the surface at least, each member had an equal say on which songs to perform during a concert, whether to hire or fire a manager, when to move to a new label, or where and when to go on tour.

"There's no 'I am the cat and you aren't,'" said guitarist Marty Balin, who organized Jefferson Airplane in 1965. "Everybody's a cat" in the group. Even though Jim Morrison's singing, composing and sexually explosive charisma on stage were the main reasons for the enormous popularity of the Doors in the late sixties, the group tried to arrive at artistic and business decisions through consensus. When Crosby, Stills and Nash began performing in public in 1969, each member staked a claim to artistic autonomy. The group's name was a conscious tribute to the artistic autonomy of the individual musicians. Instead of being called "the Spiders, or something," declared Steven Stills, the group's name implied each performer could "do what [he] wanted" in order to remain innovative and "open to new influences." "The idea," said David Crosby, the son of a Hollywood cinematographer and descendent of a signer of the Declaration of Independence, "was that we were equals in this band [and] that no one was the leader" and each performer "could try almost anything," including working with other groups or occasionally going out on his own.[34]

When Neil Young was asked to join the group for its second album he let the band know where he stood. "Before I joined Crosby, Stills and Nash," he said in 1969, "I made it clear that I belong to myself." Young wanted the income generated by his collaboration with that enormously successful band, but he was hesitant to form a permanent association with Crosby, Stills and Nash because he thought his less commercial group, Crazy Horse, was more likely to make music "people will listen to for a long time."[35]

The Grateful Dead

The unremitting individualism of rock performers was given meaning and direction by their willingness to work hard, become schooled in their craft and develop a unique approach to "selling" themselves to the public. As much as any rock-and-roll act of the time, the San Francisco band the Grateful Dead embodied this autonomy, work ethic and entrepreneurial attitude.

The band's first incarnation was in 1963-1964 as Mother McCree's Uptown Jug Band. The band performed folk songs but specialized in the bluegrass music made famous in Nashville by artists like Bill Monroe and the Carter Family. The main creative force within the band was lead guitarist Jerry Garcia. Garcia was born in 1942 and named for the Broadway composer Jerome Kern. Kern was the idol of Garcia's father, an immigrant from Spain, who was a jazz clarinetist and leader of a Dixieland band in the 1930s. In addition to Garcia, Mother McCree's included two other future members of the Grateful Dead: rhythm guitarist Bob Weir, who was raised in an affluent family in Palo Alto, and Ron "Pigpen" McKernan, a vocalist, piano player and high school dropout. McKernan's father, known as "Cool Breeze," was a disc jockey who specialized in blues music for a Berkeley radio station.[36]

In 1965 McKernan urged the band to incorporate electric guitars into its act, thereby adding rhythm and blues and rock-and-roll to its repertoire. The band's name was changed to the Warlocks to signal its new direction. The Warlocks recruited a drummer, Bill Kreutzmann, a music teacher whose mother taught at Stanford. They also added bass guitar player Phil Lesh, who was trained in classical music and jazz. When they discovered that another rock band also called themselves the Warlocks, the band searched for a new name. Toward the end of 1965, while "stoned" on the hallucinogen DMT at Lesh's home, Garcia opened an Oxford dictionary and "the first thing I saw" were the words "the grateful dead."[37]

For the next 30 years, until Garcia's death in 1995, the Grateful Dead's music, lifestyle and values made it synonymous with the sixties counterculture. The band was there from the beginning. They lived in the Haight-Ashbury during its halcyon days in 1966 and 1967. The band, along with their women companions, friends, drug connections, managers, pets and anyone who happened to drop by, lived communally in a Victorian house at 710 Ashbury Street. Members of the Grateful Dead shared counterculture views about work and capitalism. They believed most salaried employment was a pointless grind. By definition, capitalists were social parasites.[38]

The Grateful Dead helped forge the chain that linked sex, drugs and rock-and-roll during the counterculture's emergence in San Francisco. The band's bent for improvisation and electronically driven experiments with "feedback" brought the sound of "acid rock" to the "stoned," sexually charged atmosphere of the Fillmore and Avalon ballrooms in the mid sixties. The Grateful Dead was the house band for Ken Kesey's acid tests in 1965, performed at the orgiastic Trips Festival in 1966 and entertained the "Gathering of the Tribes" during the first "Human Be-In" in 1967. They did many free concerts in the streets and parks of San Francisco, believing they had a civic responsibility to do so.[39]

In June 1967 they were invited to perform at the Monterey Pop Festival. This event brought national attention and eventually substantial financial rewards to some of the bands who created the "San Francisco Sound." The Grateful Dead told the festival's promoters that the three-day concert should be free to the public. Or, if not, that the proceeds should be given to the Diggers. Neither happened. During 1966 and 1967, the band occasionally gathered late in the afternoon at the Panhandle in Golden Gate Park. While the Diggers parcelled out food to scores of hungry people, the Grateful Dead entertained the crowd. Of course, they played "for free."[40]

The ultimate counterculture band, the group's early performances were often sloppy, usually undisciplined and frequently unprofessional. Like most of those who attended their shows at the Fillmore and Avalon, the band routinely performed while stoned on one or another hallucinogenic drug, often taken in combination with marihuana. Some of their concerts veered between the incomprehensible and the chaotic, though few in the audience were in a condition to notice. Each member of the band might follow the anarchic musical path cut by his evening's choice of drugs. McKernan was the only member of the Grateful Dead who avoided psychedelic drugs. He was an alcoholic. His prodigious alcoholic binges (McKernan died at 29 from complications linked to cirrhosis of the liver in 1973) frequently forced him to miss rehearsals and seriously hampered his performances.[41]

The band's antipathy toward capitalism and the perpetual psychedelic drug haze in which its members dwelled made them the bane of record company executives and producers. In 1967 Joseph Smith, the Warner Brothers executive who signed them to the label, sent an angry letter to the band's manager. Smith, who liked the band's members personally, politely and accurately accused the group of an "inability to take care of business." He was disturbed by their desultory, "unprofessional" conduct during recording sessions, which escalated studio costs. This was especially worrisome because their early albums were not commercially successful. In response, a member of the band scrawled "Fuck You" across the letter.[42] Garcia's view of the band captured what Smith found so irksome about their approach to "business." The Grateful Dead "is an anarchy," he said. "That's what it is. . . . It doesn't have any goals. It doesn't have any plans. It doesn't have any leaders. Or real organization. And it works. . . . It doesn't work too good. It doesn't work like General Motors does, but it works okay. And it's more fun."[43]

Despite their anarchic, often self-destructive behavior both on- and offstage, members of the Grateful Dead somehow managed to invest enormous energy in honing their craft. By 1967 or so, the band learned to balance an eccentric lifestyle with a fierce work ethic. From the mid to late sixties, as the band searched for its musical voice and its members learned how to play together, they often practiced eight or more hours a day. They might do so even when booked to perform in the evenings. Garcia was obsessed with honing his guitar work in various musical genres. In addition to rock and blues, he studied bluegrass, country, jazz and even the big-band "standards" played by his late father in the 1930s and 1940s. He practiced incessantly and performed endlessly. In the late sixties Garcia joined another band, the New Riders of the Purple Sage, which played bluegrass and country music. A Grateful Dead concert might begin at 8 P.M. with Garcia and the band playing an acoustic set, followed by the Purple Sage (with Garcia on the pedal steel guitar) performing bluegrass for an hour or so. Finally, it ended, sometimes after 2 A.M., with an electric-rock performance by Garcia and the Grateful Dead.[44]

In addition to their sedulous if erratic work habits, the Grateful Dead experimented with new musical formats and studio technologies. Mickey Hart was a second drummer recruited to the band in 1967. Hart added a new dimension to its sound by incorporating an 11-count measure to his drumming. He learned this technique while studying with a handdrummer from India. It was the first use of this time signature in rock-and-roll, and it became an important part of the band's emerging style. In an attempt to capture on records the authenticity, complexity and spontaneity of their live performances, the band pioneered new recording techniques in the studio. They recorded live shows on two machines with different tape widths running at different speeds. It took them hundreds of tape "edits" and scores of hours in the studio to get the recorded sound they wanted. In 1969 the Grateful Dead was the first rock-and-roll band to use 16 track recorders in the studio.[45]

By 1966 the popularity of San Francisco bands who played at the Fillmore, Avalon and other dance halls in the city caught the attention of major record companies. Along with other companies, Columbia, RCA and Warner Brothers sent "talent scouts" to the city, hoping to sign bands to their labels who played the guitar-layered, improvisational music of the San Francisco Sound.

The Grateful Dead had no aversion to money or fame, but were deeply suspicious of major record companies. Like Frank Zappa and Neil Young, they understood that money rather than good music invariably fueled the interest of major corporations who had record divisions. Nor did the band feel comfortable with the traditional show business values of the popular music business. They were not interested in making formulaic "hit" music aimed at a nebulous mass market. They would play their music their way, in venues that were as intimate as possible, to audiences who shared their social as well as musical values. If that meant teasing a comparatively meager living from their work, so be it. "We want people to hear us," said their manager Rock Scully, but "we won't do what the system says—make single hits, take big [impersonal] gigs, do the success number. . . . We won't make bad music for bread."[46]

The band rejected overtures from record companies who refused to give them total control over the content and production of their music, or the titles and graphic designs of their albums. They finally signed with Warner Brothers in 1966, but only after the company reluctantly consented to their unprecedented demands. In addition to having absolute artistic control over their music, the Grateful Dead was given unlimited studio time to make their records. Also, they negotiated a new approach to royalty rates. The norm within the industry was to tag royalties to the number of songs featured on an album. This gave artists an incentive to fill their albums with short songs, which would fit the "Top Forty" format of AM radio stations. From the inception of rock-and-roll, songs became "hits" by being played over and again on commercial AM radio. Hence the prevalence of songs that lasted from two to three minutes during the first decade of rock-and-roll.

The Grateful Dead had no interest in this formula. Like songs composed by Dylan and Young, theirs went on for as long as it took to get their musical message across. That could mean songs that lasted 5, 10, 20, even 30 minutes. They insisted, therefore, that their royalty rate be tied to the amount of time per album side rather than the number of songs. Warner's consented to their demands. In another historically unusual arrangement, the band also retained complete publishing rights to its compositions.[47]

Only one of their demands was rejected. They insisted that Warner executive Joseph Smith "drop" LSD with the band. How else, they asked, could Smith understand their music or social values? Though Smith declined their invitation, Garcia was satisfied with the contract. "Because we held out," he said, "because we thought we were worth something, now we can do anything we want."[48]

Over the next few years, the Grateful Dead's ideas about having the right to "do anything we want" expanded well beyond artistic freedom. They became entrepreneurs, albeit of the countercultural variety. By the early seventies, the band led an organization with over 50 employees. To keep ticket prices to their shows affordable, the Grateful Dead's organization arranged its own tours, eliminating the independent and expensive promoters who scheduled dates, advertised concerts, made travel arrangements, accounted for ticket sales and shipped equipment. Also, the Dead wanted to break Bill Graham's hold on the concert business in San Francisco, and thereby reduce the cost of tickets. In partnership with the Jefferson Airplane, they leased the Carousel Ballroom in the city's downtown area and produced their own shows. In addition, the band organized a travel agency for rock groups, called Fly By Night.[49]

In 1973, after the expiration of their contract with Warner Brothers, the Grateful Dead Record Company was founded. The band made all voting members of their "family" co-owners of the corporation, including secretaries and the people who set up their equipment before concerts. Their hope was to provide fans with records made of higher quality material and to reduce their cost by eliminating distributors and major record outlets. Grateful Dead records could be bought directly from the company by mail order, or purchased in nontraditional venues like "head shops" (one member of the organization suggested selling them from Good Humor Ice Cream trucks). The band announced its plan in a letter to fans on September 4, 1973:

> We've decided to produce, manufacture, and distribute our records ourselves. . . . The [new] album will be made from the highest quality vinyl available, which has the best technical properties. In addition, it will be heavier (weigh more, that is) than most albums available in this country. It will be handled locally through independent record distributors and should be available everywhere.
>
> This adventure is a jumping-off point to get us in a position of greater contact with our [fans], [and] to put us more in command of our own ship.[50]

ROCK AND COMMERCE

The Grateful Dead and their business associates were never confused with captains of industry. Every one of their business ventures, from Grateful Dead Records to the Carousel Ballroom, were unqualified failures.[51] Nor were the Grateful Dead and other sixties rock performers so adept in business matters that they avoided being shortchanged by managers, promoters or record companies. (Lackluster sales of their early albums left the Dead deeply in debt to Warner's for expenses incurred in production and promotion.) The success or failure of their entrepreneurial gambits, however, were less important than the motivations that inspired them. Making money was, of course, one of them. But not the only or necessarily primary one. More than anything else, their goal was to get "command of our own ship," as the Grateful Dead told their fans. The major rock acts of the late sixties wanted autonomy in their art and their lives, which for most of them amounted to the same thing.

During the mid to late sixties, two unusual and unprecedented circumstances within the music industry allowed some musicians to achieve both. One was the transformation of popular music fashioned by the young composer-performers of the new rock-and-roll. The other was the pervasive confusion among executives of record companies, who did not know what to make of the new music, how to market it, or to whom.

On the first issue, the young artists were willing to take risks by plunging into uncharted musical territory. Much of the rock-and-roll created from 1965 through the early 1970s was new, experimental music. As noted earlier, the musicians delved into electronic technology as a way of exploring uncharted musical waters. In the studio, on stage and even in their homes, young artists experimented with feedback, distortion and multiple-track recorders. They took chances by improvising during performances and in recording sessions. Instruments and sounds from other musical genres and cultures were incorporated into their version of rock-and-roll.

Equally important, after 1965 rock lyricists breached the traditional topical boundaries of popular music aimed at white audiences. Most American popular music, including the pop rock of the early sixties, deliberately dodged controversial issues. Its lyrics dealt for the most part with romance, requited or otherwise. It might flirt with sexual titillation, but often sang the praises of chastity before marriage and of monogamy ever after.

From the mid sixties on, rock lyricists rudely stormed and breached the walls of permissible musical topics. However frenzied the rhythm or fervid the beat of their music, in their lyrics young composers explored the vagaries of personal experience. They wrote about sexuality discovered, desire spent, trust betrayed, hopes demolished and friendships wrecked by pettiness. The music sometimes dealt with public issues as well, such as an American government that lied, spied on its citizens and recklessly plunged the country into a pointless, grotesque war in Vietnam.

The composers of this music were remarkably confident young people. Bob Dylan consciously pushed his music and performances to a point where "nothing is predictable and you're always out on the edge." He wanted to go, he said, where "anything can happen." His goal wasn't to give audiences what they wanted, but to give them himself through his music. Record companies could take it or leave it. "I can't say if being 'non-commercial' is a put down or a compliment," Dylan declared. His audience could take it or leave it as well. "If anyone has any imagination," he said in 1965, "he'll know what I'm doing. If they don't understand my songs, they'll be missing something."[52]

Jerry Garcia welcomed the opportunity to fail. For him, making music was a perilous adventure in self-exploration and creative communication. Failure and unpredictability made his music and his life more interesting. Rather than feeling threatened by failure, Garcia welcomed adventure and uncertainty. He preferred the improvisation, spontaneity and danger of live performances to working in the studio. A well-crafted studio record sounded too polished and perfect, too safe and secure. "The aesthetics of making good studio albums is that you don't make any mistakes. And when you make a record that doesn't have any mistakes on it, it sounds fucking boring." Neil Young felt the same way about the "factory assembly-line" sound of studio recordings. "I consider it a form of suicide to make polished records."[53]

Besides the attitudes of the performers, the other unique circumstance within the industry was rampant confusion among record company executives when confronted with the new music. Neither the music, the artists who made it nor the audiences who purchased the records fit industry paradigms about the nature of popular entertainment or rock-and-roll's traditional market niche. Since rock-and-roll's inception in the mid fifties, the attitude of executives of major record labels toward the music was "it smells but it sells," as they commonly put it.[54] Their disdain for rock-and-roll was so profound that Capitol Records initially refused to release the Beatles early recordings. Though most upper-echelon executives disliked the music, they tolerated it for economic reasons. By 1964, when the Beatles struck gold in America, rock-and-roll records accounted for over 50 percent of the industry's half-billion dollars in annual sales.[55]

The new, post-1965 rock radically changed this situation. The music created by Dylan, the San Francisco groups and, eventually, the Beatles and Rolling Stones incorporated themes that transcended teen love. For the first time in the history of rock-and-roll, the music attracted a sophisticated audience, including huge numbers of college students, thoughtful teenagers and even some adults. Because of this, the music was not only more difficult to market, but its format could change radically from one album to another as young musicians experimented with new ideas and technologies. Joseph Smith, of Warner Brothers, said of the Grateful Dead, "I don't think Jack Warner will ever understand this [music]. I don't know if I understand it myself, but I really feel like they're good."[56]

Whether or not they understood the music, executives at Warner's and other major and independent labels had little difficulty comprehending the new bottom line forged by its popularity. In 1968 sales of records reached the one billion dollar mark for the first time, and rock-and-roll accounted for over 80 percent of the market.[57] Confusion within executive suites about the music and how to market it, along with its unprecedented sales potential, opened the door for young artists to attain almost total control over the production and other aspects of their work.

Executives who worked for major labels, like Smith or Mo Ostin (who headed Warner's Reprise division), grasped the economic implications of this situation. Like executives from smaller independent record companies, such as Atlantic and Electra, Ostin and Smith came to the conclusion that the way to profit from the sales potential of the new rock-and-roll was to give its creators the artistic freedom they wanted. It didn't take Smith long to realize that the Grateful Dead and the other San Francisco groups he dealt with viewed their music as more than entertainment. They saw it as a medium for self-expression and personal authenticity. "These people," Smith said of the San Francisco bands, "were using all the technology. They were very demanding about how they were positioned, packaged, and sold. They wrote these songs, and the records meant a lot more to them than Dean Martin's ever meant to him."[58]

More than any other record company executive, Mo Ostin profited from this insight. Ostin came to Warner Brothers in the early sixties when the company purchased Reprise Records, which was owned in part by Frank Sinatra, for whom Ostin worked. Before the merger, Reprise's album roster specialized in mainstream entertainment. Its prominent singers included Sinatra, Sammy Davis, Jr., and Dean Martin. It steered clear of rock-and-roll, which Sinatra despised.[59]

After Reprise was sold to Warner's, Ostin aggressively pursued the new rock acts. He lured some of the decade's most creative and idiosyncratic musicians to Reprise. Among others, he signed Young, Zappa, Jimi Hendrix and the Fugs. From Ostin's point of view, it was irrelevant whether or not he liked or understood their music. Signing these performers to Reprise, he said, was "purely pragmatic business." It "will lead to the money." And he knew the surest way to make money from these acts was to give the artists what they wanted, control of their labor. As Ostin said of Neil Young:

> [he was] totally his own person. Completely unpredictable. . . . Always willing to take risks, always willing to do something that would be viewed as maybe even dangerous. Never following trends. . . . And to try to force him to go in a particular direction to follow his last record that was successful would have in some ways destroyed him. . . . You have to encourage the artists to do whatever they think is right.[60]

It was a marriage of convenience between cultural outlaws and capitalists. On one side were autonomous artists intent upon making music viewed by some as "dangerous" to the status quo. On the other were businessmen who saw a chance to profit from it. Ostin held up his end of the deal. Ed Sanders of the Fugs said of Ostin that "no matter how chaotic our vision was, he let us pursue it and lay down our brains on tape as we saw fit."[61] And as the rock music critic and historian Fred Goodman observed, Warner Brothers eventually became the country's biggest media conglomerate because of the extraordinary profits it made in the sixties and seventies from "the seemingly antithetical [music of the] counterculture."[62]

The merger between rock and commerce was complete by the end of the decade. Some viewed it as the end of the music's capacity to challenge the political, social and sexual status quo. In 1969 the music critic Michael Lydon wrote an article called "Money: Rock For Sale." Lydon argued that commercial success undermined rock-and-roll's potential as a medium for social criticism and rebellion. What began in the mid sixties as an avant-garde burst of freedom in the music of Dylan and the San Francisco Sound ended in the late sixties as a vehicle for corporate profit. In Lydon's view, even if their contracts gave rock stars absolute artistic freedom, it would not prevent their music and talent from being be co-opted by the gigantic corporations for whom they worked:

> For all its liberating potential, rock is doomed to a bitter impotence by its ultimate subservience to those whom it attacks. . . . Rather than being liberated heroes, rock and roll stars are captives on a leash, and their plight is but a metaphor for that of all young people and black people in America. . . . [Rock stars] lost the battle for real freedom at the very moment they signed their contracts (whatever the clauses) and entered the big-time commercial sphere.[63]

More recently, Fred Goodman and Marc Eliot made much the same point.[64] Perhaps, as these critics contend, a contradiction did exist between the music's "liberating potential" (however defined) and its status as a capitalist product. Maybe what Goodman called the "authenticity" and artistic integrity of sixties rock was undermined by its emergence as a big business.[65]

But the young musicians who created the foundations for the new rock-and-roll in 1965 and 1966 were entrepreneurs to begin with. They wanted to make both art and money through their music. Al Kooper, who performed with Dylan, the Blues Project and Blood, Sweat and Tears in the sixties, made this clear in his autobiography. He made music that exploded with "energy and volume." And, as Kooper gleefully noted, in the sixties "E plus V = $$$."[66]

This entrepreneurial posture was prominent even among the San Francisco bands, who were notorious for their disdain of capitalism and the country's commercial values. They did not think of their work—building rock bands, composing songs and performing for money—as a capitalist venture. And it wasn't, at least not in the large-scale, hierarchical, "organization man" style of modern corporate capitalism. But it did parallel in important respects the small business orientation of the independent artisan-entrepreneur.

For example, in the summer of 1965 Marty Balin set out to create a band. Within a year the band he forged, Jefferson Airplane, became the first San Francisco act signed by a major record label, RCA. Balin's group was an instant commercial success. He later admitted, however, that from the beginning, "I didn't know shit about a band! I just knew I wanted to sing."[67] Balin had some experience in show business, but none in developing an economically viable rock-and-roll act. And even if he put one together, there was no place to perform rock-and-roll in San Francisco; the Fillmore and Avalon dance halls did not then exist.

The way Balin created the band was remarkably ad hoc and intuitive. By contemporary standards it was a primitive entrepreneurial gambit. Sitting in a folk music club one day, Balin saw Paul Kantner walk in carrying a 12-string acoustic guitar. He didn't know Kantner. "I never heard him play and I just went up to him and I says, 'You wanna start something,' you know? He thought I was nuts. I just said, 'Play with me.'" The nascent band needed a drummer, and Balin met Skip Spence, who played guitar. "You'd be a great drummer," he told Spence, "I can tell." Spence said he didn't know how to play the drums. "Play [the drums] for a week," responded Balin. "If you can play in a week, you can play in our group."

With the core of a group in place, Balin still needed a venue where a rock-and-roll band could perform. Short on money, he convinced some acquaintances to purchase a pizza parlor on Fillmore Street and turn it into a music club, which he called the Matrix. In exchange for their $12,000 investment, plus $1,300 to purchase instruments and equipment for the band, Balin committed his new group to perform gratis at the club at least a hundred times over a seven-year period.[68]

Balin's experience in organizing Jefferson Airplane was not atypical of the way rock groups were developed in the sixties.[69] They launched careers on their own, usually without the guidance of experienced managers, at least in the beginning. A combination of hard work, talent, perseverance and luck allowed some of these self-taught musicians to become self-made millionaires. They garnered millions of dollars for themselves, and many millions more for record companies, promoters and managers. Whether or not their financial success compromised their art, the redoubtable entrepreneurial quality they exhibited and the "rags to riches" nature of their enterprise was a modern replay of an old American myth.

In the process, they implicitly rebelled against the fragmentation of the modern work process. Spencer Dryden, a drummer with Jefferson Airplane, resented the division of labor in the music industry and American society in general. "Everything is like being cut down, cut down, cut down. Chopped into little pieces and machine run." The assembly-line quality of work and life made Americans "all think" and behave "alike."[70]

John Fogarty, the lead singer and principle composer for Creedence Clearwater Revival, was first attracted to rock-and-roll by the intensity with which Elvis Presley performed in the early stages of his career. But even as a teenager Fogarty had "a greater affinity" for Carl Perkins, a Presley contemporary and fellow southerner who wrote and first performed the fifties rock-and-roll classic "Blue Suede Shoes." Perkins lacked Presley's looks and charisma, and was only marginally successful by comparison, but he wrote and performed his own songs. The inspiration for the song was linked to the nuances of performance. The singer-songwriter controlled both. The undivided quality of Perkin's work, said Fogarty, "went right to the middle of my musical soul."[71]

More than any other rock musician, Bob Dylan paved the way in the early sixties for those who wanted to compose and perform their work, as well as supervise its production. "Tin Pan Alley! I know that scene," said Dylan of the mecca of divided musical labor. "Tin Pan Alley's gone now." And with small exaggeration he added, "I put an end to it. People can record their own songs now," and exercise control over what they created.[72]

There was an ironic quality to the creation and production of post-1965 rock-and-roll. But it had little to do with the transformation of "art" rock into an article of commerce. From the beginning, and by definition, it was a commercial product. Rather, the irony of rock resided in the incongruity between the entrepreneurial bent of the young musicians and the radical implications of their rebellion against the music industry's division of labor.

Despite their political values which, if they had any, could vaguely be categorized as antiestablishment, most rock artists did not inject overtly political themes into their music. Relatively little of the music composed by the Grateful Dead, the Band, Zappa, Young, Hendrix or Dylan, in his post-folk musical incarnation, contained explicit political "messages." In his autobiography, Levon Helm of the Band said, with some exaggeration, "none of us ever thought to write a song about all the shit that was going on back then: war, revolution, civil war, turmoil."[73]

This was not universally true. Joe McDonald and Barry Melton were red diaper babies (children of members of the Community Party of the United States). Their Berkeley-based band was called Country Joe and the Fish in reference to Mao Tse-tung's exhortation that a revolutionary should swim among the people "as a fish." A more characteristic reflection of the political and artistic values of late sixties rock musicians was made by Bob Dylan. "I'm part of no movement," he declared. "I do a lot of things no movement would allow."[74]

It was their implacable individualism, not their political views, that inspired rock artists to reject their industry's division of labor. The need to experience their work as a "whole" rather than a fragmented process, and as a seamless product of creative labor instead of an assembly-line commodity, contrasted with the specialization, hierarchy, impersonality and fragmentation of the modern workplace.

The boredom and routine of white and blue collar work was pointedly criticized by their contemporaries in the New Left. In the *Port Huron Statement,* their 1962 manifesto of principles, Students for a Democratic Society said that the simple "mechanical tasks" performed in factories was boring and demeaning. Some of it should be returned to pre-twentieth-century "manual forms, allowing men to make whole, not partial products." SDS believed much the same was true of professional work, including the narrow specialization of their college professors. The labor performed by professionals was "often unfulfilling and victimizing, accepted as a channel to status and plenty . . . [but] rarely as a means of understanding and controlling self and events." In other words, even well-paid, prestigious work was inherently undemocratic. In order for work to be fully rewarding it should "be educative, not stultifying; creative, not mechanical; self-directed, not manipulated." Most of all, work should enhance the "independence" of the worker. It should be an "expression of an inner human reality," said SDS in another document.[75]

More than any of their young contemporaries, including most political radicals, rock artists hung flesh on these ideas. Their refusal to abide by the music industry's division of labor had little to do with a commitment to radical politics. It had everything to do with their individualism, egalitarianism, rejection of hierarchy and hunger for autonomy.

These values informed the performance of their music, as well as its creation and production.

PERFORMING THE MUSIC

Prior to 1965 most rock-and-roll shows were exercises in musical continuity and performed uniformity. "Live" performances of songs seldom strayed from recorded versions. Indeed, with the exceptions of early rockers such as Presley, Berry and Jerry Lee Lewis, performers often mimicked their songs: they "lip-synched" rather than actually sang. Audiences experienced a song in performance precisely the same way they heard it again and again over the radio and on their record players. Rock acts often dressed alike, with each member of a group wearing the same clothing, although the "lead" singer might be distinguished by a different outfit. And the stage movements of a group were usually carefully choreographed and synchronized.

Pre-1965 rock-and-roll shows, like other forms of show business at the time, were engineered entertainment. They held few surprises and rarely deviated from the script. Lip-synching, which made the expectable inevitable, was common for a number of reasons. It saved money for producers of rock shows, because they did not have to hire back-up musicians (most singers at the time did not play instruments, at least when performing). And, since audiences heard the "performed" song exactly as they had heard it many times before, lip-synching lent continuity to their experience of the music. Also, whether lip-synched or not, the lyrics to most recorded rock-and-roll songs were clearly enunciated and easily understood. Audiences saw rock acts dressed alike, and witnessed their carefully coordinated movements on stage. Everything fit together, all the parts meshed. No matter how loud or implicitly lewd the music, these shows were experiences in efficiency and security. It was like American society was supposed to be in the fifties.

There was occasional rowdiness by teens during shows produced by disc jockey Alan Freed in Boston and New York. And some Americans were convinced the music subverted the morality of teenagers. They were wrong. As music historian Peter Wicke pointed out, early rock-and-roll was "nothing more than the cultural form in which the teenagers in fifties America accepted their real conditions of life."[76]

Beginning in 1965 these aspects of rock-and-roll performances gradually diminished, though they never entirely disappeared. More than was previously the case, late-sixties performers actually sang during their shows. And they played their own instruments to music they had usually composed. Synchronized physical movement on stage often gave way to helter-skelter improvisation. Band members, especially in American groups, often dressed differently from one another. Instead of the clearly enunciated lyrics of fifties rock-and-roll, the phrasing of songs from the mid to late sixties, whether recorded or presented live, might be mumbled or garbled. (This was a useful way of sneaking sexually explicit lyrics past the censors.) Even if clearly enunciated, lyrics were often difficult to interpret. They were ambiguous and open to multiple interpretations. Jerry Garcia tried "to leave a lot of possibilities for different interpretations in my lyrics." He wanted listeners to "fill in their own ideas" about the meaning.[77] In the sixties, very little about the music or its presentation was predictable.

Unpredictability was the soul of late-sixties rock-and-roll. It was performed adventure, a conscious effort by young artists to create spaces of freedom where they could enact their music and their lives as they wished. Tom Constanten, a keyboardist who joined the Grateful Dead in 1967, called their music "exploratory ventures." The idea was to create songs that evolved, and whose meanings shifted with the moods or changing lives of its creators. The performance of a song, said Constanten, should not be a "set piece, that you know where you are in it and know where you're gonna go." Rather, it should be like "you're out on an ocean in a boat and you can choose your landmarks and response to things and move in certain directions as you wish."[78] Garcia said much the same thing in describing the influence of jazz musician John Coltrane on his music.

> I've been influenced a lot by Coltrane, but I never copped his licks. . . . I've been impressed with that thing of flow, and of making statements that to my ears sound like paragraphs. He'll play along stylistically with a certain kind of tone, in a certain kind of syntax, for X amount of time, then he'll, like, change the subject, then play along with this other personality coming out. . . . It's like other personalities stepping out, or else his personality is changing, or his attitude's changing. But it changes in a holistic way, where the tone of his axe and everything changes. It's a complete vertical change, then it'll narrow down to a point, then it'll open up again.
>
> Perceptually, an idea that's been very important to me in playing has been the whole 'odyssey' idea—journeys, voyages. And adventures along the way. . . . You don't get adventure in music unless you're willing to take chances.[79]

This notion of performance as "movement" along a frontier of possibility where musicians could "take chances" was one reason most of them disliked lip-synching and tried to avoid it. Lip-synching implied that a song was a finished product indelibly etched in vinyl. For these performers the recording of a song was only a moment in its history. Subsequent presentations of the song before an audience created the possibility of investing its lyrics and music with new phrases and different intonations. The meaning of a recorded song was no more settled or defined than the life of its composer. Also, as Jimi Hendrix said, lip-synching was "phony." He was "strictly a live performer," and freedom of performance allowed him and his music to avoid becoming "classed in any [definitive] category." The life of a song, like that of its composer, was a process, and rock artists felt comfortable with the experimentation and uncertainty involved in continually redefining their recorded music.[80]

Their lives and performances were conscious explorations of contingency. As much as any rock star in the late sixties, Jim Morrison, of the Doors, the son of the youngest admiral in the history of the United States Navy, danced with danger and the unexpected, both on and off the stage. Despite their outward conformity, in their hearts "all Americans are outlaws," said Morrison. America was a blank slate of possibility, a vast, churning arena of unpredictability. Nothing was certain, everything was possible, anything could happen. That was the point of the country and its music.

> I'm interested in anything about revolt, disorder, chaos, and especially activity that appears to have no meaning. . . . Who isn't fascinated with chaos? More than that, though, I'm interested in activity that has no meaning, and all I mean by that is free activity. Play. Activity that has nothing in it except just what it is. No repercussions. No motivation. Free.[81]

For rock performers, the stage was an arena of self-exposure as well as a zone of entertainment. "I gotta risk it," said Joplin about her approach to performing. "I never hold back, man. I'm always on the outer limits of probability."[82] It meant dodging permanent self-definition, as a performer and human being. "I hate to be stuck in one thing," Neil Young declared. "I just don't want to be anything for very long. I don't know why. I just want to keep moving, keep running, play my guitar."[83] And it meant doing the unexpected while composing and performing. Steven Stills made sure that the final stanzas of "Suite: Judy Blue Eyes" had nothing to do with the song's ostensible subject. "And that little kicker at the end about Cuba was just to liven it up because [the song] had gone on forever. . . . I said 'Now that we've sung all these lyrics about one thing, let's change the subject entirely.' And we did. Even did it in a different language just to make sure nobody would understand it."[84]

Caprice and a perverse enjoyment in keeping audiences off balance motivated some of their performed improvisation. Also, performers wanted to elude the burnout and boredom characteristic of the modern work process. Bob Dylan justified his improvisations by pointing out that "life itself is improvised. We don't live life as a scripted thing. Two boxers go into a ring and they improvise. Go to sports car races, total improvisation." For Hendrix, rehearsing for a show had little to do with how he would actually perform. "We improvise an awful lot," said Hendrix. "Like we don't really rehearse a thing. It's a spontaneous performance. For instance, one of us is in a rock bag, another is just jazz, while I'm on the blues. We are all doing our separate things together. Rehearsals are only to see how the amps sound or something technical like that."[85]

These attitudes created strains between artists and the consumers of their music. Rock musicians complained about audiences that wanted them to play only their hits, and to replicate on stage the song as it was performed on record.

During a 1968 national tour by Jefferson Airplane, Marty Balin voiced resentment about fans who "want us to do the same thing over and over." Audiences wanted to hear the group's most popular songs, like "White Rabbit" and "Somebody to Love." They became restive when Jefferson Airplane played its experimental, less commercial music, or when performances of their hit songs veered from the recorded versions. Balin told the band to resist these demands. "What made the fucking group, you know? It's been our taste," not that of audiences or record companies. Airplane drummer Spencer Dryden agreed it was important to approach a song differently each time it was performed, to "start with a different beat . . . or with a different bass line. And see if we can take the same tune and relate it some other way."[86]

Jimi Hendrix had little patience with audiences unable to appreciate his improvisations, or with its expectation that he would replicate the recorded versions of his songs during performances. "I don't try to move an audience," declared Hendrix, "it's up to them what they get from the [performed] music." Nor should they expect a rote reproduction of their favorite Hendrix songs. If that's what they wanted, then "we could either bring the whole box of [recorded] tapes on stage" and not play live, or the audience "could go back home" and listen to the records.[87] Frank Zappa hoped artist and audience would think of each performance as a singular, nonreproducible experience. "The audience attending that concert," he observed, "is the only audience that is going to experience" the music as performed at that moment. "The piece exists only for them."[88] And Garcia proudly acknowledged he never heard any member of the Grateful Dead "repeat a thing in a song two nights in a row," much less duplicate its recorded music for an audience. Repetition in the performance of a song was like consistency in one's life. It signalled stagnation, boredom, routine—in other words, settlement. Garcia made this clear in 1969:

> Thinking about what [a performance] means comes after the fact and isn't very interesting. Truth is something you stumble into when you think you're going someplace else, like those moments you're playing and the whole room becomes one being. . . . But you can't look for them and they can't be repeated. Being alive means to continue to change, never to be where I was before. Music is the timeless experience of constant change.[89]

The most famous rupture between a performer and his audience, and perhaps the most important event in the history of rock-and-roll, occurred in 1965. Bob Dylan transformed himself from the country's most admired folk singer and composer to its most influential rock-and-roll musician. In this case the issue wasn't an artist's refusal to duplicate recorded versions of songs during performances. Dylan radically changed his persona as a performer. By suddenly playing rock-and-roll, a medium his fans saw as antithetical to the values they associated with folk music, Dylan undermined their belief that he shared with them a political bond through his music.

In 1963 the folk-singing, 22-year-old Dylan became the main attraction at the Newport Folk Festival. The festival was an annual gathering of folk musicians and devotees. Among its principle organizers were folk singers Pete Seeger and Theodore Bikel and musicologist Alan Lomax, all Old Leftists. The surge in folk music's popularity in the early sixties suggested to them that the political repression and torpor of the fifties was on the wane. The music was closely tied to an emerging political and existential restlessness among college students, as well as the moral transcendence and social ideals of the Civil Rights movement.

Seeger and Bikel admired Dylan's talent, but valued him even more because his popularity with both younger and older audiences alike reinvigorated the link between folk music and political activism. To Seeger and Bikel, Dylan compositions like "Blowin' in the Wind," "Masters of War" and "The Times They Are A-Changin'" were more than simply great songs produced by an incomparable artist. Dylan's music symbolized the revival of activism among ordinary citizens and the dispossessed. He was the Woody Guthrie of the sixties, a persona Dylan himself adopted at the beginning of his career.[90]

But by the mid sixties Dylan shifted gears. On July 25, 1965, he took the stage at the Newport Folk Festival. After performing a solo acoustic set of his folk songs, Dylan "went electric" and many in the audience went berserk, along with some of the festival's organizers. Dylan was joined on stage by keyboardist Al Kooper and Chicago blues guitarist Michael Bloomfield. As their electric instruments exploded into Dylan's "Maggie's Farm," cascades of boos and catcalls from the audience flooded the stage (a few cheers were heard as well). Seeger was scandalized. "You can't understand the words!" he screamed. And the noise was deafening. "If I had an ax I'd cut the cable right now," Seeger said. A day earlier Lomax, a folk-song purist, and Dylan's manager, Albert Grossman, had exchanged punches near the stage. The fight was inspired by their differences over the use of electric guitars in the performance of folk music.[91]

Dylan spent the rest of the summer touring with his new rock-and-roll ensemble, which included Kooper and a group of back-up musicians called the Hawks, who would become famous as the Band in 1969—Robbie Robertson, Levon Helm, Garth Hudson, Richard Manuel and Rick Danko. The reception Dylan received at Newport was duplicated around the country. In August the booing was relentless at New York's Forest Hills tennis stadium. Some in the audience yelled "rock and roll sucks" and worse, while Dylan and his band played songs from his watershed new album, *Highway 61 Revisited.* One member of the audience climbed on stage and knocked Kooper from his stool while he was playing the organ. Reactions were much the same in city after city. Drummer Levon Helm quit the tour, unsettled by the mounting anger of audiences. But Dylan pushed on. "They can boo till the end of time," he said. "I know that the music is real, more real than the boos." He even expressed disappointment when confronted by a relatively subdued audience at the Hollywood Bowl in Los Angeles. "I wish they had booed. It's good publicity. Sells tickets."[92]

Despite the issues that pulled performers and their fans in different directions, they had much in common. They were roughly the same age, wore the same clothing, kept their hair long and used the same drugs. Some musicians believed their commitment to personal and artistic "authenticity" was understood and shared by their fans. Joplin said she didn't have "one way of art and another way of life. They're the same for me." "Singing with Big Brother was the first time I was able to make my emotions work for me." Performance was a public display of private joy, grief or resentment. Some rock stars believed audiences could share this experience, understand the vulnerability and danger it implied and possibly incorporate it into their own lives. As one of Joplin's fans declared, "She's us. She's not a star. . . . She's all of us." Spencer Dryden said rock musicians could touch and "please the people" by "doing your own thing." If "you listen to yourself," he said, "I think you'll get it all said. Plus the people will appreciate it, 'cause they know. They know. Don't give them your projection of somebody else, or an idea you think they want, give them you."[93]

Other artists weren't as certain that their fans understood or could tolerate the ambiguity, uncertainty and honesty projected by their music and performances. Neil Young was puzzled by his success. "I'm lucky. Somehow by doing what I wanted to do, I manage to give people what they don't want to hear and they still come back."[94] Jimi Hendrix was convinced even his most ardent audiences failed to grasp what his guitar was trying to tell them. During one performance the audience appeared uncomfortable with his pace and improvisations. Hendrix told them that "you wouldn't know" good from mediocre music.[95] Even before he "went electric" Dylan had an ambiguous relationship with audiences. If he sensed they were uneasy during a performance he let them know he didn't care. "Hasn't anyone got a newspaper to read?" he would ask. Or, "Don't worry, I'm just as eager to finish and leave as you are."[96] Frank Zappa had a succinct, uncouth message for fans who urged him to play his music as they wished to hear it rather than the way he felt like playing. "We told the audience to 'get fucked.'"[97]

BOB DYLAN
DEFYING TIME THROUGH THE MUSIC

Ralph Waldo Emerson's notion of the "representative man" fit the role played by Bob Dylan in the history of rock-and-roll. Dylan's influence was pivotal in defining the music's style and substance, as well as the way in which it was conceived and performed in the late sixties. He was admired or emulated by artists as diverse in their musical styles and national origins as the Beatles, Joplin, the Jamaican composer Bob Marley, Eric Clapton and the Grateful Dead. He was the avatar of the composer-performer, the artist-artisan who controlled his labor. And he was seen by fans, distinguished literary figures and authors of numerous doctoral dissertations as a major poet who more than any other figure transformed rock-and-roll into an art form.[98]

Dylan's approach to work also made him rock's most representative figure. He was among the first to reconfigure his recorded music during performances. His improvisations and approach to work in the studio embodied the refusal of rock artists to view recorded songs as finished products. The perception of their work as improvised, impermanent and ceaselessly evolving signalled a need to cheat time as well as evade boredom and burnout. It reflected a desire to "keep moving," as Garcia said, and to evade permanent identities, as performers and human beings. This wasn't mere self-reliance or rugged individualism. It was ceaseless "movement," rock-and-roll as a medium of what Emerson called "self-infinitude." In his opinions and art, Dylan displayed these sensibilities more than any other performer.

Dylan was born Robert Zimmerman in Duluth, Minnesota, in 1941. When he was five or six years old, his parents moved to Hibbing, a small iron-mining town in the northeastern corner of the state. His father owned a furniture and appliance store in Hibbing, and his family participated in the religious and social activities of the region's small Jewish community.

Dylan's childhood and teen years appear to have been unremarkable and relatively stable. Even in remote Hibbing, he was exposed to the main currents of the suburban youth culture of the mid to late fifties. He was impressed by James Dean's screen persona as a loner, read *Mad Magazine* and listened to Chuck Berry, Buddy Holly and Elvis Presley. Access to Chicago radio stations exposed him to the electrified urban blues played by African Americans who had moved there from the South, including Muddy Waters, Otis Spann and Howlin' Wolf.

Dylan organized a rock-and-roll band when he was 14. After graduation from high school in 1959, he enrolled at the University of Minnesota in Minneapolis. He stayed for about a year, attending classes intermittently. He was more interested in singing in the coffeehouses of the city's bohemian neighborhood, known as Dinkytown. Late in 1960, the 19-year-old Dylan made his way to New York City. He settled in Greenwich Village, performing in its legendary folk music clubs, including Gerde's Folk City, the Limelight, and Village Gate. Within little more than two years, Dylan was regarded as the country's preeminent composer and performer of folk music.[99]

Those who crossed Dylan's path in the early sixties were astonished by his capacity to study and master diverse musical styles. He delved into and absorbed the nuances of the acoustic and talking blues, country, rock-and-roll, rhythm and blues and topical, protest and traditional folk music. They were equally struck by Dylan's need to fabricate his past, to improvise and constantly alter an identity severed from his actual childhood.[100]

Dylan's tales about his past varied. What he said depended upon his mood, his audience and his desire to confuse people or keep them at a distance. But the theme was consistent: he was self-created. He said he ran away to Chicago when he was 10 years old, because "I wasn't free." Returned to his home, two years later he fled once again to Chicago, where he claimed to have met blues singer Big Joe Williams. Dylan told people he rode freight trains at an early age and hitchhiked across the western states of South Dakota, New Mexico and Kansas. He was an orphan. Or, "I was never a kid who would go home. . . . I made my way all by myself." Growing up in Hibbing, he said, had "nothing to do with what I am, what I became." "There isn't a home you can't leave. I've left maybe 20 or 30 homes. It's easy to leave because all you have to do is get up and go." In a 1961 interview with *New York Times* music critic Robert Shelton, Dylan fashioned the following odyssey: "I started travelling with a carnival at the age of thirteen. I cleaned up ponies and ran steam shovels in Minnesota, North Dakota, and then on south. For a while, Sioux Falls, South Dakota was a home, and so was Gallup, New Mexico. I also lived in Fargo, North Dakota and in a place called Hibbing, Minnesota."[101]

Dylan changed his name, as if to punctuate his act of self-creation. The name change occurred when he went to college in 1959, but at that point he didn't spell it "Dylan." He called himself Bob "Dillon," inspired perhaps by the name of the fictitious western marshal from one of his favorite television shows, Matt Dillon of *Gunsmoke.* Around the same time he also affected a new singing voice. Audiences might like or dislike his harsh, whining, intrusive nasal twang, but they could not ignore it. That may have been one reason Dylan adopted it.

But the voice, along with a remarkable gift for punctuating a lyric by sudden shifts in inflection, also enabled him to invest his songs with a wide range of emotional hues and story-telling strategies. From one song or phrase to the next, Dylan's voice alternated mockery, defiance, wit, anger, pathos and irony. Almost everything, perhaps, except tenderness. Unlike most popular singers in the early sixties it was a deliberately unpolished voice. It grated against and assaulted, rather than caressed, the ear.

There was a sort of democratic sensibility to that voice. Dylan seemed to be saying that the quality of a singer's voice was less important than the emotional truth and passion channelled through it. How a performer sounded or looked mattered less than what he had to say and how he said it. In any event, it was his voice of choice. Like the name "Dillon," the nasal twang was modelled on a western figure. This time it was Dylan's real-life hero Woody Guthrie, the legendary western troubadour of Depression-era radicalism. Dylan genuinely admired and was inspired by Guthrie. But assuming Guthrie's voice, as Dylan told a friend from Minneapolis, was also part of what he called "building a character."[102] Another friend from Dylan's days in Minneapolis commented on the significance of the voice:

> It was phenomenal. Even his speech patterns began to change. That Oklahoma twang, which became much more extreme after he left here, came into his voice. That incredibly harsh gravel sound in his voice became more and more a part of him. It really became much more than identification. He *was* the people he identified with, especially Guthrie.[103]

"Building a character" became an endless process for Dylan. This was fitting for a restless artist whose capacity for mastering musical genres required him to move on or risk stagnation. It was apparent in his shift from protest folk to rock-and-roll in the mid sixties, and later in the decade from rock to acoustic and country music on albums like *John Wesley Harding* (1967) and *Nashville Skyline* (1969). After the sixties, it informed his religious interests, as he alternatively embraced versions of Judaism and Christianity. But Dylan's uneasiness with having a defined identity was most evident in the way he made and altered his music.

In the studio he roamed the frontier between improvisation and chaos. Like Young, Garcia and others, Dylan wanted to record as he was creating, warts and all. The idea was to capture on record a song at its conception, at the moment when musical nativity was cross-pollinated by the artist's emotions. Rather than produce polished, rewritten, overly rehearsed versions of his songs, Dylan wanted the recordings to capture the music while it was raw, imperfect perhaps, but nonetheless an authentic rendering of himself and the song at the moment it was born. Recorded inspiration, not unblemished, "produced" music, was his goal.

From the beginning, Dylan approached studio sessions in this fashion. During the recording of his first album in 1961, Dylan refused his producer's request to do second takes of songs. "I said no. I can't see myself singing the same song twice in a row. That's terrible." Dylan's commitment to recording spontaneous and unadorned music meant that he spent remarkably little time in the studio. It took the Beatles 129 days in the studio to produce their landmark 1967 album, *Sgt. Pepper's Lonely Hearts Club Band.* Dylan, who felt *Sgt. Pepper's* was an "indulgent" album in which the music was overwhelmed by gratuitous electronic frills, took as little as 3 days to record his albums. His view of the recording process ("Go in, cut it, and get the fuck out") allowed him to spend about 90 days in the studio to produce the 16 albums he made between the debut *Bob Dylan* in 1961 and *Desire* in 1976.[104]

Dylan's improvisational style frequently created havoc for producers and session musicians. It was not unusual for Dylan to enter the studio with fragments of lyrics, parts of melodies and vague notions about how to perform a song. Nor was he particularly concerned about telling musicians where he was headed, assuming he knew. Quite the opposite. A musician who worked on *Blood On The Tracks* (1974) said Dylan's "whole concept of making an album seems to be go ahead and play it and whatever way it comes out, well that's the way it is. It's what happens at the moment. We'd just watch his hands and pray we had the right changes."[105]

At times this led to less than adequate work. But his ability to create on the borderland between chaos and creativity could have startling results. In 1965 Al Kooper was a relatively unknown guitarist who asked Dylan's producer if he could play in the *Highway 61 Revisited* studio sessions (which lasted six days). Kooper was told to show up with his guitar, but Dylan had already engaged the redoubtable blues guitarist Michael Bloomfield. Kooper was allowed to join in but only if he played the organ. He agreed, even though he had never played the instrument professionally. As Kooper recalled:

> Check this out: there's no music to read. The song is over five minutes long. The band is so loud that I can't even hear the organ, and I'm not familiar with the instrument to begin with. The best I could manage was to . . . feel my way through the [song's] changes like a kid fumbling in the dark for a light switch. After six minutes they'd gotten the first complete take of the day down and all adjourned to the booth to hear it played back. Thirty seconds into the second verse, Dylan motions toward [producer] Tom Wilson. "Turn the organ up," he orders. "Hey, man," Tom says, "that cat's not an organ player." But Dylan isn't buying it. "Hey now don't tell me who's an organ player and who's not. Just turn the organ up." At the conclusion of the playback, the entire booth applauded the soon-to-be-a-classic "Like A Rolling Stone" and Dylan acknowledged the tribute by turning his back and wandering into the studio for a go at another tune.[106]

The *Highway 61 Revisited* session occurred in the midst of Dylan's transition from folk to rock, and the songs he composed during this period seemed as chaotic, spontaneous and unnerving as his approach to recording them. It is likely that the discordant, unfamiliar qualities of the music, as much as his shift from folk music to rock-and-roll, inspired some of the booing during his concerts in 1965 and 1966. Even some of the musicians who played with Dylan in those concerts were confused by his new sound and lyrics. He made three remarkably influential albums in little more than one year. Their cumulative impact created a space within rock-and-roll where the music could go beyond standard themes of pop music. *Bringing It All Back Home* was released in March 1965, followed by *Highway 61 Revisited* in August of that year and *Blonde On Blonde* in May 1966.

At the time music critics called the music from the three albums "folk-rock." They were neither folk nor rock. Most of the electric music on the albums sounded like idiosyncratic versions of the urban blues. It had little in common with the sound of early sixties rock-and-roll. And the lyrics could not have been further removed from the didactic political and moral tone of early-sixties protest folk music.

Dylan's lyrics did not deal with political issues. They told subjective, interior tales suffused with mythological, dreamlike, phantasmagoric imagery. The stories were refracted through a mind at once brilliant, angry, witty, spectral, insightful, mistrustful and sometimes paranoid. They were populated by a menagerie of grotesque characters who acted within appropriately bizarre settings. They told of people who had bedroom windows made of bricks ("Maggie's Farm"), were warned to "watch the plain clothes" and follow parking meters instead of leaders ("Subterranean Homesick Blues"), wore Napoleon Bonaparte masks ("On the Road Again") and who were given directions by Guernsey cows ("Bob Dylan's 115th Dream"). The songs featured lampposts with "folded arms" and utopian hermit monks ("Gates of Eden"), the ghost of Belle Starr and Jezebel the nun ("Tombstone Blues"), one-eyed midgets and sword swallowers who wore high heels ("Ballad of a Thin Man"), Einstein playing an electric violin and disguised as Robin Hood ("Desolation Row") and a preacher who wore 20 pounds of newspaper headlines stapled to his chest ("Stuck Inside of Mobile with the Memphis Blues Again").[107]

There was something beyond their behavior or appearance that made this motley cast of characters grotesque. It was their fate as strangers, to one another and themselves. Condemned to play roles dealt them by circumstance, the power of others or their own weakness, they were locked into their privacy and inauthentic lives. They had little choice but to see each other (and themselves) as aliens, warped and deformed. The country itself, Dylan seemed to be saying, lacked a center of social gravity or basis for mutuality and familiarity. Everyone orbited an America of his own, ready as Dylan sang in "Mr. Tambourine Man," to disappear into his "own parade." In these songs the United States was a huge space occupied by hustling migrants, immigrants and other strangers who randomly stumbled upon and over one other. Immersed in their material possessions, immured by mutually exclusive "American dreams," they were bereft of a usable collective past. As Dylan sang over and again in a refrain from "Like A Rolling Stone," there was "no direction home" for a "complete unknown" who was on her own. So, he inquired over and again about that exhilarating and solitary American version of freedom: "how does it feel?"

Politics and social reform were irrelevant. Political activism was fruitless in an absurd world, and even more so in a country that seemed beyond reform. Or, more to the point of Dylan's vision, beyond redemption. The America glimpsed in these songs is a land mired in conformity, violence, loneliness, mindless consumption, sexual repression, hypocrisy, missed opportunities and middle class obsessions with security and success masquerading as freedom. In other words, the country was a failed experiment.

However one interprets the lyrics in these songs, the impetus behind his creativity was Dylan's fiercely personal and idiosyncratic vision of the world and his place in it. In his music and public comments Dylan's persona was that of an old-fashioned, intensely private, self-reliant individualist. Dylan was unto himself, and he crowned himself with moral sovereignty. "It's not a question of breaking the rules," Dylan said in the mid sixties about his music and personal values. "I don't break the rules, because I don't see any rules to break. As far as I'm concerned there aren't any rules." In 1964 he told the journalist Nat Hentoff that "I'm part of no movement." He was not trying to influence others through his music. If those in the New Left or Civil Rights movements drew inspiration from his music that was their business, not his intention.[108]

Dylan's life and music were studies in the self-reliant individualism celebrated by Emerson more than a century earlier. "It is only as a man puts off all foreign support," Emerson wrote in 1841, "and stands alone that I see him to be strong and to prevail. He is weaker by every recruit to his banner."[109] Dylan had no banner and sought no recruits, notwithstanding the thousands of young people who studied his lyrics in search of moral inspiration or political insight. Dylan once said he would rather have lived during "the time of King David, when he was the high priest of Israel. I'd have loved to have been riding with him or hiding in caves with him when he was a hunted outlaw." When asked by journalists in the sixties to describe the "messages" hidden in his lyrics, Dylan produced a large light bulb and said, "keep a good head and always carry a light bulb." And when asked about the impact of his music, he said "I don't want to influence people. . . . My songs are meaningless. They don't mean nothin.'" "I've found out some things," he said.

> [T]he [New Left] movement with all their president-vice-president-secretary stuff, it's politics. Inside their own pettiness they're as bad as the hate groups. I can't ever have a fan club because it'd have to have a president, it'd be a group. . . . I'm not a believer in doing things by number. I believe the best things get done by individuals.[110]

His determined self-reliance was expressed in a variety of ways. Dylan relished the fact that he was a "self-taught" musician, one who would rather "fail on my own" than be part of a permanent musical group. "Nobody's gonna learn by somebody else showing them or teaching them" how to play music or to negotiate life. "People have to learn for themselves, by going through it all until they get to the center of it." The "center" resided within the wall of flesh, bone and consciousness that separated people from one another. There was little hope of breaching that barrier. "When I listen to other people talk," he said, "all I hear is what they're not tellin' me."[111]

But neither self-reliance, artistic imperatives, nor individualism (in its common-sense meaning) accounted for the inclinations of Dylan and other rock musicians to alter their previously recorded songs. They needed to evade permanence, to defy time, to avoid being confined or defined by their personal or musical pasts. "Definition destroys," said Dylan. "Do not create anything. It will be misinterpreted. It will not change. It will follow you the rest of your life."[112] This was the cry of a peripatetic artist who wanted to follow his own muse rather than fit the musical mold defined by his fans or record companies.

But it also indicated a need to cheat time, evade definition, perhaps even death, by incessantly reinventing himself through his various musical incarnations. And by the major alterations he made in his recorded songs over the years. If the songs never stopped evolving, neither the art nor the artist would perish. "I would not let myself decay," Dylan said. "I'm against decay. That's nature's will—decay. I am against nature. I don't dig nature at all. I think nature is very unnatural. I think the truly natural things are dreams, which nature can't touch with decay."[113] Or limit by time.

This was "movement" at an extreme. Jerry Garcia felt that being alive meant "never to be where I was before." Music was the gateway to ceaseless motion. As he said, it was the "timeless experience of constant change."[114] Such statements were mid-twentieth century expressions of what Emerson called his "central doctrine," the "infinitude of the private man." In the nineteenth century, Emerson claimed that "Before the revelations of the soul, Time, Space, and

Nature shrink away."[115] In the 1960s, Dylan suggested much the same thing. "There is no guidance at all except from one's own senses."[116]

Dodging permanence in his recorded art was Dylan's way—one that reflected the needs not only of fellow rock musicians but of many other Americans as well—of evading time. It mattered little whether time was viewed as history or as the carrier of the decay and death awaiting them in the future. Dylan said the goal of an artist should be to "stop time." In some songs he tried to "defy time, so that the story took place in the present and the past at the same time." The idea was to create "the break-up of time, and where there is no time, where you're trying to make believe that life is one narrow line."[117]

The individualism of late-sixties rock-and-roll musicians not only displayed what Tocqueville saw as the tendency of the American to depend "forever upon himself alone." Rock artists embodied as well one of the most enduring insights about the American experience gleaned by the Frenchman during his visit to the United States. The country struck him as unhinged from time. In America "the woof of time is every instant broken, and the track of generations effaced. Those who went before are soon forgotten; of those who will come after, no one has any idea."[118]

Or as Dylan said in 1993, the "songs I recorded in my past, they're almost like demos. I'm still trying to figure out what some of them are about. [I] don't allow the past to encroach upon the present."[119]

PART III

The Sixties in American History II: Students for a Democratic Society

We cannot reduce society to atoms. It doesn't work. We are terribly, objectively, knitted together.

Paul Potter, *A Name for Ourselves,* 1971

America was built by a nation of strangers.

President Lyndon Johnson,
on signing the Immigration Act of 1965

INTRODUCTION TO PART III: DIFFERENCES BETWEEN CULTURAL AND POLITICAL RADICALS

STUDENTS OF THE SIXTIES generally divide white radicalism into two categories. Diggers and serious hippies are called "cultural" radicals because they tried to change their lives and society without reference to established economic and political institutions. They simply "dropped out" of those institutions and created a "counterculture" of alternative mores and lifestyles. In hundreds of (usually short lived) rural and urban communes around the country, hippies developed their own versions of family, sexual relationships, patterns of work and economic exchange. Seekers of new personal identities, they immersed themselves in exotic experiences that were far removed from the middle-class world in which most of them had been raised. In addition to experimenting with a wide variety of communal lifestyles, they used hallucinogenic drugs and explored Native American culture, Eastern religions and astrology. Some, like the rock performers whose music permeated the world of hippies, even became hip entrepreneurs who made and sold their own handicrafts or organically grown farm produce.

By contrast, the young leftists who challenged the nation's post–World War II domestic and foreign policies were "political" radicals. During the early sixties, they created a New Left whose goal was to redeem and reconstruct American institutions, not drop out of them. A small number of left-of-liberal groups dedicated to civil rights, economic justice, the right to hold unpopular political views, nuclear disarmament and détente between the United States and the Soviet Union emerged in the late fifties and early sixties. Among them were the student division of the National Committee for a Sane Nuclear Policy (SANE), the Student Peace Union and the Student Nonviolent Coordinating Committee (organized by African American students but open to white membership during the first half of the sixties). Within a few years, Students for a Democratic Society became the best known and most influential of these organizations, at least among white college students.

Categorizing radicals as cultural or political (while recognizing, as most scholars do, that individuals like Jerry Rubin and Abbie Hoffman had a foot in both camps, and that by the chaotic late sixties the boundaries between the two became increasingly blurred) is a useful, generally valid way of separating the two main strands of youth rebellion in the sixties.[1] But there is another way to distinguish between them: each held radically different views about the relationship between the individual and society.

For instance, the counterculture promoted an extreme strain of "expressive" individualism, distilled in the psychodrama of Emmett Grogan's saga as a hunter in the American wilderness. The solitary hunter of his own identity, Grogan created himself by himself. He required neither the permission of others nor the mediation of institutions to do so. Like his Digger colleagues and the hippies of the Haight-Ashbury, Grogan believed in the sovereignty of the isolated self. The right to self-creation and self-fulfillment were largely independent of, indeed morally superior to, the ways and means of organized society.

Of course, cultural radicals valued community as well. As we saw in chapter 5, they called themselves "tribes" during the San Francisco Be-In of 1967. Hippies organized hundreds of rural and urban communes in a serious quest for new forms of intimacy and community. And they celebrated "peace," "love" and "flower power" in countless "love-ins" and "be-ins" around the country.

But the counterculture was mainly driven by a hip version of the idea of a state of nature. It was as though Diggers and hippies imagined themselves as inhabitants of a pre-social world. Since personal freedom preceded, and was morally superior to, the demands of organized society, each individual in theory was free to do as he pleased. It was not coincidental that in order to reinvent himself Grogan temporarily fled organized society. Like the trappers and adventurers who wandered the continent's unsettled spaces in the eighteenth and nineteenth centuries, Grogan was free to secede from and reenter "civilized" society at will. His freedom and independence were sui generis. They were not products of the give and take of a "social contract," in which a balance needed to be struck between personal rights and social obligations.

Cultural radicals often approached the most intimate relationships as though they were vehicles of self-discovery instead of arduously negotiated compromises between otherwise autonomous individuals. "When you have sex with a lot of people," said a young woman who lived in an Oregon commune, "you find out who you really are."[2] She expressed no interest in finding out who her partners "really" were. In his 1969 study of hippie communards, Robert Houriet took note of the extraordinary movement of individuals in and out of the communes he visited. Their need for absolute autonomy made it difficult for hippies to live together. "Everywhere," observed Houriet, there was "instability, transiency. Somebody was always splitting, rolling up his bag . . . off again in search of the truly free, un-hung-up community." Usually they searched in vain.[3]

Ideally, hippie communes were experiments in new forms of intimacy and community. But a recalcitrant individualism isolated people from one another. Hippies often lived together alone. "I was awakened by a thudding sound near my pillow," said one relatively new communard. "It was Reuben doing his matinal yoga, rolled on his back. So far, we haven't said a word to each other. Yesterday was one of the days he chose not to talk to anyone." While Reuben, cloistered within himself, did his exercises as if no one else was present, the unfortunate narrator was further disturbed by sounds of determined lovemaking coming from a couple named "Joe" and "Jean." (The previous evening, all of them happened to fall asleep in the same room.) They "began to make turbulent love," as though they were by themselves. In a way they were. "I jumped out of the [sleeping] bag and hurriedly dressed," said the embarrassed hippie.[4]

Living in a commune could be an experience that was both liberating and intimate, but all too often it was a contentious, short-lived exercise in determined self-absorption. This counterculture variety of individualism was aptly summarized by the rock musician David Crosby in 1967. A relentless advocate of the counterculture in his life and music, Crosby's definition of what he called the hippie "golden rule" was a tribute to the majesty of the isolated self: "Don't inflict your thing on me and I won't inflict my thing on you."[5]

The young political activists who organized Students for a Democratic Society (SDS) turned these assumptions on their heads. They believed the individual could not be truly human or genuinely free if he dwelled outside the bonds of society, whether in fact, myth or fantasy. SDS assumed that the needs for intimacy and community were at least as powerful as the drives for autonomy and independence. To be sure, most members of SDS were inveterate individualists who championed personal freedom and self-development. Male SDSers especially were prone to egotistical behavior. Their aggressively competitive style often led to personality clashes within the organization.

But at the same time, they believed autonomy and personal identity were neither possible nor desirable unless the individual actively participated in the social and political life of a bonded, egalitarian, democratic community. SDS tried to formulate a politics that reconciled personal autonomy with community, and a morally informed individualism with intimacy and friendship. They did so by advancing a form of political ethics in which the individual would be largely free of restraints imposed by undemocratic, remote institutions beyond his direct control. Yet he would be deeply invested in voluntary, community-based associations that at once cultivated and placed limits upon his autonomy.

Thus, beneath the categories of cultural and political radicalism, young dissidents in the sixties were divided by sharply contrasting views of the individual's relationship to society.

SEVEN

The Politics of Liberty and Community: Students for a Democratic Society, 1960–1965

I am of the opinion, that, in the democratic ages which are opening upon us, individual independence and local liberties will ever be the products of art; that centralization will be the natural government.

Alexis de Tocqueville, 1835

What is needed [is] a way to connect knowledge to power and decentralize both so that community or participatory democracy might emerge, to be connected with the problem of the individual in a time inevitably ridden with bureaucracy, large government, international networks and systems.

Tom Hayden, SDS, 1961

THE HISTORY OF STUDENTS FOR A DEMOCRATIC SOCIETY is perhaps the most widely studied and astutely evaluated expression of white radicalism in the sixties. Scholars have thoroughly mapped the organization's turbulent journey, which began in

1960 and ended in 1969.[1] Much of their work has focused on the subject of this chapter: the ideas and programs advanced in relative obscurity by members of SDS in the years 1960 to 1965. This was the period before it emerged as a major player in the anti–Vietnam War movement, and its membership swelled. And before many of its late-sixties spokespersons embraced one or another form of Marxism-Leninism. The first five years of SDS's history have intrigued scholars because its young members explicitly distanced themselves from Marxism and other "foreign" versions of radicalism. They groped for a radical perspective rooted in American political soil. During the early years of the decade they tried to formulate a radical way to "speak American," as they put it.[2]

But historians have not attempted to connect the ideas that animated early SDS to specific themes in the history of (non-Marxist or socialist) American politics. For the most part, what was "new" and not "new" about SDS's version of the New Left has yet to be defined in historical terms. Also, despite the claim that their radicalism spoke in a native tongue, SDS members never made a serious effort to place their political values within a specific historical context. One thing cultural and political radicals shared in common was their disdain for the past. To be young and a rebel in the sixties meant doing and thinking everything for the first time. Tom Hayden, the second president of SDS, was on the mark when he said of himself and his colleagues that "everything for us had to be new."[3]

But the political quandaries that inspired the ideas and programs pushed by SDS during the first half of the decade were far from new. They reprised tensions and ambiguities inherent in American political culture and society since the origins of the country's political system in the late eighteenth century. SDS's challenge to the political status quo in the sixties, and its relevance for understanding the ongoing malaise of American political culture since that decade, cannot adequately be understood or assessed outside of this historical framework.

An overview of the organization's turbulent, decade-long history is a necessary starting point for discussing these issues. What follows is a summary of SDS's history. It is not an in-depth portrait. While it barely skims the surface of the issues and complex personalities that drove the organization, hopefully it provides a useful setting for discussing the main themes presented in this chapter and the next.

A SUMMARY OF THE HISTORY OF SDS

When it was founded in 1960, Students for a Democratic Society was not a new organization; it was the most recent incarnation of the college-student division of the League for Industrial Democracy (LID). Headquartered in New York City, the LID's lineage stretched back to 1905, when Jack London, Clarence

Darrow and Upton Sinclair, among others, created the Intercollegiate Socialist Society. The main purpose of the society was to spark interest in and debate about socialism among college students. It was not especially successful. Even so, the fury unleashed by the red scare that swept the country after World War I forced the society to excise the word "socialist" from its title. In 1921 it renamed itself the League for Industrial Democracy.[4]

Along with other left-of-center organizations, the LID was largely fallow during the prosperous, politically conservative 1920s. It experienced a revival during the hard times, labor strife and political turbulence of the thirties. But by the late fifties it was a small, rudderless organization with a few hundred members. Its version of democratic socialism was barely distinguishable from post-New Deal liberalism. The LID supported organized labor. It was virulently anti-communist and avidly pro-American in the Cold War struggle with the Soviet Union. The organization was barely kept afloat financially with assistance from the International Ladies Garment Workers Union and the United Auto Workers. (UAW president Walter Reuther had been a member of the LID's student division during the thirties.)

By the late fifties the LID's student division was as moribund and irrelevant to radical politics as was its parent organization. In 1960 the Student League for Industrial Democracy (SLID) had only three campus chapters, at Yale, Columbia and the University of Michigan at Ann Arbor. It did not engage in political activism. Nor did it formulate independent positions on public issues. For the most part, the SLID sponsored discussion groups and seminars on the Cold War and the economy for the small number of students who bothered to attend them.

Robert "Al" Haber provided a good deal of the initial impetus that eventually transformed the Student League for Industrial Democracy from an innocuous discussion group into the most dynamic white radical student organization of the sixties. In 1960 Haber was a graduate student at Ann Arbor, where his father was a professor of economics. Haber was the SLID's field secretary. His visits to college campuses around the country convinced him that the political and social "consensus" of the fifties was beginning to unravel. A hard-to-define restlessness gripped some of the brightest students he met. Some of their discontent was inspired by a simmering aversion toward the professional careers and middle-class lifestyle that awaited them upon graduation. But they were moved by social issues as well, especially those raised by the Civil Rights movement.

Haber shared the concerns advanced by single-issue New Left groups that emerged more or less at the same time, like the Student Nonviolent Coordinating Committee and the Student Peace Union. But he wanted to create a multi-issue organization. It would be nonideological and avoid committing itself to a priori positions about the causes or cures of major social problems.

A nonideological stance would distance it from the communist Old Left, in the minds of both its potential recruits and inevitable critics. This was an important consideration during a time when American paranoia about communist subversion and "infiltration" was still pervasive. But more than anything else, a nonideological posture would allow the organization to define itself in light of the evolving experiences of its members. It pointed to the future rather than the past. Beyond a rock-ribbed dedication to democracy, the radical student organization envisioned by Haber would avoid, as he said later in the decade, "any imposition of any pre-determined standards or categories of analysis [that] narrows the creative potential of the movement."[5]

In 1960 Haber convinced LID officials to change its student division's name to Students for a Democratic Society. Along with a coterie of early acolytes, he worked tirelessly to recruit bright, politically committed students to the new organization. Tom Hayden was a pivotal early convert. Editor of the student newspaper at Ann Arbor during his senior year, Hayden quickly emerged as one of the fledgling group's most energetic activists and its most prolific writer. Hayden, who succeeded Haber as president of SDS in 1962, was born in 1939 and raised in a lower-middle-class suburb of Detroit. His father attended college for two years and was a bookkeeper for Chrysler. After the divorce of his parents shortly after World War II, his mother worked in a local school district library. Neither parent was politically active, but had what Hayden called a "populist" affinity for the underdog. When it came time to vote in the fifties, his father was an Eisenhower Republican, his mother a Stevenson Democrat. Like Haber, Hayden was convinced that political values "should flow from experience, not from preconceived dogmas or ideologies."[6]

Other recruits to the new organization included Todd Gitlin, SDS's third president. A student at Harvard, Gitlin was born in New York City. His parents were schoolteachers and politically liberal. Paul Booth was a student at Swarthmore. His father was an economist who had worked for the Labor Department during the New Deal, and his mother was a psychiatric social worker. The sociology graduate student Richard Flacks and his wife Mickey were children of radicals from New York. Paul Potter, the fourth president of SDS, and Rennie Davis were politically active students at Oberlin before they joined SDS. Potter was raised on a farm in Illinois. Davis, whose father was an economist who had served on the Council of Economic Advisors during the Truman administration, grew up in Virginia.

Sharon Jeffrey, another student recruit from Ann Arbor, was the daughter of former socialists who worked for the United Auto Workers and were currently active in the liberal wing of the Democratic Party. Her mother served on the Democratic National Committee in the sixties and seventies, as well as on the board of the liberal group Americans for Democratic Action. New Yorker Steve

Max was a red diaper baby who did not attend college. His father was an editor for the Communist newspaper, *The Daily Worker,* before he left the party in the late fifties. Bob Ross, whose mother was a schoolteacher and socialist, was still another Ann Arbor student who joined SDS. Finally, Carl Oglesby came to SDS in 1965 at the age of 30, and promptly became its fifth president. He joined SDS after quitting his job in the technical publications department of the Bendix Corporation, a defense contractor.[7]

Despite the eclectic social and political backgrounds of these and other members of early SDS, they shared a number of important traits. Nearly all were high achievers enrolled in elite colleges and research universities. They were, in Gitlin's words, "academic stars" and ambitious "junior achiever types." They were articulate, adept at the rough-and-tumble of debate, self-confident and well "trained in the ways of competition." "At once analytically keen and politically committed," according to Gitlin, the young activists believed they "could actually take life in [their] own hands and live it deliberately."[8]

Many of them experienced, as Hayden noted years later, the excitement and anticipation of change that accompanied the election of John F. Kennedy to the presidency in 1960. The Kennedy presidency, along with the surge of activism generated by the Civil Rights movement, made them feel that the early sixties "vibrat[ed] with potential." "Many of us were student leaders," said Hayden, "who were conditioned to believe that if you spoke out, you would get a hearing from the Kennedy administration." "[Our] backgrounds of achievement made us feel charmed."[9]

Between 1960 and 1965, SDS was a small organization led by a close-knit inner circle of friends and political allies. They were committed, in the words of their 1962 constitution, to a "vision of a democratic society, where at all levels the people have control over the decisions which affect them." Until 1965 the organization excluded from membership those who advocated authoritarianism, including communists. It welcomed to its ranks "liberals and radicals, activists and scholars, students and faculty."[10]

Its goal was to "bring forth a radical, democratic program counterpoised to authoritarian movements both of communism and the domestic right." Their hope of revitalizing American politics by creating a decentralized "democracy of individual participation" was codified in the famous *Port Huron Statement* of 1962 and in other writings. And their commitment to democratic localism was given programmatic substance in August 1963 with the creation of the Economic Research and Action Project, an ambitious attempt to organize the poor and unemployed of all races in selected cities in the North.[11]

Within a short time SDS emerged as the most energetic and intellectually creative force within the New Left. But it attracted relatively few members during the first half of the decade. It had fewer than five hundred dues-paying members in 1962 (about one-sixth that of the Student Peace Union), and only about twice that number two years later. This meager harvest was not caused by lack of effort. From the beginning SDS worked hard to recruit the increasing numbers of white middle-class students attending universities, and after 1963 it tried to organize the urban poor of all races as well. They solicited money, publicity and political support from liberal politicians and intellectuals, private foundations, wealthy individuals, labor unions and sympathetic journalists. Their manifesto of principles, the *Port Huron Statement,* was probably the best-selling and most widely discussed radical document of the sixties. It went through four editions and 60,000 copies in four years. This included one copy delivered by Haber and Hayden to presidential advisor Arthur Schlesinger, Jr., in June, 1962. According to Hayden, Schlesinger promised them he would "bring [their] views to the attention" of President Kennedy.[12]

SDS's call for a "participatory democracy" was one of the most frequently mouthed shibboleths of the decade, though it seemed to have different meanings to each person who used it, including those in SDS. A few sympathetic journalists publicized the group's activities, and it was more successful than other white radical organizations in interpreting and acting upon the ferment generated by the Civil Rights and peace movements in the early sixties.

In the process, SDS dissociated itself not only from communism, but to some degree from what Hayden called the "sectarianism" and "queer jargon" of older democratic socialists. Socialism, he said, "is a European word."[13] It was associated with ideological hairsplitting, a passion for factionalism and a vision of inevitable class conflict alien to most Americans. Nor, of course, could an organization promoting socialism hope to have an impact on American politics. And SDS was intent upon having an impact.

For intellectual inspiration, Hayden and the others leaned on the writings of radical sociologist C. Wright Mills and French existentialist Albert Camus, rather than on Marx and Lenin. Or, for that matter, on American democratic socialists like Eugene Debs, Norman Thomas (a member of the LID's board) and Irving Howe. As Todd Gitlin noted in recalling the attitude of SDS members toward Howe and the democratic socialists in the LID who had been radicals since the thirties, they "seemed to us altogether *settled*" (Gitlin's emphasis).[14] Mills's ideas about the undemocratic power wielded by economic and other elites, and his exhortations to create empowered, decentralized democratic "publics," were especially influential in early SDS.[15]

Notwithstanding their dismissive attitude toward older leftists, a good number of SDS members in the early sixties were democratic socialists. As Hayden pointed out, the "vision" of SDS "lay in the traditions of the left," though he didn't specify them. But, as Carl Oglesby noted, SDS's version of a new left was designed to "overcome" the "memories, the certitudes, and the premises of the old left," whether socialist or communist. And Haber incessantly warned against falling into the trap of adhering to the rigid "political or economic formulations" of socialism and communism. For Paul Potter, the demonization of capitalism by the Old Left was "for me and my generation an inadequate description of the evils of America." Capitalism was a "hollow, dead word tied to the thirties."[16] New Leftists like Potter sensed something more insidious than capitalism, something more fundamental to the culture, behind the urges to dominate and exploit. How these disparate views squared with SDS resting "in the traditions of the left" was unclear.

Their attitudes toward contemporary liberalism were even more ambivalent. From the beginning liberals were encouraged to join SDS. Some in SDS, most notably the red diaper baby Steve Max, envisioned an alliance (however uneasy) between liberals and New Leftists that might lead to radical change through the electoral process. Max and some others in SDS believed realignment within the two major political parties was logical if not inevitable. Ideologically, the powerful block of southern conservatives in Congress belonged in the Republican camp, despite their historical ties to the Democratic Party. If Southern conservatives became Republicans, realignment would give liberals a firm hold on the Democratic party. This might create conditions favorable to the formation of a left wing within the party. SDS-style radicals could fill that role and push the liberal majority toward advocating major structural changes in the society. It is likely that many early members of SDS envisioned some version of this scenario as their best hope for achieving radical change.[17]

For a number of reasons, however, there was little if any basis for reconciling the goals of SDS with those of modern liberalism. Hayden indicated as much in 1961 when he said the task of radicals was to forge major changes in society. Liberal reform merely assuaged, and thus essentially preserved, the country's "continuous ills."[18] Also, events during the first half of the decade gave New Leftists legitimate reason to mistrust liberals. Despite their initial attraction to Kennedy, they were disillusioned by his administration's halfhearted support for, and protection of, civil-rights activists working for racial equality under life-threatening conditions in the South. And President Lyndon Johnson's decision to seat the segregated Mississippi delegation at the 1964 Democratic National Convention, instead of the democratically elected and racially integrated Mississippi Freedom Democratic Party, outraged both African American and white activists.

Beyond such important but discrete matters, a far more fundamental issue created an irreconcilable breech between SDS and liberals. SDS was a rebellion against the premises of modern liberalism. Twentieth-century liberalism embodied the middle-class orientations that inspired the rebellion of political (and cultural) radicals in the first place: managerial "rationality," achieved status through intense competition, narrowly framed professional specialization and bureaucratic "efficiency." More than anything else, SDS activists were radical egalitarians who instinctively recoiled from the ways and means of twentieth-century American liberalism.

In studying the history of early SDS, scholars have advanced a number of reasons for its failure to attract more recruits and to create a viable left in American politics. Conceptual haziness on important issues was part of the problem. Between 1960 and 1965, SDS failed to locate precisely where it wished to stake its claim on the political spectrum. Nor was it particularly clear about what it meant by a decentralized, community-based "democracy of individual participation." It was one thing to call centralized institutions "undemocratic." It was quite another to detail how a participatory democracy would function, or to describe concretely how solutions to problems that were national in scope could flow from clusters of decentralized, local political structures. And SDS members often confounded public issues with "personal politics." Their political ideas and programs were often entwined with romantic quests for transcending alienation, longing for intimacy and achieving personal "authenticity."

Also, while the group denounced communist and other forms of dictatorship, it often seemed more intent on trumpeting the rectitude of "anti-anticommunism." This nurtured a corrosive mutual mistrust between the young activists in SDS and the virulently anticommunist social democrats in the LID (the two parted ways at mid decade). SDS seemed to think it more important to point out the dangers to civil liberties of what they called "unreasoning" anticommunism than to protect the organization from infiltration by Marxist-Leninist ideologues. Some in SDS romanticized autocratic Third World revolutionaries like Fidel Castro and Ho Chi Minh. And as we have seen, their attitudes toward potential political allies, especially liberals and social democrats, ranged from muddled to ambiguous to antagonistic.[19]

In addition, by 1963 significant differences about SDS's goals as a radical organization surfaced among the young activists, creating serious rifts within the organization. Some wanted SDS to remain a student-oriented, university-based group focused on organizing the college-educated middle class. Others favored off-campus community activism among the poor and unemployed through the Economic Research and Action Project, a crucial initiative described in the following chapter. Steve Max wanted SDS to press for concrete political objectives, such as the realignment of the Democratic and Republican Parties, while Hayden said there was a more pressing need to realign the country's moral values.[20]

Finally, these instinctively egalitarian young people had a powerful antipathy toward hierarchy. They tried to arrive at organizational decisions through consensus rather than majority rule. Consequently, decision making within SDS was an arduous, often futile process. Chaos usually reigned in the organization's national office. Few who belonged to SDS prior to 1965 were interested in the day-to-day details of running an organization. They had trouble opening, filing and answering the mail, much less building the administrative structures, hierarchy and alliances necessary to sustain a political movement.[21]

But circumstances beyond the young radicals' control also compromised their hope of forging a viable political left. By far the most important was President Johnson's decision in the spring of 1965 to drastically expand the American combat presence in Vietnam. On April 17, 1965, in Washington, D. C., SDS cosponsored the first major protest against the war. The demonstration's sponsors, including the Student Peace Union and Women's Strike for Peace, hoped a few thousand people would attend the rally. To their surprise, about 20,000 showed up, many of them students. While this number was paltry compared to the hundreds of thousands who participated in protests against the Vietnam War later in the decade, it was the largest antiwar demonstration in American history to that point. The rally featured music by folk singer Phil Ochs, and a speech by the leftist journalist I. F. Stone. Senator Ernest Gruening of Alaska, one of the few members of Congress to oppose the war from the beginning, also spoke.[22]

The day's most memorable speech was made by SDS president Paul Potter. Along with others in SDS, Potter was worried that the war and the incipient antiwar movement would deflect New Left and civil-rights groups from pressing for radical change in American society. He also feared that the war would force SDS to take positions on conditions in distant countries about which it knew little. Potter sculpted his speech with these concerns in mind.

He reminded his audience that relatively few of them were members of peace groups or concerned with foreign policy. Most simply wanted to "build a more decent society" in the United States. They were students "involved in protests over the quality and kind of education they are receiving in growingly bureaucratized, depersonalized institutions called universities." They were African Americans "struggling against the tyranny and repression" of racism, and advocates for the poor "attempting to build movements that abolish poverty and secure democracy." These "hopeful beginnings" of dissent and change were threatened by the "all-consuming priorities and psychology of a war against an enemy thousands of miles away!" But if the problems facing the American people were not in Southeast Asia but "here in the United States," Vietnam was nonetheless a stark symbol of a "system" of domination that permitted a small number of economic and political elites to decide the fates of millions, at home and around the world. He challenged his listeners to "name that system":

> What kind of system is it that justifies the United States or any other country seizing the destinies of the Vietnamese people and using them callously for its own purpose? What kind of system is it that disenfranchises people in the South, leaves millions upon millions of people throughout the country impoverished and excluded from the mainstream and promise of American society, that creates faceless and terrible bureaucracies and makes those the place where people spend their lives and do their work, that consistently puts material values before human values—and still persists in calling itself free and still persists in finding itself fit to police the world? What place is there for ordinary men in that system and how are they to control it, make it bend itself to their wills rather than bending them to its?
>
> We must name that system. We must name it, describe it, analyze it and change it. For it is only when that system is changed and brought under control that there can be any hope for stopping the forces that create a war in Vietnam today or a murder in the South tomorrow or all the incalculable, innumerable more subtle atrocities that are worked on people all over—all the time.[23]

Potter didn't "name the system." He deliberately refrained from calling it capitalism. He knew it wasn't that simple, and believed that Old Left panaceas were irrelevant to the New Left's vision, at least up to 1966 or so. Potter's speech captured the New Left's rejection of the Old Left's economic determinism, as well as the young radicals' taste for ambiguity and experimentation. He called for a movement centered on "the integrity of man and a belief in man's capacity to tolerate all the weird formulations of society that men may choose to strive for."[24] It was a brilliant evocation of the humanism and penchants for risk and adventure among alienated youth in the sixties, within and outside of the New Left.

But it was also one of the last times a member of SDS's founding generation, or "old guard" as they called themselves, would wrap early New Left sensibilities around a well-publicized speech. Public denunciations of the war were not popular in 1965. Many liberals and anticommunist socialists were incensed by the rally. Also, SDS's decision to allow communist youth groups, such as the W. E. B. DuBois Clubs and Progressive Labor, to "endorse" (though not cosponsor) the protest outraged its parent organization and led to an irrevocable break between itself and the League for Industrial Democracy. And Potter was prescient in anticipating that the war would consume young radicals and ultimately undermine their focus on domestic change.

The success and media coverage of the April 1965 demonstration made it appear, both to the general public and college students, that SDS was primarily an antiwar organization. The surge of antiwar sentiment among students over the next three years swelled SDS's membership. With most of the first generation of leaders involved in community organizing activities that were effectively independent of the organization, some SDS campus chapters emerged as the most strident and influential force in the student antiwar movement.

SDS gradually shed most of its nonideological posture and a good deal of its multi-issue orientation. The "old guard" was replaced by students who often came from different social, regional, educational and political backgrounds. According to Todd Gitlin, they were not like the rather formal, cleanshaven, tie-and-jacket-wearing early recruits to SDS. Post-1965 SDS members came from "frontier country, had long, shaggy, swooping mustaches, [and] wore blue work shirts and cowboy boots." Many were from "the Midwest and Southwest, they were not Jewish, they were more likely to come from working class families, and they were less intellectual, less articulate" than the founding generation.[25]

By the late sixties SDS was less an organization than a name appended to hundreds of autonomous campus chapters around the country. With approximately one hundred thousand members, it was the largest radical student organization in American history. SDS became famous, in fact notorious, as a fomenter of disruptive, violent antiwar protests at Wisconsin, Columbia, Harvard and other universities. But unlike the much smaller SDS of the early sixties that called for a renewal of the country's democratic traditions, its post-1965 incarnation often shouted down opponents. By leading or encouraging disruptions on scores of college campuses, SDS allowed its opponents to shift public attention from the war in Vietnam and other pressing social issues to the bad manners of obstreperous college protesters. This incarnation of SDS, rather than that of the early sixties, is the one recalled by most Americans who read newspapers or watched television newscasts in the late sixties.

In the late sixties, a variety of groups espousing doctrinaire and, to put it charitably, idiosyncratic versions of Old Left revolutionary politics, vied for control of SDS. These groups included Marxist-Leninist-Maoist groups such as Progressive Labor and the Revolutionary Youth Movements I and II. The most notorious of these was the Weatherman faction, which denounced "white skin privilege" and viewed African Americans and other victims of Euro-American imperialism as the avant-garde of an impending worldwide revolution. The few hundred members of the well-publicized Weatherman faction were driven by fantasies of sparking a violent revolution which they believed was imminent but for which no one showed up. Members of Weatherman organized themselves into small revolutionary "cells" and "cadre," in which individuals surrendered their autonomy to the will of the "collective." Susan Stern, the daughter of a wealthy New Jersey family, joined a "Weather collective" in Seattle in 1969. "Everything I did, I did as a Weatherman," recalled Stern. "The way I dressed, the manner in which I talked, what I said, my friends, whom I slept with, my eating, my sleeping, my reading, my feelings about the past, all were open to the closest scrutiny. There was no part of me left unexposed and unchanged by Weatherman."[26]

No one was killed by Weatherman's well-publicized, sporadic acts of violence except for three of its own. They accidentally detonated a bomb while assembling it in a Manhattan townhouse owned by the wealthy parents of a Weatherman.

The combination of factionalism and fantasies of revolution, along with harassment and sabotage by police "red squads" and the FBI, led to the disintegration of SDS in 1969. What began amid the optimism of 1960 as an attempt to revitalize the radical promise of American democracy, ended in pseudopolitical burlesque at the close of the decade.

This division between the pre- and post-1965 SDS was not as hard and fast as this outline suggests. The leaders of early SDS were antiauthoritarian and nonviolent. And they had few formal ties to the organization after 1966. But Hayden, Rennie Davis and other members of the "old guard" became caught up in the frustration and rage that fueled violent protests in the late sixties. After the sixties Hayden denounced Weatherman as the "id" rather than the "conscience" of the New Left, but admitted he was tempted on more than one occasion during the late sixties by the "lure of violence and martyrdom."[27]

And if early SDS was politically on target in distancing itself from liberalism and the old democratic left, the arrogance, self-righteousness and condescension it displayed in doing so presaged the behavior of less thoughtful SDSers later in the decade. As did the "old guard's" tendency to romanticize Third World autocratic figures as long as they were on the left. The old guard had more in common with the post-1965 SDS ideologues than many of them admitted.

This sketch of the history of SDS brings us back to the questions posed earlier. What were the historical sources of early SDS's radical democratic values and its criticisms of the country's political institutions? Which American political traditions resonated with SDS's desire to create decentralized, community-based enclaves of democracy? Why did they view democracy as something that transcended electoral politics? And why did their values fail to pique the interest of most Americans, even before the war on Vietnam skewed the political landscape, and before the shift in membership, circumstances and tactics altered the original trajectory of SDS?

An appropriate starting point for approaching these issues is a discussion of SDS's ideas about human nature, democracy and community. Its views of these matters were often fuzzy, scattered and incomplete. They were embryonic rather than fully developed. Nevertheless, SDS's political ideas were informed more by its members' perceptions of these three issues than by formal political theories or doctrines.

HUMAN NATURE, DEMOCRACY AND THE POLITICS OF COMMUNITY

Most members of SDS were children of the middle class who rejected its staid lifestyle, hunger for status, materialism and commitment to economic individualism. Despite their alienation from these values, the group's most important assumptions about human nature were tied to the "expressive," non-economic side of their middle-class heritage.

They believed human beings needed to be autonomous, self-reliant and free. The vast majority of people were not only capable of exercising the privileges and responsibilities of freedom, but of transcending conformity, apathy and fear of the unknown. In effect, these assumptions about human nature mirrored their own experiences and self-images. As youngsters, they had learned to think for themselves. They were trained to be prepared for and welcome the opportunities and contingencies life would inevitably send their way. Their image of human nature revolved around these middle-class notions.

SDSers believed that to be truly human the individual had to wean himself from dependence upon received wisdom or ideologies. "[D]irect experience," declared Carl Oglesby, was the only "incontrovertible" guide to personal and political behavior.[28] In 1961 Hayden said that one of the defining characteristics of the New Left was its "radicalism of style." "Radicalism of style" meant defying fear of change and pressures to conform. It reflected a determination to control one's destiny. New Leftists made "a serious personal decision to be introspective, to be exposed always to the stinging glare of change, to be willing always to reconstruct our social views. In its harshest consideration, radicalism of style demands that we oppose delusions and be free. It demands that we change our life."[29] As an SDS recruitment brochure written in 1962 or 1963 said, "we affirm that men are in control of their destinies and must accept that control."[30]

But according to Hayden, social elites "manipulated" most people into surrendering "that control." Religious, intellectual and economic leaders believed the vast majority of people were inherently unsuited for self-government and independence. Hayden made this clear in an internal memorandum written early in 1962.[31] He wrote that the neo-orthodox Christian view of human nature, embraced by many liberals and intellectuals after World War II, assumed human beings were stained by inherent penchants for sin and evil. They harbored irrational, even murderous, impulses that were barely contained by their consciences, dread of disorder or fear of punishment.

In Hayden's view, liberals believed that the majority did not want to be free. Instead they craved economic and personal security at almost any cost. Even in an ostensible democracy like the United States, most citizens tacitly surrendered to various elites and elected officials their rights to make most of the important decisions that affected them. The image of human beings as fallen, imperfect creatures who retreated from freedom legitimated liberalism's halfhearted approach to social change. Since people were "children of darkness" as well as "children of light," the best Americans could hope for in the way of improving society was gradual reform designed and implemented by elected representatives and the various experts they consulted. Visions of social transformation beyond this were at best unrealistic, at worst utopian.

Hayden believed these views made a sham of the promise of American democracy. They assumed "all men really do not desire freedom." SDS should counter this elitist view of human nature by proclaiming the "feared sovereignty of the unqualified." It should promote an image of the ordinary citizen as "a creator and self-maker rather than a pitiless [*sic*] and buffeted thing unable to reach the forces that control" him.[32]

Hayden revisited these themes in a speech to students at Ann Arbor in March 1962. He told the students that American society was shrouded in a fog of fear, apathy and conformity. Most Americans, including his educated audience, unwittingly drifted through their lives, bent upon security and fearful of change. They wallowed in "impotency," adapting themselves to the self-images and "the myriad of rules" imposed by social and political elites.

> Above all, I reject the claim that only a privileged few can be independent, the view that creativity is necessarily the function of culture-preserving elites. I believe that independence can be a fact about ordinary people. And democracy, real participatory democracy, rests on the independence of ordinary people.[33]

The idea of ordinary people as autonomous "self-makers" capable of independence informed the images of democracy and community incorporated in SDS's 1962 manifesto of principles, the *Port Huron Statement.*[34] In the document's opening passages the young radicals identified themselves as "people of this generation, bred in at least modest comfort, housed now in universities, looking uncomfortably to the world we inherit." Characteristically, they called the *Port Huron Statement* "a living document open to change with our times and experiences." Rather than a manifesto of immutable principles, it was a starting point for "our own debate and education" and "our dialogue with society."

While growing up in the forties and fifties, they were told the United States was a land of equality and freedom, endowed with governments "of, by, and for the people." These principles, along with the country's affluence and its stated goal of defending freedom throughout the world, led many of them to mature "in complacency." The world might be less than perfect, but life in America was the best of all possible worlds. By the late fifties, however, their complacency was "penetrated by events too troubling to dismiss."

More than anything else, the scourge of racism compelled them to question the commitment of their fellow countrymen to liberty and equality. The American "declaration 'all men are equal' rang hollow" in the face of racism. The Cold War standoff between superpowers armed with nuclear weapons planted in them the dread of being the "last generation in the experiment with living."

There were other problems, less morally urgent than racism or the bomb, but compelling nonetheless. An immense gulf separated the democratic ideal of Americans as proudly independent and bursting with initiative, and the "apathetic and manipulated" lives endured by most of them. A small minority of elites dominated the country and lived in "superfluous abundance." Mindless conformity, "meaningless work," unemployment or poverty were the lots of the great majority. These and other problems might appear morally intolerable, but a combination of middle-class affluence, suburban contentment, fear of change and feelings of political impotence rendered most Americans complacent or apathetic.

> [W]e ourselves are imbued with urgency, yet the message of our society is that there is no viable alternative to the present. Beneath the reassuring tones of the politicians . . . is the pervading feeling that . . . our times have witnessed the exhaustion not only of Utopias, but of any new departures as well. Feeling the press of complexity upon the emptiness of life, people are fearful of the thought that at any moment things might be thrust out of control. They fear change itself. . . . For most Americans all crusades are suspect, threatening. The fact that each individual sees apathy in his fellows perpetuates the common reluctance to organize for change.[35]

As historian Allen Matusow pointed out, the manifesto bore little resemblance to radical proclamations "of the past." Despite the cachet enjoyed by the *Port Huron Statement* during the sixties and SDS's hope that the document would "provide the infant new left with an ideology," it did not offer an apocalyptic vision of revolutionary transformation. It didn't even demand an end to capitalism. To "some, especially later [in the sixties], the statement seemed entirely too liberal."[36]

Matusow had a point. The SDS manifesto called for realignment of the major political parties, a higher minimum wage and an end to the "unreasoning anticommunism" that fueled McCarthyism and other domestic right-wing movements. It urged "controlled disarmament" between the nuclear superpowers. As for capitalism, Hayden's original draft of the manifesto said that "private enterprise is not inherently immoral or undemocratic—indeed, it may at times contribute to offset elitist tendencies."[37] This was excised from the final version to placate the socialists in SDS. Even so, the *Port Huron Statement* did not call for an end to the free enterprise system. It did say "corporations must be made publicly responsible," and that the "means of production should be open to democratic participation and subject to democratic social regulation."[38] Whatever this meant in practical terms (there were no detailed descriptions of what "democratic social regulation" meant or how it might function), it was hardly the stuff of social or economic transformation.

But if much of the document hovered somewhere between liberalism and socialism, the first formal section of the *Port Huron Statement,* titled "Values," went beyond both. It contained ideas about human nature, democracy and community that, though fragmented and lacking intellectual cohesion (as in other SDS writings), defined what was radical and historically significant about SDS.

"We regard men as infinitely precious and possessed of unfulfilled capacities for reason, freedom, and love." (Hayden's original draft said "infinitely perfectible" instead of "infinitely precious.") Human beings had "unrealized potential for self-cultivation, self-direction, self-understanding, and creativity." Thus the goal of society "should be human independence." Despite prevailing images of human nature, SDS saw no reason "why men cannot meet with increasing skill the complexities and responsibilities of their situation, if society is organized not for minority, but for majority, participation in decision-making."[39]

In this last sentence the young radicals were suggesting, however obliquely, that the republican, or representative, form of government that existed in the United States was incompatible with its democratic heritage. In addition to representative government, there should be a more direct "democracy of individual participation." A participatory democracy implied sustained involvement by all citizens in the social and political activities of their communities. It meant active participation by the individual in "those decisions determining the quality and direction of his life." In a participatory democracy society would be organized "to encourage independence in men and provide the media for their common participation."[40]

Neither in the *Port Huron Statement* nor in subsequent writings did SDS describe how a participatory democracy would function, or how it would mesh with the system of electoral politics and form of representative government created by the United States Constitution. The manifesto implied that a democracy of participation required the decentralization of political power and the active involvement of citizens in decisions that impacted their lives. By definition, this would mean a surrender of some of the decision-making power held by state and federal authorities, and its dispersal throughout hundreds, if not thousands, of communities around the country. But the *Port Huron Statement* did not identify which powers should be transferred. Nor did it describe how state- or nationwide problems could be solved through decision making at the local level. As used in the manifesto and other SDS documents, "participatory democracy," perhaps the most intriguing, inspiring and potentially explosive political idea of the sixties, was an imprecise, elusive notion.[41]

Nor did those who participated in the 1962 SDS convention in Port Huron, Michigan, where the manifesto was debated and approved, see eye to eye about what the term meant. During and since the sixties, their definitions of participatory democracy were at best heterogeneous and at worst contradictory. For Sharon Jeffrey it suggested control over one's life. "I definitely wanted to be involved in decisions that were going to affect me. How could I let anyone make a decision about me that I wasn't involved in?" For Bob Ross and other socialists in SDS, participatory democracy "had embryonic in it the idea of socialism." It was a way to "talk about socialism in an American accent."[42]

By contrast, Paul Potter believed the SDS version of democracy was "basic American civics," which, as he well knew, didn't include socialism as an option. For Potter, participatory democracy was "radical egalitarianism" in the American grain. In 1971 the socialist Richard Flacks defined it as the "abolition of hierarchy, of authority based on expertise or privilege."[43] In 1966 a member of SDS who was not at Port Huron said participatory democracy implied a "highly decentralized social system." It meant "direct democracy" carried on within political "units" small enough to allow for the "direct involvement" of individuals in the "decision-making process." Participatory democracy was the opposite of representative, or indirect, democracy. The latter encouraged "elitism" and separated elected officials "from the everyday reality of the activities being governed."[44] At times, Tom Hayden seemed to think that an exclusively representative form of government was inconsistent with a genuine, that is, participatory, democracy. "This is the central fatal fact about the United States," he said in 1962. "It is a republic [with an electoral, representative form of government] not a democracy, and nearly everyone wants to keep it that way."[45]

Though no single definition of participatory democracy held sway among the young radicals, there was some common ground about what it implied. It meant that most human beings were capable of making important public decisions. In order to make those decisions, they had to be actively engaged in a locally oriented, vibrant public life, where shared decision making could occur among equals. In other words, through the process of democratic decision making at the local level individuals expressed *both* their personal independence and their need to associate with others. Whatever else it may have meant to SDSers, participatory democracy was clearly the political axis where personal liberty and equality should intersect with community and social bonding.

The conflict between personal autonomy and the requirements of community was more than an abstraction for SDS activists. It was the social equivalent of their own inner tensions. Potter pointed out that New Leftists believed that "our commitment to the rhetoric of individualism makes us insist there is no conflict between communalism and individualism." But, "there is," he said, and an amoral, distorted version of individualism usually dominated American behavior, including that of New Leftists.[46] During her work in SDS's community organizing project in Cleveland in the mid sixties, Sharon Jeffrey said the organizers who lived among the poor in SDS's Economic Research and Action Project were group-oriented in the midst of a society which emphasized competitive individualism. Yet Jeffrey liked the idea that the organizers "were very independent. Independent thinking was encouraged and supported."[47] How the two were reconciled she didn't say. In his autobiography, Hayden admitted that during the sixties he could not tolerate "ego denial." He was unable to resist the self-absorption involved in exploring his own identity, even as he tried to submerge his ego in the interest of collective decision making and action.[48]

SDSers knew competitive individualism was the engine that drove the American social and economic machine. It led to the exploitation, poverty, elitism and corruption of democratic values they railed against. Also, it was the cause of a warped version of privacy, and of the loneliness, apathy and impersonality it fostered throughout American society. Socialized in the ways of individualism, the young radicals nevertheless shied away from the social and personal atomization it implied. Hence Hayden's (unintentionally) paradoxical 1962 definition of the New Left: it was a "movement out of privacy [and toward community] . . . by individuals who are their own leaders."[49]

In the "Values" section of the *Port Huron Statement* they dealt with this conundrum by distinguishing between what they called "authentic," or morally informed, independence and "egoistic individualism." They said the "object [of authentic individualism] is not to have one's way so much as it is to have a way that is one's own." Exploring and defining "a way of one's own" was inseparable from social relationships. Indeed, the ultimate purpose of politics was to "bring people out of isolation and into community." Politics was the "art of collectively creating an acceptable pattern of social relations." In one of the document's most important passages they tried to outline the civic space where morally informed individuality and social bonding might converge:

> Loneliness, estrangement, isolation describe the vast distance between man and man today. These dominant tendencies cannot be overcome by better personnel management, nor by improved gadgets, but only when a love of man overcomes the idolatrous worship of things by man. As the individualism we affirm is not egoism, the selflessness we affirm is not self-elimination. On the contrary, we believe in generosity of a kind that imprints one's unique individual qualities in the relation to other men, and to all human activity.[50]

Their search for a way of reconciling personal autonomy and liberty with intimacy and community revisited old dilemmas that had existed from the beginning of the American experience. How can shared values be agreed upon in a dynamic, pluralistic society that promotes economic and other forms of radical individualism? Is it even possible to develop a viable sense of community among a restless people constantly on the move and immersed in their private concerns? The United States lacks an established religion or other institutions sufficiently powerful to restrain competitive individualism. Nor will its people tolerate an overbearing government. Indeed, the notion of government as the embodiment of the "collective will of the people" does not exist in the United States. How, then, can individuals enjoy the blessings of liberty yet be restrained from engaging in immoral or exploitative behavior?[51]

The assertion that human beings possessed a "generosity of a kind that imprints one's unique qualities in relation to other men" implied that the restraint came from within the individual. SDS activists weren't the first advocates of American democracy to suggest this. Though they were unaware of the lineage, this approach to reconciling individual liberty and social cohesion revisited themes raised by Thomas Jefferson early in the nineteenth century. And for the same reasons.

Like SDS, Jefferson searched for a way of balancing individual liberty and freedom with community and fellow feeling. On one hand, he affirmed the superior claims of personal liberty against those of a powerful or meddlesome government. The "public good is best promoted by the exertion of each individual seeking his own good in his own way" with minimal interference from the state or other powerful institutions. On the other hand, Jefferson believed individual liberty and social cohesion could coexist because "nature" imbued human beings with "social dispositions" (or what SDS described as an innate "generosity" toward others). Nature "hath implanted in our breasts," wrote Jefferson in 1814, "a love of others, a sense of duty to them, a moral instinct, in short, which prompts us irresistibly to feel and succor their distresses."[52]

Thus freedom and order, individual liberty and social amity could be harmonized. If the "moral instinct" of fellow feeling was nurtured, autonomous individuals would care about and respect one another. Equally important, they would do so voluntarily. Civility and social order were not dependent solely (or even primarily) upon the coercive authority of powerful political and religious institutions.

This may have been behind Jefferson's idea of creating a host of "small republic[s]" throughout the country (roughly similar to SDS's notion of participatory democracy.) These local agencies of self-government would complement (not replace) state and federal governments. Their dual purpose was to encourage individuals to actively participate in the process of self-governance and to do so as a community. "[E]very man in the State would thus become an acting member of the common government, transacting in person a great portion of its rights and duties." These decentralized "republics" would focus on local issues of concern to residents, and hopefully help bond them as a community.[53]

The idea that human beings could exist in a "state of nature" was anathema to both Jefferson and SDS. Even before human beings formed organized societies, according to Jefferson, their instinctive need to bond with one another compelled them to create voluntary groupings. Or, as Hayden wrote in 1963, the human need for "social relations" preceded the creation of formal "institutional relations."[54]

Gary Wills has pointed out that Jefferson's belief in a moral instinct was probably grounded in his study of Scottish Enlightenment philosophers. Jefferson was well acquainted with the ideas of the Scottish philosopher Francis Hutcheson, who believed human beings possessed an innate moral sense and experienced gratification when they acted benevolently toward others. According to Wills, Jefferson's use of the phrase "pursuit of happiness" in the Declaration of Independence was not an invitation to self-absorbed individualism. Rather, it reflected Jefferson's belief that the greatest happiness possible for an individual was to be seen by his community as a benevolent person. Pursuit of the common good, the ideal of classical civic republicanism, led to personal happiness.[55]

But it is also possible that Jefferson's notion of a moral "instinct," or what he called humanity's "innate sense of justice," pointed, however embryonically, toward a more modern, more recognizably American, notion of personal liberty.

Human beings could both be free from overweening government (or other intrusive institutions) and respect the rights of others. They could pursue their own interests but not at the price of losing the intimacy and security offered by a bonded community. And they could retain their "natural rights" as individuals and forge a civilized, harmonious society based upon voluntary associations and cooperation without unnecessary interference from the state.[56]

These ideas meshed with Hayden's definition of participatory democracy in his 1988 memoir. He said the term as used by SDS in the sixties had nothing to do with urging people to participate in elections in order to send radical or liberal representatives to Congress and the state legislatures. Participatory democracy meant empowering "ordinary" people to take "command of their lives" by acting as "independent and creative human beings, expressing a new force outside of existing institutions, a society apart from the state."[57]

This was not a modern replay of the civic republicanism that existed in Jefferson's day. Classical civic republicanism (which is discussed in the next chapter) placed too many restrictions upon the individual, and too few on society's leaders, to be relevant for understanding SDS. The centerpiece of SDS's radicalism was its attempt to salvage an American version of individual liberty by embedding it within a bonded but egalitarian community setting. Their attempt to do so was vaguely drawn (and, in the end, quite unrealistic). But it helped shape their ideas about three important issues: stemming the influence of elites and experts, decentralizing political power and revitalizing community.

For SDS, the power and influence wielded by elites of one sort or another contradicted the egalitarian promise of American democracy. By contrast with the Old Left, which focused almost exclusively on the economic and political power exerted by those who controlled the "means of production," SDS challenged elites who possessed cultural and social influence as well as economic and political clout. For example, they denounced what Paul Potter called the "cult of the expert."[58] There was something fundamentally undemocratic about the prestige and influence enjoyed by scientists, lawyers, academics, critics, psychologists, physicians, policymakers and other professionally trained experts. These educated products of achieved status and middle-class ambition defined and monopolized the means of knowledge. If their nominal power was dwarfed by that of elected officials and economic elites who controlled the means of production, their influence in a technological, knowledge-driven society was nonetheless enormous.

The prestige and power possessed by educated elites did more than intimidate those with less education. It expropriated their claims to autonomy and independence. The United States considered itself a democratic society because it placed achieved status over ascribed status—equality of opportunity above inherited advantages. Anyone could become anything if they worked hard and possessed the requisite talent, regardless of their parents' station in life.

For SDS, this substituted one form of hierarchy for another. It replaced a rationale for social stratification based upon heredity or family connections with a system of hierarchy based upon meritocratic competition. Restraints upon the power of public officials to act arbitrarily were supplanted by the license given private individuals, such as employers, to do the same. According to Potter, the result was an undemocratic social order. "We stand," Potter said of the New Left, "for the destruction of the cult of the expert." The

> simplest assertion the New Left has made is that people have the capacity to make *all* the judgments about the critical things that affect their lives. . . . If a man is so estranged from his body that he has nothing to do but place it limply in the hands of a doctor, then he is philosophically, physically and emotionally in bad health, regardless of what the doctor does for him. . . . If civilization is too complicated for ordinary men to direct, then civilization is at fault and not the people. If one must have Shakespeare experts in order to "understand and appreciate" Shakespeare, it just may be that we can get along without Shakespeare.[59]

What stands out from these remarks, beyond Potter's apparent antipathy toward intellectuals and experts, is his startling faith in American democracy and its "ordinary" citizens. But Potter was no more an anti-intellectual than Thomas Jefferson was when, in 1787, he praised "ordinary" Americans in a way SDS would have endorsed. "State a moral case to a ploughman and a professor," wrote Jefferson. "The former will decide it as well, and often better than the latter."[60] For Potter the issue was not the merits or utility of education and intellect, both of which he valued. It was the inequality created by the subtle but nonetheless coercive power conferred upon a minority of experts and professionals (as well, of course, as upon the more obvious power exercised by corporate executives and elected officials). The various forms of power and influence wielded by elites diminished the autonomy and freedom of the vast majority of Americans.

For SDS, the logic of democracy implied that significant portions of political power should be in the hands of the people, not simply derived from them or exercised by their elected representatives and unelected experts. And not merely when stating a "moral case," as Jefferson put it, but in every significant realm of public decision making. In the United States the sources of political decision-making power that affected people's lives were mostly centralized and, therefore, remote. They were lodged in vast, byzantine bureaucracies, and ensconced in faraway state and national capitals. Or they were found in the interstices between power, money and influence occupied by elected officials and lobbyists for corporate, professional and other well-heeled interest groups.

In an article written for the *New Republic* in 1966, Todd Gitlin questioned the assumption of liberals that political and economic power was dispersed in American society.[61] According to New Deal and post–New Deal "managerial liberals," the inevitable but orderly conflict among competing interest groups was refereed by an ostensibly neutral central government. In this scenario, organized interest groups such as labor unions, corporations and professional associations competed at the state and federal levels for legislation favorable to their constituents. The New Deal and Great Society model of government was one in which lobbying by various interest groups supposedly created a balance between society's competing interests. Since all citizens were free to organize themselves, and "there is always room for one more interest," this system insured the survival of a democratic social order.

But the "brute reality," according to Gitlin, was far different. The vast majority of Americans knew that the sources of power were both "remote" and "indifferent" to their needs. The actual processes of day-to-day governing were substantially beyond "democratic control." In exchange for surrendering their democratic prerogatives, the majority of Americans were rewarded with economic "sustenance," ranging from upper-middle-class affluence to welfare subsistence. If one of the goals of Lyndon Johnson's War on Poverty was to rebuild inner-city slums, the job should be done "according to plans adopted by the residents," not by experts or government policymakers and bureaucrats. Gitlin went still further. Welfare programs "should be supervised by the recipients" until all Americans were guaranteed a "decent" income, even if they did not wish to work. Power of all kinds needed to be "localize[d]." Police should be elected by local residents. Neighborhood "courts" should have jurisdiction over the "quality of goods, the availability of loans, the behavior of municipal, state and federal agencies." And there should be "computerized referenda on national issues like war and compulsory health insurance."[62]

SDS did not call for the eradication of the state and federal governments. It wanted (unspecified) portions of political power to be redistributed. If democracy meant having control over the decisions that affected one's life, it followed that a good deal of power had to be situated where people actually lived: within their communities.

Tom Hayden thought the country's "most wonderful political habit" was "doing specific things about one's immediate situation." That meant localism. "The death of us all," he continued, "is signaled always by apathy towards the local community."[63] And in order for political localism to be meaningful, a sense of cohesion had to exist within communities, however pluralistic their populations. In 1961 Al Haber, echoing C. Wright Mills, said democracy is "based on the idea of a 'political' public—a body that shares a range of common values and commitments, an institutional pattern of interaction and an image of themselves as a functioning community."[64]

Richard Flacks said the solutions to problems caused by "big," paternalistic government and the unfair influence enjoyed by various elites was to create alternative models of democratic citizenship. "I don't know what such models would look like," Flacks said candidly. But they would include the "decentralizing of decision-making, the development of diverse loci of power, the breaking up of gargantuan organizations."[65] These were necessary conditions for insuring genuine democratic control over elected officials, as well as for developing a vibrant civic space within which citizens could actively participate in decision making.

In a 1965 memorandum, some SDS members expressed concern about the impunity with which President Johnson unilaterally expanded the American presence in Vietnam. Johnson was "unresponsive to challenge within" Congress, much less from the general public. They wondered "how the President is unilaterally able to make a war in Viet-Nam as well as call it off."

> Crucial decisions affecting the lives of all of us are made privately by executive advisors and military planners in terms of political and military calculations. They are not made publicly by men responsible to the people and subject to public democratic decisions in terms of moral considerations and social needs.[66]

SDS's views of human nature, democracy, community, elites and the decentralization of political power shared at least some common ground with a host of earlier reform and radical movements. These included Jacksonian democracy, agrarian Populism, the democratic socialism of Eugene Debs, New Freedom progressivism and, as historian Maurice Isserman has shown, some currents of thought within the surviving remnants of the Old Left in the late fifties.[67] But early SDS differed profoundly from each of these movements as well. It was less ideological than most of them. And unlike all of them, it renounced hierarchy of any sort, rejected centralized decision making, repudiated economic determinism and refused to tailor its ideas or strategies to fit the interests of a particular interest group or social class.

In searching for American sources of their ideas (beyond those already linked to Thomas Jefferson) it might be more useful to place SDS within a historical framework consistent with the kinds of issues they raised, the problems that most concerned them and the solutions they offered. The social and political issues raised by the young radicals were related to the first principles of American political culture, and to their lingering ambiguities and contradictions. SDS reprised issues which originated during the formative period of American political development: the late eighteenth century, and especially the period between the onset of the American Revolution and the ratification of the United States Constitution. To understand the historical genesis of what SDS was for and against, which American political traditions it reprised and why its quest for community failed, we need to revisit those beginnings.

EIGHT

The Political Ferment of the Late Eighteenth Century and SDS's Failed Quest for Community

You might as well attempt to rule Hell by Prayer [as attempt] Democracy if consolidated into one Government [over the] vast Continent of America.

An Antifederalist Expressing Opposition to the Proposed U. S. Constitution, 1788

Festering together in the debris of a realtor's whim. . . . [E]ach . . . in his own cell of consciousness, each making his own patchwork quilt of reality, collecting fragments of experience here, pieces of information there. From the tiny impressions gleaned from one another they . . . tried to make do with the way they found each other.

Toni Morrison, *The Bluest Eye*

A NOTE TO THE READER

TO THE READER WHO HAS COME THIS FAR: I give thanks and appreciation. And a warning. Placing SDS in a historical context is a different enterprise from doing so for the counterculture or rock-and-roll. It requires a lengthy, sustained detour backward in American time. Before returning to the 1960s later in this chapter, we have to spend some time in the late eighteenth century.

This is necessary because SDS was not a political movement in the usual sense of the term. Rather than organize for success at the ballot box (as did their conservative contemporaries in Young Americans for Freedom), it raised basic questions about relationships between human nature, liberty, community, political and social hierarchy and self-governance. And it engaged head-on what was (and is) perhaps the most abiding irony of American history: the country's democratic values are not reflected in its most powerful political institutions.

These issues are inseparable from pivotal events that took place between 1776 and 1788. The prototype for SDS's conviction that "ordinary" citizens were capable of governing their own lives and becoming "their own leaders" was the surge of democratic sensibilities that accompanied the American Revolution. And the problems SDS addressed—symbolized by the stoicism and passivity implicit in the American adage that "you can't fight city hall"—were directly tied to the remote form of representative government created by the framers of the Constitution.

In what follows I do not argue that SDS leaned on eighteenth-century ideas to fashion their political values. They didn't. Nor do I contend that similar words used in vastly different historical contexts necessarily carry the same meaning. They don't. For instance, the meanings of political terms like "democracy" and "republic" have changed over the centuries. What hasn't changed was what SDS forcefully and all too briefly, vaguely and vainly brought to the surface of political discourse in the sixties: the incongruity between the country's democratic ethos—its genuine commitment to the ideal of equality—and an eighteenth-century political system designed, among many other things, to exclude the majority of Americans from direct decision-making power.

These issues cannot adequately be addressed without first describing why some Americans in the aftermath of the Revolution favored the Constitution and others opposed it.

THE POLITICAL FERMENT OF THE LATE EIGHTEENTH CENTURY

The debate over the proposed Constitution, which began in the fall of 1787 and ended with ratification in the summer of 1788, was fueled by conflicting economic and social interests, as well as by ideological disputes over political power and who should exercise it. Those who lived in the older, eastern and more urban portions of the original 13 states, regardless of their occupations or social statuses, generally favored the Constitution. They had different economic and social interests from those who opposed ratification, mostly middling and subsistence farmers living in the more recently settled western areas of the various states. The young nation was divided along a variety of regional, economic and social fault lines, all of which were exacerbated by an economic depression that developed in the aftermath of independence in 1783. Disagreements over volatile issues such as protective tariffs divided manufacturers and urban laborers from merchants and farmers, while debates over currency inflation separated creditors from debtors. Americans disagreed as well about which economic groups should bear the brunt of the tax burdens to repay the national debt incurred during the War of Independence. Also, there was contention over which political entity should be responsible for paying the debt: the individual states or the federal government.[1]

Though the focus here is on the ideological divide separating those who favored ratification of the Constitution from those who opposed it, these economic and regional issues were important and should be kept in mind. For the most part, and with important exceptions on both sides, the ideological debate revolved around an unintended consequence of the American Revolution: a nascent, incomplete but nonetheless powerful impetus toward democracy in state politics. In the aftermath of 1776, the incessant calls for liberty that pervaded the rhetoric of the Revolution created unanticipated bursts of democratic sentiments in some parts of the country.

Few Americans, and certainly not most leaders of the Revolution, anticipated these developments. In two masterful and persuasive studies of the Revolutionary era, Gordon S. Wood suggested that those who led the Revolution were engaged in a "utopian" movement that went far beyond the goal of securing independence from Great Britain.[2] They expressed "extraordinarily idealistic hopes for the social and political transformation of America." While committed to the ideals of liberty and equality, they did not envision a new nation governed by an unchecked democracy, or one whose economy was driven by economic individualism.

The leaders of the Revolution hoped their new country would embrace the civic republicanism advocated by political philosophers from classical Rome and Greece to the eighteenth-century British Whigs. They hoped the United States would become a cooperative commonwealth populated by a civic-minded citizenry. Frugality, temperance and a diligent work ethic would define the character of its hard-working, overwhelmingly agrarian population. A general equality of condition would exist among the majority, based on the ownership of an adequate, though usually modest, amount of property.

The essence of this vision, and the chief premise of civic republicanism, was that personal self-interest should be subservient to the greater good of the whole society. Benjamin Rush, a signer of the Declaration of Independence, defined the type of society he hoped would spring from the Revolution when he said that "every man in a republic is public property."[3] Sam Adams dreamed of a transformed America in which selfish behavior would be restrained by each citizen's awareness that he owed "everything to the commonwealth."[4] Neither destructive social factions nor political parties would exist. Political and social leaders would be selected on the basis of their talent, accomplishments and commitment to the public welfare. By themselves, inherited wealth or family connections would not qualify an individual for public office. When the Revolutionary leaders spoke of personal liberty they often placed it within the context of this vision of a cooperative republic. According to Wood,

> Individual liberty and the public good were easily reconcilable because the important liberty in the Whig ideology was public or political liberty. In 1776 the solution to the problems of American politics seemed to rest not so much in emphasizing the private rights of individuals against the general will as it did in stressing the public rights of the collective people against the supposed privileged interests of their rulers.[5]

These goals had a "decidedly reactionary tone," in Wood's words.[6] Civic republicanism squared with neither the realities of the country's development up to that point, nor with the increasingly self-interested behavior of its enterprising people. European civic republicanism was based on the medieval image of society as a more or less stable entity composed of relatively static, hierarchical, interdependent estates. Such a society had probably never existed in America.[7] Certainly by the late eighteenth century, geographic and social mobility had eroded older European notions of stability and social stasis.

Equally out of touch with American realities was the civic republican equation of social and political leadership. Like most Americans, those who led the Revolution opposed hereditary privilege, especially the idea that inherited wealth and family connections automatically qualified an individual to stand for political office. But as civic republicans, they were committed to an alternative notion of a ruling elite. Elective office should be held by men who possessed a combination of natural talent, education, earned affluence, industry, wisdom and selfless dedication to the public weal. In other words, a self-made elite.

Also, many of the leading advocates of independence from Great Britain clung to the traditional notion of social and political "deference." This held that the majority of voters should willingly select their political leaders from their self-made "betters": a "natural aristocracy" of talent, superior intellect and civic virtue. In practical terms, this usually meant landed gentry, or self-made men of wealth, education and influence. Influence and power had to be earned. Theoretically, these attributes could be acquired by anyone from any background who possessed the requisite talent and ambition. But few Revolutionary-era leaders were "prepared to repudiate the idea of a dominating [social and political] elite" to whom the majority should defer.[8]

Neither deference nor the idea that a natural aristocracy of merit had an entitlement to hold elective public office survived the democratic and egalitarian ferment set loose by the Revolution. In the aftermath of 1776, wrote Wood,

> Equality became so potent for Americans because it came to mean that everyone was really the same as everyone else, not just at birth, not in talent or property or wealth, and not just in some transcendental religious sense of the equality of all souls. Ordinary Americans came to believe that no one in a basic down-to-earth-and-day-in-and-day-out manner was really better than anyone else. That was equality as no other nation has ever had it.[9]

From the point of view of those who framed the Constitution (many of whom, of course, played important roles during the Revolution), one of the most disturbing expressions of egalitarianism after 1776 was the incipient stirring of political democracy within some of the new states. This was perhaps most evident in the new state constitutions drafted in the years after independence was declared (only Rhode Island and Connecticut retained constitutions from the colonial period). The number of democratic elements installed in new constitutions varied from one state to another, and no state adopted universal suffrage, even for white males. But the significance of these changes was nonetheless enormous, since most political power resided in the individual states prior to the adoption of the Constitution in 1788.

For example, property qualifications for voting were reduced in most states. In Pennsylvania only 10 percent of adult males were able to vote before the Revolution. After 1776 all taxpaying white males—the vast majority of men in the state—were enfranchised. In North Carolina, Georgia and Vermont the franchise was also significantly broadened. Three states abolished the upper house of the legislature, traditionally a haven for a wealthy and well-educated elite whose principle purpose was to restrain the "passions" of those elected by a popular vote to the lower house. These states placed all legislative power in the hands of a (more or less) democratically elected assembly. Seven other states restricted the legislative role of the upper house, limiting its purview to issues like impeachment of officials accused of wrongdoing.[10]

In every state except South Carolina, elected members of the legislatures had to stand for office every year. Some believed that annual elections and democracy went hand-in-hand. They would prevent officials from becoming accustomed to power. And they were powerful symbols of the subservience of the elected to those who elected them. "Where annual elections end," said an opponent of the proposed Constitution in 1787, "slavery begins."[11]

In another expression of popular mistrust of those who sought or exercised power, most states placed restrictions on the latitude of governors. Most colonial governors had wielded significant power in the pre-Revolutionary colonies. Some new state constitutions limited the legislative sphere of governors, restricting them to administrative responsibilities. In most states governors were limited to terms of one year. Only Massachusetts allowed the governor to have a veto over bills passed by the legislature. Pennsylvania did away altogether with a single chief executive. And most states capped the number of consecutive terms all elected officials could serve.[12]

Since these changes denied a political voice to women, indentured servants, slaves, free African Americans and even substantial numbers of white males, they fell far short of universal political empowerment. Or anything approaching genuine democracy. Nor did most Americans in the eighteenth century favor an unchecked democracy (any more than they do in the twentieth century). The idea that decision-making power should directly or indirectly be in the hands of all white males conjured visions of chaos and anarchy. Prior to the Revolution, as historian Jackson Turner Main observed, the notion of an "unchecked democracy was uniformly condemned" on both sides of the Atlantic.[13] Indeed, universal white-male suffrage did not become complete in the United States until the 1820s. Even with these qualifications, the post-Revolutionary broadening of the franchise was startling and unanticipated, however embryonic and partial it may have been.

Along with increasing the number of white males who could vote, there was an important change in the social status of those elected to high office. Before 1776 most voters seemed to have acted upon the notion of political and social deference when selecting representatives to state legislatures. The artisans, proprietors of small shops and owners of small farms who were allowed to vote seldom chose people from their own ranks to represent them. Nor did many people from modest backgrounds have the temerity to stand for election to the legislature. The majority of voters usually elected those who owned large estates or significant numbers of slaves, along with wealthy merchants and well-to-do and well-educated professionals, especially lawyers. Prior to the Revolution, this elite comprised about 10 percent of the adult population, but held 85 percent of the assembly seats throughout the colonies.[14]

This changed between 1776 and 1787. In many states "ordinary" people not only voted for the first time, but increasingly chose individuals from their own ranks to represent them in the legislatures. Apparently, some voters thought that any white male possessed of "common sense" and a good reputation in his community was qualified to serve. The percentage of those elected to legislatures who were well educated or who hailed from prestigious and influential families declined in some states. In many cases they were replaced by yeoman farmers, shoe makers or other artisans with little if any formal education or experience in politics. This tendency was evident as early as 1776. In describing the sort of individuals who should be elected to design a new constitution for Pennsylvania in 1776, one citizen urged voters to ignore men of wealth and privilege:

> It is the Happiness of America that there is no Rank above that of Freeman existing in it; and much of our future Welfare and Tranquility will depend on its remaining so forever; for this Reason, great and over-grown rich men will be improper to be trusted, they will be too apt to be framing Distinctions in Society, because they will reap the Benefits of all such Distinctions. . . . Honesty, common Sense, and a plain Understanding, when unbiased by sinister Motives, are fully equal to the Task. . . . Let no Men represent you . . . who would be disposed to form any Rank above that of Freemen.[15]

These sentiments appear to have been held by some individuals beyond the borders of Pennsylvania. In 1785 the majority of New York's 56 assemblymen were middling farmers and artisans, while in 1769 most of them came from the upper ranks of New York society. In 1765, about 60 percent of the lower house of the Massachusetts legislature were either college graduates or members of prominent families. By 1784, only 9 percent were college educated, while only 6 percent were related to influential families. Similar changes in the social and economic backgrounds of legislators occurred in some other states.[16]

A third important expression of emerging democratic sentiments after 1776 was an effort to increase the number of representatives in state legislatures. This was reflected in a sizeable increase in the absolute number of assemblymen in most states, which in some cases doubled or tripled. A more equitable share of representation for the states' western districts, traditionally underrepresented in the legislatures, accounted for a good deal of the increase. But the augmentation of representatives also grew out of a desire to empower smaller communities by allowing as many of them as possible to have their own voices in the state legislature.[17]

When combined with the inclination to elect "ordinary" citizens to state office, this initiative had significant democratic implications. It suggested that representatives should be people whom voters knew, who came from their midst. It implied they should share their constituents' political values, religious persuasions, occupations or social statuses.

Still another trace of incipient democracy in the new nation was the increasing popularity of "binding" or "instructing" legislators. This practice mandated representatives to cast votes in the legislature in accordance with the will of the majority of their constituents. Obviously, a direct democracy, in which all citizens actually participated in decision making, was not feasible on statewide issues. But when casting votes on matters of general importance, state legislators could be bound to vote in line with the wishes of a majority of those who sent them to the assembly. Along with annual elections, this was a way of putting representatives on a short leash. It sent the message that they were elected to enact the will of the majority on important matters, not to exercise their own judgment. Or, worse still, to become the servants of powerful economic or social interests. The idea of binding or instructing representatives, of investing representative government with an indirect but significant dose of the people's will, appears to have had some support in the 1780s. When considering the Bill of Rights, the first Congress under the Constitution debated making instruction a part of the First Amendment. It was rejected.[18]

That the sources of political power should reside in as many communities as possible, and rest directly or indirectly in the hands of "Freemen" as much as feasible, was consistent with the structure and purview of the country's first national government. Established in 1781 under the Articles of Confederation, it was a truly federal and, therefore, deliberately weak form of central government.[19]

The narrow scope of its power and prerogatives mirrored the mistrust of centralized political power that animated the Revolution, as well as the stirring of democratic sentiments that accompanied it. Laws enacted by the central government did not supersede those of the individual states. The central government under the Articles was a "league of friendship," in the words of its establishing document, between 13 distinct states, each of which retained "its sovereignty, freedom, and independence."[20] It had no upper chamber of the legislature to house men of accomplishment and "wisdom." There was no chief executive or president. No "supreme" judiciary. It did not have a supremacy clause that elevated federal legislation over that of the individual states.

The men who wanted to replace the Articles of Confederation with a far more powerful national government had a variety of motives. One was their belief that the new nation was awash in democratic disorder and endangered by a potential tyranny of the majority. Among the other problems that alarmed them were economic dislocations caused by the postwar depression and the proliferation of divisive issues. These ranged from calls for currency inflation to disputes over the distribution of tax burdens. They were deeply disturbed as well by what they perceived as an increasing tendency among people of all ranks to behave in ways that were self-interested and self-aggrandizing. The republican image of a virtuous, civic-minded citizenry held by many during the Revolution seemed to be a mirage. As George Washington put it, the country's leaders "had too good an opinion of human nature in forming our confederation" of 1781.[21] As it turned out, people seemed far more avaricious and self-interested than they were civic minded.

But perhaps the most glaring symbol of social disarray was the spread of nascent democratic sentiments across the country, especially as they were reflected in elections for state legislators. Some of those involved in framing the proposed Constitution were scandalized by the sort of people elected to the legislatures, and alarmed by the laws they might enact. It made them feel, as one of them said, that their world was being "turned upside down."[22]

John Jay, one of the authors of the *Federalist Papers,* was taken aback by the "effrontery and arrogance" of voters who conferred "rank and Importance to men whom Wisdom would have left in obscurity."[23] Jay's feelings were shared by others who witnessed the spectacle of ordinary people standing for and being elected to statewide office. "Blustering, ignorant men," and those who literally "patch [a] shoe" for a living, suddenly held elective office. The "turbulence and follies of [an unchecked] democracy" threatened to take over the country, while a "licentious" majority seemed ready to overwhelm "the worthy" and accomplished minority.[24]

James Madison, the "father" of the Constitution, was alarmed by the spectacle of "men without reading, experience, or principle" assuming legislative office. Such men were obviously unfit for office, though not solely because of their meager education and experience. Equally telling were their ties to the local, parochial interests of those who elected them. "Is it to be imagined," wrote Madison in 1787,

> that an ordinary citizen or even an assemblyman of R[hode] Island in estimating the policy of paper money, ever considered or cared in what light the measure would be viewed in France or Holland; or even in Massachusetts or Connecticut? It was a sufficient temptation to both that it was in their interest: it was a sufficient sanction to the latter that it was popular in the State; to the former that it was [popular] in the neighbourhood.[25]

In seeking to replace the Articles of Confederation with the Constitution, Madison and the other framers hoped to limit the political impact of this parochialism. And they linked it to the tide of greed and self-interest that seemed to envelop the country after the Revolution. To some degree, the Constitution was an attempt to contain these anti-social forces by elevating to office "disinterested" individuals who placed the common good above personal or narrowly framed gain.

Madison hoped to fashion a political process in which those selected for service in the "democratic" portion of the new government, the House of Representatives, would be taken from a state's "purest and noblest characters." They would be men whose wisdom, commitment to public service and broad vision of national greatness extended far beyond the parochial and partisan interests of the "neighbourhood." This would be accomplished by creating comparatively large election districts. Representation in the proposed Constitution was not to exceed one member for every 30,000 citizens. This was an enormous number, given the sparse population in most election districts, and it likely meant that congressmen would represent extremely diverse social, ethnic and religious groups in many election districts. The first House of Representatives would contain only 65 members to represent the interests of about 3 million white people.

This scheme of representation was designed to make the United States a republic rather than a democracy, as Madison made clear in his contributions to the *Federalist Papers.* It would place the greater share of decision-making power in the hands of elected representatives rather than in those of the people. Representatives would stand between those who elected them and the levers of decision-making power.[26]

Also, limiting the number of House members and creating large election districts minimized the number of communities that would be directly represented in the most powerful legislative arena of American government. And it made it likely, if far from inevitable, that men of "attractive merit" would be elected. In order to appeal to such a broad range of constituents and diverse interests, a candidate would have to be articulate and ecumenical in vision and experience, rather than "blustering" and parochial. Taken together, these strategies might limit the purview of an "over-bearing majority."[27]

Madison hoped those elected would be men whose "cool and deliberate sense" would temper the "people against their own temporary errors," their "delusions" and "irregular passions." It meant that individuals of broad vision, those whose "wisdom may best discern the true interest of their country" would be chosen for Congress. And, of course, this applied only to the "democratic" portion of the proposed national government, the House of Representatives. Neither the members of the Senate nor the president would be directly elected by the people.[28]

The framers of the Constitution wanted to shift the center of political gravity from the states and their communities to a national government. It appeared they wanted to limit, though by no means eradicate, the range of influence exercised by local, anti-elitist, community-oriented and *potentially* democratic politics. At least this was the way some of their opponents among the Antifederalists saw it.

THE ANTIFEDERALISTS AND SDS

To put it mildly, similarities between Students for a Democratic Society and those who opposed ratification of the Constitution are not obvious. They lived in remarkably distinct American worlds. They were separated by nearly two hundred years of spectacular transformations in the ways people lived, worked, travelled, communicated, learned and defined themselves. Beyond all this, the college-educated, cosmopolitan, middle-class egalitarians in SDS would have had a hard time believing they had anything in common with Antifederalists (assuming they ever heard of them in the first place).

A majority of Antifederalists were small-to-middling farmers in a new nation in which over 80 percent of adults earned their living from agriculture. Most were barely educated or literate. Nor were many of them very knowledgeable about the world beyond their immediate communities. So far as we know, few of them advocated the absolute "unchecked" democracy championed by SDS. Indeed, many among the 15 percent or so of Antifederalists who were well educated were often overtly anti-democratic. They opposed the proposed Constitution because it threatened their sway over their own communities and states. These elite Antifederalists ranged from those SDS would have viewed as merely undesirable, such as wealthy merchants and lawyers, to those who were morally execrable, such as owners of slaves.[29]

But the issue is not similarities between the two, socially or even politically. What matters is that some of the problems the Antifederalists saw in the proposed Constitution in 1787 were the very things SDS complained about nearly two centuries later. Ultimately, two general themes linked SDS and some (by no means all) of the issues raised by the Antifederalists.

First, many Antifederalists viewed the Constitution as a physically and politically remote form of representative government. It was not only a republic rather than a democracy (as Tom Hayden noted many decades later), but it was overly centralized and subject to the unfair influence exerted by various groups of elites (Antifederalists called them "aristocrats").[30] By shifting the ultimate sources of political power from the states and communities to the central government, the Constitution, in effect, equated democracy with the right to vote (an issue implicitly raised by SDS, not the Antifederalists). And it was democratic in name only, in the sense that beyond the process of selecting representatives by majority vote, most citizens had little opportunity to exercise decision-making power on issues that impinged on their daily lives. Given SDS's commitments to decentralized power and localism, the Constitution was *the* problem, at least in terms of their political views.

Second, some of the views held by a small number of Antifederalists reinforced the embryonic democracy that surfaced in various states after 1776. They harbored in utero the democratic values advanced in subsequent decades and centuries by various reform and radical movements, including SDS. If there is a radical tradition in American political thought it revolves around the idea that no one is "more equal" than anyone else. And if American democracy, beyond the right to vote for someone you don't know, has the radical implications that SDS believed it has, it rests on the conviction that "ordinary" citizens are capable of governing themselves and their society.

Who were the Antifederalists? For one, they were not "anti"-federalist. This label was adroitly and eternally hung on those who opposed ratification of the Constitution by their adversaries and by contemporary newspapers, the vast majority of which supported adoption of the Constitution. The Antifederalists were, in fact, federalists. They wanted the country to consist of a federation of 13 sovereign republics, in which the central government's role would be restricted to areas of concern common to all the states. These included foreign policy, waging war and regulating commerce between the states.[31]

While many Antifederalists favored the move to strengthen the Articles of Confederation, they believed the proposed Constitution would create a consolidated central government whose power largely incorporated, and therefore transcended, that of the states. They wanted more political power to be retained by the individual states. And, of course, their adversaries were not true "federalists." Those who framed the Constitution or supported its ratification clearly sought a central government whose prerogatives and reach was designed to place limits on the scope of state and local political power.[32]

Antifederalism was not a marginal political position in 1787 and 1788. Jackson Turner Main estimated that 52 percent of eligible voters were Antifederalist in sentiment, and were a majority in at least six, perhaps seven, states.[33] These included Massachusetts and Virginia, without whose support the Constitution would have been defeated. (The reasons for the eventual success of the

Federalists, much of which turned on their commitment to incorporate a Bill of Rights in the new Constitution, need not concern us.)

As mentioned earlier, Antifederalism was not a monolithic movement. While all Antifederalists (like most Americans) mistrusted powerful governments, the minority of social and economic elites among their ranks feared democracy even more. In fact, some of the most vocal among them, including Patrick Henry of Virginia and Elbridge Gerry of Massachusetts, joined the Federalists in the aftermath of the Constitution's ratification. Gerry called those who favored unchecked democratic rule "levellers" and "mobites."[34]

The majority of Antifederalists were not sufficiently well heeled, well educated or literate to compose the many pamphlets and articles written in opposition to ratification. A small faction of them believed political equality was impossible unless property and wealth were evenly distributed as well. They agreed with the sentiments expressed by radicals in Philadelphia during the 1770s that "an enormous Proportion of Property vested in a few Individuals is dangerous to the Rights, and destructive of the Common Happiness of Mankind." It followed that "Every free State hath a Right by its Laws to discourage the Possession of such Property."[35] But most Antifederalists believed in the freedom to make and keep the money one earned, and understood that such freedom inevitably led to an unequal division of wealth.[36]

Most Antifederalists also believed, however, that economic inequality should not lead to political inequality. Like the vast majority of Americans at the time, most Antifederalists distrusted the hunger for power and influence that animated ambitious individuals. According to Main, what disturbed them about the proposed Constitution was "not just the abstract transfer of power" from the states to a national government. Rather, they feared it meant "the concrete transfer of power from the people to the well born," or to a self-made "aristocracy" of talent and ambition.[37]

Finally, while the majority of Antifederalists feared the specter of a strong central government and were locally oriented, they were not necessarily parochial or provincial in outlook. Indeed, as Wood pointed out, in some ways the Antifederalists were proto-pluralists.[38] On the one hand, they believed that those who lived in a particular community should share important values and experiences, whether in the ways they lived, worshiped, worked or interacted with each other. On the other hand, they clearly understood that the American people, even within the individual states and various communities, were socially and culturally heterogeneous. Several communities dispersed over large election districts could not be effectively served by a single representative, unknown to most residents, who served in a distant national or state government. Elected representatives had to be more than advocates for the people. They should emerge from the people who elected them, and be known and controlled by them.[39]

Antifederalist criticisms of the proposed Constitution were comprehensive. They questioned the potentially enormous powers of the presidency, the reach of the Supreme Court, the length of terms for senators, the government's power to tax, the dangers of a standing army in peacetime and the absence of a bill of rights, among other important facets of the proposed new government.[40] But for our purpose, their comments about how the Constitution would favor social elites and undermine local self-government are most relevant.

An Antifederalist from Boston pointed out that the House of Representatives, the supposedly "democratical" part of the new government, was anything but democratic. The small number of representatives made it inevitable that they would not bear the "likeness" of the people they represented. They could not possibly know or understand the "wants," "grievances" or "wishes" of so many constituents. Under the current form of government, state legislators were subject to annual election. The "persons elected would reside in the center of you, their interests would be yours, they would be subject to your immediate controul." But under the Constitution, representatives were made

> strangers to the very people choosing them, they reside at a great distance from you, you have no controul over them, you cannot observe their conduct, and they have to consult and finally be guided by twelve other states, whose interests are, in all material points, directly opposed to yours.[41]

Melancton Smith of New York said "natural aristocrats" would predominate in the House of Representatives. A "substantial yeoman, of sense and discernment" running for Congress was not likely to have the education, experience or connections to best an opponent who was "highly elevated and distinguished." And even if the farmer of modest means won, his lack of education and "plain and frugal" ways would make him diffident in dealing with his more worldly, experienced colleagues in the House. Smith was convinced that most, though not all, representatives would be selected from among the "great" and "talented" minority of Americans in each state. And, since the "first class of the community" easily form "associations" among themselves, they were likely to pass legislation favorable to the "few and the great."[42]

"Centinel" of Philadelphia (Federalists and Antifederalists frequently used pseudonyms in their public exchanges) said that a "masqued aristocracy," fearful of the "good sense and discernment" of the majority, created the Constitution in order to "humble that offensive upstart, equal liberty."[43] An Antifederalist from Virginia believed the Constitution in essence was "a transfer of power from the many to the few."[44] Others were certain that the rights of the people, along with the resources of the country, would be sold by their representatives in Congress to the highest bidders.[45] The lengthy terms of office for the president and the senate, and the absence of limits on the number of terms they could serve, convinced "Centinel" that "oppression and tyranny" would triumph under the Constitution. Congress would be an association of "harpies of power," the "lordly and high minded." Such individuals were bereft of "congenial feelings [for] the people."[46]

A related, and extremely important issue consistently raised by Antifederalists was the difficulty of placing so large and diverse a country under the same set of laws. The Antifederalists of Philadelphia conceded the need for a federal government. It was necessary in order to manage the country's "foreign concerns" and its "common" internal issues. But they were convinced that beyond these legitimate activities "a very extensive territory cannot be governed on the principles of freedom, otherwise than by a confederation of republics, possessing all the powers of internal government."[47] (It is worth noting that the "very extensive territory" of the United States at the time was approximately 1,000 miles in length and 800 miles in width.)

Time and again critics of the Constitution insisted that the country was too large in territory and its people too diverse in background to be governed by a uniform set of federal laws. "Agrippa" of Massachusetts believed history demonstrated that in "large states the same principles of legislation will not apply to all the parts." Differences in climate, terrain, religion and national origins forged distinctive occupations and "habits" among people in the various states. "To promote the happiness of the people it is necessary that there should be local laws . . . made by the representatives . . . who are immediately subject" to the people. "It is impossible," concluded Agrippa, "for one code of laws to suit Georgia and Massachusetts. They must, therefore, legislate for themselves."[48]

As historian Saul Cornell pointed out, the elite among the Antifederalists feared that a centralized government would impinge on their prerogatives and economic interests.[49] They were not viscerally opposed to a central government more powerful than the one under the Articles of Confederation. And most of them were as alarmed by the upsurge of democracy in the years since 1776 as they were by various facets of the proposed Constitution. By and large, their opposition to ratification was obviated by the arguments and promises of the Federalists.

But according to Cornell, some grassroots Antifederalists neither trusted those who supported ratification nor shared the framers' vision of national greatness. They were people who lived and thought locally. They leaned toward local self-government; and at least some of them believed ordinary citizens should vote and serve in high elective office. They mistrusted those who possessed or hungered for economic and political power.[50] Some agreed with Thomas Paine that legislators should cast votes "in the same manner as the whole body [of their constituents] were they present."[51] And according to Gordon Wood, the grassroots Antifederalists were the "true champions of the most extreme kind of democratic and egalitarian politics expressed in the Revolutionary era."[52]

The grassroots Antifederalists were sensitive to the undemocratic bearing of the accomplished, ambitious men whom they thought most likely to stand for election under the new government. They were aware of the "necessary qualifications of authority; such as the dictatorial air, the magisterial voice, the imperious tone, the haughty countenance" of "well-born" and self-made "aristocrats."[53] An Antifederalist from western Massachusetts warned that "these lawyers, and men of learning, or moneyed men, that talk so finely, and gloss over matters so smoothly," would be the ones who "get into Congress." Once there, they would become "the managers of this Constitution, and get all the power and all the money into their own hands." From that perch of power it would be easy for them to "swallow up all us little folks."[54]

From the perspective of these "little folks," there was "not a tincture of democracy in the proposed constitution," as one opponent of ratification said.[55] Indeed, they believed the Constitution was a betrayal of the democratic promise of 1776. What, asked an Antifederalist, "have you been contending for these ten years past? Liberty! What is liberty? The power of governing yourselves. If you adopt this Constitution, have you this power? No: you give it into the hands of a set of men who live one thousand miles distant from you. Let the people but once trust their liberties out of their own hands, and what will be the consequence?"[56]

From the perspective of 1787 and 1788 the political and social issues confronted by SDS in the 1960s were unimaginable (not least because Antifederalist predictions of "tyranny and oppression" under the Constitution did not materialize). Also, neither the Federalists nor Antifederalists would have dreamed that by 1960, the year John F. Kennedy was elected president and SDS was founded, the central government sanctioned by the Constitution would have assumed such enormous scope and power. Or that the country itself would encompass so much territory. Indeed, more than 40 years after ratification Tocqueville observed that the federal government had little direct impact on the daily lives of most Americans. They seldom thought about it. The tradition of local self-government was alive and well, especially in New England.[57]

But the Civil War and the enormous burst of industrialization and urbanization that followed it led to a significant expansion of federal power. The swelling of the federal government's purview continued into the early decades of the next century. And the crises of economic depression and world war in the 1930s and 1940s exponentially increased the size of the central government's bureaucracies, the role of experts in policy formulation, the reach of its regulatory power and its overall prestige, especially that of the executive branch.

The power, scope, remoteness and impersonality of this government created many of the problems that concerned SDS. Ironically, however, what SDS saw as among the worst aspects of the American condition were not related to the power of the central government. They flowed from its relative impotence. The very tendencies toward competitive individualism and selfishness denounced by SDS (and which the framers of 1787 themselves hoped to contain) were enhanced by the explicit limitations that the Constitution originally placed upon the power of the federal government. And by the extraordinary guarantees of personal freedom and privacy that were added to it in the Bill of Rights.[58]

Madison envisioned a government composed of enlightened, disinterested statesmen whose concern for the common good would transcend and hopefully limit the impact of uninhibited individualism. According to Gordon Wood, this hope was quickly dashed. It was stymied by a combination of the appeals to liberty and equality set loose by the Revolution, the Constitution's guarantees of personal freedom and the enterprise of a citizenry dedicated above all to relentless pursuits of money and self-interest. These developments fed the very "social competitiveness and individualism" the Constitution was supposed to contain.[59]

Within a few years after ratification, Americans were increasingly absorbed in their private concerns and activities. Their focus on privacy and self-interest was complemented by an abiding distrust of government, which many came to see as an impediment to liberty. By the early years of the nineteenth century, Americans invoked the Constitution to emphasize what Wood called "the freedom to be left alone, and in turn that freedom meant the ability to make money and pursue happiness."

> The liberty that was now emphasized was personal or private, the protection of individual rights against all government encroachments. . . . America would remain free not because of any quality in its citizens of spartan self-sacrifice to some nebulous public good, but in the last analysis because of the concern each individual would have in his own self-interest and personal freedom.[60]

Thus the major issues focused upon by SDS were tied to two distinct, somewhat paradoxical legacies of the formative years of American political development. On one side was the evolution over many decades of a powerful central government. The actual levers of power were effectively severed from the direct control of most citizens, rendering them passive and apathetic. Hence the emphasis in the *Port Huron Statement,* written 200 years after the ratification of the constitution, on issues such as personal autonomy, the powerlessness of the majority, elitism, the need to decentralize political power and participatory democracy. On the other side were the American commitments to privacy and competitive individualism, or what Wood referred to as the constitutional guarantee of being left alone. In effect, these conditions separated Americans from one another. And thus the *Port Huron Statement*'s focus on loneliness, estrangement, alienation, community and, once again, participatory democracy.

In other words, from the perspective of SDS American society was both undemocratic and atomized. Most citizens were politically powerless and thus incapable of controlling the social and economic forces that affected them. And they were too individualistic and socially isolated from one another to create the civic spaces necessary for nurturing a meaningful sense of community.

In 1963 SDS tried to change these conditions by initiating an ambitious community-organizing program, the Economic Research and Action Project. Its stated goal was nothing less than the transformation of American society. In describing his hopes for the project, Tom Hayden invoked a historic democratic moment tied to the nation's birth in the eighteenth century. "[U]ltimately," he said, "this movement might lead to a Continental Congress called by all the people who feel excluded from the higher circles of decision-making in the country."[61]

THE ECONOMIC RESEARCH AND ACTION PROJECT

The Origins of ERAP

The Economic Research and Action Project (ERAP) was implemented in the summer of 1964. Its principal architect was Tom Hayden, who said that ERAP was designed as a "northern counterpart" to the grassroots organizing carried on in the South by the Student Nonviolent Coordinating Committee.[62] Funding for ERAP projects came mostly from liberal organizations, including a $5,000 start-up grant from the United Auto Workers union.

This seed money financed the work of over 100 SDS members who moved into 9 northern and border state inner-city neighborhoods in the summer of 1964. The initial goal was to organize the unemployed in cities like Chicago and Baltimore. But when SDS's prediction of increased unemployment failed to materialize, ERAP became what historian Kirkpatrick Sale called a "protean" movement.[63] In Newark, Cleveland, Boston, Chicago, Baltimore, Trenton and the other cities, ERAP organizers tried to help those who were poor, unemployed or on welfare deal with a huge array of problems. These ranged from obtaining basic services from city agencies and slumlords to dealing with welfare departments and employers. By the summer of 1965, ERAP programs were begun in 14 additional cities. Most of the projects disintegrated rather quickly. Only those in Baltimore, Cleveland, Chicago and Newark lasted more than two years, but by 1967 they were disbanded as well.[64]

Hayden hoped ERAP would become an "interracial movement of the poor," as well as provide "SDS ideology more practical content," by organizing the country's most economically and socially marginalized populations.[65] Years after the demise of ERAP, Paul Potter observed that the projects reflected the doubts of SDS's white middle-class activists that their grievances were sufficient by themselves to effect radical change. They came to believe significant change could happen only if SDS brought people "who were getting creamed"—that is, the poor or unemployed of both races—into the movement.[66] To a considerable extent, ERAP was created on the assumption that shared conditions of poverty or unemployment would create the basis for cooperation between African Americans and whites.

But ERAP was also a way of actualizing SDS's faith in the capacity of "ordinary" citizens to run the country. As Hayden put it, ERAP's purpose was to effect "a transformation of society" by organizing "the most excluded and 'unqualified' people" at the local level.[67] In his view, the poor and unemployed of both races had the ability to make connections between their day-to-day deprivations and the wider social and economic forces that caused them. They were capable of understanding that poverty, unemployment and living in rat- and roach-infested housing were neither accidental nor the products of "character deficiencies" within themselves. By working at the community level with the poor and unemployed, ERAP might be able to forge a critical mass of local "insurgencies." These alliances between the poor and unemployed of all races might eventually coalesce into a nationwide movement to transform American society. The creation of a truly democratic country had to begin with, and be premised upon, democratic initiatives taken at the local level and involving all members of the community.[68]

To bring this about, ERAP volunteers moved into some of the nation's most forsaken and dangerous neighborhoods. They lived in conditions similar to that of their poor neighbors, sharing the dangers of inner-city crime and the deprivations of poverty. In some projects, the ERAP volunteers limited the cost of their daily food allowance to the meager government dole allotted to the neighborhood's welfare recipients. Hayden said the "spirit" of the projects was an ascetic "one of voluntary poverty and simple living."[69]

The organizers were not supposed to lead the downtrodden into the promised land of a "new society." Their task was to call attention to problems. If local residents wanted them addressed, ERAP volunteers would work with them to organize rent strikes, demonstrations over inferior municipal services in poor neighborhoods, protests against inadequate welfare benefits and so forth. The people who lived in the neighborhood would define their own grievances, develop strategies to remedy them and, with the assistance of ERAPers, lead the movement to eliminate them. This was an expression of SDS's belief in the common sense and inherent wisdom of ordinary people. They could work together, define their problems, solve them and command their own lives. In short, they could become their own leaders.[70]

The rather tricky and ambiguous role of ERAP organizers was to start the ball rolling, then get out of the way and "let the people decide," in the words of the slogan they borrowed from SNCC.[71] Norman Fructer and Robert Kramer, who worked in the Newark project, said the purpose of ERAP was to "create, then enlarge, a space in which the possible alternatives [to the present society] can be developed."[72] Selecting alternatives was the prerogative of the local residents who joined the project. ERAP organizers, public officials or other educated "experts" should be bystanders in this process.

> Various academic degrees, status, "many years of service," "an intimate knowledge of the field," are all threatened when a [local resident] project member defines qualifications in terms of direct experience, not acquaintance with the problem of making decisions or running a city agency, but acquaintance with the problem itself.[73]

ERAP was a pivotal departure for SDS. From the beginning in 1960, SDS promoted itself as a campus-based student organization. Its stated purpose was to help radicalize the swelling ranks of those who were young, alienated and college educated. In other words, those who were, or aspired to become, middle-class. Also from the beginning, SDS tried to push beyond the Old Left's economic determinism, its apocalyptic vision of a revolution sparked by the grievances of society's most exploited, abused or impoverished classes. The *Port Huron Statement* did not trace what it called the "loneliness," "isolation," "apathy" and "alienation" pervading American life to economic causes. Nor did it seek remedies in economic solutions.[74]

But the political rationale for ERAP, developed at SDS's national convention in 1963, was overtly economic. Formulated by Hayden and Richard Flacks, it predicted surging unemployment throughout the economy. Automation created by the "cybernetic revolution" would imperil the jobs of industrial workers, while a thaw in the Cold War would generate unemployment in the country's massive defense industry. Working- and middle-class employees would be adversely affected.[75]

Hayden, Flacks and other ERAP supporters in SDS assumed that the surge in unemployment would happen almost immediately, leading to an "increasing crisis in the U.S. economy" by the second half of the decade. ERAP organizers, therefore, should create local vehicles of protest that connected the plight of the new unemployed to those "whose economic role in the society is marginal or insecure" to begin with, and was almost certain to deteriorate as the decade progressed. Isolated "local insurgencies" could not by themselves transform society. ERAP projects were supposed to be "transitional." But a critical mass of local movements might create "in embryo" the "foundation for a national radicalism" capable of "transform[ing] American politics" and the country's economic institutions.[76]

Those who favored ERAP—in addition to Flacks and Hayden, they included Rennie Davis, Sharon Jeffrey, Potter, and Gitlin—believed it was time for SDS to leave the sanctuary of the campus. Hayden said radicals should move beyond the "academic crap" and sterile "intellectuality" of campus life and act on their radical convictions. SDS should go off campus, to where "the people" and the "action" were.[77]

ERAP's economic rationale and its focus on the inner-city poor caused the first major rift among SDS's small, close-knit inner circle. Steve Max and Al Haber were especially irked by ERAP. Max said the community-organizing projects smacked of "liberal" and "utopian" sentimentality.[78] ERAP implicitly romanticized the poor and other victims of an unjust economy. Worse, those in the ERAP camp largely ignored organized labor, disenchanted students and realignment politics as important players in the movement for radical change. It was wrongheaded, according to Max, to think a radical movement could be spearheaded by the most marginal and desperate portions of the population. Those who were poor, unemployed or victims of racism found it difficult enough to survive day-to-day. They were not in the position, materially or psychologically, to lead a mass movement. Much less one based at the local level, which by definition could not affect the policies and programs of major corporations and the national government.[79]

Al Haber also criticized Hayden and the others for their economic focus, and for undermining SDS's original mission of radicalizing students. He described ERAP as "anti-intellectual."[80] It was a romantic plunge "into the ghetto" by middle-class radicals who were alienated from their own backgrounds, and felt guilty about their privileged place in society. ERAP lacked "radical direction, clarity of goals, or significant differentiation from social reform." "Action," Haber noted, "is not radical because its form is different or 'gutsy.'" It was hard to distinguish the immediate goals of ERAP projects from those of Lyndon Johnson's antipoverty program. Is "radicalism subsisting in a slum for a year or two, or is it developing your individual talents so you can function as a radical in your 'professional' field and throughout your adult life?"[81] Picking up on Haber's use of the terms "ghetto" and "slum," another SDS critic of ERAP went further. The people in ERAP were "ghetto-jumping." They confused living in "sackcloth and ashes" in the "slum" with genuine radicalism.[82]

Even though Hayden convinced a majority of SDS's governing body to approve ERAP, and to channel a good deal of the organization's personnel and funds into launching and sustaining the community projects, the criticisms by Haber and Max were on the mark. Despite claims made by Hayden during and since the sixties that ERAP was different from the liberal reformism of "missionaries, or social workers," it was not always easy to distinguish between the two.[83] After all, President Johnson's War on Poverty called for the "maximum feasible participation" of the poor in program development.[84]

And ERAP was not the first time in the country's history that young middle-class Americans seeking meaning and adventure in their lives, and a deeper sense of community in their society, moved into inner-city "slums." Social settlement workers, the sort of "liberal" reformers Hayden disdained, had done the same thing at the turn of the century by moving into inner-city immigrant ghettos. In some ways their motives were similar to those of ERAP organizers. Part of the "prospectus" for the Baltimore project linked the abundance of "bars and pool halls" in the "slum area" organized by ERAP to the "unhealthy social lives" of the city's poor.[85] These sentiments could have been expressed by Jane Addams, the pioneer social settlement activist, over 60 years earlier about conditions in Chicago.[86]

Equally important, the hope that shared, "objective" economic deprivations might unite the races and make ERAP an "interracial movement of the poor" was, to say the least, exuberantly optimistic. If nothing else, the scores of racial disturbances that occurred from the mid sixties on, beginning with the deadly uprising in the Watts ghetto in Los Angeles in the summer of 1965, made it unlikely that whites and African Americans could engage in a meaningful dialogue, much less form a united front for radical change. Finally, the prediction that unemployment would surge, particularly within the working class, was wrong. The opposite happened. "Just as we got to Chicago," said an ERAP organizer, "lines at the unemployment compensation center started to get shorter."[87] The same was generally true in other ERAP cities.

Despite these legitimate criticisms and ultimately fatal shortcomings, ERAP was a logical extension of important values stressed in the *Port Huron Statement.* ERAP may have been a wrongheaded, naive, conceptually foggy enterprise. But it was a concerted attempt to actualize participatory democracy by empowering citizens to take command of their lives. And to do so at the local level, where a sense of community might be created through voluntary, egalitarian associations. As Hayden put it, a democratic society had to have "its origin" in voluntary "social relations" before it could fashion or alter "institutional relations." Radicals, he said, had to help create "locally autonomous insurgent political organizations" as a necessary prelude to securing changes in the wider society.[88] "Movement," said Gitlin in 1964, "becomes meaningful when the people directly afflicted organize for change, for it is then that people are sensing their own possibilities as men, their power to make things happen."[89]

Whether or not this approach made sense politically is not the point. Nor is it particularly pertinent whether or not ERAP deviated from SDS's original purposes. In some ways it did, in others it didn't. What mattered was that SDS's ideas about human nature, democracy and community revolved around the need for the individual to be actively engaged in local, voluntary public associations. A democratic polity required some degree of shared values, experiences or aspirations among its people. From the beginning, SDS's vision of a politically decentralized democracy of participation was tied to the prospect of reviving or creating a "political public" at the neighborhood level. The rest, they vaguely assumed, would somehow follow.

The ERAP projects demonstrated the futility and irony of this vision, though not entirely because of the questionable economic and racial assumptions that guided them. ERAPers implicitly assumed that the world of the inner-city poor would somehow be more socially cohesive than was their own impersonal, competitive, status-hungry, middle-class world. ERAPers might find the rudiments of community in the ghetto. At the very least, shared experiences of poverty, racism and unemployment would provide "objective," if wobbly, frameworks for united action among disparate populations. Upon these foundations the outlines of a vibrant civic territory might be drawn. In fact, however, what ERAP organizers found in those impoverished neighborhoods was a variation of the same atomized, random society they were alienated from.

Some ERAP Experiences

ERAPers Norman Fructer and Robert Kramer noted that community organizing

> necessitates a confrontation with the level of each individual's consciousness; what is at stake is not only how he judges his past experience, who or what he holds responsible for his deprivation, and what possibility he sees for political action, but also how rigorous his demand for change is, and what levels of his

> political and moral responses have been inhibited by the failure of any protest or political organizations to penetrate his neighborhood and make adequate roles available to him.[90]

ERAP programs, especially those in Baltimore, Chicago, Cleveland and Newark, were often very useful to local residents. But not in the ways envisioned by Fructer, Kramer and other SDS activists.

ERAP organizers, especially the women, helped those living in substandard housing get better deals from rent-gouging slumlords. They obtained day care services for welfare mothers who wanted to work and assisted the poor in navigating unsympathetic local welfare bureaucracies. ERAP organizers and their local allies among the poor were successful at times in achieving small but concrete improvements in the lives of neighborhood residents. Playground facilities for poor children were created or improved, traffic lights installed at busy intersections and school lunch programs initiated. And there were moments, perhaps few and fleeting but nonetheless morally significant, when ERAP organizers succeeded in creating a bridge between the races. During an ERAP meeting in Cleveland, "Negroes and poor whites listened to each other talk about the problems of welfare, unemployment, housing and about the powerlessness of the unorganized poor."[91]

The hope of sparking a radical "consciousness" within the residents ultimately depended upon transforming their presumed shared interests into a genuine sense of community and a base for political activism. But despite what bound local residents together in the "objective" terms defined by SDS—unemployment, ethnicity, race, poverty, the fact that they weren't middle class—the neighborhoods themselves, like the country at large, lacked a center of civic gravity.

For one thing, their populations were heterogeneous in terms of ethnicity, regional origins and religious values. In the neighborhood in which the Cleveland project was located, long-term residents who had come from eastern Europe had little in common with recently arrived immigrants from Puerto Rico. The whites who had moved to Chicago after losing their jobs in the coal mines of West Virginia or eastern Kentucky did not share much in the way of culture or experience with unemployed men born and raised in that city. And white southern migrants possessed a tradition of independence that made them wary of collective social action.

Even in ERAP neighborhoods that were ethnically homogeneous, such as the one in Newark, which was entirely African American, the residents often disagreed about which problems were most pressing, their causes, and what to do about them. The populations in the various ERAP cities often possessed little if any sense of identification with the neighborhood or their neighbors. And their aspirations and interests were as privatized and scattered as their ethnic, national and regional origins were heterogeneous.

These problems were evident in even one of the most effectively run ERAP programs, the Cleveland Community Project (CCP). The CCP staff included experienced SDS activists Sharon Jeffrey and Paul Potter, and was located in the city's largely white, low-income Near West End district. In addition to long-term residents of eastern European extraction, the district included new residents from the South and Puerto Rico. The CCP focused on the issues of public housing, welfare and unemployment. Its staff dutifully researched federal, state and municipal regulations regarding public housing, the history of welfare in Cleveland and recent patterns of unemployment in the city. During their frequent meetings, the staff discussed the "radicalness" of these issues, and how they might help residents connect them to broader economic, social and institutional forces.[92]

CCP organizers combed the community for what they called "indigenous" residents who would, they hoped, actively participate in the project and eventually assume its leadership. They arranged meetings during which welfare mothers and unemployed men were invited to share their experiences and aspirations with each other. In July 1964, after a few weeks on the job, the CCP staff was struck by the daunting magnitude of their enterprise. In one of their weekly reports they confirmed with disarming honesty the rather muddled assumptions that had brought them to Cleveland in the first place. SDS "has never developed even the bones of what a program for a community would look like." They quickly discovered that "most people do not generally look to the 'neighborhood' for their associations." Nonetheless, they felt that "this is an argument in *favor* [their emphasis] of such an attempt here in Cleveland since many of us are wed, at least by faith, to the conception of people organizing in their own communities, and growing more radical as basic needs go unmet."[93]

But in Cleveland as in other ERAP programs, it was hard to find local residents who agreed among themselves about defining their "basic needs" or what to do about them. Nor was it easy to get local residents to attend ERAP meetings. Few showed up regularly. At the end of the summer projects in 1964, the Newark program, led by Tom Hayden, convinced about 30 local residents to attend meetings at one time or another. In Chicago about 10 did so, while Cleveland recruited 20, and Baltimore only 5.[94]

Few of the local residents who attended these meeting grew "more radical." For instance, unemployed men had little in common with one another besides the fact they were out of work. When the Cleveland ERAP staff tried to organize them, they found that married men without jobs were desperate for work but had little time for "active participation in the organization." Men who were recently laid off were "more bitter" than the others and more willing to get involved with the CCP. But they were "impatient" and focused primarily on "getting a job for themselves right now." They had little interest in the wider economic or political forces that caused unemployment, or the difficulties others experienced in finding work.[95]

Another group of men without jobs, the "long-term" unemployed, "often were resigned to their position" and too "depressed" for active participation in the organization. Nearly all of these men saw their plight in private rather than political or social terms. During one meeting at the CCP headquarters, an attempt by the ERAP staff to convince the men that unemployment was "a social rather than personal problem, fell totally flat, and did not elicit any discussion or response."[96] The same was generally true of ERAP programs in other cities.

The attempt to organize tenants in Cleveland's public-housing projects came up against similar obstacles. The projects housed people from diverse social and ethnic backgrounds. Some were long-time residents, others were new to the neighborhood, while still others came and went after a relatively short stay. When the CCP staff tried to develop tenant councils to deal with a range of issues in the projects, and to connect the tenants' problems to those of the unemployed, there was little response. Tenants mostly complained about the behavior of their neighbors' children or discussed conflicts between adults in the projects. Also they expressed concern about antagonizing municipal housing officials (as well as their fear of the undercover police "red squads" who spied upon and harassed ERAP projects in every city).[97]

Variations on these themes surfaced when the CCP tried to organize mothers on welfare. The staff wanted to "attack the present system of welfare which tends to reduce people to a position of total dependency and isolation."[98] While the mothers were open to practical assistance from the CCP in dealing with welfare bureaucrats, the broader strategy left them mostly cold. To some extent, this was because the mothers were overwhelmed by their domestic responsibilities and poverty. But there were other factors as well. At one meeting the discussion of welfare "on nearly all levels was generally poor. Severe personality clashes aggravated the situation and there was a major dispute over a racial matter."[99]

Not all the meetings went so poorly. Some helped residents discover common ground on one issue or another. But the CCP staff was dismayed by the general lack of focus during the meetings. And they were conflicted about their own roles in leading the discussions. They had hoped to cultivate leadership skills in "ordinary" citizens by giving them the opportunity to confront the social and political conditions that affected them. As one of their recruitment brochures noted, ERAP was "probably the only institution in the world where a destitute alcoholic can stand up and give a lecture, occasionally brilliant but usually incoherent, on political strategy and be listened to with complete respect."[100]

But such grand examples of participatory democracy in action did not cultivate organizational or leadership skills in local residents. And the CCP staff came to realize that it was one thing to attract residents to a meeting, a hard enough chore, and quite another to inculcate them with middle-class skills concerning "agenda, the role of the chairman and secretary, committees, and the general operation of a meeting." This frustrated the organizers because

> it raised so many questions about leadership within a group such as this and its potential for dealing with difficult questions. It raised such specific questions as, 1) to what extent should CCPers exert themselves in a meeting in order to maintain order, 2) to what extent should we enter into the meeting to provide direction and ideas. . . . The CCPers disagreed a bit on these points.[101]

An irony of the ERAP experience was that in order to reach the "indigenous" population there were times when the SDS activists found themselves acting like those they were trying to organize, rather than the other way around. In an effort to channel the energies of the street-wise, unemployed young males who lived in the area in which the Chicago ERAP program was located, Rennie Davis found himself "virtually drunk all week." According to Davis, the young men who hung around the streets

> are the potential revolutionary force in Uptown, Chicago, if there can be said to be such a force. They are the force that is least afraid of the police, do have some sense of justice—and are willing to act on that sense. . . . Complications are very great. One is that to work with them really requires that you live their way . . . that you run, and fight and drink and do the things they do, and still have the capacity to direct it towards something.[102]

ERAP was early SDS's last major initiative. It was the organization's most "practical" and daring attempt to actualize participatory democracy. And its most glaring failure. In the late sixties and early seventies, amid the rubble of white radicalism's dashed hopes, some of those who worked in ERAP projects dissected the reasons for its demise. And, by implication, for the related failure of early SDS to forge a viable democratic left.

Todd Gitlin worked in the Chicago ERAP program for two years. In 1970 he echoed some of Steve Max's and Al Haber's earlier criticisms of ERAP.

Gitlin suggested that he and his ERAP colleagues were "tempted to romanticize the poor, to imagine them Noble Savages" who were generally innocent of the materialism and competitive individualism at large in the rest of society.[103] In post-1960s reflections on his experiences in the Cleveland project, Paul Potter said ERAP was bound to fail because it burdened poor people with the task of realizing another class's dream of radical social change. It was also incompatible with the spirit of the *Port Huron Statement.* The economic rationale behind ERAP was SDS's version of "vulgar Marxism." But the real problem was the inability of the disaffected middle-class students who created SDS to define an approach to radical change based on their own experiences and aspirations. If the poor and unemployed were the primary agents of radical social change, asked Potter pointedly, "then who were the middle-class people who came to work with them?"[104]

These self-criticisms were on target. Yet something else, something far more disturbing, was at the heart of ERAP's failure. And SDS's. The problem wasn't simply that SDS picked the wrong groups to organize. Or that they hitched their radical dreams to the grievances of other social classes.

Would the young radicals have been successful in creating a viable democratic left had they organized among their own kind in upper-middle-class suburbs? Or among unionized workers? Might they have been more likely to advance their cause had they stuck to the original plan of radicalizing college students and faculty?

Obviously these questions cannot be answered. But it is worth noting that members of these groups were no less heterogeneous in their personal backgrounds than were the inner-city poor. Nor were they more likely to become radicalized once they realized, as many of them already did, that a good deal of what happened to them every day was the result of political and economic decisions made by others. Most important, and just like the poor, members of these groups were driven primarily by self-interest. Their behavior was as dissociated from wider public issues and moral concerns as that of any Americans, rich, poor, black or white.

Like some reformers and radicals who came before them, early SDS tried to reconcile individual liberty with democratic fellow feeling, to bridge the gap in American life between individualism and community. It was far too late, just as it probably was at the dawn of the Republic, when Thomas Jefferson tried to affirm individual liberty by tying it to an innate, self-governing "moral sense." Certainly, by the middle of the twentieth century, neither institutional nor moral imperatives compelled Americans to feel collective responsibility for one another in any realm of public life.

SDS'S FAILED QUEST FOR COMMUNITY

Students for a Democratic Society's ideas about community were no more precise than was their theory of participatory democracy. They criticized what they called the "estrangement" and "loneliness" at the heart of American life. And they hoped both could be overcome by creating small, intimate groupings of "political publics." But SDS never concretized what this vision of community might look like, just as they failed to adequately describe how voluntary associations at the local level could evolve into zones of democracy-in-action across the country.[105] SDS simply assumed that if numerous local reservoirs of democratic participation were created they would add up to something greater than the sum of electoral politics and representative government.

This fuzzy thinking was complemented by SDS's tendency to use language and raise issues normally avoided by political movements that hope to change society. Seemingly irrelevant personal concerns were woven into the young radicals' descriptions of the country's political, social and economic ills. One moment they described the economic consequences of automation or the need to seek détente with the Soviet Union in more or less standard political language. The next moment they would echo Paul Potter in decrying the "impossibility" of love and intimacy in America's atomized society.[106] As historian Alan Brinkley correctly pointed out, by confounding the personal with the political SDS helped lead the student movement down the path of "narcissistic cultural impulses that were essentially apolitical."[107]

Despite all this it would be a mistake to underestimate the historical significance of early SDS. Or to think things could have turned out differently had they been less "apolitical." SDS came close to grasping, and bringing to the surface of political discourse, how deeply entwined were the country's centralized political system, its essentially unrestrained economic individualism and the intractable dedication of its people to privacy. Also, their emphasis on localism and community tacitly reasserted in the 1960s what some Antifederalists believed in 1787: the United States was too large in territory and too diverse in regional cultures to be consolidated under a single government. Much less to pass itself off as a democracy. There were a few passing moments of clarity, such Hayden's statement that the country's "fatal" flaw was its status as a republic rather than a democracy. But SDS never focused on the Constitution as the key political issue. Even if they had, who would have listened?

By contrast, SDS was explicit in describing the corrosive social and personal effects of competitive, obsessive individualism and privacy. But this was as fruitless as naming the Constitution as the main political problem. Whatever else it may be, the United States is a huge theater of high-energy "movement," where human atoms are far more likely to randomly bounce off and past one another than to attract or coalesce. The course of American social and political development did not merely liberate its people from Old World traditions of civic responsibility. It overtly devalued public life.

Thus many Americans not only disparage politicians and government. They shy away from all but the most symbolic public representations of their collective existence as a people. This fragmentation is only partially related to the astonishing array of ethnic, class, regional and religious divisions that separate them. Even when they celebrate shared ideals that transcend these divisions, they fall back on those that reinforce their society's unswerving commitments to competitive individualism and privacy: family, self-reliance, hard work, social mobility, individual initiative and equality of opportunity.

Of course, privacy and dissociation are not the whole story. Americans routinely associate with one another outside the realms of commerce and family. Since Tocqueville, observers of the American scene have noted the passion of its citizens for creating private organizations and joining voluntary associations of one sort or another. They belong to a wide range of religious organizations and neighborhood civic groups. They join bowling leagues and softball teams. They give generously to charity and readily help neighbors in need. But these activities, however worthy, are not what SDS meant by "political publics." They are not politically empowered voluntary associations that enable individuals to actively participate in making the decisions that govern their lives. Nor are they substitutes for what Americans lack as a people: culturally-legitimated imperatives to create *collective* moral and social obligations toward each other that are at least as powerful as their commitments to competitive individualism, self-interest and privacy.

This is the case even in areas of obvious mutual concern. For instance, a fitting symbol of Americans' unstinting dedication to mutual isolation is their country's status as the only affluent western industrial society without a publicly funded system of national health care. That would raise the specter of "socialism"—even though capitalist nations in western Europe fund such systems through taxation. (Is it possible that the various red scares over the past century were means—no doubt unconscious—of reaffirming Americans' isolation from one another, as much as they were shields against perceived threats from the contagions of domestic and foreign communism?) The commitment of Americans to go it alone is equally evident in their attitudes toward social-welfare programs. During the 1996 congressional debate on welfare reform, Republican representative John Kasich of Ohio reminded his fellow citizens that Americans are "not entitled to anything but opportunity."[108] And "opportunity," of course, is a private matter.

John Lewis, a Democrat from Georgia and an important leader of the Civil Rights movement in the sixties, tried to counter Kasich's point during debate in the House of Representatives. "Where is the compassion? Where is the sense of decency. . . . What does it profit a great nation to conquer the world, only to lose its soul?"[109] If his use of the word "soul" referred to an essence of collective identity, some shared moral principle that binds each American to all Americans, Lewis would have been hard put to locate it (except, it should be added, within the relatively small number of citizens who, like himself, somehow came into possession of that moral rudder.)

These issues, and much else besides, indicate that even had they not made serious blunders or been diverted by the Vietnam War, SDS could not have succeeded. Its call for a decentralized, community-based democracy of participation had no meaning in a society whose institutions and culture were far more likely to create public voids than civic spaces. Its criticisms of social elites were pointless in a country in which the private use of power, however arbitrarily exercised, is seen as morally legitimate as long as it is "earned" through the competitive crucible of equality of opportunity. And the young radicals' desire to bring people out of privacy could hardly resonate in a culture whose citizenry thrived on it, no matter the "loneliness" and "estrangement" it incurred.

The idea and ideal of community has a long history in the United States.[110] But even when its parameters are carefully drawn, as SDS generally failed to do, the notion of community rarely goes beyond idyllic visions of life in small towns, or moral exhortations to restrain selfishness and other deplorable expressions of individualism run amok. This was highlighted in two important and well-received books that, though published after the sixties, are relevant to our discussion of SDS.

In *Habits of the Heart,* (1986) Robert Bellah and his colleagues claimed that individualism had grown "cancerous" in American life. American freedom "turns out to mean being left alone by others." It is "strangely without content," because it is largely an end in itself, lacking moral resonance or "any purpose to involvement with others except individual satisfaction." During the course of American history its people were incrementally cut off from two traditions that historically had set boundaries on overly selfish or self-interested behavior: civic republicanism and Puritanism's "biblical" communitarianism.[111]

In Bellah's view, the idea of personal liberty that surfaced in the eighteenth century was a legitimate reaction against the oppressive forms of domination sanctioned by the civic-republican and biblical traditions. These included domination of men over women, masters over servants and slaves, leaders over deferential followers and rich over poor. But Bellah's research indicated that competitive individualism was not entirely dominant in American life. The white middle-class individuals interviewed for his book evinced "all the classic polarities of American individualism." They embraced it, but at the same time felt lonely and severed from others. "[T]he deep desire for autonomy and self-reliance" was "combined with an equally deep conviction that life has no meaning unless shared with others in the context of community."[112]

Habits of the Heart is a compelling jeremiad against the moral, social and personal corrosion caused by privacy and uncontrolled individualism. But while Bellah astutely analyzes these conditions, and adroitly presents the stories of Americans whose lives are forlorn and fragmented by them, he offers little more than moral exhortation as a way out of this dilemma. For instance, he suggests individuals should try to overcome their mutual estrangement by working to create a common past. They should share "narratives" of continuity about their communities, ethnic origins and religious beliefs. And he calls for the creation of a new form of personal liberty, one in which legitimate expressions of individualism might be morally informed by reconstituted, less oppressive versions of the civic-republican and biblical traditions.[113] But how those traditions could be made less "oppressive" is not clear. Nor does Bellah clarify how a sense of community or narratives about a shared history can be fashioned in a geographically mobile, ethnically plural, innately competitive culture.

Like Bellah and, ironically, in some ways like Students for a Democratic Society, Michael Sandel's book, *Democracy's Discontent* (1996), dissected (from a rather conservative perspective) the undemocratic consequences of liberalism's version of competitive individualism. Moral relativism and a "procedural" liberalism that asserts "the priority of fair procedures over particular" social and moral ends has fostered an "impoverished civic life" in the United States.

> [T]he liberal vision of freedom lacks the civic resources to sustain self-government. This defect ill-equips it to address the sense of disempowerment that afflicts our public life. The public philosophy by which we live cannot secure the liberty it promises, because it cannot inspire the sense of community and civic engagement that liberty requires. . . . [A] procedural republic that banishes moral and religious argument from political discourse makes for an impoverished civic life. . . . [I]ts image of citizens as free and independent selves, unencumbered by moral or civic ties they have not chosen, cannot sustain the public spirit that equips us for self-rule.[114]

Like Bellah, Sandel warned that Americans, both individually and collectively, might find themselves "slipping into a fragmented, storyless condition." They could lose "the capacity for narrative" essential for a sense of continuity as well as for "competing interpretations of the character of a community, of its purposes and ends." This loss would "amount to the ultimate disempowering of the human subject, for without narrative there is no continuity between present and past, and therefore no responsibility," and "no possibility of acting together to govern ourselves."[115]

But what if discontinuity *is* the main point of the American experience? What if the traditional appeal of the country—to prospective immigrants, for example—is the uncertainty inherent in the unregulated form of gambling known as "equality of opportunity"? And what if an indeterminate life in a random society, despite its negative moral, political and social consequences, is the primary tale of the American "narrative"? Weren't these things implied, in effect, by Thomas Jefferson when he said that the "dead are not even things"? And decades later by Thoreau, when he declared, "old deeds for old people, and new deeds for new"? Or still more decades down the American road by the Diggers, when they proclaimed, "throw out the old! Simply throw it out!"?

These sentiments and the behavior they implicitly justify are tributes of recognition to the actual promise of American life.

The New Left ended in spasms of death and despair in the late sixties. Beginning with the march on the Pentagon in November 1967, which signalled a more militant antiwar mood among young people, through the end of the decade, the country seethed with conflict. There were the assassinations of Martin Luther King and Robert Kennedy and the killings of students at Jackson State and Kent State universities; conspiracy trials and scores of bloody confrontations between police and young black and white protesters on streets and campuses; Weatherman bombs and venomous expressions of mutual disdain between young and old, white people and black and, in some cases, parents and children; and routine violations by government officials of the rights of citizens to dissent, along with bold (and widely supported) displays of police brutality toward dissidents.

By 1969 the leaders of early SDS found themselves a world removed from the optimism that had ushered John Kennedy into the presidency and their organization into existence. Not to mention the confidence that had inspired them to deliver a copy of the *Port Huron Statement* to his White House. At decade's end, they gathered up their losses and searched for community within cloistered remnants of a movement rapidly losing momentum.

Tom Hayden and other activists were found guilty of planning a riot during the 1968 Democratic National Convention. While awaiting appeal on his conviction, he joined a commune in Berkeley called the Red Family collective.[116] In the late sixties, the movement splintered into hordes of mutually exclusive bands of neo-Marxists, feminists, environmentalists, and other (mostly single-issue) groups. Some moved to rural communes to shield themselves from the fury and gore of the time.

Hayden eventually was asked to leave the collective, whose members found him guilty of having a "powerful" personality and of proclivities toward "male chauvinism." He decided to visit Ireland, where he hoped to explore his ethic roots. He was looking for what Bellah and Sandel called a "narrative" of continuity, one that might shed light on his own journey to radicalism. He could not find it in America.

> I was trying to understand how the various Haydens, Garitys, Foleys, and Duceys were driven by a combination of desperation and hope to seek *their* identities as Americans, how their Irish ethnicity had been dissolved over a century and replaced by the bland, middle-class American identity of my parents. Not only was this new identity lacking in cultural richness, but I realized that its attainment involved an erasure of a historical consciousness of having once been oppressed.[117]

American officials warned Irish authorities that Hayden might cause "trouble" in Northern Ireland. He was not granted a visa.[118]

In the immediate aftermath of the sixties, other leaders of early SDS sought solace and intimacy in communes or "New Age" therapies. In 1973 Sharon Jeffrey went to the Esalen Institute in California, where for "the first time in my life I had nothing to say."[119] Rennie Davis was despondent, not only over the collapse of the New Left but because when he looked inside himself, "all I saw was ego."[120] He tried to overcome this state by submitting to the philosophy of self-denial preached by a 15-year-old guru in India. Prior to becoming a member of the Berkeley faculty, Todd Gitlin joined a male consciousness-raising group as a way of "greasing" his withdrawal from politics.[121]

In the winter of 1970 Carl Oglesby joined a commune in Vermont. He had become a member of SDS in 1965 and served as its fifth president that year. In an antiwar speech in the fall of 1965 Oglesby had laid the blame for the Vietnam fiasco at the feet of what he called American "corporate liberalism." Nevertheless, he supported Robert Kennedy's run for the presidency in 1968 (though not his corporate liberal agenda). "I knew damn well that I would fight like a maniac to bring SDS into the Bobby Kennedy coalition . . . because to me anything else was silly."[122] Through the spring of 1968 he believed it was still possible for SDS to assume "its proper place in American politics, on the left wing of the Democratic Party."[123]

But Kennedy was murdered, leaving the field to "Nixon and the militarists." "We had nothing left to say. I could bitch and moan about the incongruities of the Weatherman manifesto, but that didn't mean I had an alternative." Leaving it all behind and heading for the solitude of Vermont was Oglesby's only "alternative." "It was almost the best part of the struggle," he said. "The best part of the struggle was the surrender."[124]

Paul Potter, perhaps the most thoughtful SDSer, died of cancer in 1986. In his 1971 political memoir he still tried to make sense of it all. He continued to search for the elusive moral juncture where liberty and community might converge in America, the quest that drove SDS from the start. But by this time he was going in circles, trapped in a forlorn hunt for an American way to be both free and to express "the depth of the need for other people."

> For example, no one would have a highway built through his neighborhood (assuming that there was someone interested in building highways) unless he wanted it. But no one would think of not wanting it if the society needed it. The correlative of that would be that the society would not think it needed it unless it really needed it. A difference of opinion between one man and the community over whether a highway was needed would be a clear sign to everyone that things had to be worked out very carefully.[125]

A decade of radical activity had come to this. Yet, in an ironic way Potter's example suited both his dilemma and his country's way of life. What more fitting way to close a sixties dream of community in America than with a discussion about a highway?

AFTERWORD

A Fiction of the Past

Perchance, when, in the course of ages, American liberty has become a fiction of the past—as it is to some extent a fiction of the present—the poets of the world will be inspired by American mythology.

Henry David Thoreau, "Walking," 1862

WHEN PEOPLE UTTER THE WORDS "THE SIXTIES" they can mean almost anything. Were these years the good old days when youth, ecstasy and commitment were synonymous? Or was the decade an extended national trauma from which the country has yet to fully recover? Did the movements spawned in those years succeed or fail, nourish a renewal of national ideals or foster moral decline? Did one serve in Vietnam? Oppose the war? Both? There were many sixties, depending on an individual's political values, race, ethnicity, region of origin, gender, sexual orientation and musical taste. Whatever one's values or connections to the sixties, it is impossible to ignore either the extraordinary changes wrought by the decade's numerous movements or their continuing impact on nearly every feature of American life.

The African American, women's and gay movements of the 1960s were epochal turning points in the history of race, gender and sexuality. The pace of progress enjoyed by each group has been uneven. But there will be no return to the days before the sixties, when legal discrimination against these groups pervaded society and facile, even violent, expressions of personal prejudice could be aimed at blacks, women, gay men or lesbians with almost total impunity. Also, the surge of ethnic pride that erupted during the late sixties among both minority and white groups continues to eddy through society, in debates over multiculturalism and in many other ways.

The specter of the antiwar movement, and of the domestic upheavals that accompanied it, lingers (no doubt distastefully) in the memories of those who walk the corridors of power in Washington. More important, it is a reminder to ordinary citizens that they can challenge, and if need be obstruct, the capacity of those in power to pursue irrational policies. And that lost war remains a monument to the dark side (and blind side) of a grand national fantasy: that technological sophistication and managerial "rationality" enable Americans to eradicate or control what they fear or don't understand. Including the protean quality and inherent disorderliness of their own brand of freedom.

In addition, the various sixties movements initiated or helped accelerate changes that liberalized the culture in a variety of ways. Among many other things, the Supreme Court's decision legalizing abortion in 1973 was inconceivable without the surge of feminism in the late sixties. Arguably, the extraordinary freedom of expression that defines contemporary popular culture is in part a legacy, however dubious, of the counterculture's casual approach to sexual matters and the license taken by rock artists in composing their lyrics. Finally, the resurgence of political and social conservatism over the last three decades is to some degree tied to sixties movements. The emergence of neoconservatism and the rise of the religious right were reactions to a number of developments, not least of which were the fears of conservatives that feminism undermined traditional "family values" while the counterculture's "anything goes" attitude encouraged moral relativism.[1]

The various expressions of white radicalism described in this book were directly and indirectly linked to all of these movements and shifts in sensibility. They played central roles in making the sixties "the sixties." But there is irony and paradox here. Unlike the other movements, the democratic ideals of early SDS, the Digger version of personal freedom and rock musicians' demands for autonomy in the workplace have had little if any residual impact on the ways and means of American society. Although these diverse strains of white radicalism raised basic questions about personal liberty, democracy, work, political power and community, it is hard to see what, if anything, came of it all.

Of course, some of the blame for this has to be shouldered by the young radicals. The New Left and counterculture were blemished by lack of focus, disunity, naiveté, self-righteousness, condescension toward their opponents and, during the final years of the decade, sporadic violence by a small number of radicals. Also, their casual and often public indulgence in a wide variety of personal excesses was not likely to win many adherents to their causes. By themselves, however, these inadequacies cannot explain an enduring paradox in the history and legacy of white radicalism.

The young radicals discussed in this book promoted core American values. They were self-reliant and competitive. They mobilized personal initiative as a means of achieving control over their lives. They championed democracy, localism, community, individualism and autonomy. In these and other ways they were thoroughly American. And in the early years of the decade they behaved responsibly enough and tried, however haltingly, to reach out to established institutions. It will be recalled that SDS delivered a copy of the *Port Huron Statement* to the Kennedy White House and worked with labor unions like the United Auto Workers. And if the street antics and ebullient individualism of the Diggers, who often wore costumes to disguise themselves, put off many who witnessed them, this behavior did not occur in a vacuum in terms of cherished American traditions. The perpetrators of the Boston Tea Party disguised themselves as Indians to make a point, and a determined, often rowdy, individualism is well within the American grain. Yet during and since the sixties most people responded to the ideals and values of white radicals with chilly indifference, perplexity or outright hostility.

This happened for reasons that went well beyond the radicals' blunders and excesses. Early SDS exposed a startling contradiction between the American axiom that "all politics are local" and the American reality that ultimate political power isn't. Most Americans have little interest in confronting this incongruity. Their general dissociation from public life, as well as the paucity of politically empowered local civic organizations necessary for genuine democracy to flourish, are inseparable from their obsessions with privacy and the primacy of self-interest. The Diggers pushed the "act" of American self-creation beyond its economic script, a social improvisation the vast majority simply will not tolerate. The case of rock musicians and their attitudes toward work raises other issues. Rock artists were not inherently anticapitalist; they were dedicated entrepreneurs—though they disdained the hierarchy and power of corporations. But their commitment to autonomy on the job, whether expressed through opposition to alienated, divided labor, an aversion to compulsive, boring work or their antipathy toward the hierarchical structure of the modern corporation, potentially challenged an arrangement that may be more deeply rooted in American culture than capitalism itself. Had their demand for autonomy in the workplace somehow been projected onto all workers (admittedly a complex task), it would have conflicted with the nearly untrammeled right of owners and managers in most industries to determine the conditions of work—and to a great extent, therefore, the physical and psychological conditions of life—of their employees. It would have undermined the enormous power of managers and owners which, if legitimately earned through meritocratic competition, is nearly boundless—

even when it is inspired by unremitting greed, exercised arbitrarily or routinely damaging to the dignity and well-being of employees.

In the end, white radicals reprised myths which harbored intimations of American liberty, rather than the country's actual history. Nothing remotely resembling the unchecked democracy favored by SDS has ever existed in the United States. Throughout the country's history very few people have taken advantage of the freedom of improvisation celebrated by the Diggers. Much less, like rock performers, have many ever enjoyed (or even demanded) workplace autonomy and dignity appropriate to their jobs and skills. Yet these currents of the radical youth culture flowed from myths and themes implicit in the culture, despite the fact that most Americans have seldom acted upon them.

Young radicals in the 1960s reasserted potentials of American liberty that Henry David Thoreau called "fictions of the past." In the essay "Walking," published in the *Atlantic Monthly* shortly after his death in 1862, Thoreau discussed the "art" of "sauntering." He took daily walks, not for exercise but as strolls toward freedom. Thoreau said purposeful walking was the art of moving away from "a freedom and culture merely civil," one that focused mainly on personal security and social order. The "minister and the school committee and every one of you will take care of that," he reminded his readers. Instead he walked toward "Nature . . . absolute freedom and wildness," where he could be a "free man." Accordingly, in his daily walks he found himself inevitably heading west or southwest. "It is hard for me to believe that I shall find fair landscapes or sufficient wildness and freedom behind the eastern horizon." The moon and sun seemed larger in the American West than in Europe or New England, the heavens higher, the stars brighter. The physical grandeur of free, sparsely settled American space was "symbolical of the height to which the philosophy and poetry and religion of her inhabitants may one day soar." Not even "Adam in paradise" was more "favorably situated than the backwoodsman in this country."

For Thoreau, the future of his country was not presaged in its "lawns and cultivated fields," its settled zones of "dullness" and "tameness." It was foretold in the fables and heroic myths spun from the trek West and the wondrous encounters with "the Platte . . . the St. Lawrence, and the Mississippi." Of course, the western wilderness would eventually disappear. At some point the West would become but another version of the settled East. American liberty, beyond its formal, legal or economic expressions, would survive mainly in remembrances of the wilderness encounter inscribed in its myths. When the West and the freedom it symbolized was tamed, and American liberty inevitably became a fiction of the past (Thoreau noted this was already happening in 1862), "the poets of the world will be inspired by American mythology."[2]

Except for some rock-and-roll artists, there weren't many "poets" among sixties radicals. But their ranks were swollen with those inspired by the democratic vistas associated with the wilderness, the frontier and the West—and by other intimations of liberty that Thoreau referred to as "American mythology." They acted on those fictions. They believed in the myths of liberty, equality, autonomy and democracy. Their America was a spacious theater of freedom and unpredictability. They eagerly anticipated its bracing adventures and unforeseeable opportunities. And they looked forward to engaging head-on the risks demanded by its promise of freedom.

Of course, these were all fictions of the American past. Yet, as the Digger Emmett Grogan once said, everything he had "ever heard about America was true."

NOTES

CHAPTER 1

1. Paul Potter, "Student Discontent and Campus Reform," *Papers of Students for a Democratic Society,* State Historical Society of Wisconsin (Social Action Collection). Microfilm, reel 4, series 2.A, no. 29, (July 1965), 15. (Hereafter called *SDS Papers.*)
2. Terry Anderson, *The Movement and the Sixties* (New York: Oxford University Press, 1995), 135.
3. Ibid., 242.
4. The quotes are from Stanley Rothman and S. Robert Lichter, *Roots of Radicalism,* 400. On the middle class origins of sixties cultural and political radicals, see Richard Flacks, *Youth and Social Change* (Chicago: Markam, 1971); Charles Hampden-Turner, *Radical Man* (Cambridge, Mass: Schenkman, 1970); Kenneth Keniston, *Youth and Dissent* (New York: Harcourt, Brace, Jovanovich, 1971), and *Young Radicals* (New York: Harcourt, Brace, Jovanovich, 1968); Richard Rapson, ed., *The Cult of Youth in Middle-Class America* (Lexington, Mass.: D. C. Heath, 1971); D. Westby and R. Braungnant, "Class and Politics in the Family Backgrounds of Student Political Activists," *American Sociological Review* 31 (1966): 690-692; Lewis Yablonsky, *The Hippie Trip* (New York: Pegasus, 1968); Philip Slater, *The Pursuit of Loneliness* (Boston: Beacon Press, 1970; and Christopher Jencks, "Is It All Dr. Spock's Fault?" *New York Times Magazine,* 3 March 1968.
5. Godfrey Hodgson, *America in Our Time: From World War II to Nixon* (New York: Doubleday, 1976), 351-352.
6. See Flacks, *Youth,* 31 and Flacks, "Revolt of the Young Intelligentsia: Revolutionary Class Consciousness in Post-Scarcity America," in *The New American Revolution,* Roderick Aya and Norman Miller, eds. (New York: Free Press, 1971), 223-229.
7. Hippie quoted in Anderson, *Movement,* 256. On consumerism and the counterculture, see Keniston, *Youth and Dissent,* 314; Allen Matusow, *The Unraveling of America: A History of Liberalism in the 1960s* (New York: Harper and Row, 1984), 306-307; David Farber, *The Age of Great Dreams: America in the 1960s* (New York: Hill and Wang, 1994); and Daniel Bell, *The Cultural Contradictions of Capitalism* (New York: Basic Books, 1976).

    On rebellion among college students in the sixties and how it took intellectuals by surprise, see Nathan Glazer, *Remembering the Answers* (New York: Basic Books, 1970). On the history of college campus culture, see Helen Lefkowitz Horowitz, *Campus Life: Undergraduate Cultures from the End of the Eighteenth Century to the Present* (Chicago: University of Chicago Press, 1987). For an excellent history of student radicalism in the 1930s, see Robert Cohen, *When the Old Left Was Young: Student Radicals and America's First Mass Student Movement, 1929-1941* (New York: Oxford University Press, 1993). Student radicalism during the thirties differed from the sixties in a number of ways. For my purposes, however, the most important difference between them was that students in the thirties, for the most part, expressed their discontent through established radical agencies like Marxism. Students in the sixties generally created their own forms of cultural and political radicalism.

    On the middle-class family as an agent of social change, see Paula Fass, *The Damned and the Beautiful: American Youth in the 1920's* (New York: Oxford University Press, 1977); Loren Baritz, *The Good Life: The Meaning of Success for the American Middle Class* (New York: Harper and Row, 1990); and Steven Mintz and Susan Kellogg, *Domestic Revolutions: A Social History of American Family Life* (New York: Free Press, 1988).
8. See Keniston, *Youth and Dissent* and *Young Radicals.*
9. On the distribution of income in the United States during the twentieth century, see Elizabeth Hoyt, *American Income and Its Use* (New York: Harper and Row, 1954); Gabriel Kolko, *Wealth and Power in America* (New York: Praeger, 1962); and Richard Parker, *The Myth of the Middle Class* (New York: Harper and Row, 1972).
10. Lance Morrow, "Turn On, Tune In, Trash It," *Time,* 6 May 1996, 92.

11. See William Broad, "Campus Turmoil of 60's Reveals Themes Echoed in Unabom Manifesto," *New York Times,* 1 June 1996, 8; Bob Wiemer, "The Unabomber Is a Typical '60s Lout," *Newsday,* 15 April 1996, 30. See also, "An Unlikely Legacy of the 60's: The Violent Right," *New York Times,* 7 May 1995, 1.
12. Allen Bloom, *The Closing of the American Mind* (New York: Simon and Schuster, 1987).
13. Dick Armey quoted in Fred Barnes, "Revenge of the Squares," *New Republic,* 13 March 1995, 29; Newt Gingrich quoted in Edward Macedo, ed., "Introduction," *Reassessing the Sixties* (New York: Norton, 1997), 9.
14. See Edward Rothstein, "Voices From the 60's, in Harmony," *New York Times,* 3 May 1997, 18; Neil MacFarquhar, "Sounds of Spring at Columbia," *New York Times,* 15 April 1996, B1; and Will Durst, "A 60's Summer Through a 90's Lens," *New York Times,* 4 October 1997, 15. For a recent evaluation of the sixties, see Macedo, ed., *Reassessing the Sixties.* Other important perspectives on the period include: David Burner, *Making Peace with the 60s* (Princeton, N.J.: Princeton University Press, 1996); William Chafe, *The Unfinished Journey: America since World War Two* (New York: Oxford University Press, 1991); Morris Dickstein, *Gates of Eden: American Culture in the Sixties* (New York: Basic Books, 1977); and James J. Farrell, *The Spirit of the Sixties* (New York: Routledge, 1997).
15. On the relationships between the rise of sixties feminism and the roles of women in the Civil Rights movement and New Left, see Sara Evans, *Personal Politics* (New York: Vintage, 1979).

CHAPTER 2

1. "The Younger Generation," *Time,* 5 November 1951, 47. For a sampling of important contemporary works on conformity and related issues in the fifties, see Vance Packard, *The Status Seekers* (New York: David Mckay, 1959); William Whyte, Jr., *The Organization Man* (New York:Doubleday, 1956); David Riesman, *Abundance for What? and Other Essays* (New York: Doubleday, 1964), and *The Lonely Crowd: A Study of the Changing American Character* (New Haven: Yale University Press, 1950); C. Wright Mills, *White Collar* (New York: Oxford University Press, 1953); and Paul Goodman, *Growing Up Absurd* (New York: Vintage, 1956).
2. Laura Joplin, *Love, Janis* (New York: Villard, 1992), 23-24, 37-39, 125-126, 239, 268.
3. Studies of the family backgrounds of individuals who were political or cultural radicals prior to 1965 show that the majority came from middle-class families in which at least one parent was a professional. After 1965, with the surge of antiwar sentiment, the ranks of active protestors among young people was enlarged considerably, along with the diversity of their social-class backgrounds. On the class origins of young radicals, see Seymour Martin Lipset, "The Activists: A Profile," in *Confrontation: The Student Rebellion and the Universities,* Daniel Bell and Irving Kristol, eds. (New York: Basic Books, 1968), 45-57; D. Westby and R. Braungant, "Class and Politics in the Family Backgrounds of Student Political Activists," *American Sociological Review* 31 (1966), 690-692; William Watts and D. Whittaker, "Some Socio-Psychological Differences between Highly Committed Members of the Free Speech Movement and the Student Population at Berkeley," *Applied Behavior Science* 2 (1966), 41-62; Stanley Rothman and S. Robert Lichter, *Roots of Radicalism: Jews, Christians and the New Left* (New York: Oxford University Press, 1982), 20-24; Kirkpatrick Sale, *SDS* (New York: Random House, 1973), 89-90, 204-206; Allen Matusow, *The Unraveling of America* (New York: Harper and Row, 1984), 306-308; Jeanne Block Norma Haun and M. Brewster Smith, "Some Psychological Aspects of Student Radicalism," *Youth and Society* 1 (March, 1970): 261-280, and "Subjective Correlates of Student Activism," *Journal of Social Issues* 25 (1969); Rex Weiner and Deanne Stillman, *Woodstock Census: The National Survey of the Sixties Generation* (New York: Viking Press, 1979), 17-18; and Kenneth Keniston, *Young Radicals* (New York: Harcourt, Brace, and World, 1968), 306-307.
4. George Kennan ("X"), "The Sources of Soviet Conflict," *Foreign Affairs,* July 1947, 580-582.
5. Quoted in Terry Anderson, *The Movement and the Sixties* (New York: Oxford University Press, 1995), 10-11. On membership figures for the Communist Party of the United States in the 1930s and 1950s, see Harvey Klehr, *The Heyday of American Communism: The Depression Decade* (New York: Basic Books, 1984), 413, and Maurice Isserman, chapter 1 in *If I Had a Hammer: The Death of the Old Left and the Birth of the New Left* (New York: Basic Books, 1987), respectively. For a recent history of Americans who spied for the Soviet Union, see Allen Weinstein and Alexander Vassiliev, *The Haunted Wood: Soviet Espionage in America—The Stalin Era* (New York: Random House, 1998).
6. On the "consensus" of the fifties, see Godfrey Hodgson, chapter 4 in *America in Our Time: From World War II to Nixon* (New York: Doubleday, 1976). On the history of the forties and fifties, see Eric Goldman, *The Crucial Decade—And After* (New York: Knopf, 1965); John Diggins, *The Proud Decades: America in War and Peace, 1941-1960* (New York: Norton, 1988); Marty Jezer, *The Dark Ages: Life in the U. S., 1945-1960* (Boston: South End Press, 1981); Benita Eisler, *Private Lives: Men*

and Women of the Fifties (New York: Franklin Watts, 1986); James Gilbert, *Another Chance: Postwar America, 1945-1968* (New York: Knopf, 1981); William Graebner, *The Age of Doubt: American Thought and Culture in the 1940s* (Boston: Twayne, 1991); Douglas Miller and Marion Nowak, *The Fifties: The Way We Really Were* (New York: Doubleday, 1977); Stephanie Coontz, *The Way We Really Were* (New York: Basic Books, 1992); William Chafe, *The Unfinished Journey: America since World War II* (New York; Oxford University Press, 1991); and Loren Baritz, *The Good Life: The Meaning of Success for the American Middle Class* (New York: Harper and Row, 1990).

7. Hodgson, *America,* 76.
8. R. W. B. Lewis, *The American Adam* (Chicago: University of Chicago Press, 1955), 195-196.
9. Jack Newfield, *A Prophetic Minority* (New York: New American Library, 1966), 41.
10. See Jezer's preface to *The Dark Ages.*
11. Eisler, *Private,* 37.
12. William Whyte, Jr., "The Class of '49," *Fortune,* June 1949, 85-87; "Younger Generation", *Time,* 46-47.
13. "Arise Ye Silent Class of '57", *Time,* 17 June 1957, 97.
14. Riesman, *Abundance,* 167.
15. George Gallup and Evan Hill, "Youth," *Saturday Evening Post,* 23-30 December 1961, 64-69.
16. "The Careful Young Men," *Nation,* 9 March 1957, 197-208.
17. David Riesman, "The Found Generation," in *Abundance.*
18. Ibid., 315-322.
19. Daniel Miller and Guy Swanson, *The Changing American Parent* (New York: Wiley, 1958), 40-50.
20. Quote from "Editorial," *McCall's,* May 1954, 29. On demographic trends, the family and the suburban migration, see Steven Mintz and Susan Kellogg, *Domestic Revolutions: A Social History of American Family Life* (New York: Free Press, 1988), 179-185; Richard Easterlin, *Birth and Fortune* (Chicago: University of Chicago Press, 1987); Landon Jones, *Great Expectations: America and the Baby Boom Generation* (New York: Cloward, McCann and Geohegan, 1980); and Kenneth Jackson, *Crabgrass Frontier* (New York: Oxford University Press, 1985).
21. Baritz, *Good Life,* 199.
22. Elaine Tyler May, *Homeward Bound: American Families in the Cold War Era* (New York: Basic Books, 1988), 3-15. For an astute analysis of the idealization of family life in the forties and fifties, see Warren Susman, "Did Success Spoil The United States? Dual Representations in Postwar America", in *Recasting America,* Lary May, ed. (Chicago: University of Chicago Press, 1989), 19-37.
23. Daniel Bell, "The Mood of Three Generations," in *The End of Ideology* (New York Free Press, 1960).
24. Ibid., 299-314.
25. Norman Podhoretz, *Breaking Ranks* (New York; Harper and Row, 1979), 28.
26. Norman Podhoretz, "The Know-Nothing Bohemians," in *Doings and Undoings: The Fifties and After in American Writing* (New York: Farrar, Strauss, 1964), 144-157.
27. Quote from William Whyte, Jr., "The Transients," *Fortune,* May 1953, 114. On "teamwork" on the job, see "U. S. A.: The Permanent Revolution," *Fortune,* February 1951, 178 and Daniel Bell, "Work and its Discontents," in *Ideology,* 230-248.
28. Packard, *Status,* 123-124, 116-117.
29. David Halberstam, *The Fifties* (New York: Villard, 1993), 488-489 and chapters 10-12.
30. Arthur Schlesinger, Jr., *The Vital Center* (Boston: Houghton-Mifflin, 1949), 167.
31. Mills, *White Collar,* xii-xv, 9, 34, 64.
32. Quote from Whyte, *Organization Man,* 78. On the impact of the Great Depression, see also Baritz, *Good Life,* 113. For a longitudinal study of the psychological impact of the Great Depression, see Glen Elder, *Children of the Great Depression* (Chicago: University of Chicago Press, 1974).
33. Roosevelt and New Deal supporter quoted in Michael Kammen, *Spheres of Liberty: Changing Perceptions of Liberty in American Culture* (Ithaca, N.Y.: Cornell University Press, 1986), 149-150. On visions of the post-Depression American economy as "mature" and relatively static, see Robert M. Collins, "Growth Liberalism in the Sixties," in *The Sixties: From Memory to History,* David Farber, ed. (Chapel Hill: University of North Carolina Press, 1994), 12.
34. Hodgson, *America,* 19. See also Eugenia Kaledin, *Mothers and More: American Women in the 1950's* (Boston: Twayne, 1984), 11.
35. "Permanent Revolution," *Fortune,* 64.
36. "The Leisured Masses," *Business Week,* 12 September 1953, 142.
37. On the baby boomers and education, see Jones, *Great Expectations,* 82-87 and James Brooks, *The Great Leap* (New York: Harper and Row, 1966), 9-11, 32-33.
38. The first quotation is from Harold Vatter, *The U. S. Economy in the 1950's* (New York: Norton, 1963), 1, 23-31; the second is from Gilbert Bruck and Stanford Parker, "The Changing American Market,"

Fortune, August 1953, 98-102. On the performance of the economy in the fifties, see Miller and Nowak, *Fifties,* 7-8, 116; Coontz, *Way We Really Were,* 23-24; Ronald Oakley, *God's Country: America in the Fifties* (New York: Dembner, 1986), 228-231.

39. "The Promise of the Next 100 Years," *Fortune,* August 1949, 84.
40. Baritz, *Good Life,* 184. On poverty and the maldistribution of income in the fifties, see Richard Parker, *The Myth of the Middle Class* (New York: Harper and Row, 1972); Gabriel Kolko, *Wealth and Power in America* (New York: Praeger, 1962).
41. Jones, *Great Expectations,* 2.
42. See Riesman, *Abundance,* 234; and Gilbert, *Another Chance,* 4.
43. See Diggins, *Proud;* William O'Neill, *American High: The Years of Confidence, 1945-1960* (New York: Free Press, 1986); Scott Donaldson, *The Suburban Myth* (New York; Columbia University Press, 1969); Herbert Gans, *The Levittowners: Ways of Life and Politics in a New Suburban Community* (New York: Harper and Row, 1967).
44. Daniel Bell, "America as a Mass Society," in *Ideology,* 34-35.
45. William Whyte, Jr., "How Hard Do Executives Work?" *Fortune,* January 1954, 109.
46. Eisler, *Private,* 90.
47. Whyte, "Transients," 214-221.
48. William Whyte, Jr., "The Outsize Life," *Fortune,* July 1953, 85.
49. Riesman, *Abundance,* 266-267.
50. On images of masculinity in American history, see Anthony Rotundo, *Manhood in America* (New York: Basic Books, 1995), and Michael Kimmel, *Manhood in America: A Cultural History* (New York: Free Press, 1996).
51. See May, *Bound,* 87; Baritz, *Good Life,* 216; and Wini Breines, *Young, White and Miserable: Growing Up Female in the Fifties* (Boston: Beacon, 1992), 31. On the negative impact of television on traditional images of patriarchy, see Lynn Spigel, *Make Room for TV: Television and the Family Ideal in Postwar America* (Chicago: University of Chicago Press, 1992), 62.
52. Arthur Schlesinger, Jr., "The Crisis of American Masculinity," in *The Politics of Hope* (Boston: Houghton, Mifflin, 1963), 237-244.
53. Schlesinger, "The New Mood in Politics," in Ibid., 86.
54. Goodman, *Absurd,* 12, 14, 36, 122-129.
55. William Whyte, Jr., "The Wives of Management," *Fortune,* October 1951, 86.
56. Ibid., 150, 111;
57. J. Fred MacDonald, *Who Shot the Sheriff? The Rise and Fall of the Television Western* (New York: Praeger, 1987), 48-60.
58. On the ratings for television westerns, see ibid, 55; and Jay Harris, ed., *TV Guide: The First Twenty-Five Years* (New York: Simon and Schuster, 1978), 283.
59. Richard Slotkin, *Gunfighter Nation* (New York: Athenaeum, 1992), 348.
60. MacDonald, *Sheriff,* 48.
61. Robert Athearn, *The Mythic West in Twentieth Century America* (Lawrence, Kans.: University of Kansas Press, 1986), 10-13.
62. Jane Tompkins, *West of Everything: The Inner Life of Westerns* (New York: Oxford University Press, 1992), 6, 13-15.
63. Ibid.
64. On family TV programs in the fifties, see Halberstam, *Fifties,* 509-514.
65. MacDonald, *Sheriff,* 51-52.
66. Arness quoted in ibid., 63.
67. Ibid., 75-76.
68. Ibid, 76.
69. *Rebel Without a Cause* (1955).
70. *High Noon* (1952).
71. *Man in the Gray Flannel Suit* (1956).
72. *Twelve Angry Men* (1957).
73. *Shane* (1953). For an excellent analysis of Hollywood films of the forties and fifties, see Peter Biskind, *Seeing Is Believing* (New York: Pantheon, 1983).
74. Slotkin, *Gunfighter,* 352.

CHAPTER 3

1. Else Frenkel-Brunswick, "Differential Patterns of Social Outlook and Personality in Family and Children," in Margaret Mead and Martha Wolfenstein, eds., *Childhood in Contemporary Cultures* (Chicago: University of Chicago Press, 1955), 386-393.
2. Ibid., 386-389, 390-393.
3. Barbara Ehrenreich, *Fear of Falling: The Inner Life of the Middle Class* (New York: Harper Collins, 1989), 12, 13-15.
4. Ibid. See also, David Aberle and Kaspar D. Naegele, "Middle Class Fathers' Occupational Role and Attitudes Toward Children", in Philip Olsen, ed., *America as a Mass Society* (New York: Free Press, 1963), 409-410; Steven Mintz and Susan Kellogg, *Domestic Revolutions: A Social History of American Family Life* (New York: Free Press, 1988), 123.
5. See Martha Ericson Dale, "Child-Rearing and Social Status," in Judson Landis and Mary Landis, eds., *Readings in Marriage and the Family* (New York: Prentice-Hall, 1952), 260-263; Evelyn Millis Duvall, "Conceptions of Parenthood," *American Journal of Sociology* 52 (November 1946): 193-203; Melvin Kohn, "Social Class and Parental Values," *American Journal of Sociology* 64 (January 1959): 337-351; Mirra Komarovsky, *Blue Collar Marriage* (New York: Random House, 1962).
6. Ericson, "Child-Rearing," 262-263.
7. Quoted in Duvall, "Parenthood," 200. On this issue, see also Kohn, "Social Class," 342-343.
8. Quoted in Kohn, "Social Class," 350. See also Duvall, "Parenthood," 200-203; Dale, "Child-Rearing," 261.
9. Kohn, "Social Class, 350.
10. Ibid, 342-345.
11. Quoted in Dale, "Child-Rearing," 263. See also Duvall, "Parenthood," 195-199.
12. Kohn, "Social Class," 348-351.
13. Bruno Bettelheim, *Dialogues with Mothers* (New York: Free Press, 1962).
14. Ibid., 1, 87-99.
15. Earl Selby and Dorothy Selby, "It's All in the Family," *Ladies' Home Journal*, August 1950, 110.
16. "Playgrounds of Tomorrow," *McCall's*, November 1955, 14.
17. Judith Chase Churchill, "How Much Can You Predict about Your Child," *McCall's*, January 1956, 46, 75.
18. Marthedith Stauffer, "I'm the Housekeeper with Ten Thumbs," *Ladies' Home Journal*, February 1950, 186.
19. Bettelheim, *Dialogues*, 55-57.
20. Selwyn James, "I. Q. Tests for Babies," *McCall's*, November 1955, 8.
21. Don Wharton, "First Baby A Year Later", *McCall's*, September 1953, 39.
22. Brett Harvey, *The Fifties: A Woman's Oral History* (New York: Harper Collins, 1993), 105-106.
23. Kenneth Keniston, *Young Radicals* (New York: Harcourt, Brace and World, 1968), 56-57.
24. Philip Olsen and Carlton Daley, "The Education of the Individual," in Olsen, *Mass Society*, 419-434.
25. Laura Joplin, *Love, Janis* (New York: Villard, 1992), 39-40.
26. David Katz, *Home Fires* (New York: Harper Collins, 1992), 84.
27. John Fischer and Ann Fischer, "The New Englanders of Orchard Town, USA," in Beatrice Whiting, ed., *Six Cultures: Studies in Child-Rearing* (New York: Wiley, 1963), 1003.
28. Rubin quoted in J. Anthony Lukas, *Don't Shoot: We Are Your Children* (New York: Random House, 1972), 355, 383.
29. Midge Decter, *Liberal Parents/Radical Children* (New York: Coward, McCann and Geohagan, 1975), 27-28.
30. Elizabeth Pope, "A *McCall's* Report Card on Report Cards," *McCall's*, February 1955, 82-84.
31. Elizabeth Pope, "Are We Teaching Our Children to Cheat?," *McCall's*, April 1956, 175.
32. "Let The Parents Speak," *Ladies' Home Journal*, October 1954, 57.
33. Keniston, *Radicals*, 52-53.
34. Ibid.
35. Ibid., 63.
36. Ibid., 52-53. See also, Joan Morrison and Robert Morrison, eds., *From Camelot to Kent State* (New York: New York Times Books, 1987), 124-129.
37. Keniston, *Radicals*, 70-71.
38. Timothy Leary, *Flashbacks: An Autobiography* (Los Angeles: J. P. Tarcher, 1983), 377.
39. Loren Baritz, *The Good Life: The Meaning of Success for the American Middle Class* (New York: Harper and Row, 1990), 205.
40. Keniston, *Radicals*, 73.

41. Philip Slater, *The Pursuit of Loneliness* (Boston: Beacon Press, 1970), 63-65.
42. Rubin quoted in Lukas, *Don't Shoot,* 351.
43. Hilda Bruch, "It's All in the Way You Say No," *McCall's,* October 1953, 111-116.
44. Bettelheim, *Dialogues,* 160-178.
45. Ibid., 185-187.
46. Ibid., 48-50.
47. Ibid., 112-115.
48. Harvey, *Fifties,* 108.
49. Hilda Bruch, *Don't Be Afraid of Your Child* (New York: Farrar, Strauss, and Young, 1952), 155, 157; see also Eisler, *Private,* 211-212, 216.
50. "How to Run a Happy Home," *McCall's,* August 1952, 34-35.
51. Ibid; Herman Bundesen, "The Overprotective Mother," *Ladies' Home Journal,* March 1950, 243-244.
52. On changes in child-rearing during World War II, see William Tuttle, Jr., chapter 6 in *Daddy's Gone to War: The Second World War in the Lives of America's Children* (New York: Oxford University Press, 1993). On the rise of the "democratic" and "companionate" middle class family, see Mintz and Kellogg, chapter 3 in *Domestic Revolutions;* Paula Fass, chapter 2 in *The Damned and the Beautiful: American Youth in the 1920's* (New York: Oxford University Press, 1977). See also, Elliott West, *Growing Up in Twentieth-Century America* (Westport, Ct.: Greenwood Press, 1996) and Christina Hardyment, *Dream Babies: Three Centuries of Good Advice on Child-Rearing* (New York: Harper and Row, 1983).
53. John Andrew III, *The Other Side of the Sixties* (New Brunswick, N.J.: Rutgers University Press, 1997), 1-10.
54. On the middle class backgrounds of radicals, see Seymour Martin Lipsit, "The Activists: A Profile," in *Confrontation: The Student Rebellion and the Universities,* Daniel Bell and Irving Kristol, eds. (New York: Basic Books, 1968), 45-57; D. Westby and R. Braungant, "Class and Politics in the Family Backgrounds of Student Political Activists," *American Sociological Review* 31 (1966): 690-692; and William Watts and D. Whittaker, "Some Socio-Psychological Differences between Highly Committed Members of the Free Speech Movement and the Student Population at Berkeley," *Applied Behavior Science* 2 (1966): 41-62.
55. See Ibid., and W. J. Rorabough, *Berkeley at War: The 1960s* (Oxford University Press, 1989), 33-34.
56. Andrew, *Other Side,* 147-149, 105-109, 223-231.
57. Ibid., 146-150.

CHAPTER 4

1. Paul Potter, *A Name For Ourselves* (Boston: Little, Brown, 1971), 112.
2. On the roles played by the modern middle class in the development of the planned society, see Robert Wiebe, *The Search for Order, 1877-1920* (New York: Hill and Wang, 1967).
3. Ibid. See especially chapters 5 and 6.
4. Ibid. See also Jerry Isreal, ed., *Building the Organizational Society* (New York: Free Press, 1972). On distinctions between "expressive" and economic individualism, see Gerald M. Platt and Rhys H. Williams, "Religion and Ideology in Electoral Politics," *Transaction* 25 (July-August, 1988): 38-45.
5. Laura Joplin, *Love, Janis* (New York: Villard, 1992), 36.
6. Jerry Rubin, *Growing Up at Thirty-Seven* (New York: M. Evans, 1976), 62-63.
7. Bruno Bettelheim, *Dialogues with Mothers* (New York: Free Press, 1962), 70-71.
8. Hayden quoted in James Miller, *Democracy Is in the Streets: From Port Huron to the Siege of Chicago* (New York: Simon and Schuster, 1987), 270.
9. Todd Gitlin, "The Dynamics of the New Left," *Motive* 31 (November 1970): 65-66.
10. Hayden quoted in Miller, *Democracy,* 309.
11. Potter, *Name,* 104-108.
12. First quote from Potter is from Philip Slater, *The Pursuit of Loneliness* (Boston: Beacon, 1970), 58, and the second quote is from Sara Evans, *Personal Politics* (New York: Vintage, 1979), 110.
13. Joan Morrison and Robert Morrison, eds., *From Camelot to Kent State* (New York: Times Books, 1987), 124-129.
14. Ibid., 138.
15. Bettelheim, *Dialogues,* 199.
16. Flacks quoted in Kirkpatrick Sale, *SDS* (New York: Random House, 1973), 94.
17. Tom Hayden, *Reunion: A Memoir* (New York: Random House, 1988), 44.
18. Ibid., 6-21.

19. The first quote is from Jerry Rubin, *Growing Up at Thirty-Seven,* 53; and the second quote is from J. Anthony Lukas, *Don't Shoot: We Are Your Children* (New York: Random House, 1972), 385.
20. Geoffrey O'Brien, *Dream Time: Chapters from the Sixties* (New York: Viking, 1988), 4-5.
21. Quoted in Lukas, *Don't Shoot,* 269.
22. Thomas King Forcade, ed., *Underground Press Anthology* (New York: Ace, 1972), 51-53.
23. Rubin quoted in Morrison, *Camelot,* 279.
24. George Gallup and Evan Hill, "Youth," *Saturday Evening Post,* 23-30 December 1961, 66, 69.
25. Abbie Hoffman, *The Best of Abbie Hoffman* (New York: Four Walls, Eight Windows, 1989), 27-28, 53.
26. Coyote quoted in Bill Graham and Robert Greenfield, *Bill Graham Presents* (New York: Doubleday, 1992), 186.
27. Slick quoted in Ibid.,195.
28. Mario Savio, "An End to History," in Mitchell Cohen and Dennis Hale, eds., *The New Student Left* (Boston: Beacon, 1966), 254-255, 257.
29. Potter, *Name,* 115-116.
30. On putting one's "body on the line" in the South, see Casey Hayden, Preface to Mary King, *Freedom Song: A Personal Story of the 1960s Civil Rights Movement* (New York: William Morrow, 1987), 7-10.
31. Potter, *Name,* 118.
32. Ibid.
33. Todd Gitlin, *The Sixties* (New York: Bantam, 1987), 107.
34. Casey Hayden, Preface to *Freedom Song,* 8.
35. Ibid., 7.
36. Lukas, *Don't Shoot,* 288-289.
37. Elizabeth Sutherland, ed., *Letters from Mississippi* (New York: McGraw-Hill, 1965), 23.
38. Ibid., 22-23.
39. Harris quoted on manhood in Godfrey Hodgson, *America in Our Time from World War II to Nixon* (New York: Doubleday, 1976), 309. See also David Harris, *Dreams Die Hard* (New York: St. Martin's, 1982), 81.
40. Savio quoted in Lewis Feuer, *The Conflict of Generations* (New York: Basic Books, 1969), 504.
41. Ronald Fraser et al., *1968: A Student Generation in Revolt* (New York: Pantheon, 1988), 91.
42. Paul Lauter "The Free University Movement," *SDS Papers,* reel 3, series 2.A, no.16 (no date), 1-4.
43. Ibid.
44. Ibid.
45. Tom Hayden, "Student Social Action," *SDS Papers,* reel 37, series 4.B, no.160 (March 1962), 1-10.
46. Hayden, *Reunion,* 75-77.
47. Jerry Garcia quoted in Editors of *Rolling Stone, Garcia* (Boston: Little, Brown, 1995), 127.
48. Lewis Yablonsky, *The Hippie Trip* (New York: Pegasus, 1968), 28, 71.
49. Jerry Rubin, *We Are Everywhere* (New York: Harper and Row, 1971), 76.
50. Hoffman, *Best,* 80.
51. Rubin quoted in David Farber, *Chicago '68* (Chicago: University of Chicago Press, 1988), 20 (emphasis added); Garcia in *Garcia,* 95.
52. Haber quoted in Miller, *Democracy,* 144.
53. Ibid.
54. Paul Potter, "The Intellectual as an Agent of Social Change," *SDS Papers,* reel 38, series 4.B, no.275 (1963), 5.
55. Kesey quoted in Paul Perry and Ken Babbs, *On the Bus* (New York: Thunder's Mouth Press, 1990), 22-23.
56. Garcia in *Garcia,* 95.
57. Timothy Leary, *The Politics of Ecstasy* (New York: Putnam, 1968), 64-66, 159, 242-246.
58. Quoted from ibid., 65-66,170, 242-46, 278. On related issues, see Leary et al., *The Psychedelic Experience* (Secaucus, N.J.: Citadel Press, 1964), 11; and Leary, *Flashbacks: An Autobiography* (Los Angeles: J. P. Tarcher, 1983), 149.
59. Quoted in R. E. L. Masters and Jean Houston, *The Varieties of the Psychedelic Experience* (New York: Holt, Rinehart, and Winston, 1966), 72. On the "trip" as a solipistic experience, see also Yablonsky, *Trip,* 29-30; and Leary, *Ecstasy,* 30, 65-76, 125-129; Leary, *Flashbacks,* 46, 119, 253.
60. Yablonsky, *Trip,* 169-170.
61. Leary, *Ecstasy,* 263.
62. For incisive discussions of cultural polarities in American history, see Michael Kammen, *People of Paradox* (New York: Vintage, 1972); and Erik H. Erikson, *Childhood and Society* (New York: Norton, 1950), 285-293.

63. Alexis de Tocqueville, *Democracy in America,* ed. J. P. Mayer, trans. George Lawrence (New York: Anchor, 1969), 281.
64. Frederick Jackson Turner, *The Frontier in American History* (New York: Holt, 1920).
65. Thomas Jefferson to Francois de Marbois, 14 June 1817, *Thomas Jefferson: Writings,* ed. Merrill Peterson (New York: Library of America, 1984), 1410.
66. On the frequency of migrations by farmers in the early nineteenth century, see John Mack Faragher, *Sugar Creek: Life on the Illinois Prairie* (New Haven: Yale University Press, 1986), 51-59.
67. British official quoted in Gordon S. Wood, *The Radicalism of the American Revolution* (New York: Vintage, 1991), 128.
68. Tocqueville, *Democracy,* 215.
69. Marvin Meyers, *The Jacksonian Persuasion* (Stanford: Stanford University Press, 1957), 104.
70. Flint quoted in Faragher, *Sugar Creek,* 51-52.
71. On the Boone narratives, see Richard Slotkin, *Regeneration Through Violence: The Mythology of the American Frontier, 1600-1860* (Middletown, Connecticut: Wesleyan University Press, 1973), chapter 9.
72. Henry David Thoreau, "Walking," in Carl Bode, ed., *The Portable Thoreau* (New York: Viking, 1947), 623-624.
73. Gatlin quoted in Dee Brown, *The Westerners* (New York: Holt, Rinehart, and Winston, 1974), 82.
74. Wood, *Radicalism,* 308.
75. Ibid., 133-134.
76. Brownson quoted in Michael Kammen, *Mystic Chords of Memory* (New York: Knopf, 1991), 42.
77. Ralph Waldo Emerson, "Self-Reliance," in Gordon Haight, ed., *Ralph Waldo Emerson* (Roslyn, New York: Walter J. Black, 1941), 132.
78. Henry David Thoreau, *Walden* in *The Portable Thoreau,* 264
79. Francis Parkman, *The Oregon Trail* (1847, reprint, New York: Random House, 1949), 79-80. On the idea of a discontinuous American past, see R. W. B. Lewis, *The American Adam* (Chicago: University of Chicago Press, 1955) and Quentin Anderson, *The Imperial Self* (New York: Knopf, 1971).
80. Jefferson to Madison, 6 September 1789, *Writings,* 959-963.
81. Jefferson to Major John Cartwright, 5 June 1824, Ibid., 1193-1194.
82. Thoreau, *Walden,* in *The Portable Thoreau,* 403.
83. William R. Taylor, *Cavalier and Yankee* (New York: Harper and Row, 1961), 98.
84. Hector St. John de Crevecoeur, *Letters From An American Farmer* (New York: Signet, 1963), 65-67. On the western migrations as preservations of community, see Thomas Bender, *Community and Social Change in America* (New Brunswick, N.J.: Rutgers University Press, 1978) and T. Scott Miyakawa, *Protestants and Pioneers: Individualism and Conformity on the American Frontier* (Chicago: University of Chicago Press, 1989).
85. Jones, *O Strange,* 379-388.
86. For an excellent local study of this issue, see Mary Ryan, *Cradle of the Middle Class: The Family in Oneida County, NY, 1790-1865* (Cambridge, Mass.: Cambridge University Press, 1981).
87. For a sampling of works on the family and female domesticity, see Barbara Welter, "The Cult of True Womanhood," *American Quarterly* 18 (1966): 151-174; Welter, "The Feminization of American Religion, 1800-1860," in Mary Hartman and Lois W. Banner, eds., *Clio's Consciousness Raised* (New York: Harper and Row, 1974), 137-157; William E. Bridges, "Warm Hearth, Cold World," *American Quarterly* 21 (1969); Steven Mintz and Susan Kellogg, *Domestic Revolutions* (New York: Free Press, 1988), especially chapter 6; Carroll Smith-Rosenberg, *Disorderly Conduct: Visions of Gender in Victorian America* (New York: Oxford University Press, 1985).
88. On the attractions of life and community in small towns, see James Oliver Robertson and Janet C. Robertson, *All Our Yesterdays: A Century of Family Life in an American Small Town* (New York: Harper Collins, 1993); Hal S. Barron, *Those Who Stayed Behind* (Cambridge: Harvard University Press, 1984); Steven Hahn and Jonathan Prude, eds., *The Countryside in the Age of Capitalist Transformation* (Chapel Hill: University of North Carolina Press, 1985); David Lamb, *A Sense of Place* (New York: Random House, 1993).
89. On utopian movements and the "simple life," see Keith Melville, *Communes in the Counterculture* (New York: Morrow, 1972); Laurence Veysey, *The Communal Experience* (New York: Harper and Row, 1973); Peter Schmitt, *Back To Nature: The Arcadian Myth in Urban America* (New York: Oxford University Press, 1969; Rosabeth Moss Kanter, *Commitment and Community: Communes and Utopias in Sociological Perspective* (Cambridge: Harvard University Press, 1972); David Shi, *The Simple Life: Plain Living and High Thinking in American Culture* (New York: Oxford University Press, 1985).
90. James Axtell, *The European and the Indian* (New York: Oxford University Press, 1981), 59-60.
91. Rubin, *We,* 41, 42-43.

92. Hoffman, *Best,* 29.
93. Ibid., 42, 100.
94. On the attitudes of jurors during the Chicago conspiracy trial, see J. Anthony Lukas, *The Barnyard Epithet and Other Obscenities: Notes on the Chicago Conspiracy Trial* (New York: Harper and Row, 1970), 26.
95. Hayden, *Reunion,* 405.
96. On working-class Americans in the sixties and their attitudes toward the upheavals of the decade, see Robert Coles and Jon Erikson, *The Middle American* (Boston: Little, Brown, 1971); Peter Schrag, "The Forgotten Americans," in William Chafe and Harvard Sitcoff, eds., *A History of Our Time* (New York: Oxford University Press, 1991), 395-407 (originally published in *Harper's,* August 1969); James Michener, *Kent State: What Happened and Why* (New York: Random House, 1971); Richard Lemon, *The Troubled Americans* (Boston: Atlantic/Little, Brown, 1971); Sar Levitan, ed., *Blue Collar Workers: A Symposium* (New York: Harper and Row, 1971); Donald Warren, *The Radical Center* (South Bend, Ind.: University of Notre Dame Press, 1976); Bill Moyers, *Listening to America* (New York: Harper and Row, 1971); and Maurice Friedman, ed., *Overcoming Middle Class Rage* (Philadelphia: Westminster Press, 1971. For an insightful historical essay on this issue, see David Farber, "The Silent Majority and Talk about Revolution," in Farber, ed., *The Sixties: From Memory to History* (Chapel Hill: University of North Carolina Press, 1994), 291-316.
97. Coles, *Middle American,* 137-138
98. The quote about a "good, safe job" is from ibid., 92. On middle Americans hoping to escape the "rat race," see Schrag, "Forgotten," 403-405.
99. On middle American animosity toward liberals and their children, see Lemon, *Troubled,* 24-30; and Coles, *Middle American,* 105.
100. Ibid., 52-53.
101. 'Middle American: Man and Woman of the Year," *Time,* 1 January 1970, 12.
102. Michener, *Kent State,* 454-455.
103. Ibid., 448-449.
104. Diana Trilling, *We Must March My Darlings* (New York: Harcourt, Brace, Jovanovich, 1977), 127-133, 140-141.
105. George F. Kennan, *Democracy and the Student Left* (Boston: Atlantic Monthly Press, 1968), 12-14, 170-171.
106. Norman Podhoretz, "The Idea of Crisis," *Commentary,* November 1970, 4.
107. Daniel Bell, *The Cultural Contradictions of Capitalism* (New York: Basic, 1976), 9, 87-88.

CHAPTER 5

1. Jerry Hopkins, ed., *The Hippie Papers* (New York: Signet, 1968, 17-18; see also "The Digger Papers," a collection of their leaflets in *The Realist,* August 1968.
2. Nicholas von Hoffman, *We Are the People Our Parents Warned Us Against* (Chicago: Ivan R. Dee, 1989, originally published in 1968), 140.
3. Emmett Grogan, *Ringolevio: A Life Played for Keeps* (New York: Citadel, 1990), 247; Charles Perry, *The Haight-Ashbury: A History* (New York: Random House, 1984), 97.
4. Grogan, *Ringolevio,* 238-239; "Digger Papers," 5-8.
5. "In the Clear," *San Francisco Chronicle,* 30 November 1966, 1; Grogan, *Ringolevio,* 253-258; "The Frame," *Berkeley Barb,* 4 November 1966, 1, 5.
6. Don McNeill, *Moving Through Here* (New York: Knopf, 1970), 121.
7. "Digger Papers," 6.
8. Grogan, *Ringolevio,* 277.
9. George Metevsky [*sic*], "Delving the Diggers," *Berkeley Barb,* 21 October 1966, 3.
10. R. G. Davis, *The San Francisco Mime Troupe: The First Ten Years* (Palo Alto: Ramparts Press, 1975).
11. W. J. Rorabough, *Berkeley at War: The 1960s* (New York: Oxford University Press, 1989), 144.
12. For the Diggers' influence on other cultural radicals, see Abbie Hoffman, *The Best of Abbie Hoffman* (New York: Four Walls, Eight Windows, 1989), 17-21. On the relationship between the Beat movement and the Diggers, see David Burner, *Making Peace with the Sixties* (Princeton: Princeton University Press, 1996), chapter 4.
13. Grogan, *Ringolevio,* 318.
14. "Digger Papers," 2-3.
15. Kevin Starr, *America and the California Dream* (New York: Oxford University Press, 1973), 51-61.

16. Whitman quoted in Henry Nash Smith, *Virgin Land: The American West as Symbol and Myth* (New York: Vintage, 1950), 48.
17. Starr, *Dream,* 61, 240-241; Doris Muscatine, *Old San Francisco* (New York: Putnam, 1975), 11.
18. Roger Lotchin, *San Francisco: 1846-1956* (New York: Oxford University Press, 1974), 100-104.
19. Ibid, 342-347.
20. Muscatine, *San Francisco,* 11; Oscar Lewis, *Bay Window Bohemia* (New York: Doubleday, 1965), 8.
21. Starr, *Dream,* 61.
22. Lewis, *Bay,* 26-27.
23. Starr, *Dream,* 264.
24. Ibid., 240-241.
25. Richard Miller, *Bohemia:The Protoculture Then and Now* (Chicago: Nelson-Hall, 1977), 216-220.
26. Ibid., 67.
27. Ann Charters, *Kerouac* (New York: St. Martin's Press, 1973), 238-241.
28. Howard Becker, ed., *Culture and Civility in San Francisco* (Chicago: Transaction, 1971), 6, 8-9.
29. Miller, *Protoculture,* 316-230, 244.
30. David Horowitz, *Student* (New York: Ballantine, 1962), chapters, 2, 7, 8.
31. On the FSM and the various student uprisings at Berkeley during the sixties, see Rorabough's excellent history of the period, *Berkeley at War.*
32. Ibid., 28.
33. Ibid., 30-31.
34. Ibid., 31-47.
35. Mario Savio, "An End to History," in Alexander Bloom and Wini Breines, eds. *Takin' it to the Streets* (New York: Oxford University Press, 1995), 111.
36. Clark Kerr, "The Uses of the University," in Immanuel Wallerstein and Paul Starr, eds., *The University Crisis Reader,* Vol. 1 (New York: Vintage, 1971), 84-86.
37. Michael Rossman quoted in Ronald Fraser et al., *1968: A Student Generation in Revolt* (New York: Pantheon, 1988), 96. On the socioeconomic backgrounds of FSM activists, see Rorabough, *Berkeley at War,* 33-34.
38. Paul Perry and Ken Babbs, *On the Bus* (New York: Thunder's Mouth Press, 1990), 185-186.
39. Ibid., 47.
40. On the history of the secret testing of hallucinogens by the United States government, see Martin Lee and Bruce Shalin, *Acid Dreams* (New York: Grove Press, 1985).
41. Perry and Babbs, *Bus,* 36.
42. Tom Wolfe, *The Electric Kool-Aid Acid Test* (New York: Bantam, 1968), 65.
43. Perry, *Haight-Ashbury,* 55. On Bill Graham and his career, see Bill Graham and Robert Greenfield, *Bill Graham Presents* (New York: Doubleday, 1992), and John Glatt, *Rage and Roll: Bill Graham and the Selling of Rock* (New York: Birch Lane Press, 1993).
44. Graham and Greenfield, *Graham,* 3-28.
45. Perry, *Haight-Ashbury,* 41-50.
46. Ralph Gleason, *The Jefferson Airplane and the San Francisco Sound* (New York: Signet, 1969), 5-7, 60; on the Trips Festival, see Perry, *Haight-Ashbury,* 43-46, and Graham and Greenfield, *Graham,* 137-138.
47. Graham and Greenfield, *Graham,* 142.
48. Ibid.
49. On the history of the San Francisco Sound, see Jack McDonough, *San Francisco Rock* (San Francisco: Chronicle Books, 1985) and Joel Selvin, *Summer of Love* (New York: Dutton, 1994).
50. Bill Thompson quoted in Graham and Greenfield, *Graham,* 166.
51. Henry David Thoreau, "Walking," in Carl Bode, ed., *The Portable Thoreau* (New York: Viking, 1947), 604.
52. For typical examples of media coverage of the Haight-Ashbury in the mid sixties, see "Happenings Are Happening," *Time,* 4 March 1966; "The Nitty-Gritty Sound," *Newsweek,* 19 December 1966; "Drop-outs With a Mission," *Newsweek,* 6 February 1967; and Hunter Thompson, "The 'Hashbury' is the Capital of the Hippies," *New York Times Magazine,* 14 May 1967.
53. The word "hippie" antedates the sixties. In his autobiography, Malcolm X said that young whites who frequented Harlem in the 1940s and emulated the "hip" talk of black musicians were called "hippies" by black people. Malcolm X with Alex Haley, *The Autobiography of Malcolm X* (New York: Ballantine, 1964), 94.
54. Perry, *Haight-Ashbury,* 171.
55. Ibid., 253.

56. Ibid., 78-88; Gene Anthony, *Summer of Love: Haight-Ashbury at its Highest,* (Millbrae, Ca: Celestial Arts, 1980), 58-61, 94; Leonard Wolf, ed., *Voices from the Love Generation* (Boston: Little, Brown, 1968), xlii, xxix-xxx; and Helen Perry, *The Human Be-In* (New York: Basic Books, 1970), 99-100. See also Sherri Cavan, *Hippies of the Haight* (St. Louis: New Critics Press, 1972).
57. Davis, *Mime Troupe,* 154. On the Mime Troupe, see "Mime Troup [*sic*] Always Set to Shuffle," *Berkeley Barb* (July 28, 1967), 9.
58. Davis, *Mime,* 31.
59. R. G. Davis, "Radical, Independent, Chaotic, Anarchic Theatre vs. Institutionalized, University, Little, Commercial, Ford and Stock Theatres," *Studies on the Left,* Spring 1964, 36. On the history of mime and related issues, see Anthony Caputi, *Buffo: The Genius of Vulgar Comedy* (Detroit: Wayne State University Press, 1978).
60. Davis, *Mime,* 32, 39-40.
61. Davis, "Radical," 36-37.
62. David, *Mime,* 70; Grogan, *Ringolevio,* 235-236; and Wolf, *Love Generation,* 255-256.
63. Claude Schumacher, ed., *Artaud on Theatre* (London: Methuen, 1989), xxiii, 92, 107-109.
64. Grogan, *Ringolevio,* 318.
65. "The Ideology of Failure," *Berkeley Barb* (September 22, 1967), 3.
66. Peter Coyote, *Sleeping Where I Fall* (Washington, D.C.: Counterpoint, 1998), 70.
67. Grogan, *Ringolevio,* 238.
68. Grogan, *Ringolevio,* 318, 238.
69. Coyote quoted in ibid., v.
70. "Digger Papers," 3.
71. Berg quoted in Grogan, *Ringolevio,* 300.
72. Ibid.
73. Ibid., 300-301; "Digger Papers," 3.
74. See the testimony of a Digger about free store "customers" who emptied the stores in Joan Morrison and Robert Morrison, eds., *From Camelot to Kent State* (New York: New York Times Books, 1987), 320-321.
75. Coyote, *Sleeping,* 90.
76. "Love Community, Conspiracy Clash," *Berkeley Barb,* 10 March 1967, 1, 7.
77. Perry, *Haight-Ashbury,* 261. On nineteenth-century images of a pastoral industrialism, see Leo Marx, *The Machine in the Garden* (New York: Oxford University Press, 1964).
78. "Digger Papers," 4-6.
79. Ibid.
80. Ibid., 9.
81. Perry, *Haight-Ashbury,* 108-109, 114-115.
82. Grogan, *Ringolevio,* 299.
83. Ibid., 278.
84. "Love Community," 1, 7; Perry, *Haight-Ashbury,* 259-260.
85. Grogan, *Ringolevio,* 248, 278.
86. Abbie Hoffman, *Soon to be a Major Motion Picture* (New York: Perigree Books, 1980), 97-98.
87. For two versions of the Digger fiasco at the SDS conference, see Todd Gitlin, *The Sixties: Years of Hope, Days of Rage* (New York: Bantam, 1987), 227-230, and Grogan, *Ringolevio,* 385-403.
88. On the Alan Burke episode, see Grogan, *Ringolevio,* 253-256.
89. Wolf, *Love Generation,* 113-134.
90. Coyote quoted in von Hoffman, *We Are the People,* 132.
91. "Digger Papers," 3-4.
92. Radical Whigs quoted in Michael Kammen, *Spheres of Liberty: Changing Perceptions of Liberty in American Culture* (Ithaca, N.Y.: Cornell University Press, 1986), 31.
93. Henry David Thoreau, *Walden,* in *The Portable Thoreau,* 343.
94. Ralph Waldo Emerson, "The American Scholar," in Mark Van Doren, ed., *The Portable Emerson* (New York: Penguin, 1957), 34-35.
95. William James, *Essays in Pragmatism* (New York: Hafner, 1948), 144-145, 43.
96. Berg quoted in Wolf, *Love,* 260.
97. Ibid.
98. Emerson, "American Scholar," 39.
99. Coyote quoted in Wolf, *Love,* 117-118 and in Derek Taylor, *It Was Twenty Years Ago Today* (New York: Simon and Schuster, 1987), 191-192.
100. Grogan, *Ringolevio,* 367.

101. Richard Slotkin, *Regeneration through Violence: The Mythology of the American Frontier,* (Middletown, Conn.: Weslyan University Press, 1973), 6.
102. Peter Coyote, Introduction to *Ringolevio,* ix.
103. Grogan, *Ringolevio,* 367.
104. Ibid., 367-378.
105. On the mountain men and their experiences, see Robert M. Utley, *A Life Wild and Perilous: Mountain Men and the Paths to the Pacific* (New York: Holt, 1997), and Henry Nash Smith, chapter 8 in *Virgin Land: The American West as Symbol and Myth* (New York: Vintage, 1950).
106. Frederick Jackson Turner, *The Frontier in American History* (New York: Holt, 1920), 4.
107. Hector St. John de Crevecoeur, *Letters from an American Farmer* (New York: Signet, 1963), 71-72.
108. On attitudes toward the West and the frontier, see Richard Slotkin, *Gunfighter Nation* (New York: Athenaeum, 1992) and *Regeneration Through Violence;* Smith, *Virgin Land;* R. W. B. Lewis, *The American Adam* (Chicago: University of Chicago Press, 1955). Roderick Nash, *Wilderness and the American Mind* (New Haven, Conn.: Yale University Press, 1973). On turn-of-the-century fears that an urban, sedentary life would undermine American individualism and "rigor," see Dominick Cavallo, *Muscles and Morals: Organized Playgrounds and Urban Reform, 1880-1920* (University of Pennsylvania Press, 1981), chapter 2.
109. Quoted in Nash, *Wilderness,* 153.
110. Lewis, *Adam,* 91-101.
111. Ibid.
112. Thoreau, "Walking," 610-611.
113. Slotkin, *Regeneration,* 506-507. On Daniel Boone, see John Mack Faragher, *Daniel Boone* (New York: Holt, 1992).
114. Grogan's views on women were typical within the counterculture. See the interviews of Haight-Ashbury hippies and Diggers in Wolfe's *Love Generation.*
115. On the counterculture and the Native American, see Anthony, *Summer of Love,* 147, Perry, *Haight-Ashbury,* 172, Hopkins, *Hippie,* 20; and Grogan, *Ringolevio,* 280.
116. von Hoffman, *We Are The People,* 137-138.
117. For Jefferson on Native American society, see Thomas Jefferson, *Notes on the State of Virginia* in Merrill Peterson, ed., *Thomas Jefferson: Writings* (New York: Library of America, 1984), 220.
118. Hopkins, *Hippie,* 21.
119. James Fenimore Cooper, *The Last of the Mohicans* (New York: Simon and Schuster, 1957), 420.
120. D. H. Lawrence, *Studies in Classic American Literature* (New York: Viking, 1923), 59.
121. Slotkin, *Regeneration,* 556.
122. Thoreau, *Walden,* 456-457.
123. Turner, *Frontier,* 2-3.
124. On the demise of the Haight-Ashbury, see Perry, *Haight-Ashbury,* 220-221, Grogan, *Ringolevio,* 445-446, von Hoffman, *We,* 15, David Smith and John Luce, *Love Needs Care: A History of San Francisco's Haight-Ashbury Free Medical Clinic* (Boston: Little, Brown, 1971), 155-160, 207-216, 253-264, and David Smith et al., "The Health of the Haight-Ashbury," in Becker, ed., *Culture and Civility,* 81, 90-96.
125. "Digger Papers," 8; Smith and Luce, *Love,* 207-209.
126. Smith, "Health," 81-96.
127. von Hoffman, *We Are The People,* 15.
128. Perry, *Haight-Ashbury,* 287.
129. Ibid., 227.
130. Ibid., 287-288.
131. Peter Coyote, "The Free-Fall Chronicles: Crossing the Free Frame of Reference" (C/Netscape/DiggersT3, HTM), 6.
132. "Digger Papers," 8.
133. Kesey quoted in Perry, *Bus,* 47.
134. Grogan, *Ringolevio,* 492.
135. Jack Kerouac, *On the Road* (New York: Viking, 1955), 156.
136. Coyote, Introduction to *Ringolevio.*
137. On the counterculture's legacies, see Harvey Mansfield, "The Legacy of the Late Sixties," in *Reassessing the Sixties,* Stephen Macedo, ed. (New York: Norton, 1997); Peter Clecak, *America's Quest for the Ideal Self* (New York: Oxford University Press, 1983); Timothy Miller, *The Hippies and American Values* (Knoxville: University of Tennessee Press, 1991). On the counterculture's role in inspiring the neoconservative movement, see Peter Steinfels, *The Neoconservatives* (New York: Simon and Schuster, 1979). For specific comments on the hippie legacy, see David Burner, *Making Peace with the 60s*

(Princeton, N.J.: Princeton University Press, 1996), 222; William Chafe, *The Unfinished Journey* (New York: Oxford University Press, 1991), 411-412; Allen Matusow, *The Unraveling of America* (New York: Harper and Row, 1985), 305-307; Daniel Yankelovich, *The New Morality* (New York: McGraw-Hill, 1974), 3-9, 13-22, 23-29. By contrast, see Yankelovich's earlier polls in *Generations Apart* (New York: CBS, 1969). See also, David Caute, *The Year of the Barricades: A Journey Through 1968* (New York: Harper and Row, 1988), 462.

138. Emerson quoted in Yehoshua Arieli, *Individualism and Nationalism in American Ideology* (Cambridge, Mass.: Harvard University Press, 1964), 278.

CHAPTER 6

1. Dylan quoted in John Bauldie, ed., *Wanted Man: In Search of Bob Dylan* (New York: Citadel Press, 1991), 107.
2. On the sybaritic lifestyles of rock musicians during the sixties, see Joel Selvin, *Summer of Love* (New York: Dutton, 1994), 169, 185, and David Downing, *A Dreamer of Pictures: Neil Young* (New York: Da Capo, 1994), 114, 131. For an unrelenting odyssey through the hedonistic world of rock-and-roll, see David Crosby's autobiography, *Long Time Gone* (New York: Doubleday, 1988).
3. Quoted in Gleason, "Correspondence," *Rolling Stone,* 18 October 1969, 3. On rock and politics, see Ralph J. Gleason, "Like a Rolling Stone," in Jonathan Eisan, ed., *The Age of Rock: Sounds of the American Cultural Revolution* (New York: Vintage, 1969), 72.
4. John Sinclair, *Guitar Army* (New York: Douglas Books, 1972), 14-15, 31-37, 43-45, 103; Fred Goodman, *Mansion on the Hill: Dylan, Young, Geffen, Springsteen and the Head-on Collision of Rock and Commerce* (New York: Times Books, 1997), 183.
5. Gleason, "Rolling Stone," 72.
6. On the sixties dance halls, see Bill Graham and Robert Greenfield, *Bill Graham Presents* (New York: Doubleday, 1992), Ralph J. Gleason, *Jefferson Airplane and the San Francisco Sound* (New York: Signet, 1969), and Jack McDonough, *San Francisco Rock* (San Francisco: Chronicle Books, 1985).
7. Joplin quoted in Godfrey Hodgson, *America in Our Time* (New York: Doubleday, 1976), 341. One survey in the late-sixties found that 70 percent of young rock fans did not think lyrics were especially important. See James Harmon, *The New Music and the American Youth Subculture* (Ann Arbor: University of Michigan Microfilms, 1971), 229. For studies of rock and politics in the sixties, see Robin Denselow, *When the Music's Over: The Story of Political Pop* (Boston: Faber and Faber, 1989), Jerome Rodnitsky, *Minstrels of the Dawn: The Folk-Protest Singer as a Cultural Hero* (Chicago: Nelson-Hall, 1976), and Robert Rosenstone, "'The Times They Are A-Changin': The Music of Protest," *Annals of the American Academy of Political and Social Science,* March 1969, 131-141. On the difficulty of measuring the impact of lyrics on listeners of music, see David Riesman, "Listening to Popular Music," in *Mass Culture: The Popular Arts in America,* Bernard Rosenberg and David Manning, eds. (New York: Free Press, 1957), 408-417.
8. Among other things, British rock musicians—with important exceptions such as Cream and the Rolling Stones—were often more studio- and art-rock-oriented. They were more likely than their American counterparts to come from working- class backgrounds and to invest their songs with class conscious themes. They were also more adept at business matters and more organized and professional in their performances. For example, see Goodman, *Mansion,* 27-28, and Selvin, *Summer of Love,* 26-27.
9. See Arnold Shaw, *The Rock Revolution* (London: Crowell-Collier, 1969), 3-5.
10. Bob Weir quoted in Richard Goldstein, "San Francisco Bray," in *The Penguin Book of Rock and Roll Writing,* Clinton Heylin, ed. (New York: Viking, 1992), 159; Robbie Robertson quoted in Graham and Greenfield, *Graham,* 272; and Frank Zappa quoted in Peter Wicke, *Rock Music: Culture, Aesthetics and Sociology* (New York: Cambridge University Press, 1987), 93.
11. Muddy Waters quoted in John Collis, *The Blues* (London: Salamander Books, 1997), 57.
12. On the history of early rock-and-roll, see Ed Ward, Geoffrey Stokes, and Ken Tucker, *Rock of Ages: The Rolling Stone History of Rock and Roll* (New York: Rolling Stone/Summit, 1986); Greil Marcus *Mystery Train: Images of America in Rock 'n' Roll* (New York: Dutton, 1975) and Marcus, ed., *Stranded: Rock and Roll for a Desert Island* (New York: Knopf, 1979); Arnold Shaw, *The Rock Revolution* and Shaw, *The Rockin' Fifties* (New York: Hawthorn, 1974); David Pichaske, *A Generation in Motion: Popular Culture and Music in the Sixties* (New York: Schirmer, 1979); Carl Belz, *The Story of Rock* (New York: Oxford University Press, 1969); Simon Firth, *The Sociology of Rock* (London: Constable, 1978); David Szatmary, *Rockin' In Time: A Social History of Rock and Roll* (Upper Saddle, N.J.: Prentice-Hall, 1996); Ben Fong-Torres, ed., *The Rolling Stone Rock and Roll Reader* (New York: Bantam, 1974); Kit Kiefer, ed., *They Called It Rock: The Goldmine Oral History of Rock 'n' Roll, 1950-*

1970 (New York: Billboard, 1989); Jim Miller, ed., *The Rolling Stone Illustrated History of Rock and Roll* (New York: Random House, 1976); and Jon Pareles and Patricia Romanowski, eds., *The Rolling Stone Encyclopedia of Rock and Roll* (New York: Summit, 1983).

13. Szatmary, *Rockin'*, 26-28, 61-66; Ward et al., *Rock*, 229; Shaw, *Rockin' Fifties*, 15-18; Langdon Winner, "The Strange Death of Rock and Roll," in Marcus, *Will Stand*, 39-40; Belz, *Rock*, 26-27; on Pat Boone and Fats Domino, see Paul Du Noyer, *The Story of Rock 'n' Roll* (Miami: Carlton, 1995), 46-47.
14. On the ways and means of early rock-and-roll, see Ward, *Rock*, part 1.
15. Ibid; Szatmary, chapter 3 in *Rockin'*.
16. Szatmary, *Rockin'*, 65.
17. Marc Eliot, *Rockonomics* (New York: Franklin Watts, 1989), 94-95.
18. Ibid., 95.
19. On the ways in which record companies, managers and disc jockeys controlled early rock performers, see Ibid., especially chapters 4, 5 and 6.
20. Frank Zappa, *The Real Frank Zappa Story* (New York: Poseidon, 1989), 37; McDonough, *San Francisco Rock*, 135; Ward, *Rock*, 334-335; Gleason, *Airplane*, 29; and the sketches of San Francisco musicians in Selvin, *Summer of Love*, 355-365.
21. Zappa, *Real*, 51-52, 158-159.
22. Ibid., 83.
23. Ibid., 141.
24. Ibid., 83-84.
25. Ibid. Sandy Troy, *Captain Trips: A Biography of Jerry Garcia* (New York: Thunder's Mouth Press, 1995), 155.
26. Dylan quoted in Anthony Scaduto, *Bob Dylan* (New York: Great American Library, 1971), 254; Hendrix quoted in Harry Shapiro and Caesar Glebbeek, *Jimi Hendrix: Electric Gypsy* (New York: St. Martin's Press, 1992), 262-263.
27. On Neil Young's early years, see Downing, chapter 1 in *Dreamer*. Young quoted in Bill Flanagan, *Written in My Soul* (Chicago: Contemporary Books, 1986), 121.
28. Goodman, *Mansion*, 63.
29. Ibid., 67; Bill Flanagan, *Written In My Soul* (Chicago: Contemporary Books, 1986), 128-129.
30. Ibid., 121. Editors of *Rolling Stone*, *Neil Young: The Rolling Stone Files* (New York: Hyperion, 1994), 243-247.
31. Ibid., 123.
32. Ibid; Downing, *Dreamer*, 36.
33. Editors of *Rolling Stone*, *Young*, 243.
34. Crosby, *Long Time Gone*, 152, 192-195; Jerry Hopkins and Danny Sugarman, *No One Gets out of Here Alive* (New York: Warner Books, 1980), 82; Gleason, *Jefferson Airplane*, 278-279; Steven Stills quoted in Chet Flippo, liner notes to *Crosby, Stills and Nash Box Set* (Atlantic Records, 1991), unpaginated.
35. Ben Fong-Torres, "Crosby, Stills, Nash, Young, Taylor and Reeves," *Rolling Stone* (December 2, 1969), 24; Pichaske, *Motion*, 129.
36. Sandy Troy, *Captain Trips*, 6.
37. Ibid., 51-65.
38. Editors of *Rolling Stone*, *Garcia* (Boston: Little, Brown, 1995), 66.
39. Ibid.
40. Ibid, and 88; Troy, *Captain Trips*, 104.
41. Selvin, *Summer of Love*, 193.
42. Ibid, 155.
43. Editors of *Rolling Stone*, *Garcia*, 123.
44. Selvin, *Summer of Love*, 156; Troy, *Garcia*, 134, 142.
45. Selvin, *Summer of Love*, 155-157; McDonough, *San Francisco Rock*, 135.
46. Ibid., 11-12; Marcus, *Will Stand*, 64-65.
47. Selvin, *Summer of Love*, 94-95.
48. Troy, *Captain Trips*, 96.
49. Ibid., 155; Editors of *Rolling Stone*, *Garcia*, 67, 108-109.
50. Troy, *Garcia*, 164.
51. Ibid., 177.
52. Quotes from Dylan in sequence from Robert Shelton, *No Direction Home: The Life and Music of Bob Dylan* (New York: William Morrow, 1986), 450; Cameron Crowe, liner notes to Bob Dylan's *Biograph*

(Columbia Records, 1985), 22; Levon Helm, *This Wheel's on Fire* (New York: William Morrow, 1993), 133.

53. Young quoted in Downing, *Dreamer,* 224-225. See also Editors of *Rolling Stone, Garcia,* 183;
54. Goodman, *Mansion,* 52.
55. Ibid.
56. Selvin, *Summer of Love,* 94.
57. On rock and commerce, see Goodman, *Mansion;* Marc Eliot, *Rockonomics* (New York: Franklin Watts, 1989); Steve Chapple and Reebee Garofalo, *Rock 'n' Roll Is Here to Pay* (Chicago: Nelson-Hall, 1977); and George Lipshitz, "'Who'll Stop The Rain?' Youth Culture, Rock 'n' Roll, and Social Critics," in David Farber, ed., *The Sixties: From Memory to History* (Chapel Hill: University of North Carolina Press, 1994), 206-234.
58. Goodman, *Mansion,* 79-80.
59. Ibid., 49-57.
60. Ibid., 133.
61. Ed Sanders quoted in Fred Goodman, "How a Legend Tapped the Rock Underground," *New York Times,* 29 January 1995, Arts and Leisure Section, 23.
62. Goodman, *Mansion,* xi.
63. Michael Lydon, "Money: Rock for Sale," in Heylin, *Penguin Book of Rock and Roll Writing,* 482.
64. See Goodman, *Mansion* and Eliot, *Rockonomics.*
65. Goodman, *Mansion,* x-xii.
66. Al Kooper, *Backstage Passes: Rock 'n' Roll in the Sixties* (New York: Stein and Day, 1977), 94.
67. Balin quoted in Gleason, *Jefferson Airplane,* 278.
68. Balin to Kantner quoted in ibid.; For Balin on Spence, see Selvin, *Summer of Love,* 34; on the Matrix, see Selvin, *Summer of Love,* 14-17.
69. For a host of stories about the ad hoc ways in which the San Francisco bands were formed, see Selvin, *Summer of Love.*
70. Dryden quoted in Gleason, *Jefferson Airplane,* 238
71. Fogarty quoted in Tom Piazza, "The Lost Man of Rock and Roll," *New York Times,* 10 November 1996, Arts and Leisure Section, 14.
72. Dylan quoted in Crowe, liner notes to *Biograph,* 22.
73. Helm, *Fire,* 220.
74. Dylan quoted in Shelton, *Dylan,* 202-203, 287, 344. On Country Joe, the Fish and Mao, see Selvin, *Summer of Love,* 29-30;
75. All but the last quote are from Students for a Democratic Society, *The Port Huron Statement,* [Reprinted in James Miller, *Democracy Is in the Streets: From Port Huron to the Siege of Chicago* (New York: Simon and Shuster, 1987)], 364, 338, 333; On the independence of workers, see Students for a Democratic Society, "America and the New Era," in Massimo Teodori, ed., *The New Left: A Documentary History* (Indianapolis, Indiana: Bobbs-Merrill, 1969), 181.
76. Wicke, *Rock Music,* 47. See also Shaw, *Revolution,* 17; Shaw, *Rockin' Fifties,* 179; Belz, *Rock,* 30.
77. Editors of *Rolling Stone, Garcia,* 127.
78. Constanten quoted in Troy, *Garcia,* 123.
79. David Glans and Jackson Blair, "Talking with Garcia," in Editors of *Rolling Stone, Garcia,* 155.
80. Shapiro and Glebbeek, *Hendrix,* 345. On lip-synching, see also Helm, *Fire,* 204.
81. Morrison quoted in *Rolling Stone,* 14 June 1969, 8; "Interview: Jim Morrison," *Rolling Stone* (July 26, 1969), 12.
82. Joplin quoted in *Time Magazine: 1968, A Special Collector's Edition* (1991), 54.
83. Young quoted in Flanagan, *Written,* 118.
84. Stills quoted in Flippo, liner notes *Crosby, Stills, Nash,* unpaginated.
85. Dylan quoted in Bauldie, *Dylan,* 124; Hendrix quoted in Shapiro and Glebbeek, *Hendrix,* 205.
86. Gleason, *Jefferson Airplane,* 230, 259-262.
87. First Hendrix quote from Shapiro and Glebbeek, *Hendrix,* 345; second quote from "Interview: Jimi Hendrix," *Rolling Stone,* 9 March 1968, 12.
88. Zappa, *Real,* 177.
89. Garcia on repetition in Troy, *Garcia,* 206. Garcia on music and truth in Michael Lydon, "Dead Zone," in Editors of *Rolling Stone, Garcia,* 64.
90. Goodman, *Mansion,* 7-9.
91. Ibid.
92. "They can boo" in Sy and Barbara Ribakove, *Folk-Rock: The Bob Dylan Story* (New York: Dell, 1966), 59. On epithets by Dylan's audience and his wish they would boo more, see Helm, *Fire,* 133-135. For more on Dylan's performance at Newport and its aftermath, see Bauldie, *Dylan,* 57-66.

93. Janis Joplin quoted in Laura Joplin, *Love, Janis* (New York: Villard, 1992), 126, 179, 293, 232; Dryden quoted in Gleason, *Jefferson Airplane*, 252-253.
94. Young quoted in Matt Damsker, *Rock Voices* (New York: St. Martin's Press, 1980), 36.
95. Shapiro and Glebbeek, *Hendrix*, 329, 205.
96. Shelton, *Dylan*, 370.
97. "Interview: Frank Zappa," *Rolling Stone*, 20 July 1968, 11.
98. For Dylan's influence on other musicians, see Shelton, *Dylan*, 225-238; Crowe, liner notes to *Biograph*, 24, 31; Ward, *Rock*, 315; and Derek Taylor, *It Was Twenty Years Ago Today* (New York: Simon and Schuster, 1987), 85-86.
99. Shelton, *Dylan*, 1-68.
100. Clinton Heylin, *Bob Dylan* (New York: Summit, 1991), 54. Nat Hentoff told Dan Wakefield that Dylan lied to him about running away from home, among other things. See Dan Wakefield, *New York in the 50's* (Boston: Houghton-Mifflin, 1992), 158-159.
101. On Dylan's tales of his early years, see Shelton, *Dylan*, 110. "There isn't a home" quoted in Ribakove, *Dylan*, 26.
102. Jim Miller, "Bob Dylan," *Witness*, Vol. 2, no. 2/3 (Summer/Fall, 1988), 54
103. Shelton, *Dylan*, 75.
104. Dylan quoted on singing the same song twice in Ribakove, *Dylan*, 37. On his attitude toward *Sgt. Pepper's*, see Clinton Heylin, *Bob Dylan: The Recording Sessions, 1960-1994* (New York: St. Martin's Press, 1995), 184. For Dylan's approach to working in the studio, see Heylin, *Dylan*, xi-xii, 47, 105. For more on these issues, see Paul Williams, *Performing Artist: The Music of Bob Dylan* Lancaster, Pa.: Underwood-Miller, 1990), 151.
105. Heylin, *Sessions*, 105.
106. Kooper, *Backstage*, 55-56.
107. For a collection of Dylan's lyrics, see Bob Dylan, *Lyrics: 1962-1985* (New York: Knopf, 1986).
108. Dylan quoted on breaking the rules in Shelton, *Dylan*, 344, and in Nat Hentoff interview in Shelton, *Dylan*, 202-203. For more information on Dylan's impact upon young people in the sixties, see Rex Weiner and Deanne Stillman, *Woodstock Census: The Nationwide Survey of the Sixties Generation* (New York: Viking, 1979), 69. Shelton, *Dylan*, 287, 344, 202-203.
109. Ralph Waldo Emerson, "Self-Reliance," in Gordon Haight, ed., *Ralph Waldo Emerson* (Roslyn, New York, 1941), 145.
110. Dylan on King David in Crowe, liner notes to *Biograph*, 33; on "keeping a good head" in Heylin, *Bob Dylan*, 117. For Dylan on the New Left, see Shelton, *Dylan*, 287. For more on these issues, see Rodnitsky, *Minstrels*, 109.
111. Scaduto, *Dylan*, 254; Shelton, *Dylan*, 191.
112. Bauldie, *Dylan*, xiv.
113. Shelton, *Dylan*, 60.
114. Editors of *Rolling Stone*, *Garcia*, 64.
115. On the private man, see Emerson, "Self-Reliance," 136. On time and space, see Emerson, "The Over-Soul," in Haight, ed., *Emerson*, 209. On "self-infinitude" and American culture, see Quentin Anderson, *The Imperial Self* (New York: Knopf, 1971), and R. W. B. Lewis, *The American Adam* (Chicago: University of Chicago Press, 1955).
116. Shelton, *Dylan*, 159.
117. Damsker, *Rock Voices*, 2; Flanagan, *Written*, 96.
118. Alexis de Tocqueville, *Democracy in America*, Richard Heffner, ed. (New York: Mentor, 1956), 194.
119. Dylan quoted in *Newsday*, 10 September 1993, 92.

INTRODUCTION TO PART III

1. For a sampling of works that distinguish between the counterculture and New Left along these lines, see Allen Matusow, chapters 10 and 11 in *The Unraveling of America* (New York: Harper and Row, 1984); Godfrey Hodgson, chapters 15-17 in *America in Our Time from World War II to Nixon* (New York: Vintage, 1976); James Farrell, chapters 6 and 8 in *The Spirit of the Sixties* (New York: Routledge, 1997); and David Burner, chapters 4 and 5 in *Making Peace with the Sixties* (Princeton, N.J.: Princeton University Press, 1996).
2. Hippie quoted in Robert Houriet, *Getting Back Together* (New York: Coward, McCann and Geohegan, 1969), 108
3. Ibid., xxxiv. See also, Lewis Yablonsky, *The Hippie Trip* (New York: Pegasus, 1968), 71.
4. Houriet, *Together*, 31.

5. Crosby quoted in Jerry Hopkins, ed., *The Hippie Papers* (New York: Signet, 1968), 220. On the counterculture, see Keith Melville, *Communes in the Counter Culture* (New York: William Morrow, 1972); Timothy Miller, *The Hippies and American Values* (Knoxville: University of Tennessee Press, 1991); Theodore Roszak, *The Making of a Counterculture* (New York: Doubleday, 1969); Richard Fairfield, *Communes U.S.A.: A Personal Tour* (New York: Penguin, 1972).

CHAPTER 7

1. Important works on the history of SDS and the New Left include Wini Breines, *Community and Organization in the New Left, 1962-1968: The Great Refusal* (New York: Praeger, 1982), and Breines, "Whose New Left," *Journal of American History* 75, September 1988, 528-545; Peter Clecak, *America's Quest For The Ideal Self* (New York: Oxford University Press, 1983), and Clecak, *Radical Paradoxes: Dilemmas of the American Left, 1945-1970* (New York: Harper and Row, 1973); Sara Evans, *Personal Politics: The Roots of Women's Liberation in the Civil Rights Movement and the New Left* (New York: Vintage, 1979); Paul Berman, *A Tale of Two Utopias: The Political Journey of the Generation of 1968* (New York: Norton, 1996); Todd Gitlin, *The Sixties* (New York: Bantam, 1987), and Gitlin, *The Whole World is Watching: The Mass Media in the Making and Unmaking of the New Left* (Berkeley: University of California Press, 1980); Maurice Isserman, *If I Had A Hammer: The Death of the Old Left and the Birth of the New Left* (New York: Basic Books, 1987); James Miller, *Democracy Is in the Streets: From Port Huron to the Siege of Chicago* (New York: Simon and Schuster, 1987); Jack Newfield, *A Prophetic Minority* (New York: New American Library, 1966); Kirkpatrick Sale, *SDS* (New York: Random House, 1973); James Weinstein, *Ambiguous Legacy: The Left in American Politics* (New York: New Viewpoints, 1975); Doug Rossinow, "'The Break-through to New Life': Christianity and the Emergence of the New Left in Austin, Texas, 1956-1964," *American Quarterly* 46, September 1994, 309-340; and Stanley Rothman and S. Robert Lichter, *Roots of Radicalism: Jews, Christians and the New Left* (New York: Oxford University Press, 1982).
2. See comments by SDSers in Miller, *Democracy*, 144-145.
3. Hayden, quoted in Milton Viorst, *Fire in the Streets* (New York: Simon and Schuster, 1979), 192. On SDS's assumption that they had little to learn from older democratic leftists like Irving Howe, see Gitlin, chapter 7 in *Sixties*.
4. On the history of the LID, see Sale, *SDS*, 673-693.
5. Al Haber, "Non-exclusionism: The New Left and the Democratic Left," *SDS Papers*, reel 37, series 4B, no. 134 (undated), unpaginated.
6. Tom Hayden, *Reunion: A Memoir* (New York: Random House, 1988), 5-6.
7. On the backgrounds of various SDSers, see sketches in Miller, *Democracy;* for Carl Oglesby, see Joan Morrison and Robert Morrison, eds., *From Camelot to Kent State* (New York: Times Books, 1987), 297-307.
8. Gitlin, *Sixties*, 105-106.
9. Hayden, *Reunion*, 74, 102.
10. "Draft Constitution," *SDS Papers*, reel 1, series 1, no.6, (May 20, 1962), 1.
11. The Economic Research and Action Project is discussed at length in the following chapter.
12. Hayden, *Reunion*, 102. Among those from whom SDS solicited money and support were entertainers and sports figures, including Jerry Lewis, Tennessee Ernie Ford, Stan Musial, Jackie Robinson, and Leontyne Price. They also sought funds from Edward R. Morrow, Jacqueline Kennedy, and various foundations, including the Eleanor Roosevelt Fund, the Gerber Foundation, and the Stern Family Fund. New York liberal congressman William Fitts Ryan was an early supporter of SDS, calling it a "vital" political group, and UAW president Walter Reuther described it as the "vanguard of student organizations." Journalists who looked favorably upon SDS included Jack Newfield and Andrew Kopkind. See *SDS Papers*, reel 10, series 2.A, no. 130 (undated) and reel 11, series 2.B, no. 14 (May 24, 1964), unpaginated.
13. Hayden quoted in Miller, *Democracy*, 54. On socialism and related issues, see "Tom Hayden to Executive Committee," *SDS Papers*, reel 1, series 1, no. 6 (1962), 2.
14. Gitlin, *Sixties*, 174.
15. Tom Hayden, "A Letter to the New (Young) Left," in Mitchell Cohen and Denis Hale, eds., *The New Student Left* (Boston: Beacon Press, 1966), 2-9, originally published in the *Activist* (Winter, 1961); Hayden, *Reunion*, 76-80.
16. Oglesby quote from Carl Oglesby, ed., *The New Left Reader* (New York: Grove Press, 1969), 13; Hayden quoted in Viorst, *Fire*, 192; Haber quote from Al Haber, "Aims and Purposes of SDS: Some Comments," *SDS Papers*, reel 1, series 1, no.6 (1962) unpaginated, undated; Potter quote from Paul Potter, *A Name for Ourselves* (Boston: Little, Brown, 1971), 101. See also Jim Williams, "Haber's

Critique of the N.C.: Reflections of a Southern Hillbilly SDS'er," Ibid., reel 2, series 2.A, no. 9 (undated), 1-2; and Viorst, *Fire,* 192.

17. Steve Max, "Movements and the Political Arena," *SDS Papers* reel 38, series 4.B, no. 239 (undated), 1-4; Richard Flacks, "Discussion Bulletin," Ibid., reel 35, no series number (Spring 1965) 1-6; Sale, *SDS,* 111-112.
18. Hayden, "Letter to the (Young) New Left," 8.
19. Gitlin, *Sixties,* 172.
20. "Hayden to Executive Committee," *SDS Papers,* reel 1, series 1, no. 6, (undated), 8.
21. On the lack of structure and organization in SDS's central office, see C. Clark Kissinger, "There's A Change Gotta Come," *SDS Papers,* reel 37, series 4.B, no. 198 (undated).
22. An excellent description of the demonstration and the controversy surrounding it is in Gitlin, *Sixties,* 177-188.
23. Paul Potter, "Speech to the April 17, 1965, March on Washington," in *The Sixties Papers: Documents of a Rebellious Decade,* Judith and Stewart Albert, eds. (New York: Praeger, 1985), 220.
24. Ibid., 222, 224. On October 27, 1965, during another antiwar march on Washington, SDS's new president, Carl Oglesby, did "name the system." He called it "corporate liberalism." If Potter's refusal to name the system was consistent with the early New Left's willingness to abide ambiguity and avoid the Old Left's economic categories, Oglesby's equally evocative speech was a portent of the direction toward which the left of the late sixties was headed.
25. On the backgrounds of post-1965 SDS members, see Gitlin, *Sixties,* 186.
26. Susan Stern, *With the Weathermen: The Personal Journal of a Revolutionary Woman* (New York: Doubleday, 1975), 102. On the Weathermen, see Harold Jacobs, ed., *Weatherman* (Berkeley, Ca.: Ramparts Press, 1970).
27. Hayden, *Reunion,* 422.
28. Carl Oglesby, ed., *The New Left Reader* (New York: Grove Press, 1969), 14.
29. Hayden, "Letter to New (Young) Left," 6.
30. "Cabot-Max Draft for the New SDS Organizational Brochure," *SDS Papers* reel 4, series 2.A, no. 25, (undated).
31. Tom Hayden, "Manifesto Notes: A Beginning Draft," *SDS Papers* reel 1, series 1, no. 6, (March 12, 1962), 1-4.
32. Ibid., 2, 3, 4.
33. Hayden, "Student Social Action," *SDS Papers,* reel 37, series 4.B, no. 160, (March, 1962), 5, 7.
34. Citations from the *Post Huron Statement* are from the reprint in the appendix to Miller, *Democracy Is in the Streets.*
35. Ibid., 329-330.
36. Matusow, *Unraveling,* 312-313.
37. Hayden, *Reunion,* 97-98.
38. *Port Huron Statement* in Miller, *Democracy,* 332, 333.
39. Ibid., 355, 362, 363.
40. Ibid.
41. There is an incisive discussion of this issue in Miller, chapter 8 in *Democracy.*
42. Jeffrey and Ross quoted in Miller, *Democracy,* 144.
43. Potter quote from Potter, *Name,* 113, 144; Flacks quote from Richard Flacks, "Revolt of the Young Intelligentsia," in Roderick Aya and Norman Miller, eds., *The New American Revolution* (New York: Free Press, 1971), 236.
44. Donald McKelvey, "Some Notes on Participatory Democracy," *New Left Notes,* 6 May 1966, 8.
45. "Tom Hayden to Executive Committee," 5.
46. Potter, *Name,* 115.
47. Jeffrey quoted in Miller, *Democracy,* 207.
48. Hayden, *Reunion,* 446, 442.
49. "Hayden to Executive Committee," 7.
50. *Port Huron Statement* in Miller, *Democracy,* 332, 333.
51. For a brilliant analysis of the relationship between individualism and American political culture, see Yehoshua Arieli, *Individualism and Nationalism in American Ideology* (Cambridge, Mass.: Harvard University Press, 1964).
52. Jefferson to Thomas Law, 13 June 1814, *Thomas Jefferson: Writings,* Merrill Peterson, ed. (New York: Library of America, 1984), 1137.
53. Jefferson to William Johnson, 12 June 1823, in Ibid., 1470-1471; Jefferson to Major John Cartwright, 5 June 1824, in Ibid., 1192-1193.

54. Tom Hayden, "To All The Guys at ERAP." *SDS Papers* reel 10, series 2.B, no. 1 (undated), 4. Jefferson was not alone among the revolutionary generation in assuming the existence of an innate moral sense. See Eric Foner, *Tom Paine and Revolutionary America* (New York: Oxford University Press, 1976), 92-93.
55. Gary Wills, *Inventing America: Jefferson's Declaration of Independence* (New York: Doubleday, 1978), 248-255; Willard Randall, *Thomas Jefferson: A Life* (New York: Henry Holt, 1993), 204.
56. Jefferson quoted in Arieli, *Individualism,* 98.
57. Hayden, *Reunion, 98.*
58. Potter, *Name,* 95.
59. Ibid., 101, 107, 110, 111, 120.
60. Jefferson to Peter Carr, 10 August 1787, *Jefferson,* 902.
61. Todd Gitlin, "Power and the Myth of Progress," in Massimo Teodori, *The New Left: A Documentary History* (Indianapolis, Ind.: Bobbs-Merrill, 1969).
62. Ibid., 188-191.
63. "Hayden to Steve Johnson," *SDS Papers* reel 4, series 2.A, no. 25, (May 10, 1963), 3.
64. Haber quoted in Miller, *Democracy,* 69.
65. Richard Flacks, "Is the Great Society Just a Barbecue," in Teodori, *New Left,* 195.
66. Martin Roysher and Charles Laffer, "Memorandum," in *SDS Papers* reel 6, series 2.A, no. 60, (undated).
67. See Isserman, *If I had a Hammer,* Chapter 5.

CHAPTER 8

1. On social and economic conditions and conflicts during the 1780s, see Merrill Jensen, *The New Nation* (New York: Vintage, 1950), and Jackson Turner Main, chapters 2 and 3 in *The Antifederalists* (Chapel Hill: University of North Carolina Press, 1961).
2. Gordon S. Wood, *The Creation of the American Republic* (New York: Norton, 1969), 53-75; see also Wood, *The Radicalism of the American Revolution* (New York: Knopf, 1992). I find Wood's interpretations of late eighteenth-century American political culture most convincing. There are, of course, numerous and excellent studies in this field. A few that I found particularly useful for this chapter were Bernard Bailyn, *The Ideological Origins of the American Revolution* (Cambridge: Harvard University Press, 1967), and Pauline Maier, *From Resistance to Revolution: Colonial Radicals and the Development of American Opposition to Britain, 1765-1776* (New York: Knopf, 1972). For a collection of essays that emphasize social and economic conflicts among the colonists as factors in the Revolution, see Alfred Young, ed., *The American Revolution: Explorations in the History of American Radicalism* (DeKalb: Northern Illinois University Press, 1976).
3. Rush quoted in Wood, *Creation,* 61.
4. Adams quoted in Ibid.
5. Ibid., 61.
6. Ibid., 59.
7. See Wood, *Radicalism,* 124-145.
8. Wood, *Creation,* 479-480.
9. Wood, *Radicalism,* 234.
10. Main, *Antifederalists,* 17-19; Jackson Turner Main, "Government by the People: The American Revolution and the Democratization of the Legislatures," *William and Mary Quarterly* 23, July 1966, 391-397.
11. Main, *Antifederalists,* 12.
12. Ibid., 42.
13. Main, "By the People," 391.
14. Ibid., 396-397.
15. Pennsylvania radicals quoted in Eric Foner, *Tom Paine and Revolutionary America* (New York: Oxford University Press, 1976), 129.
16. Main, "Government," 398-407.
17. Ibid., 401.
18. Cass Sunstein, "Democracy Isn't What You Think," *New York Times Book Review,* 18 August 1996, 29.
19. See discussion in Wood, *Creation,* 354-363.
20. "Articles of Confederation and Perpetual Union," reprinted in Richard Brown, *Major Problems in the Era of the American Revolution, 1760-1791* (Lexington, Mass.: D. C. Heath, 1992), 390-391; on the relationship between the Articles of Confederation and the Antifederalists, see Main, *Antifederalists,* 17.

ion, 472.

/.

78. See also Main, "By the People,' 406-407 and Michael Kammen, *Spheres of Liberty* (Ithaca, .: Cornell University Press, 1986), 37-52.

nes Madison, "Vices of the Political System of the United States," in Brown, *Era of the American Revolution,* 470-471.

James Madison, "Federalist" no. 63, and "Federalist no. 10," in Jacob Cooke, ed., *The Federalist* (Middletown, Conn.: Wesleyan University Press, 1961), 425, 57, 63-64.

27. Ibid.
28. Ibid.
29. Main, *Antifederalists,* 177-184.
30. Ibid., 263.
31. On the social composition and political views of the Antifederalists, see Main, *The Antifederalists;* Saul Cornell, "Aristocracy Assailed: The Ideology of Backcountry Antifederalism," *Journal of American History* 76, March 1990, 1148-1171; John Kaminsk, "Antifederalism and the Perils of Homogenized History," *Rhode Island History* 42, February 1983, 30-37; Cecilia Kenyon, "Men of Little Faith: The Antifederalists on the Nature of Representative Government," *William and Mary Quarterly* 12, January 1955, 3-43; Herbert Strong, *What the Antifederalists Were For* (Chicago: University of Chicago Press, 1981); Robert Rutland, *The Ordeal of the Constitution: The Antifederalists and the Ratification Struggle of 1787-1788* (Norman: University of Oklahoma Press, 1966); Stephen Boyd, *Antifederalism and the Acceptance of the Constitution* (Millwood, N.Y.: KTO Press, 1979); Issac Kramnick, "The 'Great National Discussion': The Discourse of Politics in 1787," *William and Mary Quarterly* 45, January 1988, 548-560. Published collections of Antifederalist writings include: Cecilia Kenyon, ed., *The Antifederalists* (Indianapolis, Ind.: Bobbs-Merrill, 1966); Morton Borden, ed., *The Antifederalist Papers* (East Lansing: Michigan State University Press, 1965); W. B. Allen, Gordon Lloyd, and Margie Lloyd, eds., *The Essential Antifederalist* (New York: University Press of America, 1985); J. R. Pole, ed., *The American Constitution: The Federalist and Antifederalist Papers* (New York: Hill and Wang, 1987).
32. Wood, *Creation,* 525.
33. Main, *Antifederalists,* 249.
34. Cornell, "Aristocracy Assailed," 1169.
35. Philadelphia radicals quoted in Foner, *Paine,* 133.
36. Wood, *Creation,* 490-491.
37. Main, *Antifederalists,* 130.
38. Wood, *Radicalism,* 259.
39. Cornell, "Aristocracy Assailed," 1159, Wood, *Creation,* 516.
40. For an excellent collection of comprehensive Antifederalist criticisms of the proposed Constitution, see Kenyon, ed., *The Antifederalists.*
41. Kenyon, ed., *Antifederalists,* 108; 382-383.
42. Ibid., 383-384.
43. Ibid., 17-18.
44. Pole, ed., *Constitution,* 34-36.
45. Ibid., 46-47.
46. Kenyon, ed., *Antifederalists,* 55-56.
47. Ibid., 39.
48. Ibid., 133.
49. Cornell, "Aristocracy Assailed," 1157.
50. Ibid.
51. Daniel Wheeler, ed., *The Life and Writings of Thomas Paine,* vol. 2 (New York: Vincent Parke and Company, 1908), 4-6.
52. Wood, *Creation,* 516.
53. Cornell, "Aristocracy," 1166, 1167.
54. Kenyon, ed., *Antifederalists,* 72.
55. Ibid., 184.
56. Wood, *Creation,* 521.
57. Alexis de Tocqueville, *Democracy In America,* ed. J. P. Mayer, trans. George Lawrence (New York: Anchor Books, 1969), 61-70.
58. See discussion in Wood, chapter xv in *Creation.*
59. Wood, *Radicalism,* 217-218, 225, 230, 253-254.

60. Wood, *Creation,* 608-612; see also 601-602, 607-608. Of course, competitive individualism ar obsessions with money and commerce were incremental processes that developed over a long perioc of time. On issues related to commerce and individualism in the early- to mid-nineteenth century, see Mary Ryan, *Cradle of the Middle Class* (New York: Cambridge University Press, 1981), and Paul E. Johnson, *A Shopkeeper's Millennium* (New York: Hill and Wang, 1978).
61. Tom Hayden, "The Politics of 'The Movement,'" in Alexander Bloom and Wini Breines, eds., *"Takin' It to the Streets": A Sixties Reader* (New York: Oxford University Press, 1995), 95.
62. "*Rolling Stone* Interview: Tom Hayden," *Rolling Stone,* 26 October 1972, 42. Histories of SDS (and other sixties movements) which include excellent material on ERAP include, Wini Breines, *Community and Organization in the New Left, 1962-1968: The Great Refusal* (New York: Praeger, 1982), Sara Evans, *Personal Politics: The Roots of Women's Liberation in the Civil Rights Movement and the New Left* (New York: Vintage, 1979), Todd Gitlin, *The Sixties* (New York: Bantam, 1987), James Miller, *Democracy is in the Streets: From Port Huron to the Siege of Chicago* (New York: Simon and Schuster, 1987), and Kirkpatrick Sale, *SDS* (New York: Random House, 1973).
63. Sale, *SDS,* 133.
64. Ibid., 134-140.
65. Tom Hayden and Carl Wittman, "An Interracial Movement of the Poor," *SDS Papers,* reel 36, series 4.B, no. 151, (1963).
66. Paul Potter, *A Name For Ourselves* (Boston: Little, Brown, 1971), 147-148.
67. Hayden quoted in "Convention Report," *SDS Papers,* reel 2, series 2.A, no.2 (1963), 1-3.
68. Ibid.
69. Tom Hayden, *Reunion: A Memoir* (New York: Random House, 1988), 128.
70. Rennie Davis, "ERAP Projects: Toward an Interracial Movement of the Poor," *SDS Bulletin,* June 1964, 1, 19, 21.
71. Hayden, "Convention Report," *SDS Papers,* 1-3.
72. Norm Fructer and Robert Kramer, "An Approach to Community Organizing Projects," *Studies on the Left* 6, March-April 1966.
73. Ibid., 40-41, 48-50. For a sympathetic journalist's portrait of ERAP, see Andrew Kopkind, *Thoughts of the Young Radicals* (New York: New Republic Press, 1966).
74. See discussion of the *Port Huron Statement* in chapter 7.
75. Richard Flacks, "Draft Statement # 2," *SDS Papers,* reel 2, series 2.A, no.9 (1964), 1-23; "The Triple Revolution," Ibid., reel 36, series 4.B, no.1 (1964), 1-13.
76. See Hayden and Wittman, "An Interracial Movement of the Poor," Ibid., reel 36, series 4.B, no.151, (1963), 17; "Convention Report," Ibid reel 2, series 2.A, no.2, (1963); "America and the New Era," Ibid., (1963); Fructer and Kramer, "Organizing," 37-38, 31-36, 40-41.
77. Hayden quoted in Wini Breines, *Community,* 128.
78. Steve Max, "On the SDS Conception of the Positions of the Left, the Liberals and the Right In America," *SDS Papers,* reel 38, series 4.B, no.240, (undated), 1-4.
79. Ibid., and Steve Max, "Movements and the Political Arena," Ibid., reel 38, series 4.B, no.239, (undated), 1-3; Max and Doug Ireland, "Draft Statement: 1964 Convention," Ibid., reel 2, series 2.A, no.9, (1964), 5, 20-27.
80. Al Haber, "A Reply to the President's Report," Ibid., reel 35, no series number, (March, 1964), 23-25.
81. Ibid., and Al Haber, "Memorandum," Ibid., reel 2, series 2.A, no.6, (Sept., 1963), 2-3; Haber, "Minutes of National Council Meeting," Ibid., reel 2, series 2.A, no.6, (Dec. 28, 1963), 6-7.
82. Jim Williams, "Haber's Critique of the N. C.: Reflections of a Southern Hillbilly SDS'er," Ibid., reel 2, series 2.A. no.9, (undated), 2.
83. Tom Hayden, "All the Guys at ERAP," *SDS Papers,* reel 10, series 2.B, no.1 (undated), 4; Hayden, *Reunion,* 130; "Rolling Stone Interview: Tom Hayden," 42.
84. Max, "SDS Conception," *SDS Papers,* 3-4.
85. Peter Davidowicz and Kimberly Moody, "Prospectus for the Baltimore Research and Action Project," *SDS Papers,* reel 36, series 4.B, no.62 (May, 1964), 6.
86. Jane Addams, *Twenty Years at Hull-House* (1910; reprint, New York: New American Library, 1960).
87. Sale, *SDS,* 134.
88. Hayden, "Convention Report," *SDS Papers,* 3. The words "locally autonomous" were italicized by Hayden. Hayden, "All the Guys," 4.
89. Todd Gitlin, "The Battlefields and the War," *SDS Papers,* reel 10, series 2.B, no.2 (undated), 1. See also Gitlin, "The Radical Potential of the Poor," in Massimo Teodori, *The New Left: A Documentary History* (Indianapolis, Indiana: Bobbs-Merrill, 1969), 136-149; Rennie Davis, "The War on Poverty: Notes on Insurgent Response," *SDS Papers,* reel 36, series 4.B, no.68 (undated), 3-8.
90. Fructer and Kramer, "Organizing," 31-36, 48-51, 54-61.

sion of the role of women in ERAP and SDS is in Evans, chapters 6 and 7 in *Personal* ccessful interactions between whites and blacks in ERAP sponsored meetings, see Connie eveland Conference of the Poor," *Studies on the Left* 5, Spring 1965, 71.

Community Project Report," *SDS Papers,* reel 10, series 2.B, no.2 (July 23, 1964), 6-7; 1-2.

nd Community Project Report," Ibid. (27 July 1964), 2-3.

d Flacks, "Organizing the Unemployed: The Chicago Project," in Mitchell Cohen and Dennis , eds., *The New Student Left* (Boston: Beacon Press, 1966), 144. On the participation of local dents in ERAP activities, see Sale, *SDS,* 136-138.

Cleveland Community Project Report," *SDS Papers* (July 27, 1964), 1-2.

Ibid., 2-3.

"Cleveland Community Project Report," in Ibid. (August 9, 1964), 5.

Ibid., 1.

9. "Cleveland Community Project Report," Ibid. (September 20-27, 1964), 1.
00. Richard Rothstein, "A Short History of ERAP," *SDS Papers,* reel 11, series 2.B, no.21 (March 1966), 3.
101. "Cleveland Community Project Report," Ibid (September 20-27, 1964), 1; Ibid. (August 9, 1964), 1.
102. Davis quoted in Norman Fructer, "Chicago: Join Project," *Studies on the Left* 5, Summer 1965, 113. On the ERAP experience in Chicago, see Todd Gitlin, *Uptown: Poor Whites in Chicago* (New York: Harper and Row, 1970).
103. Todd Gitlin, "The Dynamics of the New Left," *Motive* 31, November 1970, 44.
104. Paul Potter, *Name,* 138-152.
105. For example, see comments of the Cleveland Project staff on pages 6-7 in its report of July 23, 1964. *SDS Papers,* reel 10, series 2.B no. 2. The best description and analysis of SDS's quest for community is, Breines, *Community and Organization in the New Left.*
106. Potter, *Name,* 115, 120.
107. Alan Brinkley, "Dreams of the Sixties," *New York Review of Books,* October 22, 1987, 16.
108. Kasich quoted in "Clinton to Sign Welfare Bill," *New York Times,* 1 August 1996, 22.
109. Ibid.
110. R. Jackson Wilson's *In Quest of Community: Social Philosophy in the United States, 1860-1920* (New York: Wiley, 1968), remains a valuable study of the history of the idea of community. See also Robert Wiebe, *The Segmented Society: An Introduction to the Meaning of America* (New York: Oxford University Press, 1975), and Thomas Bender, *Community and Social Change in America* (New Brunswick, N.J.: Rutgers University Press, 1978).
111. Robert Bellah et al., *Habits of the Heart: Individualism and Commitment in American Life* (New York: Harper and Row, 1986), 150.
112. Ibid
113. Ibid, vi, vii, 23-25, 33, 143-144, 277.
114. Michael Sandel, *Democracy's Discontents: America in Search of a Public Philosophy* (Cambridge, Mass.: Harvard University Press, 1996), 6.
115. Ibid., 349-351.
116. Hayden, *Reunion,* 425-428.
117. Ibid., 432.
118. Ibid., 432 (Hayden's emphasis).
119. Miller, *Democracy,* 319
120. Hayden, *Reunion,* 462.
121. Gitlin, *Sixties,* 427.
122. Oglesby quoted in Joan Morrison and Robert Morrison, eds., *From Camelot to Kent State* (New York: Times Books, 1987), 304.
123. Ibid.
124. Ibid., 306-307.
125. Potter, *Name,* 119.

AFTERWORD

1. On the origins of neoconservatism and its relation to the sixties, see Peter Steinfels, *The Neoconservatives* (New York: Simon and Schuster, 1979).
2. Henry David Thoreau, "Walking," in *The Portable Thoreau,* Carl Bode, ed., (New York: Viking, 1947), 617, 603-605, 607-609, 611, 616.

INDEX